D1345955

Corporate Criminal Liability

AUSTRALIA
Law Book Co
Sydney

CANADA and USA
Carswell
Toronto

HONG KONG
Sweet & Maxwell Asia

NEW ZEALAND
Brookers
Wellington

SINGAPORE and MALAYSIA
Sweet & Maxwell Asia
Singapore and Kuala Lumpur

Corporate Criminal Liability

Amanda Pinto Q.C.
&
Martin Evans

THOMSON

SWEET & MAXWELL

LONDON
SWEET & MAXWELL
2008

Published in 2008 by
Sweet & Maxwell Limited of
100 Avenue Road London NW3 3PF
www.sweetandmaxwell.co.uk
Typeset by YHT Ltd, London
Printed and bound in Great Britain by
MPG Books Ltd, Bodmin, Cornwall

No natural forests were destroyed to make this
product, only farmed timber was used and
replanted.

A CIP catalogue record for this book is available
from the British Library

ISBN 978-0-421-89410-5

PREFACE

On Sunday April 14, 1912, a dinner was held in the First Class Restaurant of *RMS Titanic* in honour of the Captain, Edward J Smith. The Titanic was on her maiden voyage from Southampton to New York. At 9pm New York time, Captain Smith excused himself and went up to the bridge. During the day warnings had been received in the wireless room of ice in the region. Up on the bridge, Captain Smith ordered a sharp lookout to be kept and then retired for the night.

At 9.05pm, a message was received by the radio operator of the Titanic from SS California: "We are stopped and surrounded by ice" to which he replied: "Keep out. I am busy. I am working Cape Race."[1] The California's warning was never passed to the bridge.

That Sunday night was clear but moonless. At about 11.30pm, high up in the crow's nest, the lookout, Fred Fleet, noticed a slight haze in the distance. Surprisingly, Fleet did not have the benefit of binoculars to help him spot icebergs. He was to give evidence in the Wreck Commissioner's Court that had his employer followed its normal practice and provided binoculars, the disaster would have been averted.[2] Too late did the bridge hear his alarm: "*Iceberg. Right ahead*". Within seconds, the Titanic had scraped alongside an iceberg which tore a gaping hole on the starboard side below the waterline.

Of the 2,201 passengers and crew aboard, only 711 survived. Huge loss of life was inevitable because there were only sufficient lifeboats for 1,178 people.[3] As is well known, of those lifeboats launched, few were filled to

---

[1] Meaning "go off air"; Wreck Commissioner's Court Minutes of Evidence, Pt 4 qq 8992–8999.
[2] Wreck Commissioner's Court Minutes of Evidence, Pt 4 qq 7401–17403 p.390.
[3] A capacity of 216 more than the 962 required under the Merchant Shipping Act 1894 for a vessel above 10,000 tons—the Titanic was of 46,328 tons.

capacity.[4] Even after the disaster, there were those, like Mr Holt M.P., who scoffed at the idea of sufficient lifeboats for all passengers and crew. During a House of Commons debate on the sinking of the Titanic, he said: "Boats for all [is] one of the most ridiculous proposals ever put forward".[5] In America, a Senate Inquiry was held to investigate the wreck, chaired by Senator William Alden Smith. The Committee was able to say:

> "... that the ice positions so definitely reported to the Titanic just preceding the accident located ice on both sides of the track or lane which the Titanic was following, and in her immediate vicinity. No general discussion took place among the officers; no conference was called to consider these warnings, no heed was given to them. The speed was not relaxed, the lookout was not increased, and the only vigilance displayed by the officer of the vessel was by instructions to keep 'a sharp lookout for ice' ".

In England, the Government immediately ordered a formal inquiry. On April 23, 1912, Charles Bigham, Lord Mersey of Toxteth, President of the Probate, Divorce & Admiralty Division of the High Court was appointed Wreck Commissioner by the Lord Chancellor.

The Titanic was the flagship of the White Star Line, part of a powerful Anglo-American cartel responsible for most transatlantic trade. The Managing Director of White Star Line, Joseph Bruce Ismay, was on board and survived the wreck. Ismay knew perfectly well that the Titanic was steaming towards ice. During the London Inquiry, he was cross-examined by the Attorney-General, Sir Rufus Isaac:

Q: And you knew also that you would be approaching ice that night?
A: I expected so, yes.
Q: And therefore it behoved those responsible for the navigation of the ship to be very careful?
A: Naturally.
Q: And more particularly, if you were approaching ice in the night it would be desirable, would it not, to slow down?
A: I am not a navigator.
Q: What was the object of continuing at full speed through the night if you expect to meet ice?
A: I presume the man would be anxious to get through the ice region. He would not want to slow down upon the chance of fog coming on.
Q: So that, of course, the object would be to get through it as fast as you could?

---

[4] The first lifeboat launched, No.7, had only 28 occupants; it had a capacity of 65. Not all the lifeboats were even launched, but of the 19 that were, only six were filled to capacity or near it.
[5] R.D. Holt M.P., House of Commons Debate October 7, 1912.

A: I presume that if a man on a perfectly clear night could see far enough to clear an iceberg he would be perfectly justified in getting through the ice region as quickly as he possibly could. Assuming the weather was perfectly clear, I should say the Captain was perfectly justified in going full speed.

Q: And according to your view, what do you say as to the weather conditions?

A: So far as I could judge, it was a perfectly fine, clear night.[6]

Earlier, the Attorney-General had asked about the speed of the Titanic at the time of the collision:

Q: But really Mr Ismay, if you will just search your recollection a little. Remember that this question of speed interested you very materially. You, a Managing Director of the company, were interested in the speed of the vessel?

A: Naturally.

Q: Your intention was, before you reached New York, to get [from 75 revolutions] the maximum speed of 78?

A: The intention was that if the weather should be found suitable on the Monday or the Tuesday that the ship would then have been driven at full speed, 78.[7]

The Report of the United States Senate Committee concluded that Ismay's presence on board had subconsciously encouraged the Captain to go as fast as possible, though it cleared him of giving any specific instruction to do so.[8] It was generally suspected that Ismay let it be known that the company wanted the Titanic to better the record time for the transatlantic crossing, set by another White Star liner, the *Olympia*, the year before.

The speed of the Titanic was gradually increased after leaving Queenstown, Ireland. Just prior to the collision, the ship was making her maximum speed of the voyage—not less than 21 knots, or 24¼mph.

In his report, the Wreck Commissioner observed:

"The question is what ought the Master to have done. I am advised that with the knowledge of the proximity of ice which the Master had, two courses were open to him: The one was to stand well to the southward instead of turning up to a westerly course; the other was to reduce speed materially as night approached. He did neither. ... Why, then, did the Master persevere in his course and maintain his speed? The answer is to be found in the evidence. It was shown that for many years past, indeed, for a quarter of a century or more, the practice of liners using this track when in the vicinity of ice at night had been in clear weather

---

[6] Wreck Commissioner's Inquiry, Day 16, qq 18,428–18,448.
[7] ibid. at qq 18,375–18,379.
[8] See fn.46 28.5.12 S.Rept 806 (6127).

In this case a manslaughter prosecution was brought[14]—against P&O European Ferries (Dover) Ltd, (who by then had taken over Townsend Car Ferries), together with some of its directors, Mark Stanley and Leslie Sabel. Before the prosecution had even completed its case, the trial judge, Turner J., ruled that as a matter of law there was no evidence upon which the jury could properly convict any of the five most senior executives of P&O on trial or the company. It was necessary, he said, for the prosecution to prove that the risk of the vessel putting to sea with her bow doors open would have been "obvious to the hypothetically prudent master or mariner".[15] Turner J.'s ruling was predictable in the circumstances because the prosecution had called a number of ships' masters who were or had been in the employment of the Defendant company, all of whom said that it had not occurred to them that *any* risk existed, let alone an obvious one.[16] Worse still, the prosecution was unable to adduce, from any marine expert unconnected with the Defendant company, evidence to the effect that the risk was obvious.

During the 75 years between these two maritime disasters, important developments in the law concerning the responsibility of corporations for criminal acts had taken place. Since 1944 it had been possible to prosecute a company for crimes requiring proof of mens rea. Ultimately however, despite Sheen J.'s damning conclusions the case against P&O failed.

That a prosecution was brought at all represented a departure from conventional juristic thinking; at that time there was no clear authority establishing that a corporation could be convicted of manslaughter.

The willingness on the part of the prosecution to bring the *Herald* case no doubt reflected a shift in the public perception of corporations and of blame. The extent to which corporate crime is now the subject of public debate mirrors the increasing anxiety about public safety and a general loss of trust in corporations.

Corporate crime is about very much more than cases of manslaughter; indeed, the number of successful prosecutions of a corporation for this offence can be counted on the fingers of one hand, but cases of corporate killing have demonstrated most vividly the gap between public expectation and legal experience. In the light of the repeated, and the authors would submit inevitable, failure of corporate manslaughter prosecutions under the common law, the government has at last passed the Corporate Manslaughter and Corporate Homicide Act 2007 designed to convict companies when deaths are caused by just the sort of systemic failures highlighted in the cases running from the Titanic to the most recent rail disasters. The question remains whether the Act will have its success measured in terms of

---

[14] Following the finding by the inquest jury that the deaths of the passengers and crew were caused unlawfully.

[15] *Stanley & Others* October 19, 1990 (CCC) transcript p.18F.

[16] *ibid* at 17D-F.

the number of prosecutions resulting in convictions, or whether the fact of very few prosecutions actually indicates that the message that such management failures will be publicly censured has been heeded in the corporate world and greater care taken to operate corporate enterprises safely.

In the following chapters we chart and explain the developments in the law of corporate criminal liability and consider, amongst other things, why the Herald of Free Enterprise prosecution and others like it foundered so spectacularly.

CONTENTS

PART IV—CORPORATION AND HUMAN RIGHTS

PART V—SPECIFIC OFFENCES

ACKNOWLEDGEMENTS

We are grateful to James Richardson for his permission to use the Schedule of Offences under the Companies Act 2007 that first appeared in Criminal Law Week.

We would like to thank Suzanna Wong and Marie Anderson, our editorial team, for their support and patience and our long-suffering families who have had to endure considerable disruption during the writing of this edition!

TABLE OF CASES

TABLE OF CASES

TABLE OF STATUTES

*[Paragraph numbers in **bold** refer to where legislation is reproduced]*

xli

TABLE OF STATUTORY INSTRUMENTS

Part I

PRINCIPLES OF CORPORATE LIABILITY

HISTORICAL BACKGROUND TO CORPORATE CRIMINAL LIABILITY

INTRODUCTION

It has for many years been commonplace for corporations to be prosecuted **1.1** for criminal offences. Numerous Acts of Parliament contain provisions specifically making a body corporate liable for offences created by the Statute in question. Even if there is no such provision, the Interpretation Act 1978[1] provides that, unless the contrary intention appears, the word "person" in a statute or subordinate legislation is to be construed as including "a body of persons corporate or unincorporate". This definition applies to any Act: "whenever passed relating to an offence punishable on indictment or on summary conviction".[2] The first Interpretation Act to contain this provision was enacted in 1889, but an identical provision was enacted as early as 1827.[3] It is now conclusively recognised that companies may properly be indicted for common law offences as well as statutory, and for offences requiring proof of a criminal state of mind as well as those of strict liability.

It is submitted that there is a plain necessity for corporate criminal liability, although not all commentators agree.[4] Ashworth has described the aims of the criminal law in this way[5]:

"The first is to protect those interests which are most central to life in society (leaving less important interests to be protected by government regulation or civil actions) ... The second aim of the criminal law is to

---

[1] ss.5 and 11 and Sch.1.
[2] s.22, Sch.2 para.4(5). This does not apply to any Statutes passed before 1889; Sch.2 para.4(1)(a).
[3] Criminal Law Act 1827, s.14.
[4] Various objections to corporate criminal liability were considered by the Law Commission and are set out at pp.29 to 36 of Law Commission Working Paper No.44, 1973.
[5] *Defining Offences Without Harm in Criminal Law: Essays in Honour of J.C. Smith*, P. Smith edn (London, Butterworths, 1987).

establish an authoritative framework for the official response to lawbreaking."

Corporations are a ubiquitous feature of modern life and frequently engaged with their employees and the public in hazardous ways. The criminal law would be seriously deficient if harmful conduct carried on by those entities could not be prosecuted and punished. As Lord Denman said as long ago as 1846[6]:

"There can be no effectual means for deterring from an oppressive exercise of power for the purpose of gain, except the remedy by an individual against those who truly commit it, that is the corporation acting by its majority, and there is no principle which places them beyond the reach of the law for such proceedings."

Although a corporation may lack the capacity to have morals:

"...its members can be induced by an effective sanction to make its outward conduct conform to a standard, and where they can control its directors, public policy demands that they should be responsible in their corporate capacity."[7]

Other common law and civil law jurisdictions have also developed responses to corporate liability for crime. Recently, in recognition that corporations conduct business trans-nationally, there has been pressure to harmonise responses to some aspects of corporate misconduct.[8] By way of example, in 1983, the Council of Europe appointed a committee to examine the possibility and advisability of introducing the principle of criminal liability of corporate bodies into the legislation of Member States.[9] In 1988, the Council specifically recommended that Member States consider the promotion of corporate criminal liability.[10] The principles by which those states should be guided in their law and practice include the following propositions:

(a) enterprises should be able to be made liable for offences committed in the exercise of their activities, even where the offence is alien to the purpose of the enterprise;

---

[6] In *Gt Northern Railway Co Case* (1846) 9 Q.B. 315.

[7] C.R.N. Winn (1929) "*The Criminal Responsibility of Corporations*" (1929) 3 Camb. L.J. 398. The American courts have often taken a robust view to corporate wrongdoing: "There is but one vulnerable point about these existences called corporations—and that is, the pocket of the monied power that is concealed behind them; and if that is reached, they will wince." *Goddard v Grand Trunk Railway* 57 Me. 202.

[8] e.g. Environmental offences (Convention on the protection of the environment through criminal law, Strasbourg, 4 xi 1998; art.9 and Resolution 77(28)); Bribery and Corruption (Council of Europe Criminal Law Convention on Corruption. Strasbourg, 1999; art.18); Consumer Protection (Recommendation R(82)15) and Economic Crime (Recommendation No. R(81)12); Tachograph offences ((EEC) No. 3820/ 85).

[9] Decision CDPC/68/070582.

[10] Recommendation No. R(88)18.

(b) liability should attach irrespective of whether a natural person can be identified;

(c) the enterprise should be exonerated where its management is not implicated and has taken all necessary steps to avoid the offence;

(d) enterprise liability should be additional to any individual management liability;

(e) the imposition of appropriate sanctions ... particularly suited to enterprises including fines and confiscation of property.[11]

Because the EU institutions have no authority to legislate in the area of criminal law, there has been no move towards a standardised response to corporate crime, but there does exist a well developed system of administrative sanction, for example in respect of anti-trust violations. Nevertheless, the combined effect of various international conventions is to exert powerful pressure on any state to introduce or develop corporate criminal liability. For example, the Trade Marks Act 1994 was enacted to implement Council Directive 89/104 EEC which was designed to harmonise the laws of Member States relating to trade marks.

Given that corporations must exist in the same society (or societies) as their customers and their employees, it is not unreasonable to "impute to corporations social duties including the duty not to offend all relevant parts of the criminal law."[12] Prosecutions have a vital declaratory effect:

"The public nature of criminal prosecutions plays an important role in conveying cultural messages about types of behaviour and offences."[13]

The catalogue of criminal offences which a company cannot commit as principal is very small indeed: certainly it includes murder[14] (because the only lawful sentence, life imprisonment, can only be inflicted upon an individual in his personal capacity) and bigamy (since a corporation can't marry one person, let alone more than one at a time),[15] some driving offences,[16] incest, rape and some other sexual offences. A company may be a criminal conspirator,[17] although it cannot conspire only with its sole director because a conspiracy requires the agreement of two separate minds. If the mind of the director is treated as being the mind of the company, there

---

[11] Appendix to Recommendation No. R(88)18.

[12] per Turner J. in *R. v P&O European Ferries (Dover) Ltd* (1991) 93 Cr.App.R. 72, 83.

[13] Professor Celia Wells, *Corporations and Criminal Responsibility*, 2nd edn (Oxford, OUP, 2001), p.30.

[14] And any other offence in respect of which the only sentence is one of imprisonment: *Hawke v Hulton & Co* [1909] 2 K.B. 93. Until 1925 this included all felonies: see para.2.3 below. A corporation can be convicted of an offence punishable by a fine—s.32 of the Magistrates Courts Act 1980 and s.30 of the Powers of Criminal Courts Act 1973.

[15] As a principal; a company set up to procure multiple marriages could be indicted for bigamy as a secondary party.

[16] *Richmond upon Thames LBC v Pinn and Wheeler* (1988) 87 L.G.R. 659 DC.

[17] *R. v ICR Haulage* [1944] K.B. 551, 554.

on which Queen Elizabeth I signed the Royal Charter then necessary for incorporation.[26] The Royal Charter conferred on the East India Company the exclusive right to trade with the East Indies for 15 years without interference from the Crown.

The East India Company is considered by some to be the first "modern" joint stock company in England.[27] However, when it was first incorporated, the East India Company was quite unlike a modern corporation. For a start, the individual members of the company continued to trade on their own account, initially at least. It was convenient for traders to group together for the purposes of trading overseas and "company" was the name usually adopted for such organisations. If there was a pooling of stock (for example, to fund and equip a voyage) the joint stock[28] was divided up on the ship's return according to the original share. From 1614 to 1653, joint stock was subscribed by the members for a fixed period of years rather than on a voyage by voyage basis. Thereafter, the East India Company established a permanent joint stock, and after 1692, individual members were prohibited from trading on their own account. Only then did the company become a true joint commercial enterprise.

Before 1862, there was, in practical terms, little to distinguish between unincorporated partnerships and incorporated companies. Early corporations were more like guilds, exercising control over the right to engage in specific business activities.[29] One of the main reasons for seeking incorporation was to obtain monopolistic rights[30] or special powers.[31] Incorporation was difficult and costly to obtain until the enactment of the Joint Stock Companies Act 1844, but there were advantages to it even during the infancy of company law, which reflected the fact that the law recognised an incorporated company as having a separate legal existence. A corporation (unlike a partnership) was capable of existing in perpetuity. A corporation could own property and could sue in its own right. It could also invite investment from the public. This aspect was, in due course, the reason for the first interest shown by the criminal law in the operation of corporations.

---

[26] In the seventeenth century, a company could only be incorporated by Act of Parliament or by Royal Charter. This did not change until 1844 when the Joint Stock Companies Act first introduced a restricted form of incorporation by registrations. However, after the English Revolution of 1688 the prerogative powers of the Crown to grant charters were curtailed. Any monopolistic or other special powers decided by a company were thereafter granted by statute. See Gower, *Principles of Modern Company Law*, (London, Sweet & Maxwell, 1997).

[27] C. Stone, *Where the Law Ends: The Social Control of Corporate Bodies*, (New York, Harper Row, 1975), p.15.

[28] In the sense of stock in trade, not stocks and shares.

[29] Bernard, "*The Historical Development of Corporate Criminal Liability*" (1954) Criminology, 22:3, 4.

[30] For example in respect of foreign trade, as in the case of the East India Company.

[31] For example, of compulsory purchase, necessary when constructing canals or railways.

EARLY REGULATION OF CORPORATIONS

The ultimately reckless scheme devised by the South Sea Company to attract **1.4** investment from the public in order to purchase the whole of the national debt provoked the passing in 1720 of what came to be known as the Bubble Act.[32] This was the first Act of Parliament to include provisions regulating companies. It was not a success. According to Holdsworth[33]:

> "What was needed was an Act which made it easy for joint stock companies to adopt a corporate form and, at the same time, safeguard both the shareholders in such societies and the public against frauds and negligence in their promotion and management. What was passed was an Act which deliberately made it difficult for joint stock societies to assume a corporate form and contained no rules at all for the conduct of such societies if, and when, they assumed it."

In the event, the Act did nothing to prevent, and may even have helped to precipitate the spectacular collapse of the South Sea Company, nor were investors protected from the fraud of its directors. However, by s.21 of the Act, brokers dealing in securities of illegal companies (i.e. those not authorised by Act of Parliament or Crown charter to raise or transfer stock) were liable to penalties. This was the first appearance in the criminal law of a corporate dimension, albeit not an offence in respect of which a company could be convicted. Despite its being signally unsuccessful legislation, the Bubble Act was not repealed until 1902; criminal prosecutions of brokers under the Act are reported into the nineteenth century.[34]

The crash of the South Sea Company undoubtedly set back the development of corporations in England. The Law Officers of the Crown were extremely wary of granting a charter outside the range of commercial endeavours identified by Adam Smith[35] as being suitable for a joint stock company (banking, fire and marine insurance, making and maintaining canals and bringing water to cities). As a result, much domestic commercial activity was undertaken by unincorporated companies which had no separate legal identity, could not sue or be sued and could not be prosecuted for any criminal offence.

Until at least the middle of the nineteenth century, company law developed somewhat haphazardly. The first modern company law statute was the Joint Stock Companies Act of 1844, introduced following the report[36] of the Parliamentary Committee on Joint Stock Companies under the chairmanship of the then President of the Board of Trade, William Gladstone. This

---

[32] 6 Geo. 1, c.18.
[33] 32 H.E.L., Vol.8, pp.219–220, quoted in Gower's *Principles of Modern Company Law*, 6th edn (London, Sweet & Maxwell, 1997), p.25.
[34] *R. v Dodd* (1808) 9 East 516; *R. v Stratton* (1809) 1 Camp. 549n.
[35] Adam Smith, *"The Wealth of Nations"* Vol.V, Ch.1, Pt III, art.1.
[36] 1844 B.P.P. Vol.VII.

legislation was passed in the period of rapid expansion of the railways. As had happened in the eighteenth century with the growth of the canal network, the demand by railway companies for incorporation in order to acquire the special powers (in particular, powers of compulsory purchase) necessary for construction required the passing of numerous private Acts of Parliament. This was neither satisfactory nor efficient. The 1844 Act provided, for the first time, for restricted incorporation by registration,[37] and, to that end, established the Registrar of Companies.[38] Hereafter, a registered company had the legal status of a corporation.

LIMITED LIABILITY

1.5 In an ordinary partnership, each partner is personally liable for all debts of the firm, whereas the members of an incorporated company have no individual liability to the company's creditors. The liability of the members is only to the company and is satisfied if they pay the calls properly made upon them by the company or its liquidator. The creditors of a limited company cannot look to the members to make good the debt; creditors are restricted to the property of the company, including such further amounts as the members may be required to contribute in respect of shares held by them in the capital or in accordance with any guarantee contained in the memorandum of association. The calls made on the members may be limited or unlimited dependent upon the status of the company. By reducing and defining the potential risk to members (investors), limited liability has opened the way for modern companies to raise the necessary capital for their business, either privately or on the stock market. For this reason, only in exceptional circumstances does the law allow a creditor of the company to pierce the veil of incorporation and fix the shareholders with personal liability.[39]

Although the limited liability of corporations had been recognised since the eighteenth century, recognition of the benefits it bestowed upon the members was slow to develop. The 1844 Joint Stock Companies Act did not introduce limited liability; that did not become generally available until 1856.[40] Even after the Limited Liability Act 1855 there were in fact instances where investors in major corporations were exposed to unlimited liability for the corporation's debts; this frequently resulted in the investors' ruin.

Under the Joint Stock Companies Act 1856, for the first time, incorporation with limited liability could be obtained when seven or more people

---

[37] Instead of by a special Act of Parliament or by Royal Charter.

[38] s.19.

[39] See *Standard Chartered Bank v Pakistan National Shipping Corpn and Others (Nos 2 and 4)* [2003] 1 A.C. 959 HL per Lord Mustill at para.37.

[40] Although it was first put on a statutory footing by the Limited Liability Act 1855, repealed and replaced the following year by the Joint Stock Companies Act 1856.

signed and registered a memorandum of association with the Registrar of Companies. In the years immediately following enactment, the number of applications for incorporation increased dramatically. Six years later, in 1862, the legislation was consolidated and amended. The new Act dropped the words "Joint Stock" from the short title and remained in force (though much amended) until 1908; this was the first Companies Act.

The laissez-faire doctrine which encouraged Parliament to enact the Acts of 1844 and 1856 can be exemplified by these words:

"...and it must be remembered that no one needs to trust a limited company unless he so pleases, and that before he does so he can ascertain, if he so pleases, what is the capital of the company and how it is held."[41]

The Joint Stock Companies Act 1844 had made full publicity a legal requirement in order to guard against fraud, and full publicity has been at the core of company law ever since.[42]

The essence of an incorporated company is that it has a separate legal **1.6** personality distinct from its shareholders, so it can enjoy rights and be subject to duties in its own right like any other person. But unlike a natural person, a corporation is capable of existing in perpetuity. Although this was the clear effect of the companies legislation of the mid-nineteenth century, it was not until 1897 that this apparently uncontroversial proposition received the unambiguous approval of the judiciary, when the case of *Salomon v Salomon & Co Ltd* was considered by the House of Lords.[43]

SALOMON V SALOMON & CO LTD[44]

Mr Salomon was a boot and shoe manufacturer from Whitechapel, London. **1.7** He had been trading for over 30 years and had built a thriving business. He decided to turn his private business into a limited company. All the formalities and requirements of the Companies Act 1862 were duly observed. His old business was sold to the new company, Aron Salomon and Company Limited. The subscribers to the memorandum were himself, his wife and five

---

[41] *Salomon v Salomon & Co Ltd* [1897] A.C. 22, 46 HL, per Lord Herschel.

[42] As was observed by Lord Watson in *Salomon v Salomon & Co Ltd* above, at 40:

"The unpaid creditors of the company, whose unfortunate position has been attributed to the fraud of the appellant, if they had thought fit to avail themselves of the means of protecting their interests which the Act provides, could have informed themselves of the terms of purchase by the company, of the issue of debentures to the appellant, and of the amount of shares held by each member."

[43] The transfer of partnership to a company formed by the partners had already been held to be a sale to a distinct person: "We have two parties, one party consisting of several individuals, and the other party consisting of a corporation." per Lindley L.J. in *Foster & Sons v Commissioners for the Inland Revenue* [1894] 1 Q.B. 516, 528.

[44] *Salomon v Salomon & Co Ltd* [1897] A.C. 22.

of his grown-up children. All but six of the 20,007 shares in the company were held by Mr Salomon; the remaining shares were held by the other directors.

Unhappily, the business collapsed, due apparently to a great depression in the boot and shoe trade and the withdrawal of orders from public bodies which were the principal source of profit. Mr Salomon did what he could. He borrowed money from a Mr Broderip, secured against debentures, but the business did not improve and the loan could not be repaid. Mr Broderip commenced proceedings and a receiver was appointed. The company went into liquidation and the assets were sold. Although the proceeds of sale were sufficient to pay Mr Broderip, unsecured creditors were left without redress.

The receiver took proceedings against Mr Salomon. At first instance, Vaughan Williams J. found that the company had an action against Mr Salomon because it (the company) was Mr Salomon in another form; in effect, the company was his agent and so he was held to be liable to indemnify the company against its trading debts. Mr Salomon appealed but lost, a strong Court of Appeal[45] declaring that the formation of the company and the issue of debentures to Mr Salomon were "contrary to the true intent and meaning of the Companies Act 1862".

1.8   The House of Lords unanimously allowed the appeal of Mr Salomon, holding that he was quite entitled to set up a company to carry on what was, in essence, his business. Lord Halsbury observed[46]:

> "I am wholly unable to follow the proposition that this was contrary to the true intent and meaning of the Companies Act. I can only find the true intent and meaning of the Act from the Act itself; and the Act appears to me to give a company a legal existence with rights and liabilities of its own, whatever may have been the ideas and schemes of those who brought it into existence.
>
> Either the limited company was a legal entity or it was not. If it was, the business belonged to it and not to Mr Salomon. If it was not, there was no person and no thing to be an agent at all, and it is impossible to say at the same time that there is a company and there is not."

Lord Herschel stated[47]:

> "I am at a loss to understand what is meant by saying that A. Salomon and Co. Limited is but an 'alias' for A. Salomon. It is not another name for the same person. The company is *ex hypothesi* a distinct legal persona."

---

[45] Including Lindley L.J. whose dictum in *Foster & Sons v Commissioners for the Inland Revenue* is quoted above (fn.43).

[46] [1897] A.C. 22, 31.

[47] ibid. at 42.

To form a company under the 1862 Act, all that was required was that a memorandum of association was signed by seven persons who each took at least one share. Once that was done, Lord Macnaghten had no doubt that a body corporate was created and it mattered not whether the signatories were relations or strangers[48]:

> "The company attains maturity on its birth. There is no period of minority—no interval of incapacity. I cannot understand how a body corporate thus made 'capable' by statute can lose its individuality by issuing the bulk of its capital to one person, whether he be a subscriber to the memorandum or not. *The company is at law a different person altogether from the subscribers to the memorandum.*" [emphasis added]

Their Lordships made it absolutely clear that a company properly incorporated is a distinct legal entity, capable of owning and dealing with property, suing and being sued and contracting on its own behalf.[49] Who owns the shares and in what proportion is irrelevant. The company's acts are not the shareholders' acts, even if one of them also has sole control of its affairs.[50] At the time of the dictum of Lord Holt (1701),[51] it is doubtful the principle that "a company is at law a different person altogether from the subscribers to the memorandum" had any foundation at all and so his observation was probably correct. Once the company began to be recognised as a separate legal entity, the dictum was ignored.

COMPANY CONSTITUTION

A corporation can only act within the scope of the powers given to it at **1.9** birth. The Joint Stock Companies Act 1856 required the constitution of a registered company to be set out in two separate documents:

(a) the memorandum of association, and

(b) the articles of association.

This requirement still applies today.

The memorandum must contain the basic constitution of the company, its name, objects, domicile, share capital (if any) and whether it is limited or public. All matters concerning the administration of the company are to be found in the articles of association, the terms of which (unlike the

---

[48] [1897] A.C. 22, 50 and 51.

[49] See *Lee v Lee's Air Farming* [1961] A.C. 12 PC where it was held that a company and its sole governing director were separate and distinct legal entities; the fact that he exercised sole control over the company did not prevent him from being the servant of the company and taking orders from it.

[50] *Inland Revenue Commissioners v Sansom* [1921] 2 K.B. 492.

[51] See para.1.2 above; fn.21.

memorandum) may be altered by special resolution of the company.[52] The articles of association will provide for the appointment of a board of directors, set out the powers vested in it and, customarily, confer on the board of directors all the company's powers (except as otherwise provided). Accordingly, the directors of a modern company will be responsible for policy decisions as well as general administration of the company's affairs. Such is the primacy of the board that a decision taken by it cannot be altered by the members in general meeting. The day-to-day management of the company will (depending on its size) typically be delegated by the board to a managing director or directors; indeed a provision to this effect commonly appears in the articles of association.

These two instruments are important so far as corporate criminal liability is concerned because they represent the starting point for determining whose acts may be identified as those of the corporation itself. Lord Diplock regarded them as paramount:

> "My Lords, a corporation, incorporated under the Companies Act 1948, owes its corporate personality and its powers to its constitution, the memorandum and articles of association. The obvious and the only place to discover by what natural persons its powers are exercisable, is in its constitution...
>
> In my view, therefore, the question: 'what natural persons are to be treated in law as being the company for the purposes of acts done in the course of its business' ... is to be found by identifying those natural persons who by the memorandum and articles of association or as a result of action taken by the directors, or by the company in general meeting pursuant to the articles, are entrusted with the exercise of the powers of the company."[53]

In a later case, *Meridian Global Funds Management Asia Ltd v Securities Commission*, Lord Hoffmann said[54]:

> "A company exists because there is a rule (usually in a statute) which says that a *persona ficta* shall be deemed to exist and to have certain of the powers, rights and duties of a natural person. But there would be little sense in deeming such a *persona ficta* to exist unless there were also rules to tell one what acts were to count as the acts of the company. It is therefore a necessary part of corporate personality that there should be rules by which acts are attributed to the company. These may be called 'the rules of attribution.'

---

[52] i.e. by a resolution in general meeting passed by a 75% majority of members voting after at least 21 days notice has been given of the intention to pass it as a special resolution.

[53] *Tesco Supermarkets Ltd v Nattrass* [1972] A.C. 153, 199. See below.

[54] *Meridian Global Funds Management Asia Ltd v Securities Commission* [1995] 2 A.C. 500, 506.

The company's primary rules of attribution will generally be found in its constitution, typically the articles of association..."

Directors and shareholders are protected from being held liable in respect of the company's obligations because the law treats a company as a distinct legal person. Only if a director assumes responsibility for the provision of services provided by the company may he be personally liable to a third party for loss occasioned by the negligent performance of that service by the company. The personal liability of a director has been explained in these terms[55]:

> "What matters is not that liability of the shareholders of a company is limited but that a company is a separate entity, distinct from its directors, servants or other agents. The trader who incorporates a company to which he transfers his business creates a legal person on whose behalf he may afterwards act as a director. For present purposes, his position is the same as if he had sold his business to another individual and agreed to act on his behalf."

Recognition that a company was a legal person with rights and obligations was the foundation of the development of principles of corporate criminal liability.

---

[55] *Williams v Natural Life Health Foods* [1998] 1 W.L.R. 830, 835; [1998] 2 All E.R. 577, 581j, per Lord Steyn.

CHAPTER 2

EARLY DEVELOPMENT OF CORPORATE CRIMINAL LIABILITY

For more than 200 years after the granting of the Royal Charter by Queen **2.1**
Elizabeth I which effected the incorporation of the East India Company,
corporations in practice enjoyed a common law immunity from prosecution
for any criminal offence. The reasons for this were both theoretical and
procedural, but, even after each was removed, there remained a reluctance
on the part of some judges to accept that there could be a general principle
of corporate criminal liability.[1]

THEORETICAL OBSTACLES

The theoretical basis for Sir John Holt's rejection of corporate criminal **2.2**
liability lay in his conclusion that a corporation was incapable of an act of
understanding and had no will to exercise.[2] The reasoning can be summarised thus: "a company cannot act in its own person for it has no person,
it can only act through directors, who are the agents of the company".[3] As
Lord Blackburn said, ". . . a body corporate never can either take care or
neglect to take care, except through its servants . . .".[4] Although the directors, as natural persons, may have a state of mind with legal significance (for
example: knowledge, intention, malice or belief), a corporation has no such
capacity.[5] A corporation is not like an individual; as Baron Thurlow is
reported to have said:

---

[1] See, e.g. Finlay J. in *R. v Cory Bros and Co Ltd* [1927] 1 K.B. 810.
[2] The *Case of Sutton's Hospital* (1612) 10 Rep. 1a, 32b.
[3] per Cairns L.J. in *Ferguson v Wilson* (1866) L.R. 2 Ch.App. 77, 89.
[4] *Mersey Dock Trustees v Gibbs* (1866–67) L.R. 1 HL 93, 104.
[5] "A corporation is incapable of malice or motive": per Lord Bramwell in *Abrath v N.E. Ry*
(1886) 11 App. Cas. 247, 251; "A company has no mind and cannot have an intention": per
Lord Reading C.J. in *R. v Grubb* [1915] 2 K.B. 683, 690.

> "Did you ever expect a corporation to have a conscience when it has no soul to be damned and no body to be kicked."[6]

This succinctly reflects the tension between criminal law, with its focus on an individualistic model of responsibility and punishment, and the corporate entity, which has been variously described as: *"an abstraction"*,[7] *"an impalpable thing"*[8] and *"a metaphysical entity"*.[9]

It is a maxim of the criminal law that "the deed does not make a man guilty unless his mind be guilty".[10] It was generally assumed that a corporation could not commit an offence which included a criminal state of mind:

> "By the general principles of criminal law, if a matter is made a criminal offence, it is essential that there should be something in the nature of *mens rea*, and therefore, in ordinary cases, a corporation aggregate cannot be guilty of a criminal offence."[11]

Moral blame, an exclusively human attribute, being regarded as the cornerstone of criminal responsibility, it is perhaps not surprising that the lack of soul identified by Baron Thurlow set corporations apart.

PROCEDURAL OBSTACLES

2.3 For a long time, the perceived theoretical difficulties in prosecuting corporate defendants were compounded by procedural factors.[12] As a general rule, the sentence on conviction for a felony was imprisonment or death,[13] neither of which could be visited upon a body corporate.[14] A fine could only be imposed on conviction for a felony if such powers were expressly provided by statute.[15] Although a corporation could be brought before a court of summary jurisdiction by virtue of the Summary Jurisdiction Act 1848,[16]

---

[6] Poynder, *Literary Extracts* (1844) Vol.1.

[7] per Lord Haldane L.C. in *Lennard's Carrying Co Ltd v Asiatic Petroleum Co Ltd* [1915] A.C. 705, 713.

[8] per Jessel M.R. in *Flitcroft's Case* (1882) 21 Ch D 519, 533.

[9] per Lord Blackburn in *The Pharmaceutical Society v London & Provincial Supply Association Ltd* (1880) 5 App. Cas. 857 HL.

[10] *"Actus no facit reum, nisi mens sit rea"*.

[11] Halsbury's Laws of England; 2nd edn, Vol.VIII, p.111; also see judgment of Channel J. in *Pearks, Gunston and Tee v Ward* [1902] 2 K.B. 1, 11.

[12] *DPP v Kent & Sussex Contractors Ltd* [1944] 1 K.B. 146, 157 per Hallet J.

[13] The only exception to which was manslaughter, which became punishable with a fine in 1828; 9 Geo. 4 c.31, s.9.

[14] In America, the Supreme Court took a more pragmatic view; in *US v Van Schaick* 134 F 592 (2nd Cir. 1904), the court peremptorily dismissed the argument that a corporation could not be convicted of the offence because the only sentence provided by statute was imprisonment, saying that "the social utility of such prosecutions clearly outweighed such an 'inadvertent' oversight by Congress.".

[15] The presumption against fines was finally removed by s.13 of the Criminal Justice Act 1948.

[16] *Evans & Co Ltd v London County Council* [1914] 3 K.B. 315.

until 1925, a defendant tried on indictment was required to attend in person at a trial at Assizes or quarter sessions. A corporation, being a *persona ficta* could only appear by attorney.[17] The only solution was to remove the indictment by writ of certiorari into the King's Bench where a corporation *could* appear by attorney.[18] The problem was removed by s.33(3) Criminal Justice Act 1925, which permitted a corporation to enter in writing by its representative a plea of guilty or not guilty.

THE EARLY LIMITS OF CORPORATE CRIMINAL LIABILITY

It is apparent from dicta in various nineteenth century cases that the judges **2.4** then regarded the compass of corporate criminal liability as being very narrow, extending only to public nuisance,[19] criminal libel[20] and, most significantly, breach of statutory duty. Historically, each of these had developed as an exception to the principle that a master was not to be held criminally liable for the wrongs of his servant unless he had authorized or aided and abetted them. The court did not want to encourage any unwarranted extension of the ambit of corporate criminal liability. Bramwell B. stated that he wished to guard himself against "... it being supposed that ... the general rule that the principal is not criminally responsible for the act of his agent is infringed."[21]

On the assumption that a corporation could neither act nor think itself, the courts were confronted with the problem of how, if at all, a corporation could commit a criminal offence; if it could not act, how could it cause a certain event forbidden by the criminal law (the actus reus), and if it could not think, how could it form the requisite state of mind in relation to the causing of the event forbidden by law (the mens rea)? Over time the courts developed two distinct rules of attribution, first vicarious liability, and, much later, the doctrine of identification.

VICARIOUS LIABILITY

At common law, a principal is not responsible for the act of his agent unless **2.5** he has commissioned (or "commanded") the offence; the doctrine of

---

[17] In *R. v Daily Mirror Newspapers Ltd* [1922] 2 K.B. 530, it was held that a limited company could not be committed for trial on indictment.
[18] *Birmingham & Gloucester Railway Company* [1914] 3 K.B. 315.
[19] *R. v Stephens* (1886) L.R. 1 Q.B. 702.
[20] *R. v Holbrook* (1878) 4 Q.B.D.
[21] In *R. v Stephens* (1886) L.R. 1 Q.B. 702.

respondeat superior[22] or vicarious liability forms no part of the criminal law of England and Wales[23]:

> "It is a point not to be disputed but that in a criminal case the principal is not answerable for the act of his deputy, as he is in civil cases; they must each answer for their own acts, and stand or fall by their own behaviour."[24]

In *R. v Huggins*,[25] the warden of the Fleet (H) was charged with the murder of a prisoner whose death had been caused by the servant of H's deputy. Lord Raymond C.J. ruled that, "He only is punishable, who immediately does the act or permits it to be done". The crime of the servant could not make H guilty without "the command of the superior"; as the murder was committed without his knowledge or command, H could not be guilty.

The doctrine of vicarious liability developed out of medieval concepts of the master/servant relationship. Originally restricted to cases where the wrong was expressly *commanded* by the master,[26] by the beginning of the eighteenth century it was accepted by the civil courts that the master (or employer) could be held liable for acts done at his implied, as well as his express, command. Such implied command could be inferred from the general terms of the servant's employment.

By the beginning of the next century, the courts had rejected the "command theory" of vicarious liability, accepting instead that liability depended upon the nature of the relationship between the employer and his employee. The employer was liable for the civil wrong of his employee provided the act was done in the course of his employment.[27] Given that an employer was unlikely to command his employer to commit a tort, still less to admit doing so, the courts were prepared to regard the employer as liable provided the act of the employee was sufficiently connected with his employment that it could be characterised as doing some authorised task in an unauthorised manner.[28] Attention was focussed on whether the wrong was done within the scope of the servant's employment.

2.6   However, vicarious liability was at that time restricted to civil wrongs committed against the public. Although there might be liability to the wider public for industrial accidents, the courts did not entertain the argument that an employer might be liable in negligence for harm done to one servant by another in the course of his employment.[29]

The difference in approach between the civil and criminal courts can be

---

[22] A phrase criticised by Lord Reid for doing no more than stating the rule baldly in two words; *Staveley Iron and Chemical Co v Jones* [1956] A.C. 627, 643.

[23] In the United States, vicarious liability does form the basis of corporate criminal liability.

[24] *Huggins* (1730) 2 Ld. Ray. 1574; (1730) 2 Str. 883, 885; 92 E.R. 518, per Raymond C.J.

[25] ibid.

[26] In fact, this is not vicarious liability at all but primary, inchoate liability.

[27] *Reedie v London & N.W. Ry* (1849) 4 Ex. 244.

[28] *Kirby v National Coal Board* [1958] S.C. 514, 533.

[29] See, e.g. *Vose v Lancs. & Yorks. Ry* (1858) 27 L.J. Ex. 249 per Pollock C.B.

demonstrated by reference to the case of *Lloyd v Grace, Smith & Co.*[30] The respondent was a firm of solicitors in Liverpool who employed a conveyancing manager who deceived one of the firm's clients into signing her properties to him. There was no suggestion of impropriety on the part of the firm. In the House of Lords, the plaintiff's appeal was allowed (unanimously). Lord Macnaghten made it clear that an employer is (civilly) liable for fraud committed by an employee:

> "And I think it follows ... a principal must be liable for the fraud of his agent committed in the course of his agent's employment and not beyond the scope of his agency, whether the fraud be committed for the principal's benefit or not."[31]

Summarising the position, Lord Macnaghten explained the rule in these terms:

> "... who is to suffer for this man's fraud? The person who relied on Mr Smith's accredited representative, or Mr Smith, who put the rogue in his own place and clothed him with his own authority?"[32]

Mr Smith, the principal, was civilly liable to the firm's client. The fraudulent employee was no doubt guilty of various criminal offences in his own right, but, in the absence of any encouragement or complicity, neither then nor today would Mr Smith also be criminally liable for the wrongdoing of his clerk.

It had already been held that a corporation could be civilly liable for the fraud of its agents:

> "Strictly speaking, a corporation cannot itself be guilty of fraud. But where a corporation is formed for the purpose of carrying on a trading or other speculation for profit, such as forming a railway, these objects can only be accomplished through the agency of individuals; and there can be no doubt that if the agents employed conduct themselves fraudulently, so that if they had been acting for a private employer, the person for whom they were acting would have been affected by their fraud, the same principles must prevail where the principal under whom the agent acts is a corporation."[33]

---

[30] [1912] A.C. 716 HL.
[31] At p.731.
[32] At p.738.
[33] *Ranger v Gt Western Ry Co* (1854) 86–87, per Lord Cottenham L.C.

Once it was recognised in the civil courts that an individual could be liable to pay damages to another for the wrongful or negligent act of his servant, it was only a matter of time before vicarious liability was relied upon in the prosecution of criminal offences which did not require proof of mens rea.[34] As Lord Atkin said[35]:

> "Once it is decided that this is one of those cases where the principal may be held liable for the act of his servant, there is no difficulty in holding that a corporation may be the principal."

BREACH OF STATUTORY DUTY

2.7 The State has long been concerned with the regulation of business activity for the benefit and protection of the public. The Magna Carta[36] provided for uniformity of weights and measures for wine, ale, corn and cloth, and by 1353, those using unjust weights and balances were liable to financial and corporal penalties.[37] The regulations that existed were as much concerned with the protection of the honest trader from unfair competition[38] as they were with the welfare of the population from adulteration of food. Up to the mid-nineteenth century, regulation followed on a piecemeal basis,[39] but in 1860 Parliament consolidated various regulations in the area of food safety

---

[34] "The real difficulty was to make out how any man, any natural man, could be vicariously liable to pay damages for the wrongful act or negligence of his servant, which he had in no way authorised and might even expressly have forbidden. When this was overcome, the difficulty of ascribing wrongful intention to an artificial person was in truth only a residue of anthropomorphic imagination." Sir Frederick Pollock in: *"Has the Common Law Received the Fiction Theory of Corporations?"*—Essays in the Law, 179.

[35] *Griffiths v Studebaker Ltd* [1927] 1 K.B. 102. Similarly, Bernard has said: "It was only a short step from the idea of a master as a human person to the master as a corporate person" Bernard (1984) *"The Historical Development of Corporate Criminal Liability"*; Criminology, 22:3.

[36] Magna Carta (25 Edw. 1 c.36).

[37] 27 Edw. III s.2 c.10:

> "Because we have perceived that some Merchants do buy wool and other merchandises by one weight, and sell by another, and also make deceitful draughts upon the weight, and also use false measures and yards, in great deceit of Us and of all the Commons, and of lawful Merchants We will establish that one weight, one measure and one Yard, be through all the Land, as well out of the Staple as within; ... and that he, which doth against the same, to the damage of the Seller, shall forfeit to Us the value of the merchandise so weighed and measured; and the Party that will complain him, shall have the quatreble of that which he shall be indamaged; and the Trespasser shall have one year's imprisonment, and be ransomed at the King's will..."

[38] Regulations were introduced as a result of pressure from guilds. The Guild of Pepperers existed in the reigns of Henry II and Henry III and was granted powers to garble (sift) spices and other foods by the Crown. The Garblers' powers were gradually extended to include various goods sold by grocers and druggists; Butterworths *Law of Food and Drugs A(2)*.

[39] The adulteration of tea was prohibited by Acts of 1730 and 1777, of coffee by Acts of 1718 and 1724, and of bread by Acts of 1758, 1822 and 1836; Butterworths *Law of Food and Drugs A(3)*.

in the Adulteration of Food and Drink Act.[40] From 1872,[41] local authorities were required to appoint inspectors to check for adulteration and enforce compliance with weights and measures regulation, considerably strengthening the effectiveness of the law.

The Adulteration of Food and Drink Act was just one of many Acts which had a public welfare character by which Parliament imposed vicarious liability.[42] Where Parliament has strictly proscribed the doing of a particular thing, if the thing happens, the person responsible will be guilty of an offence.[43] Where the person who does the proscribed thing is the servant or agent of a company and does so within the course and scope of his employment, his principal is vicariously liable for his misconduct. The employer need not be proved to have commanded, participated or even known of the criminal conduct of his servant, provided the conduct is referable to the employment relationship, or, to put it another way, was within the scope of his employment. This establishes the legal nexus on which the employer's liability is constructed.

Whether an act is committed within the scope of an individual's employment is a mixed question of law and fact. The approach of the courts has developed over time but it is now clear that the focus of attention is not the wrong itself but rather what the employee was engaged in when it was committed. This is why in criminal law there can be vicarious liability when the act has been expressly forbidden,[44] or even if the corporation is itself the victim of the employee's misconduct.[45] The argument that an employee who seeks to defraud his employer can never be acting within the scope of his employment has been rejected on policy grounds. Almost any criminal act committed by an employee would put him in breach of his contract of employment, and so outside the terms of his employment, though not the scope. If it were so simple to avoid liability, the public welfare policy on which vicarious liability is constructed would be completely undermined.

---

[40] Adulteration of Food and Drink Act 1860 (23 & 24 Vict. c.84). The Act followed the report of a Select Parliamentary Commission in 1855. The provisions of the Act were extended to drugs by the Pharmacy Act 1868.

[41] By the Adulteration of Food and Drink Act 1872.

[42] Other contemporaneous public welfare legislation include: the Public Health Act 1875, the Sale of Food & Drugs Act 1875 and the Merchandise Marks Act 1887.

[43] In *Bond v Evans* (1888) 21 Q.B.D. 249, Stephen J. said:

> "I think the meaning is that the landlord of licensed premises must prevent that which the Act prohibits from being done on his premises, and if he does not prevent it so much the worse for him."

[44] *Coppen v Moore; Re Ready Mixed Concrete (No.2); Canadian Pacific Railway Co v Lockhart* [1942] A.C. 591, 600 per Lord Thankerton.

[45] *Moore v I Bresler* [1944] 2 All E.R. 515.

VICARIOUS AND PERSONAL LIABILITY DISTINGUISHED

2.8 It is necessary to distinguish between liability for the acts of another (true vicarious liability) and liability for breach of a personal duty. In the latter category, although the act may be committed by an employee, it is the employer's own failure to prevent the harm that renders him liable. The person committing the act does not himself commit the offence because it can only be committed by the person fixed with the duty. Such duties have been described as non-delegable, not because the person fixed with the duty must carry it out personally (impossible in the case of a corporation), but because the responsibility cannot be delegated.

An example of a personal duty is to be found in s.31(1) of the Merchant Shipping Act 1988 which imposes on the "owner of a ship", a duty "to take all reasonable steps to secure that the ship is operated in a safe manner". The Divisional Court has held that although the section excludes mens rea because of the public interest in protecting life and property at sea, it did not follow that ship owners are vicariously liable for the actions of all employees however lowly. A ship owner was criminally liable only in respect of the failure to take such steps as it was reasonable for him to take in the circumstances.[46]

Whether the duty imposed by statute is vicarious or personal depends upon:

> "the object of the statute, the words used, the nature of the duty laid down, the person upon whom it is imposed, the person by whom it would in ordinary circumstances be performed, and the person upon whom the penalty is imposed".[47]

2.9 If the duty is strict (or "absolute"), the principle of vicarious liability is invoked.[48] Where a statute imposes a strict duty, an employer or principal will be liable for the acts of his employees or agents whether he has authorised them or not:

> "A master is not criminally responsible for a death caused by his servant's negligence, and still less for an offence depending on the servant's malice; nor can a master be held liable for the guilt of his servant in receiving goods knowing them to be stolen. And this principle of common law applies also to statutory offences, with this difference, that it is in the power of the Legislature, if it so pleases, to enact ... that a

---

[46] *Seaboard Offshore Ltd v Secretary of State for Transport* [1993] 3 All E.R. 25.
[47] per Atkin J. in *Mousell Bros Ltd v London and North Western Ry Co* [1917] 2 K.B. 836, 845.
[48] Not all offences of strict liability also involve vicarious liability. By way of example, the offences of dangerous and careless driving are strict, in that neither involves proof of any mens rea, but vicarious liability does not apply.

man may be convicted and punished for an offence although there was no blameworthy condition of mind about him."[49]

In these circumstances a corporation can properly be convicted for a breach of duty it did not encourage and may even have taken steps to prevent. In *Coppen v Moore (No.2)*,[50] the shop owner, Mr Coppen had given a clear written order forbidding staff from misdescribing goods for sale; Lord Russell C.J., referring to an earlier case of *Bond v Evans*,[51] stated:

> "The Court in fact came to the conclusion that having regard to the language, scope, and object of those Acts, the Legislature intended to fix criminal responsibility upon the master for acts done by his servant in the course of his employment, although such acts were not authorized by the master, and might even have been expressly prohibited by him."[52]

Many statutes are passed with this object[53] and "construed by the court in the way most effective for maintaining public order".[54]

Although many offences which attract vicarious liability are strict, it is not true to say that vicarious liability attaches only to offences with no fault element. By way of example, the offence of supplying liquor to a constable on duty requires proof of knowledge, but the courts have held[55] that the licensee may be convicted for the supply by a member of staff provided that the member of staff knew the person served was a constable on duty. If the court had held otherwise, it would "render the enactment wholly inoperative".[56]

Given that there exists a presumption that some criminal state of mind is **2.10** required to prove a criminal offence,[57] the first step is to determine whether any particular statutory offence requires proof of mens rea or not. The court will presume that mens rea is an element of an offence unless Parliament has clearly indicated to the contrary either expressly or by necessary implica-

---

[49] *Chisholm v Doulton* (1889) 22 Q.B.D. 736, 741, per Cave J. and see *Coppen v Moore (No.2)*, below.
[50] [1898] 2 Q.B. 306.
[51] (1888) 21 Q.B.D. 249.
[52] *Coppen v Moore (No.2)* [1898] 2 Q.B. 306, 311–313.
[53] per Viscount Reading C.J. in *Mousell Bros v London & N.W. Ry* [1917] 2 K.B. 836, 844.
[54] *Mullins v Collins* (1874) L.R. 9 Q.B. 292, 295 per Archibald J.
[55] (1874) L.R. 9 Q.B.
[56] per Quain J. at p.295.
[57] *Woolmington v DPP* [1935] A.C. 462, 481; *Gammon (Hong Kong) Ltd v Att-Gen of Hong Kong* [1988] A.C. 1 PC.

tion.[58] The presumption can be displaced dependant upon the wording of the section. Where an offence had as its purpose the protection of public health, the courts would readily conclude that a person could be convicted absent a criminal state of mind. For example, in *Hobbs v Winchester Corporation*,[59] Farwell L.J. decided that the need to protect the public from unsound food required the imposition of liability on the supplier irrespective of fault on his part.

The problem inherent in this approach is that it can lead to the conviction of the morally blameless, a factor to be taken into account by the court when determining whether the particular provision does impose strict liability. As Devlin J. recognised, whilst there may be sound policy reasons for making a person responsible for the acts of another in order to discourage thoughtlessness or inefficiency, to punish because of an act done by someone over whom he could not reasonably have been expected to influence or control, is unjustified.[60]

This dilemma continues to trouble the courts. To Lord Reid, the conviction of the morally blameless was "an injustice which brings the law into disrepute".[61] However, the possibility of "absurd results" should not deter the court from concluding that the offence is one of strict liability, as Steyn L.J. said in *R. v British Steel*[62]:

> "...so called absurdities are not peculiar to this corner of the law; at the extremities of the field of application of many rules surprising results are often to be found. That circumstance is inherent in the adoption of general rules to govern an infinity of particular circumstances."

RAILWAYS

2.11 Corporate criminal liability developed on the back of the expansion of the canal and, in particular, the railway network. The construction and operation of railways by corporations in the nineteenth century was the cause of significant injury to the public and workers as well as damage to property. A conspicuous degree of control over the expansion of the railway network was maintained by the Legislature because, in order to be granted the powers of compulsory purchase they needed, the railway companies had

---

[58] *R. v A (a minor)*. The position post Human Rights Act 1998 was considered by Dyson L.J. in *Muhamed* [2002] EWCA Crim 1856.

[59] [1910] 2 K.B. 471, 481:

> "The knowledge or possible means of knowledge of the butcher is not a matter which affects the public; it is unsound meat which poisons them; and I think the Legislature intended that the butcher should sell unsound meat at his peril."

[60] *Reynolds v GH Austin & Sons Ltd* [1951] 2 K.B. 135, 149.

[61] *Tesco Supermarkets Ltd v Nattrass* [1972] 1 A.C. 153, 169.

[62] [1995] 1 W.L.R. 1350, 1363.

to be incorporated by an Act of Parliament, which permitted construction of the railway in accordance with statutory regulations. Prosecutions were occasionally brought in respect of conduct said not to be in conformity with the powers conferred on the company by the Legislature. In the earliest reported case, the prosecution relied upon non-feasance by the company where the particular failure was proscribed on pain of criminal sanction.[63]

In *R. v Birmingham and Gloucester Railway Company*,[64] Patterson J. giving the judgment of the Court of Queen's Bench,[65] rejected the argument that an indictment could not lie against a corporation:

> "Only one direct authority was cited for this proposition: and it is the dictum of Lord Holt in an *Anonymous* case. The report itself is as follows: 'Note: *Per* Holt Chief Justice. A corporation is not indictable, but the particular members of it are'. What the nature of the offence was to which the observation was intended to apply does not appear, and as a general proposition it is opposed to a number of cases which show that a corporation may be indicted for breach of a duty imposed upon it by law, though not for a felony, or for crimes involving personal violence as for riots or assaults."

The *Birmingham and Gloucester Ry* case involved strict liability for non-feasance in that it failed to construct connecting arches over a railway line it had built so preventing safe crossing of the line by human and other traffic. As the breach was one of omission, there was no human offender in respect of whom the court need have concern. However, courts were soon compelled to recognise that there was no practical distinction to be drawn between *non-feasance* and *misfeasance*. In 1846, four years after the *Birmingham & Gloucester Ry* case, another railway company was prosecuted for breach of duty, this time for committing rather than tolerating a wrong.

The *Great North of England Railway Co*[66] case concerned a highway which was habitually used "by and for all the liege subjects on foot and with their horses and carriages". According to the prosecution, on July 3, 1846, workmen employed by the defendant company "with force and arms unlawfully and injuriously" cut a trench through and/or dug up the highway "to the great damage and common nuisance of all Her Majesty's liege subjects."

For the defendant company it was argued that no indictment for *mis-* **2.12** *feasance* could lie against a corporation. The company was convicted and appealed. Lord Denman C.J. resoundingly dismissed that submission

---

[63] In *R. v Severn & Wye Ry Co* (1819) 2 B. & Ald. 646, it was assumed that a railway company could be indicted for failing to maintain its permanent way.

[64] (1842) 3 Q.B. 223, 232.

[65] The indictment was removed by writ of certiorari into the Queen's Bench where a corporation could appear by attorney, because a corporation could not enter a plea on arraignment at Assizes or quarter sessions (see para.2.3, above).

[66] (1846) 9 Q.B. 315.

(observing that"no assumption could ever be more unfounded"), and then went onto state[67]:

> "The law is often entangled in technical embarrassments; but there is none here. It is as easy to charge one person, or a body corporate, with erecting a bar across a public road as with the non-repair of it; and they may as well be compelled to pay a fine for the act or for the omission."

The distinction between *non-* and *mis-feasance* became untenable. In a later case,[68] a company was prosecuted for an offence contrary to s.4 of the Shops Act 1912. The court observed that the offence could either be characterised as failing to close or keeping open; in either case the essence of the offence was disobedience to the statute.

PERSONS—"NATURAL" AND "LEGAL"

2.13 The nature and extent of the liability imposed by a criminal provision is a question of construction. Ordinarily, the section will make it an offence for a *person* to do, or to fail to do a particular thing. These two early railway cases concerned prosecutions for conduct not in conformity with the powers conferred on the defendant companies by Parliament; neither required proof of any mental element. The responsibility lay upon the corporation itself, rather than with any individual officers. Liability was imposed directly, not vicariously, on the company. Whether either company was a "person" was not in issue since the particular statute did not proscribe conduct by a "person"; each was prosecuted for offences under the Act of Parliament which brought it into being.

Whether the word "person" in a general statute could be treated as including a corporation was first considered in a civil case concerning a Jamaican civil statute prescribing rules for substituted service. The Privy Council decided that as there was nothing in the context nor in the object of the provision indicating an intention to limit its application, the word "person" was apt to describe a corporation as well as a natural person.[69]

The first criminal case that confirmed this point and considered the circumstances in which "person" applied to a corporation was *The Pharmaceutical Society v London & Provincial Supply Association Limited*.[70] This was a prosecution brought under the Pharmacy Act 1868 against a small unincorporated company that had obtained registration under the Companies Acts 1862–67. Only one of the members was a qualified registered chemist and he was employed on a salary to work in the shop and dispense

---

[67] (1842) 3 Q.B. 223, 325.

[68] *Evans & Co Ltd v London CC* [1914] 3 K.B. 315.

[69] *The Pharmaceutical Society v London & Provincial Supply Association Ltd* (1880) 5 App. Cas. 857 HL.

[70] (1880) 5 App. Cas. 857 HL.

drugs. The House of Lords held that because the Pharmacy Act required pharmacists to qualify and obtain registration with the society, these were conditions required of a human person rather than a legal one. However, the outcome of the case depended upon a question of construction rather than any conceptual obstacle. The Lord Chancellor, Lord Selbourne, said[71]:

> "There can be no question that the word 'person' may, and I should be disposed myself to say prima facie does, in a public statute, include a person in law: that is, a corporation, as well as a natural person."

This case was decided before the enactment of the Interpretation Act 1889, s.2(1) of which provided that references to a "person" in any statute should, "unless the contrary intention appears, include a body corporate". However, the case established the principle that in order to determine whether any particular statutory offence applied to a company, it was necessary to analyse the language, scope and object of the Act in question. Perhaps the clearest statement of this principle was made by Atkin J.[72]:

> "Regard must be had to the object of the statute, the words used, the nature of the duty laid down, the person upon whom it was imposed, the person by whom in ordinary circumstances it would be performed, and the person upon whom the penalty is imposed."

An early case in which it was held that "person" did *not* include a cor- **2.14** poration was *Wills v Tozer*[73] which concerned the entitlement of the defendant company to vote in an election for commissioners of Teignmouth harbour.[74] The court held that the language of the Act showed that voters had to be *natural* persons. The head note provides:

> "The word 'person' when used in a statute, does not include a corporation where the statute contains expressions that are repugnant to that construction."

Similarly, in *Hawke v Hulton & Co*,[75] "person" as used in s.41 of the Lotteries Act 1823 could not include "corporation", because the section provided that "every person publishing a proposal for a lottery should be deemed a rogue and vagabond and punished by imprisonment and whipping"!

This process of statutory analysis is not only of historical interest. In the relatively recent case of *Richmond upon Thames LBC v Pinn and Wheeler*,[76] the court used precisely the same tools to conclude that since the act of driving a lorry was a physical act which could be performed only by a

---

[71] At 861.
[72] *Mousell Bros Ltd v London & N.W. Ry* [1917] 2 K.B. 836, 845.
[73] (1904) 53 W.R. 74 Ch D.
[74] Under the Teignmouth Harbour Act 1853.
[75] [1909] 2 K.B. 93.
[76] (1989) 87 L.G.R. 659 DC.

natural person, the word "person" when used in s.142 of the Road Traffic Regulations Act 1984 ("no person shall drive any goods vehicle during proscribed hours") did not include a legal person.

Although s.2(1) of the Interpretation Act 1889 only repeated what had already been enacted,[77] it seemed to have a greater impact on the courts than its predecessor with the result that the courts began to explore the circumstances in which a company might be held liable for the misconduct of its employees. Inevitably, as more and more companies were incorporated under the Companies Acts 1862–98, the courts had to determine whether a company was guilty of a statutory offence, the actus reus of which was, as a matter of fact, committed by an employee of the company.

2.15   Justification for the imposition on a company of criminal responsibility for the conduct of its employees was cogently explained by the US Supreme Court[78] as follows:

> "The act of the agent may be controlled, in the interest of public policy, by imputing his act to his employer and imposing penalties on the corporation for which he is acting."

Dean Roscoe Pound succinctly explained the rationale for strict liability[79]:

> "Such statutes are not meant to punish the vicious will, but to put pressure upon the thoughtless and inefficient to do their whole duty in the interests of public health or safety or morals."

"SELLING"

2.16   As has already been observed, a company is *ex hypothesi*, a distinct legal person.[80] But if the company is engaged with the public in the sale of goods or provision of services, it is with people that the customer has contact. The lexicon of commerce is far older than that of the modern joint stock company. Because ordinary words like "buy" and "sell" were employed in public welfare and consumer protection legislation, the courts had to consider a vocabulary that reflected the interpersonal nature of the commercial transactions they described.

In *Coppen v Moore (No.2)*,[81] the defendant was an individual trader, not a limited company. He owned six shops including one in Richmond, Surrey. Mr Moore, a customer, wanted to buy ham. A salesman employed by the appellant pointed to a number of small hams in the window saying they

---

[77] s.14 Criminal Law Act 1827.
[78] In *N.Y.C. & H.R. Ry Co v US* 212 US 481.
[79] *The Spirit of the Common Law*, L.Q.R. 64, p.176; as quoted by Devlin, J. in *Reynolds v GH Austin & Sons Ltd* [1951] 2 K.B. 135, 149.
[80] *Salomon v Salomon & Co Ltd* [1897] A.C. 22.
[81] [1898] 2 Q.B. 306.

were Scotch: he wrote that description on the invoice. The ham in question was in fact American. Mr Coppen was charged with an offence contrary to s.2(2) of the Merchandise Marks Act 1887, namely selling goods to which a false trade description was applied. It emerged in evidence that Mr Coppen (who was not at the store at the time of the sale) had given clear instructions on the importance of accurately describing hams to staff at all his shops.

His instruction was ignored by the salesman. The appellant relied on the general principle "*nemo reus est nisi mens sit rea*"; he personally had not sold the misdescribed ham, he had given clear instructions that it should not be misdescribed. He did not have any criminal state of mind, indeed he was unaware at the time that the offence had been committed.

Lord Russell decided the issue of liability by looking at the offence **2.17** creating section of the Act, finding that it was clearly the intention of the Legislature to make the master criminally liable for for acts done by his servant in contravention of the Act where such acts were done, as in this case, within the scope or the course of their employment, observing, in a phrase that would echo down the years:

> "... when the scope and object of the Act are borne in mind, any other conclusions would to a large extent render the Act ineffective for its avowed purpose".[82]

Mr Coppen was the seller, not the actual salesman. Accordingly, he was guilty of selling goods to which a false trade description had applied.

Four years later, "selling" was again considered by the Divisional Court. In *Pearks, Gunston & Tee Ltd v Ward*,[83] the appellant, a limited joint stock company, was convicted of selling butter which was not "of the nature, substance and quality demanded".[84] It was argued by the appellant that the company was not liable to the penalties imposed upon the "person", relying upon *The Pharmaceutical Society v London and Provincial Supply Association*.[85] Lord Alverstone C.J. was of the view that "the sale is just as much a sale, if by a corporation, as if by an individual person". Although *Coppen v Moore (No.2)* was not referred to, Channell J. sat on both cases, so it is reasonable to presume that the earlier case had some influence over the court. In his judgment in the later case, Channell J. explained that the reason why a corporation could be convicted of what he termed a quasi-criminal offence was because the legislature thought it so important to prevent the particular act from being committed that it absolutely forbids it:

> "Where the act is of this character, then the master who, in fact, has done the forbidden thing through his servant, is responsible and is liable to a penalty. There is no reason why he should not be, because

---

[82] *Coppen v Moore (No.2)* [1898] 2 Q.B. 306, 314.
[83] *Pearks, Gunston & Tee Ltd v Ward* [1902] 2 K.B. 1, 11.
[84] Contrary to s.6 of the Sale of Food and Drugs Act 1875.
[85] Below, (1880) 5 App. Cas. 857 HL.

the very object of the Legislature was to forbid the thing absolutely. It seems to me that exactly the same principle applies in the case of a corporation. If it does the act which is forbidden, it is liable."

Thus, by the beginning of the twentieth century, it was well settled that a corporation could be convicted of a criminal offence provided that it fell within the categories of public nuisance, criminal libel or what Channell J. called quasi-criminal or regulatory offences. As has been shown, the basis of such liability was an extension of the responsibility of the master for the acts of his servants. The courts had yet to grapple with the question as to whether there might be any corporate criminal liability for offences in respect of which mens rea had to be proved. This was the next important development for corporate criminal liability.

LIABILITY FOR MENS REA OFFENCES: PRE 1944

INTRODUCTION

Encouraged, no doubt, by s.2(1) of the Interpretation Act 1889,[1] by the turn **3.1** of the nineteenth century, the criminal courts accepted that a corporation could be liable for a wide range of criminal offences within the regulatory sphere. Despite the lengthy gestation, there is no particular conceptual difficulty in the idea of a legal person selling or constructing. More difficult than the concept of a legal person selling or constructing is that of a corporation having a state of mind, a routine ingredient in criminal offences. Did such an ingredient in the description of a criminal offence indicate "a contrary intention" so as to exclude from liability a body of persons corporate or unincorporated? Could a legal person have a state of mind at all? The answer the judges gave to this question was "yes", but that answer, when eventually given, was given hesitantly and hedged about with qualifications.

Before 1911, there is no report to suggest that an appellate court had considered the conviction of a company for an offence which required proof of some criminal state of mind, but in that year the Divisional Court heard an appeal by Mr Chuter,[2] a food inspector. The case concerned milk. The inspector had bought some from a milkman which was found, on analysis, to have been diluted. The milkman was prosecuted under s.6 of the Sale of Food & Drugs Act 1899; the respondent was the company who had supplied the milk to him. The milkman was acquitted because the court was satisfied that he had no reason to believe that the milk was not in accordance with the warranty given to him by the respondent. The respondent was also acquitted

---

[1] The phrase "subject to the appearance of a contrary intention, the word person in a statute or subordinate legislation is to be construed as including a body of persons corporate or unincorporate" had first appeared some sixty years earlier in the Criminal Law Act of 1827.
[2] *Chuter v Freeth Pocock Ltd* [1911] 2 K.B. 832 DC.

because the magistrate was of the opinion that "only such person could commit the offence as was capable of believing, and a corporation having no mind could not exercise that faculty". The appeal by the prosecutor was allowed, Lord Alverstone C.J. giving the judgment of the court[3]:

> "Where a person is capable of giving a warranty that person is liable to a fine. There is no reason why a warranty should not be given by a corporation. It can give a warranty through its agents, and through its agents it can believe or not believe, as the case may be, that the statements in the warranty are true. Further, the question in this case has in substance been decided by Channell J. in *Pearks, Gunston & Tee v Ward*."

Pearks, Gunston & Tee v Ward was, as has been discussed, a case under s.6 of the Sale of Food & Drugs Act 1875, an offence of strict liability. In the earlier case, at the end of his judgment, in a passage that was strictly obiter, Channell J. (considering the position under ss.3 and 5 of the same Act)[4] inclined to the view that a corporation could be convicted of offences requiring mens rea.

In the lower court, the magistrate had dismissed the summons against the company. It was a defence under the 1899 Act for a person who gave to a purchaser a false warranty, to prove that when he gave the warranty, he had reason to believe that it was true; the magistrate relied on the verb *"believe"*, as showing the offence could not be committed by a corporation. The Divisional Court said he was wrong; the *Case of Sutton's Hospital*[5] was thus consigned to legal history.

3.2   In *Chuter*, the effect of the legislation was to remove from the prosecution the burden of proving knowledge (mens rea) on the part of the seller; a prima facie case was established on proof of the prohibited act. The statute provided the accused with a defence if he proved (on the balance of probabilities) that he did not have knowledge at the time of the offence. Despite the fact that *Chuter* was a case of strict liability, it was relied upon a few years later (in 1917) in *Mousell Bros Ltd v London & North West Ry Co Ltd*, the first case in which the liability of a company for an offence which required proof of mens rea was considered by an appellate court.

MOUSELL BROS LTD V LONDON & NORTH WEST RY CO LTD[6]

3.3   By s.98 of the Railways Clauses Consolidation Act 1845,[7] the owner of goods (or other persons responsible for them), was required to provide to

---

[3] *Chuter v Freeth Pocock Ltd* [1911] 2 K.B. 832, 836.
[4] [1902] 2 K.B. 1, 12.
[5] (1612) 77 All E.R. 937.
[6] *Mousell Bros Ltd v London & North West Ry Co Ltd* [1917] 2 K.B. 836.
[7] 8 & 9 Vict. c.20.

the collector of tolls for the railway an exact account of the goods to be carried; and by s.99 of the Act, if such a person gave a false account *with intent to avoid* the payment of tolls, he committed an offence. On two separate occasions in November 1916, the appellant company had delivered to the respondents lorry loads of its goods for carriage on the railway. On each occasion, the driver handed over a consignment note which in fact misdescribed the loads. It was not suggested that the directors of the appellant company were themselves parties to the false descriptions.

The court concluded that the object of the statute was to forbid the giving of a false description of goods carried on the railway and so to protect the railway company from being cheated into carrying goods at less than the due rate.[8] Plainly, a criminal state of mind was necessary on the part of the person giving the false account. The magistrate had found as a fact that the consignment notes contained incorrect descriptions of the goods; this had been done on the instructions of the manager in order to avoid payment of the proper tolls. The manager had the authority of the company to complete the consignment notes. He was not the owner of the goods, although he might have been a person responsible for them. In any event, he was not prosecuted.

The resolution of the case depended upon statutory construction. Both judges (Viscount Reading C.J. and Atkin J.) were clear that even in 1845, the duty imposed on the owner or other person having care of the goods to be carried by the railway would in most cases have been carried out by the servant of the owner of the goods. Accordingly, they concluded that the Legislature intended to fix responsibility for this quasi-criminal offence upon the principal if the forbidden act was done by his servant within the scope of his employment.

Viscount Reading C.J. saw nothing to distinguish a limited company from **3.4** any other principal.[9]

Dealing with the question of intent, Atkin J. was entirely satisfied that the owner of goods, the principal, was liable if his servant gave a false account with the state of mind required by the Act:

> "I see no difficulty in the fact that an intent to avoid payment is necessary to constitute the offence. That is an intent which the servant might well have, inasmuch as he is the person who has to deal with the particular matter. The penalty is imposed upon the owner for the act of the servant if the servant commits the default provided for in the statute in the state of mind provided for by the statute. Once it is decided that this is one of those cases where a principal may be held liable criminally for the act of his servant, there is no difficulty in holding that a corporation may be the principal. No *mens rea* being necessary to make the

---

[8] per Viscount Reading C.J., 845.
[9] *Mousell Bros Ltd v London & North West Ry Co Ltd* [1917] 2 K.B. 836, 845.

principal liable, a corporation is in exactly the same position as a
principal who is not a corporation."

In each of these cases, the criminal responsibility of the corporation was
established on the basis of *vicarious* liability for the act or acts of its servant
acting within the scope and course of his employment. In none was the
question of *personal* liability of the corporation an issue, notwithstanding
the decision of the House of Lords in *Salomon*.

R. v CORY BROS & CO LTD[10]

3.5 The first reported occasion in which a prosecution was brought against a
company for the offence of manslaughter (obviously *not* an offence of strict
liability), arose out of the miner's strike of August 1926. The defendants
were a private mining company, Cory Bros & Co Ltd, and three of its
employees. It appears that the directors of the company responded to the
strike by erecting an electric fence around the colliery power house to discourage pilfering. Soon afterwards, an unemployed miner (who was not
pilfering but ratting) tripped and fell against the fence and was electrocuted.
Private prosecutions were brought against the company and the engineers
responsible for the electric fence.[11] At the Assizes, Finlay J. quashed the
indictment holding that he was "bound by the authorities which show quite
clearly that as the law stands an indictment will not lie against a corporation
either for a felony or for a misdemeanour of the nature set out in the second
count of this indictment".[12]

Finlay J.'s decision was not inevitable. His scrutiny of the law was
minimal; he referred to only four cases,[13] the most recent of which was
decided in 1891. Absent from the decision, despite the submissions of the
prosecution, is any analysis of the reasons why, in the passages cited from
the *Birmingham & Gloucester Ry* case, Patterson J. had said[14]:

> "...a corporation may be indicted for breach of a duty imposed on it
> by law though not for a felony or for crimes involving personal
> violence..."

or why in the *Great North of England Ry* case, Lord Denman had said[15]:

---

[10] [1927] 1 K.B. 810.
[11] Supported by the dead man's union: the South Wales Miners' Federation.
[12] At 817.
[13] The four cases were: *Birmingham & Gloucester Ry*, *Great North of England Ry*, *R. v Tyler* and
The Pharmaceutical Society v London and Provincial Supply Association.
[14] *Birmingham & Gloucester Ry* (1842) 3 Q.B. 223, 232. As early as 1851, the same judge had
held that a corporation could be civilly liable (in trespass) for assault and battery; *Eastern
Counties Ry v Broom* (1851) 6 Ex. 314, 325.
[15] *Great North of England Ry* (1846) 9 Q.B. 315, 326.

"Some dicta occur in old cases: 'A corporation cannot be guilty of treason or felony.' It might be added 'of perjury, or offences against the person.'"

It seems highly unlikely that a decision of such significance as erecting an electric fence around the power house during a strike would have been taken other than by the board of directors; the engineers who were charged (but acquitted) would have had little practical alternative but to obey the company's orders. In a critical commentary of the decision written in 1929, Winn[16] wrote:

"... the *intra vires* decisions and commands of the board of directors, are factually, and should be legally, the decisions of the corporation ... A corporation should be answerable criminally as well as civilly for the acts of its primary representatives."

Less than 20 years later in *DPP v Kent & Sussex Contractors Ltd*,[17] Hallet J. said:

"Finlay J. referred to certain types of crime in respect of which according to old authorities by which he considered himself to be bound, a body corporate could not be held liable. It may be that those authorities will require reconsideration some day in the light of the development to which I have already referred ..."

Although *R. v Cory Bros Ltd* no longer represents the law,[18] it is typical of the uneven development of corporate criminal liability. Early judicial opposition to corporate liability was couched in terms of procedural obstacles, but the opposition persisted even after those obstacles were removed. Well after the law had changed, old cases were relied on as precedent for the conclusion that corporations could not be guilty of a felony.

---

[16] *"The Criminal Responsibility of Corporations"* (1929) 3 C.L.J. 398.

[17] [1944] 1 K.B. 146, 157.

[18] *R. v P&O European Ferries (Dover) Ltd* (1991) 93 Cr.App.R. 72; *Att-Gen's Reference (No.2 of 1999)* [2000] 2 Cr.App.R. 207.

CHAPTER 4

THE DOCTRINE OF "IDENTIFICATION"

THE 1944 CASES

The report of *R. v Cory Bros Ltd* does not reveal whether the prosecution **4.1** case rejected by the judge on the ground that a corporation could not be personally, as opposed to vicariously liable and it is not clear how the prosecution put its case against the company. However, in a trio of cases reported in 1944,[1] there was no doubt that the crucial issue was the *personal* liability of the companies in question.

It has already been noted that until 1944, all the cases of criminal responsibility of corporations were based on vicarious liability. Beginning with the offences of strict liability, where the corporation was liable for the conduct of its employee without proof of any criminal state of mind, the courts eventually extended the vicarious liability of corporations to include offences where some mental element was required.[2]

Corporations only became liable for offences beyond the confines of regulatory or quasi-crimes when the courts decided that those who managed or controlled the affairs of a company could be regarded as *embodying* a company. To put it another way, once the courts acknowledged that the acts (including the states of mind) of its human agents could in certain circumstances be regarded in law as the acts of the corporation itself, criminal liability could be imposed on it for virtually any offence. According to the doctrine of vicarious liability, the company can be responsible for the acts of its employees but they remain the acts of the employees. But from 1944, a company could be criminally liable on the basis that the acts of certain employees were regarded as being *the acts of the company itself*. This is direct, personal liability, not vicarious liability. The first of the trio of cases

---

[1] The first of these cases, *DPP v Kent & Sussex Contractors Ltd*, was in fact decided in late 1943, but was not reported until the following year.
[2] e.g. "with intent to avoid payment"; *Mousell Bros Ltd v London & North West Ry Co Ltd* [1917] 2 K.B. 836.

which established this principle was *DPP v Kent & Sussex Contractors Ltd*,[3] decided in November 1943.

DPP v Kent & Sussex Contractors Ltd[4]

4.2 The company was prosecuted[5] for offences of: (i) issuing a record which was false in a material particular in that it misstated the journeys and mileage of a company vehicle with intent to deceive, and (ii) furnishing false information. The records were submitted on behalf of the company by the transport manager, to obtain petrol coupons. The magistrates found that the record was false in the material particular alleged, to the knowledge of the transport manager, but acquitted the defendant on the ground that, since the offences charged "an act of will or state of mind" which could not be imputed to a company, a company could not in law be guilty of them.

Was a company capable of an act of will or state of mind, so as to be able to form an intention to deceive or to have knowledge of the truth or falsity of a statement? Although *Mousell Bros* was referred to by the court with approval, the appeal was not decided on vicarious principles, but on the basis of the company itself having the required state of mind—an intent to deceive.

In his judgment Viscount Caldecote L.C.J. said this[6]:

> "It is necessary to bear in the mind the position of a company, which is quite different from that of a private individual, a real person. It could not be better put than Lord Blackburn puts it in *The Pharmaceutical Society v London & Provincial Supply Association* where he says: 'a corporation may in one sense, for all substantial purposes of protecting the public, possess a competent knowledge of its business, if it employs competent directors, manager and so forth but it cannot possibly have a competent knowledge in itself. The metaphysical entity, the legal "person", the corporation, cannot possibly have a competent knowledge.'
>
> "...although the directors or general manager of a company are its agents, they are something more. *A company is incapable of acting or speaking, or even thinking except in so far as its officers have acted, spoken or thought.*"[7] [emphasis added].

4.3 Hallett J. considered that it would be strange and undesirable if a body corporate desiring to obtain petrol coupons and furnishing dishonest

---

[3] [1944] 1 K.B. 146.
[4] ibid.
[5] Under the Motor Fuel Rationing Order, 1941, issued under the Defence (General) Regulations 1939.
[6] ibid. at 154–155.
[7] ibid. at 156.

information for that purpose should be able to escape the liability which would be incurred in like case by a private person. He referred to *Pearks, Gunston and Tee Ltd v Ward*,[8] *Mousell Bros*[9] and *Law Society v United Service Bureau Ltd*[10] all cases of vicarious, not imputed liability.

It was all the more remarkable that this case heralded the first appearance of the "doctrine of identification" in the criminal law since there was no reference to the judgment of Viscount Haldane L.C. in the civil case of *Lennard's Carrying Co Ltd v Asiatic Petroleum Co Ltd*,[11] to which the origin of the principle can be directly traced. Viscount Haldane had said[12]:

> "A corporation is an abstraction. It has no mind of its own any more than it has a body; its active and directing will must consequently be sought in the person of somebody who for some purposes may be called an agent, but who is really the directing mind and will of the corporation, the very *ego* and centre of the personality of the corporation."

Perhaps for that reason, the Divisional Court gave no consideration to whether the transport manager represented the "directing mind and will" of the company. Nevertheless, within a few months, the decision of the Divisional Court was approved by the Court of Appeal, Criminal Division.

R. v ICR HAULAGE CO LTD[13]

The factual background to the case is of some importance. The appellant **4.4** was a private company (incorporated under the Companies Act) engaged in the haulage business; the criminal charge arose out of a contract for the supply and delivery of hardcore and ballast to a firm called Rice & Sons Ltd, a public works contractor. The prosecution alleged that the defendants, who included the company, the managing director, two ICR drivers and two Rice & Sons employees, conspired together to defraud Rice & Sons Ltd by charging it for hardcore in excess of that which was in fact delivered.

Thus the company was charged, together with its managing director, with a common law offence of conspiracy to defraud—requiring proof of a criminal state of mind. The principal defendants were all convicted. On appeal, it was argued for the company that it could not be indicted for conspiracy or indeed any offence involving mens rea as an essential ingredient.

Stable J., giving the judgment of the court, rejected that submission. *DPP*

---

[8] [1902] 2 K.B. 1.
[9] [1917] 2 K.B. 836.
[10] [1934] 1 K.B. 343, 349.
[11] [1915] A.C. 705.
[12] ibid. at 713.
[13] [1944] K.B. 551; (1944) 30 Cr.App.R. 31.

v Kent & Sussex Contractors was specifically approved ("with both the decision and the reasoning on which it rests, we agree").[14] The judge recognised that *Mousell Bros* was a case of vicarious liability and so did not answer the question for the Court in the instant case. Concluding his judgment, Stable J. said this[15]:

> "We are not deciding that in every case where an agent of a limited company acting in its business commits a crime the company is automatically to be held criminally responsible ... Whether in any particular case there is evidence to go to a jury, that the criminal act of an agent, including his state of mind, intention, knowledge or belief is the act of the company, ... must depend on the nature of the charge, the relative position of the officer or agent and the other relevant facts and circumstances of the case."

It was unnecessary for the court to consider "the relative position of the officer or agent" to determine whether his act was the act of the company, because the appellant was, in effect, a one man band. All the decisions were taken by Mr Robarts, the managing director, who was also a defendant. His acts were plainly the acts of the company.

4.5   In his judgment in the landmark case of *Tesco Supermarkets v Nattrass*,[16] Lord Reid doubted whether "the nature of the charge" was a relevant factor in determining whether the state of mind and act of an agent may be the state of mind and act of a company:

> "If the guilty man was in law identifiable with the company, then whether his offence was serious or venial his act was the act of the company."

It is submitted that if Stable J. was intending to indicate that the nature of the charge may determine the level or capacity of the employee whose act may be identified with the company, his dictum is consistent with the opinion of Lord Hoffmann in *Meridian*.[17]

MOORE V I BRESLER LTD[18]

4.6 The last of the trio, *Moore v I Bresler Ltd* was heard in October 1944 by a Divisional Court; the leading judgment was given by Viscount Caldecote L.C.J., as it had been in *DPP v Kent and Sussex Contractors Ltd*. The company, together with the company secretary, a man called Sydney Bresler

---

[14] At 39.
[15] At 39, 40.
[16] [1972] A.C. 153, 173; see below.
[17] *Meridian Global Funds Management Asia Ltd v Securities Commission* [1995] 2 A.C. 500, 511; see below.
[18] [1944] 2 K.B. 515.

(who was also the general manager) and the sales manager of its Nottingham branch, Phillips, were prosecuted under s.35(2) of the Finance (No.2) Act 1940, by which it was an offence for any person, for the purpose of the Act, to make use of any document which was false in a material particular *with intent to deceive*. The offence creating section employed almost identical wording to that used under the regulations[19] considered in *DPP v Kent and Sussex Contractors Ltd*. With the object of defrauding the company, Bresler and Phillips sold handbags intended for sale to the public. They pocketed the money and produced false documents to conceal the sales. Accordingly, the company was embezzled by its own employees. The company, through the natural defendants, submitted tax returns which showed a lower sales figure than they should have (because the figures were supressed), and thus, evaded its liability under the Act. The Recorder allowed the company's appeal[20] on the ground that it was the victim of a fraud by its employees whose misconduct was outwith the scope of their authority.

Viscount Caldecote did not regard the fact of the victim of the fraud being the company as significant; what mattered was that[21]:

> "... These two men were important officials of the company, and when they made statements and rendered returns, they were clearly making those statements and giving those returns *as the officers of the company, the proper officers to make the returns*. Their acts, therefore ... were the acts of the company."

Humphrey J. agreed[22]:

> "Being a limited company, the company could only act by means of human agents. It is difficult to imagine two persons whose acts could more effectively bind the company or who could be said in the terms of their employment to be more obvious as agents for the purpose of the company than the secretary and the general manager of that branch and the sales manager of that branch."

The case is remarkable for the width of the class of agents of the company whose acts were "imputed" to the company as its own. For Viscount Caldecote it was enough that the two men were "the proper officers to make the returns". The "directing mind and will" test was not considered. *Moore v I. Bresler Ltd* was approved by the Privy Council in *Meridian Global Funds Management Asia Ltd v Securities Commission*.[23] Giving the judgment of the Board, Lord Hoffmann said[24]:

---

[19] The Defence (General) Regulations 1939.
[20] At the Quarter Sessions, on appeal from the magistrates' court.
[21] [1944] K.B. 515, 516.
[22] At 517.
[23] [1995] 2 A.C. 500 PC.
[24] ibid. at 512.

"Likewise in a case [*Moore v I. Bresler Ltd*] in which a company was required to make a return for Revenue purposes and the statute made it an offence to make a false return with intent to deceive, the Divisional Court held that the *mens rea* of the servant authorised to discharge the duty to make the return should be attributable to the company ... Each is an example of an attribution rule for a particular purpose, tailored as it always must be to the terms and policies of the substantive rule."

These three cases mark the first appearance in the criminal law of the "doctrine of identification" which governs the criminal liability of a corporation in cases which do not fall within the scope of vicarious liability. Although they have been described as "revolutionary",[25] they are vulnerable to critical analysis; none considered the "directing mind and will" test, or even cited Viscount Haldane's dictum.

THE BIRTH OF THE DOCTRINE

4.7 In contrast to the disjointed progress of corporate criminal liability generally, the origin of the doctrine of identification can be traced definitively to *Lennard's Carrying Co Ltd v Asiatic Petroleum Co Ltd.*[26]

The case concerned a tank steamer, the *Edward Dawson*, designed for the carriage of oil in bulk. She was bound for Rotterdam loaded with a cargo of 2,011 tons of benzine. The ship put to sea with leaking boilers; during the voyage they salted up and became useless. Powerless, the ship was driven aground off the Dutch coast during a gale with the result that the tanks ruptured allowing benzine to escape. This caused an explosion; both ship and cargo were lost.

The ship was owned by Lennard's Carrying Co Ltd and let on a time charter to the Anglo-Saxon Petroleum Co Ltd. An action was brought by Asiatic Petroleum Co Ltd, the owners of the cargo, alleging failure to deliver the cargo, alternatively that the cargo was lost due to the ship being unseaworthy. The appellant owner relied upon s.502 of the Merchant Shipping Act 1894 which provided that:

"The owner of a British sea-going ship, or any share therein, shall not be liable to make good to any extent whatever any loss or damage happening without his actual fault or privity, in the following cases."[27]

The managers of the appellant company were John M. Lennard & Sons Ltd. Mr John M. Lennard (the natural person) was the registered managing owner of the ship and also a director of the appellant company. In the lower court, Bray J. had found that when the ship left port she was unseaworthy

---

[25] Welsh, "*The Criminal Liability of Corporations*" (1946) 62 L.Q.R. 345, 358.
[26] [1915] A.C. 705 HL.
[27] Which included loss and damage by reason of fire on board ship.

by reason of defects in her boilers. The defects were obvious and serious. Had the owner been a natural person, only (*his*) fault or privity could defeat the statutory protection. Accordingly, the court had to determine whether the corporate owner had proved that whatever the faults of Mr Lennard might have been, they were his alone and could not/ought not to be attributed to the company.

On appeal it was argued for the appellant that the fault or privity of Mr **4.8** Lennard could not be attributed to the company. Although he had been appointed managing owner by the board, he was nothing more than the appellant's agent; he was not the *alter ego* of the company and he did not represent the company so as to make his fault the fault of the company. Giving the judgment of the court, Viscount Haldane L.C. rejected that argument. He specifically considered whether the acts and state of mind of Mr Lennard could be attributed to the company:

> "My Lords, a corporation is an abstraction. It has no mind of its own any more than it has a body of its own; its active and directing will must consequently be sought in the person of somebody who for some purposes may be called an agent, but who is really the directing mind and will of the corporation, the very ego and centre of the personality of the corporation. That person may be under the direction of the shareholders in general meeting; that person may be the board of directors itself, or it may be, and in some companies it is so, that person has an authority co-ordinate with the board of directors given to him under the articles of association, and is appointed by the general meeting of the company, and can only be removed by the general meeting of the company."[28]

The House of Lords approached the question as one of construction and evidence. Vicarious liability was excluded by the section, but where there was fault of a servant, a ship owner had to show that the fault was not his in order to exclude the normal consequences of vicarious liability. This would depend on whether the person was "merely a servant or agent of the company, or a person for whom the company was liable because his action was the very action of the company itself."

Mr. Lennard took the active part in the management of the ship on behalf of the owners, and he was registered as the person designated for this purpose in the ship's register. There was a burden was on the company to prove that he wasn't "the directing mind and will of the company", in other words somebody for whom the company was liable because his actions were the actions of the company itself. The company failed to produce its articles or memorandum of association and Mr Lennard did not give evidence. By calling no evidence it failed to discharge that burden.

---

[28] [1915] A.C. 705, 713.

4.9   In the absence of evidence from Mr Lennard, it is not possible to know what he did, but what appears to have been critical to Viscount Haldane's conclusion was the fact that he was "registered as the person designated for [managing the ship] in the ship's register", in other words, he was the very person given the responsibility of managing the ship by the appellant company.

Viscount Haldane's dictum was probably influenced by the clear distinction drawn between agents and organs in German company law.[29] A German limited liability company (GmbH) is required by law to appoint one or more directors ("Geschaftsfuhrer") who are the company organs and for legal purposes represent the company. The knowledge of any one director however obtained is the knowledge of the company. In both English and German law, whether a person is an "organ" of the company or not depends upon the context of the powers which in law has an express or implied authority to exercise on behalf of the company.[30]

"The directing mind and will of the company" appears to be less a term of art than a matter of construction depending on the context and the meaning of the section under consideration. In his analysis of the judgment, Lord Hoffmann[31] doubted whether Viscount Haldane was expounding a general "metaphysic of companies":

> "In *Bolton (Engineering) Co. Ltd. v Graham & Sons Ltd.* [1957] 1 Q.B. 159, Denning L.J. certainly regarded it as a generalisation about companies 'as such' when, in an equally well known passage, at p. 172, he likened a company to a human body: 'It has a brain and nerve centre which controls what it does. It also has hands which hold the tools and act in accordance with the directions from the centre.'"

> "But this anthropomorphism, by the very power of the image, distracts attention from the purpose for which Viscount Haldane L.C. said at p.713, he was using the notion of the directing mind and will, namely to apply the attribution rule derived from section 502 to the particular defendant in the case...."

Lord Hoffmann thought that the discomfort some commentators had expressed about the phrase "directing mind and will" arose from concentrating on that particular phrase rather than the purpose for which Viscount Haldane L.C. was using it. Although it would often be the most appropriate description of the person designated by the relevant attribution rule, "... not every such rule has to be forced into the same formula".

---

[29] Gower, *Principles of Company Law*, 6th edn. (London, Sweet & Maxwell), p.230, fn.44.

[30] per Hoffmann L.J. in *El Ajou v Dollar Land Holdings Ltd* [1994] 2 All E.R. 685, 705.

[31] *Meridian Global Funds Management Asia Ltd v Securities Commission* [1995] 2 A.C. 500, 509.

TESCO SUPERMARKETS LTD V NATTRASS

This case, decided by the House of Lords in 1971, established that the **4.10**
doctrine of identification applied, in principle, to all offences not based upon
vicarious liability. The decision established that a corporation could be
convicted of a non-regulatory offence requiring proof of mens rea if the
natural person who had committed the actus reus of the offence could be
identified with the corporation.

The findings of fact and law made by the lower courts were significant
factors in the eventual decision, as was a concession made by the prosecution. It is important to have in mind that the issue in this case was whether
the company, which was prosecuted for an offence contrary to s.11(2) of the
Trade Descriptions Act 1968, could rely on the defence provided by s.24(1)
of the same Act.

The factual background can be stated shortly. In September 1969, Tesco
Supermarkets had an offer on Radiant washing powder; during the currency
of the offer, giant size boxes were sold at 2s. 11d. instead of 3s. 11d. The
offer was advertised in the window of Tesco stores generally, and in particular, in Northwich, as well as in the local and national press. A shopper
(Mr Coane) wanted to buy a box of reduced price powder but could only
find boxes marked at the full price. When he enquired, he was told that there
were no giant size packets at the offer price and so he was charged the full
price. He complained to his local weights and measures inspector who
brought the prosecution.

Section 11(2) of the Trade Descriptions Act 1968 provided: **4.11**

> "If any person offering to supply any goods gives, by whatever means,
> any indication likely to be taken as an indication that the goods are
> being offered at a price less than that at which they are in fact being
> offered, he shall, subject to the provisions of this Act, be guilty of an
> offence".

The offence is one of strict liability and in the absence of any defence, an
employer is vicariously liable for any breach on the part of his employee.
The store was advertising a lower price for a product than that at which it
was offered to the customer on the day. Accordingly, the offence was made
out. The word "person" applied to Tesco Supermarkets, which was the
seller.[32]

Section 24(1) provided a defence:

> "In any proceedings for an offence under this Act it shall, subject to
> subsection (2) of this section, be a defence for the person charged to
> prove—(a) that the commission of the offence was due to a mistake or
> to reliance on information supplied to him or to the act or default of

---

[32] Not in issue in the case, but see, e.g. *Coppen v Moore (No.2)* [1898] 2 Q.B. 306.

another person, an accident, or some other cause beyond his control; and (b) that he took all reasonable precautions and exercised all due diligence to avoid the commission of such an offence by himself or any person under his control."

The company sought to rely on the statutory defence. It gave notice (under s.24(2)) to the effect that any contravention of s.11(2) was due to the act or default of the store manager, Mr Clements. It called evidence to explain how it came to pass that Mr Coane was unable to buy a reduced price packet of Radiant: the evening before his visit, an employee, Miss Rogers, finding that there were no more of the specially marked boxes of Radiant in stock, refilled the empty shelves with full price boxes. She neglected to tell her manager, Mr Clements, that the store had run out of offer price stock or that she had put full price boxes on display. The following morning, Mr Clements merely endorsed his daily return "all special offers OK" without actually checking to see whether that was so. Mr Clements gave evidence that had he realised there were no reduced price boxes left in stock, he would either have removed from the window the poster which advertised the offer or reduced the price of the powder displayed in the shop.

4.12   The company adduced evidence to demonstrate that it had a clear and thorough system of training and supervision of store managers. At first instance the magistrates found as a fact that Tesco had exercised all due diligence, but convicted the company because they held that Mr Clements, the store manager, was not "another person" within the meaning of the provision.

In the Divisional Court,[33] the case proceeded on a different footing. The respondent, the prosecuting authority, conceded that Mr Clements *was* "another person" for the purposes of s.24(1). The basis for concession was that if a natural person were the owner of the goods, "another person" would be anyone other than himself. In the context of a corporation, another person was anyone other than those identified as being the company. The court agreed with the concession on the ground that "another person" was anyone other than a person mentioned in s.20(1) of the same Act, namely a director, manager, secretary or other similar officer of the body corporate. It was held that "manager" in s.20(1) referred to someone in a position of managing the affairs of the company.[34] Accordingly, the Divisional Court rejected the basis upon which the appellant was convicted

---

[33] Reported at [1971] 1 Q.B. 133; [1970] 3 W.L.R. 572; [1970] 3 All E.R. 357.

[34] See *Registrar of Restrictive Trading Agreements v WH Smith & Son Ltd* [1969] 1 W.L.R. 1460; [1969] 3 All E.R. 1065. See also *Gibson v Barton* (1875) L.R. 10 Q.B. 329:

"A manager would be, in ordinary talk, a person who has the management of the whole affairs of the company; not an agent who is to do a particular thing; or a servant who is to obey orders, but a person who is intrusted with power to transact the whole of the affairs of the company." (per Blackburn J. at p.336).

by the Northwich justices, but the conviction was nevertheless affirmed because the court was satisfied that:

> "Mr. Clements was a person to whom the appellants had delegated in respect of that particular shop their duty to take all reasonable precautions and exercise all due diligence to avoid the commission of such an offence."

Fisher J., who delivered the only (reasoned) judgment, divided "due diligence" into a two stage process. A defendant had to show first that he had an "efficient system for the avoidance of offences under the Act, secondly the proper operation of that system".[35] Since the person to whom the court found the company had delegated due diligence, had failed properly to operate the system, the company could not satisfy s.24(1)(b); therefore it had not acted with due diligence.

The Divisional Court certified[36] that a point of law of general public importance was involved, namely:

> "Whether a person charged with an offence under s.11(2) Trade Descriptions Act 1968 in a retail shop owned by him would have a defence under s.24(1) of the said Act if:—(a) he instituted an efficient system to avoid the commission of offences under the Act by any person under his control; (b) he reasonably delegated to the manager of the shop the duty of operating the system in that shop; (c) the manager failed to perform such duty efficiently; (d) the offence charged was committed by reason of such failure; (e) such failure by the manager is the act or default of another person relied on under s.24(1)(a)."

So it was that the case came before the House of Lords. The concession made in the lower court (but not at trial) was maintained, and the question as to whether Mr Clement was "another person" was not pursued by the Crown before their Lordships.[37] Although the appeal was unanimously allowed, each of their Lordships said something slightly different, so it is necessary to consider each in turn.

Lord Reid delivered the first speech. He considered the nature of the **4.13** personality which by a fiction the law attributes to a corporation[38]:

> "A living person has a mind which can have knowledge or intention or be negligent and he has hands to carry out his intentions. A corporation has none of these: it must act through living persons, though not always one or the same person. Then the person who acts is not speaking or acting *for* the company. He is acting *as* the company and his mind which directs his act is the mind of the company. There is no question

---

[35] [1970] 3 W.L.R. 572, 582; [1970] All E.R. 357 at 366b.
[36] Under s.1(2) of the Administration of Justice Act 1960.
[37] per Lord Morris, 178C.
[38] At p.170E–G.

of the company being vicariously liable. He is not acting as a servant, representative, agent or delegate. He is an embodiment of the company or, one could say, he hears and speaks through the persona of the company, within his appropriate sphere, and his mind is the mind of the company. If it is a guilty mind then that guilt is the guilt of the company."

Attempts to apply Lord Denning's words[39] to all servants of a company who exercise some managerial discretion under the direction of superior officers of the company were misconceived. For Lord Reid, only someone was 'the directing mind and will' of the company, and controlled what it did could be identified with the company so as to make his guilt the guilt of the company.

The person who speaks and acts as the company is not "another"; the natural person identified as a matter of law with the company is the company. Lord Reid disapproved of the term *alter ego* because it was suggestive of a bifurcation between company and agent; a natural person has no *alter ego*, no more does a corporation.[40]

4.14   In order to determine whether a given person was acting as the company, it was necessary to establish his position and authority vis-à-vis the board of directors which normally speaks and acts for the company. In this case the board never delegated any part of their functions; they set up a chain of command through regional and district supervisors, but they remained in control. The shop managers had to obey their general directions and also take orders from their supervisors.[41] Since Mr Clements was a subordinate to whom the board had not delegated part of its functions of management, he was not "the company". Accordingly, he was "another person" within the meaning of s.24(1) and his acts or omissions were not the acts of the company itself.

Lord Morris characterised vicarious liability as anomalous[42]:

"In general, criminal liability only results from personal fault. We do not punish people in criminal courts for the misdeeds of others. The

---

[39] *HL Bolton (Engineering) Co Ltd v TJ Graham & Sons Ltd* [1957] 1 Q.B. 159, 172:

"A company may in many ways be likened to a human body. They have a brain and a nerve centre which controls what they do. They also have hands which hold the tools and act in accordance with directions from the centre. Some of the people in the company are mere servants and agents who are nothing more than hands to do the work and cannot be said to represent the mind or will. Others are directors and managers who represent the directing mind and will of the company, and control what they do. The state of mind of these managers is the state of mind of the company and is treated by the law as such."

[40] At p.171H; none of the other Law Lords appeared to share Lord Reid's anxiety; the term *alter ego* is littered throughout the other judgments without adverse comment.

[41] At p.175A.

[42] At p.179F.

principle of *respondeat superior* is applicable in our civil courts but not generally in our criminal courts."

He regarded s.20 as giving an indication (which was not necessarily all-embracing) of those who may personify "the directing mind and will" of the company. Delegation was not a feature of the case; Tesco had not delegated to Mr Clements the duty of taking precautions and exercising diligence.[43] He was employed by Tesco but was not a delegate to whom the company passed on its responsibilities[44]:

> "He was, so to speak, a cog in the machine which was devised; it was not up to him to devise it."

Tesco had used all due diligence; Mr Clements was "another person" and not the delegate of the company.

For Viscount Dilhorne, the question was not whether the company was **4.15** criminally liable and responsible for the act of a particular servant but whether it could escape from that liability by proving that it exercised all due diligence and took all reasonable precautions, and that the commission of the offence was due to the act or omission of another person. Only a person in actual control of the operations of a company or of part of them and who is not responsible to another person in the company for the manner in which he discharges his duties in the sense of being under his "orders" could be identified with the company; anyone in a lesser role (which included Mr Clements) was "another person".[45]

Lord Pearson regarded s.20 of the Act[46] as providing "a useful indication of the grades of officers who may for some purposes be identifiable with the company", but that list was not intended to be exhaustive and Lord Pearson added that "in any particular case the constitution of the company should be taken into account".[47] Mr Clements was responsible for supervising the details of the operations in the branch; this could not normally be regarded as a function of higher management (which would devise the operations, not supervise them). He was neither the *ego* of the company, nor its delegate.

Since the majority of business of the type the Trade Descriptions Act was aimed at was conducted by corporations, "in the majority of cases, the physical acts or omissions which constitute or result in an offence under the statute will be those of servants or agents of an employer or principal on whose behalf the business is carried on". Lord Diplock acknowledged that[48]:

---

[43] At p.180F–G.
[44] At p.181A.
[45] At p.187F–H.
[46] s.20 is the "consent and connivance" provision and identifies "... any director, manager, secretary or other similar officer of the body corporate...".
[47] At p.191A.
[48] At p.194D.

"...the most effective method of deterrence is to place upon the employer the responsibility of doing everything which lies within his power to prevent his employees from doing anything which will result in the commission of an offence."

Lord Diplock regarded it as axiomatic that in enacting the Trade Descriptions Act, Parliament intended "to give effect to a policy of consumer protection with a rational and moral justification. A policy would be neither rational nor just if it penalised those who were innocent of any carelessness or wrongful intent". The magistrates had found as a fact that Tesco had used due diligence to devise an effective system to prevent the commission of offences by its employees and had ensured, so far as was reasonably practicable that the system was carried into effect. In those circumstances, Tesco "was entitled to rely on a default by a superior servant in his supervisory duties as a defence under section 24(1)".[49] A corporation may exercise legal rights and be subject to legal duties, but it is an abstraction and incapable itself of doing any physical act or being in any state of mind.[50]

", and if the agent is a natural person, it matters not whether the principal is also a natural person or a mere legal abstraction—*Qui facit per alium facit per se; qui cogitat per alium, cogitat per se.*"[51]

4.16 Unlike the position in civil law where the physical acts and state of mind of the agent are ascribed to the principal, the criminal law does not recognise the liability of a principal for the criminal acts of his agent because, outside offences of strict liability, the criminal law does not ascribe to the one the state of mind of the other. Where, as here, the offence provided a defence of "due diligence", the corporation proved that defence by showing that it had acted "without negligence". In such a case, the court has to identify those natural persons who are to be treated as being the corporation itself. If none has acted negligently, the corporation has a defence. A corporation incorporated under the Companies Act 1948 owes its corporate personality and its powers to its constitution, the memorandum and articles of association. According to Lord Diplock, "the obvious and only place to look to discover by what natural persons a corporations powers are exercisable, is in its constitution". The articles of association, if they follow Table A, provide that the business of the company shall be managed by the directors and that they may "exercise all such powers of the company" as are not required by the Act to be exercised in general meeting. Since Table A also vests in the directors the right to entrust and confer upon a managing director any of the powers of the company which are exercisable by them it may also be necessary to ascertain whether the directors have taken any action under this

---

[49] At p.198C.
[50] At p.198H.
[51] Applying the maxim *Qui facit per alium facit per se; qui cogitat per alium, cogitat per se*: "He who acts through another so acts himself, he who knows by another knows himself".

provision or any other similar provision, providing for the coordinate exercise of the powers of the company by executive directors or by committees of directors, and other persons. To discover what natural persons are to be treated in law as being the company it is necessary to identify those who by the memorandum and articles of association or as a result of action taken by the directors, or by the company in general meeting are entrusted with the exercise of the powers of the company.[52]

So far as Lord Diplock was concerned, the persons identified by s.20 of the Act: "correspond with those who, under the articles and memorandum of association of a company exercise the powers of the company itself".[53]

Lord Reid stated that whether a person was to be regarded as the company, so that any act by him could be attributed to the company, was a matter of law for the judge:

> "It must be a question of law whether, once the facts have been ascertained, a person in doing particular things is to be regarded as the company or merely as the company's servant or agent. In that case any liability of the company can only be a statutory or vicarious liability."

CRITICISM OF *TESCO SUPERMARKETS LTD V NATTRASS*

By limiting the class of persons who may be identified as the company to the **4.17** "company officers": those who by the memorandum and articles of association or as a result of action taken by the directors, or by the company in general meeting are entrusted with the exercise of the powers of the company (Lord Diplock), or those identified by s.20 of the Trade Descriptions Act (Lord Pearson), their Lordships narrowed the effective scope of corporate criminal liability. In all but the simplest and smallest corporations, the board of directors will be some distance from those at the interface between the corporation and the public. Where the board of directors is to any degree remote from the operation of the business of the corporation, it is unlikely to incur liability in the absence of criminal conduct by one of the directors.

On the one hand, the decision in *Tesco* confirmed the trio of cases from the 1940s which first introduced the principle of identification into the criminal law; hereafter, a corporation could in principle be personally liable for almost any non-regulatory criminal offence, however serious. On the other hand, the narrow definition of which persons might be identified with it meant that a corporation would be liable for such an offence only where one of those senior officers was himself guilty of the crime as a principal. The identification principle makes possible the conviction of small

---

[52] At p.199F.
[53] At p.200C.

companies if not large ones. This is an inadequate response to corporate wrong-doing. As was pointed out by Gobert[54]:

> "One of the prime ironies of *Nattrass* is that it propounds a theory of corporate liability which works best in cases where it is needed least and works least in cases where it is needed most."

The Trade Descriptions Act 1968, under which Tesco was prosecuted, is undoubtedly a piece of consumer protection legislation specifically designed to regulate an area of business activity. Mr Clements was the Tesco manager at fault for failing to ensure that no offence was committed in his store; in short, he was negligent. In the circumstances, it is somewhat surprising that the case was treated as one which invoked the doctrine of identification at all. Only by persuading their Lordships that s.11(2) was to be construed as if it were an offence requiring proof of mens rea could Tesco distinguish between the company and its store manager. The case could have been approached in terms of whether Mr Clements was acting within the scope of his employment. As Tesco employed him and was responsible for ensuring the proper performance of his duties, there was nothing especially repugnant about the notion that Tesco should have been held to be responsible for what he did in its shop.

Ultimately it can be argued there was no good reason why Tesco should have avoided a conviction, albeit that it had established a system (which failed) to avoid the commission of such offences. The "person" offering to supply washing powder was the company, not the store manager (or the shop assistant). The company set the price and decided to run the promotion; it provided all the promotional material and the reduced price stock. The company had a good system, but not one sufficient to prevent the commission of the offence. However, the finding of fact made by the magistrates that Tesco had acted with due diligence was decisive.

4.18   The absence of fault on the part of the principal was not in itself a reason to avoid conviction. As Viscount Reading C.J. had said in *Mousell Bros Ltd v London & North West Ry Co Ltd*[55]:

> "Under the Food and Drugs Acts there are again instances well known in these courts where the master is made responsible, even though he knows nothing of the act done by his servant, and he may be fined or rendered amenable to the penalty."

This passage was quoted by Lord Morris in *Tesco*, but was distinguished because the offence in *Mousell Bros* did not provide a due diligence defence.

Viscount Dilhorne thought that the due diligence defence would seldom avail an accused company if "another person" was limited to a person not

---

[54] "*Corporate Criminal Liability: four models of fault*", Legal Studies (1994) 14: 393, 401.
[55] *Mousell Bros Ltd v London & North West Ry Co Ltd* [1917] 2 K.B. 836.

employed by it.[56] However, it could be argued that the point of the defence was to excuse a defendant only when something occurred that was entirely out of its control. Employees failing properly to perform their allotted tasks can hardly be regarded as beyond the control of the employer. If the offence were treated as one of vicarious liability, a corporation seller could not escape conviction for the default of its employee acting within the scope of his employment, but only where the offence was due either to some extraneous factor over which, or to the act of a person over whom, it had no control.

The problem with the decision in *Tesco* is that the case has been understood as providing a practically exhaustive list of those whose acts or state of mind can be attributed to any corporation. This is to concentrate on the identity of company officers instead of the aim of the statutory provision in question. Over twenty years later, this misapprehension was corrected by Lord Hoffmann in *Meridian Global Funds Management Asia Ltd v Security Commission*,[57] (*Meridian*) a decision of the Privy Council.

4.19 The merit of the doctrine of identification is that it provides a mechanism whereby criminal acts may be attributed to a corporation; the drawback is the apparently narrow class of officers of the company whose acts in law are attributable to their employer. This principle of criminal law does nothing to encourage those officers who might be identified with it to involve themselves in the general management and operation of the company; what follows can be termed "organised irresponsibility". The House of Lords stressed in *Tesco* that only when the board has delegated the whole of its authority to a particular manager would criminal fault on his part be attributable to the corporation. Accordingly, a corporation that allows a degree of (but not full) autonomy to a subordinate employee (such as a store manager) will not, on *Tesco* principles, be liable for his criminal misconduct.[58] The Health & Safety Executive has identified a trend on the part of many organisations to decentralise safety services.[59] The division of a corporation into "brains" and "hands" is inappropriate in the common situation where the company is diffuse; the board would ordinarily be responsible for the culture of the corporation setting the priorities which affect the behaviour of those on the shop floor. The model of a "ladder of responsibility" referred to in *Tesco* is a somewhat simplistic tool with which to analyse decision-making in a large modern corporation let alone a multi-national enterprise.[60]

---

[56] At p.185A.

[57] [1995] 2 A.C. 500 PC.

[58] See, for example, *R. v Redfern and Dunlop Ltd* [1993] Crim.L.R. 43; the decision in this case must now be read in the light of the judgment of Lord Hoffmann in *Meridian Global Funds Management Asia Ltd v Securities Commission* [1995] 2 A.C. 500 PC. The acts of Redfern in that case should, it is submitted, have been attributed to the company, Dunlop.

[59] (1989) 157 Health & Safety Bulletin 16.

[60] See Clarkson "*Kicking Corporate Bodies and Damming Their Souls*" (1996) 59 M.L.R. 557; J. Gobert "*Corporate Criminality; Four Models of Fault*" (1994) 14 Legal Studies 393.

The difficulties involved in convicting corporations for serious crimes (rather than regulatory offences) has ensured that such prosecutions remain a rarity. A conviction for a general, as opposed to a regulatory offence is only likely where the corporation is very small, such as a one-man band or family business, because in this type of case, if an offence has been committed within the company, it is likely to have been committed by the director or other senior officer.[61] In the case of a substantial corporation, a director will seldom have sufficient proximity to the unlawful act to be personally liable and without such personal liability on the part of a person who is the "directing mind and will" of the corporation, liability cannot be attributed to it.[62] The effect of *Tesco*, at first glance, has been to limit criminal liability for practical purposes to the very bottom of the corporate scale.

THE RULES OF ATTRIBUTION

4.20 Whatever criticisms there may be of the decision in *Tesco Supermarkets Ltd v Nattrass* it remains the general basis of corporate liability in English criminal law. Moreover, the principles set out in the speeches have been adopted in other Commonwealth jurisdictions.[63]

The principle was reaffirmed by the Court of Appeal in *Att-Gen's Reference (No.2 of 1999)*.[64] A prosecution for manslaughter was brought against Great West Trains as a result of the Southall rail disaster. Two questions were referred to the Court by the Attorney-General, the second of which was:

> "Can a non-human defendant be convicted of the crime of manslaughter by gross negligence in the absence of evidence establishing the guilt of an identified human individual for the same crime?"

The answer was a blunt "No". Rose L.J. stated[65]:

> "In our judgment, unless an identified individual's conduct, characterisable as gross criminal negligence, can be attributed to the company, the company is not, in the present state of the common law, liable for manslaughter".

---

[61] See, e.g. *R. v OLL and Kite, Independent*, December 1994; *R. v JF Alford (Transport) Ltd* [1997] 2 Cr.App.R. 326.

[62] [2002] 2 Cr.App.R. 207.

[63] See, e.g. *Hamilton v Whitehead* (1988) 166 C.L.R. 121: High Court of Australia; *Canadian Dredge Dock Co Ltd v The Queen* (1985) 19 D.L.R. (4th) 314: Canadian Supreme Court; *Nordik Industries Ltd v Regional Controller of Inland Revenue* (1976) 1 N.Z.L.R. 194: Supreme Court of New Zealand.

[64] [2002] 2 Cr.App.R. 207. See Ch.13.

[65] ibid. at 217.

The "identified individual" being referred to by the Court was a person identified as the embodiment of the company itself.

The doctrine of identification enables the court to attribute to a corporation the acts and/or state of mind of a particular officer. Accordingly, in determining whether a corporation may have committed a criminal offence it is first necessary to determine which theory of liability will be applied by the Court. This is a question of law and construction.[66] Where corporate liability depends upon *attribution* to the company of the misconduct of an employee, the question is whether the corporation is responsible in law for that individual's misconduct. After *Tesco*, it seemed as if the answer to this question would be that the corporation could only be liable if the person committing the act was a member of the board of directors, because only such an officer could count as the "directing mind and will".

A corporation is a legal fiction (*persona ficta*); it is a creature of statute existing and given certain powers, rights and duties by statute. But a properly constituted corporation remains lifeless without human agents to act for it. As Lord Hoffmann has pointed out, there is, in fact, no such thing as "the company as such, no *ding an sich*".[67] Since a company has no intrinsic capacity to act, there must be rules according to which acts by human agents can be attributed to, or count as the acts of, the corporation. These are the "rules of attribution". Typically, they are found in the articles of association and will, for example, permit a decision of the board of directors to be a decision of the company. Of course, the articles of association cannot provide for every eventuality, indeed they provide only the "primary rules of attribution". To avoid the necessity of a formal decision of the board of directors before any action can be taken which will count as the act of the company, a company, like a natural person, may use "general rules of attribution, namely the principles of agency".[68] In this way, a corporation is able to transact business through the agency of its employees. Through a combination of the primary and general rules of attribution, the acts of an employee can count as the acts of the company. It is both trite and necessary that agents of the company below the level of the board of directors can legally bind the company. In the context of any particular criminal offence, it is necessary to determine whether the act of any particular agent of a company can be attributed to the company. Where an offence attracts vicarious liability, the company will be liable for the misconduct of any employee acting within the scope of his employment. Where vicarious liability does not apply, an insistence in every case on the primary

---

[66] So, in *Seaboard Ltd v Secretary of State for Transport* [1994] 1 W.L.R. 541, the House of Lords decided that s.31 Merchant Shipping Act 1988 imposed personal, not vicarious liability, whereas in *Tesco Supermarkets Ltd v London Borough of Brent* [1993] 2 All E.R. 718, the Video Recordings Act 1984 (selling videos to the underage) was held to impose vicarious liability because to hold otherwise would have defeated the aim of the legislation.

[67] In *Meridian* [1995] 2 A.C. 500, 507A.

[68] At p.506F.

rules of attribution alone as the basis for corporate liability would very often defeat the intention of the legislature. In these circumstances "the court must fashion a *special* rule of attribution for the particular substantive rule".[69]

4.21   The approach of the court in any case to the particular substantive rule in issue should be first to determine whether it was intended that it should apply to a corporation at all. This is a matter of interpretation; since the case of *The Pharmaceutical Society v London & Provincial Supply Association Ltd*,[70] the courts have determined whether a particular criminal offence with which it is concerned may be committed by a corporation. If the rule in question does apply to a corporation, it must next be determined by whose act the corporation will be rendered liable.[71]

This approach to corporate liability is explained by Lord Hoffmann giving the judgment of the Privy Council in *Meridian*:

> "By applying the usual canons of interpretation, taking into account the language of the statutory provision, its content and policy, it is possible for the court to ascertain whose act (or knowledge or state of mind) was for this purpose intended to count as the act etc. of the company".[72]

The brief facts of the case were that K was the chief investment officer (and formerly managing director), and N the senior portfolio manager, of the appellant company. As part of a fraudulent scheme to gain control of a cash-rich, publicly listed New Zealand company, K & N sought to purchase, through apparently respectable nominees, a 49 per cent controlling share holding in the target company (E.N.C.). The New Zealand Securities Amendment Act, 1988, required formal disclosure by any person who became a "substantial security holder" in a public issuer; the aim of the regulation was to help boards and investors resist predatory raids by requiring immediate disclosure to both the target company and the stock exchange, of the identity of any person acquiring a substantial interest of any kind in the company's shares.

It was common ground that Meridian had actually acquired a relevant interest in the 49 per cent holding of E.N.C. and had not given notice as

---

[69] At p.507 E.

[70] [1874–1880] All E.R. Rep. Ext. 1363.

[71] In the context of s.3 of the Health and Safety at Work Act 1974, Lord Hoffmann said:

> "[The argument] is based on what seems to me to be a confusion between two quite different concepts: an employer's vicarious liability for the tortious acts of another and a duty imposed upon the employer himself. Vicarious liability depends (with some exceptions) on the nature of the contractual relationship between the employer and the tortfeasor. There is liability if the tortfeasor was acting within the scope of his duties under the contract of employment. But s.3 of the Act is not concerned with vicarious liability. It imposes a duty upon the employer himself." *R. v Associated Octel Co Ltd* [1996] 1 W.L.R. 1543, 1547.

[72] [1995] 2 A.C. 500, 507e-f.

required, because the existence of the holding was deliberately concealed from it by K & N. At first instance, Heron J. held that Meridian *knew* that it was a substantial security holder; he arrived at this conclusion by attributing to Meridian the knowledge of K & N. It "seemed obvious"[73] to the judge that if K & N had authority from Meridian to enter into the transaction, their knowledge that they had done so should be attributed to it.

In the Privy Council, the appellant argued that it had neither actual nor **4.22** constructive knowledge that it had acquired a "relevant interest". Neither K nor N were officers identified in its constitutional instruments as being the "directing mind and will" of the company. Only a director or person given powers that he exercises independently of the board could be the "directing mind and will". Since K performed his duties under the supervision of the managing director, he was not the "directing mind and will"; K had some discretion, but did not have ultimate responsibility for the company's investment activity—there had been no delegation to him of the company's ultimate responsibility.[74]

Their Lordships rejected the proposition that for the purposes of the particular statute, only the acts or state of mind of the board could be attributed to the company. The court analysed the intention of the legislation:

> "The policy of section 20 of the [Act] is to compel, in fast-moving markets, the immediate disclosure of the identity of persons who become substantial security holders in public issuers. Notice must be given as soon as that person knows that he has become a substantial security holder. In the case of a corporate security holder, what rule should be implied as to the person whose knowledge for this purpose is to count as the knowledge of the company? Surely the person who, with the authority of the company, acquired the relevant interest. Otherwise the policy of the Act would be defeated. Companies would be able to allow employees to acquire interests on their behalf which made them substantial security holders. It would not have to report them until the board or someone else in senior management got to know about it. This would put a premium on the board paying as little attention as possible to what its investment managers were doing".[75]

Lord Hoffmann stated:

> "...it is a question of construction in each case as to whether the particular rule requires that the knowledge that an act has been done, or the state of mind with which it was done, should be attributed to the company."[76]

---

[73] *Meridian* [1995] A.C. 500 per Lord Hoffmann at p.505 F.
[74] Adopting the approach of the House of Lords in *Tesco v Nattrass*.
[75] [1995] 2 A.C. 500, 511D–E.
[76] [1995] 2 A.C. 500, 511H.

Lord Hoffmann reviewed a number of earlier decisions in terms of the special rule of attribution fashioned by the court to suit the particular statutory context. So, in *Director General of Fair Trading v Pioneer Concrete (UK) Ltd*,[77] executives of the company acting within the scope of their employment (and to the commercial advantage of their employer) made a restrictive arrangement in breach of an undertaking given by the company to the Restrictive Practices Court. The Board was unaware of the arrangement and had expressly forbidden its employees from entering such agreements. The House of Lords held that for the purpose of deciding whether the company was in contempt, the acts and state of mind of an employee who entered into an arrangement in the course of his employment should be attributed to the company:

> "This attribution rule was derived from a construction of the under-taking against the background of the Restrictive Trade Practices Act 1976: such undertakings by corporations would be worth little if the company could avoid liability for what its employees had actually done on the grounds that the board did not know about it. As Lord Templeman said (at p.465), an uncritical transposition of the construction in *Tesco Supermarkets Ltd v Nattrass*:

> "... would allow a company to enjoy the benefit of restrictions out-lawed by Parliament and the benefit of arrangements prohibited by the courts provided that the restrictions were accepted and implemented and the arrangements were negotiated by one or more employees who had been forbidden to do so by some superior employee identified in argument as a member of the 'higher management' of the company or by one or more directors of the company identified in argument as 'the guiding will of the company'."[78]

Lord Hoffmann also referred to *El Ajou v Dollar Land Holdings plc*.[79] This was a civil case in which the plaintiff was a victim of a fraud seeking the recovery of money. Without his knowledge, his money had been used to invest in a fraudulent share selling scheme. F, a non-executive director of the defendant company, was instrumental in arranging the investment of funds obtained by the fraud (and knowing them to be so) in the defendant company (DLH). F played no part in the business decisions or management of DLH, but in respect of the particular transaction, he had made all the arrangements and signed the agreements without seeking or receiving specific authorisation from the board. At first instance, Millet J. dismissed the claim on the ground that F's knowledge could not be attributed to DLH.

4.23 The Court of Appeal allowed the appeal. Each of the judges expressly

---

[77] Also known as *Re Supply of Ready Mixed Concrete (No.2)* [1995] 1 A.C. 456.
[78] *Meridian* [1995] A.C. 500, 508G.
[79] [1994] 2 All E.R. 685 CA.

referred to the judgment of Viscount Haldane in *Lennard's* case.[80] Nourse L.J. observed that the doctrine of identification had developed "with no divergence of approach in both Criminal and Civil jurisdictions, the authorities in each being cited indifferently in the other".[81] As for the "directing mind and will" he emphasised that "management and control was not something to be considered generally or in the round. It is necessary to identify the natural persons having management and control in relation to the act or omission in point".[82] Though always highly relevant, the primary rules of attribution may not be decisive.

Rose L.J. referred to passages in the speeches of Lords Diplock, Reid and Pearson in *Tesco*, in which each of their Lordships considered the identity of those who were to be treated as the directing mind and will of the company.[83] He then observed:

> "There are, it seems to me, two points implicit, if not explicit in each of these passages. First, the directors of a company are prima facie likely to be regarded as its 'directing mind and will' whereas particular circumstances may confer that status on non-directors. Secondly, a company's 'directing mind and will' may be found in different persons for different activities of the company."[84]

The third member of the court was Hoffmann L.J. (as he then was). Having quoted from Viscount Haldane's celebrated dictum,[85] he went on:

> "[He] therefore regarded the identification of the directing mind as primarily a *constitutional* question, depending in the first instance upon the powers entrusted to a person by the articles of association. The last sentence about Mr. Lennard's position shows that the position reflected in the articles may have to be supplemented by looking at the actual exercise of the company's powers. A person held out by the company as having plenary authority or in whose exercise of such authority the company acquiesces, may be treated as it's directing mind."[86]

He concluded:

> "The authorities show clearly that different persons may for different purposes satisfy the requirements of being the company's directing mind and will."[87]

---

[80] *Lennard's Carrying Co Ltd v Asiatic Petroleum Co Ltd* [1915] A.C. 705 HL.
[81] [1915] A.C. 705, 695G.
[82] ibid. 695.
[83] [1972] A.C. 153, 200, 171 and 190 respectively.
[84] At 699j.
[85] In *Lennard's* [1915] A.C. 705 HL.
[86] 705e–g.
[87] 706e.

On the facts of the case, F committed the company to the transaction and knew that the funds paid into the DLH account had been fraudulently obtained. His knowledge could be attributed to the company so that, in equity, the company was in knowing receipt of trust property. By parity of reasoning, the acts and knowledge of the company secretary who knowingly submitted false returns in *Moore v I Bresler Ltd*[88] were properly attributed to the company.

The statutory framework of the particular rule is critical in determining the scope of liability. Under s.441 of the Companies Act 1948[89] the court could make an order compelling the production to the Director of Public Prosecutions of company documents where "there is shown to be reasonable cause to believe that any person had while an officer of the company, committed an offence in connection with the management of the company's affairs ..." According to the primary rules of attribution, an "officer of the company" is a person who has the management of the whole affairs of the company, e.g. the managing director. However, where the statutory context demands it, "officer" may be widely construed. So, in the case of *Re A Company*, there were reasonable grounds to suspect that a departmental manager overcharged customers (to the benefit of the company) by sending out fraudulently inflated invoices. According to the primary rules of attribution, he was not an "officer of the company". However, Lord Denning M.R. stated that the meaning of the word "officer" depended upon the context in which it was used:

> "I would not restrict the words too closely. The general object of the Act is to enable the important officers of the State to get at the books of the company when there has been a fraud or wrongdoing. It seems to me that whenever anyone in a superior position in a company encourages, directs or acquiesces in defrauding creditors, customers, share-holders or the like, then there is an offence being committed by an officer of the company in connection with the company's affairs."[90]

It is submitted that the scope of the "directing mind and will" is now to be determined according to whether the particular rule requires that the knowledge that an act has been done, or the state of mind with which it was done, should be attributed to the company. The court in every case must "by applying the usual canons of interpretation, taking into account the language of the statutory provision, its content and policy ... ascertain whose act (or knowledge or state of mind) was for this purpose intended to

---

[88] [1944] 2 All E.R. 515.
[89] Now the Companies Consolidation (Consequential Provisions) Act 1985.
[90] *Re A Company* [1980] Ch 138, 143, cf. *Registrar of Restrictive Trading Agreements v WH Smith and Son Ltd* [1969] 3 All E.R. 1065, where, in a case concerning the power to order attendance for interrogation, Lord Denning was not prepared to give "manager" or "officer" an extended meaning. See also *R. v Boal* (1992) 95 Cr.App.R. 272.

count as the act etc. of the company".[91] It is submitted that by following this approach, the concerns that have been expressed over the limitations imposed by the doctrine of identification are ameliorated. It should be borne in mind that Rose L.J. who gave the judgment of the Court of Appeal in *Att-Gen's Reference (No.2 of 1999)*[92] had already explained that a company's "directing mind and will" may be found in different persons for different activities of the company.[93] He did not overrule his earlier observations in the later case.

It is necessary to establish whether the natural person or persons in **4.24** question have the status and authority in law to make their acts the acts of the company so that the natural person is to be treated, for these purposes, as the company itself. This depends on the specific rule under consideration.

In a trial on indictment, the judge must determine as a matter of law whether, assuming the facts be proved to the satisfaction of the jury, the criminal act of the officer, servant or agent, including his state of mind, intention, knowledge or belief is the act of the company. The judge should invite the jury to consider whether or not there are established those facts which the judge decides, as a matter of law, are necessary to identify the person concerned with the company.[94] Failure to do so will imperil any conviction.[95]

---

[91] *Meridian* [1995] 2 A.C. 500, 507E–F.
[92] [2002] 2 Cr.App.R. 207.
[93] *El Ajou*, at p.699j.
[94] per Eveleigh J., *R. v Andrews Weatherfoil Ltd* [1972] 1 All E.R. 65, 71.
[95] e.g. *R. v Andrews Weatherfoil Ltd*, above; *R. v Redfern and Dunlop Ltd* [1993] Crim.L.R. 43.

CHAPTER 5

THE PRINCIPLE OF DELEGATION

The principle of delegation developed independently of corporate criminal **5.1** liability and has had little impact upon it. It can arise where a statute imposes a duty on a particular category of person[1] and makes breach of the duty an offence. The liability is personal, not vicarious; the offence can only be committed by the office holder, but he cannot avoid his statutory obligations by delegating to another. The person under the duty may be convicted of the offence where he has delegated the duty to another and that other commits the prohibited act. The mens rea of the delegate will be imputed to the licence holder.

By way of example, in *Allen v Whitehead*,[2] the owner of a café was prosecuted under s.44 of the Metropolitan Police Act 1839 by which it was an offence "knowingly to permit or suffer prostitutes or persons of notoriously bad character to meet together and remain in a place where refreshments are sold and consumed". The particular offence could only be committed by the keeper, not the manager or any other employee, but an offence was only committed if the keeper "*knowingly*" permitted or suffered prostitutes, etc. to use the premises. The owner employed a manager to run the business for him and following warnings from the police, he instructed the manager not to permit prostitutes to congregate on the premises. The manager ignored his instruction. The court found that the defendant himself did not know what went on in his absence but convicted him on the basis that he had delegated his responsibility under the act to the manager. Both the acts and the mens rea of the manager were imputed to the owner as a consequence of his delegation.

The delegation principle can be seen as a pragmatic response by the courts to legislation of a regulatory character penalising a particular class of person. The doctrine applies to public licence holders, most commonly publicans and others holding a liquor licence. So, in *Linnett v Metropolitan*

---

[1] e.g. a licence holder.
[2] [1930] 1 K.B. 211.

Police Commissioner,[3] a licensee of a public house was convicted of "knowingly permitting disorderly conduct" even though, having left control to another man, he had absented himself from the premises and was unaware that disorderly conduct had occurred whilst he was away. His conviction was affirmed by the Divisional Court on the ground that the mens rea of the person to whom he delegated his duty was imputed to the licensee.

5.2   Lord Goddard C.J. said[4]:

> "The point does not, as I say, depend merely on the fact that the relationship of master and servant exists; it depends on the fact that the person who is responsible in law as ... the licensee of the house has chosen to delegate his duties, powers and authority to somebody else ... if the manager chooses to delegate the carrying on of the business to another, whether or not that other is his servant, then what that other does or what he knows must be imputed to the person who put the other into that position."

If the courts did not apply the doctrine, a person under the specific duty could ignore it with impunity provided only that he appointed someone else in his place and took care to ensure he remained ignorant of the general running of his business.[5] This would wholly undermine the regulation of these persons.

The authorities make it clear that for the doctrine to be invoked the licence holder must have delegated the whole of his authority to another.[6] In effect it must be shown that the licensee is not managing the business himself but has delegated the management to someone else.

In *Tesco Supermarkets Ltd v Nattrass*, the Divisional Court decided the case on the basis that Tesco had delegated its duty to exercise all due diligence to the store manager. The House of Lords rejected this approach. Lord Morris said[7]:

> "There was no delegation of the duty of taking precautions and exercising diligence. There was no such delegation to the manger of the particular store ... His duties as the manager of the store did not involve managing the company. He was one who was being directed. He was one who was employed but he was not a delegate to whom the company passed on its responsibilities."

In *R. v Winson*,[8] Lord Parker made it clear that it was only necessary to invoke the doctrine where the particular offence required proof of mens rea.

---

[3] [1946] K.B. 290 DC.
[4] At pp.295–296.
[5] *Police Commissioner v Cartman* [1898] 1 Q.B. 655 per Lord Russell C.J.
[6] *Vane v Yiannopoullos* [1965] A.C. 486; [1964] 3 All E.R. 820 HL, cf. *Howker v Robinson* [1973] 1 Q.B. 178; [1972] 2 All E.R. 786 DC.
[7] *Tesco Supermarkets v Nattrass* [1972] A.C. 153; [1971] 2 All E.R. 127.
[8] [1969] 1 Q.B. 371, 382; [1968] 1 All E.R. 197.

Where liability is strict, the person under a duty is liable for the act of his employee or agent irrespective of the nature, scope or extent of the delegation. In *Tesco Ltd v Nattrass*, the Divisional Court and House of Lords both characterised the defence under s.24 as introducing a mens rea element into an otherwise strict liability offence. It may be that this is the reason why Lord Parker in the latter case (he was presiding in the Divisional Court) was attracted to the doctrine of delegation. In any event, the doctrine has remained on the periphery; it has been criticised,[9] but has not disappeared altogether.[10]

---

[9] e.g. in *Vane v Yiannopoullos* [1965] A.C. 486.
[10] As predicted by Lord Reid in *Tesco Supermarkets Ltd v Nattrass* [1972] A.C. 153, 173G.

Part II

DIRECTORS' LIABILITY

CHAPTER 6

DIRECTORS' LIABILITY

THE CIVIL LAW

In the law of tort, the normal position is that a director[1] of a limited **6.1**
company is not personally liable for the tortious acts or omissions of the
company.[2] The foundation for the general rule is the concept of the separate
personality of a corporation:

> "What matters is not that the liability of the shareholders of a company
> is limited but that a company is a separate entity, distinct from its
> directors, servants or other agents. The trader who incorporates a
> company to which he transfers his business creates a legal person on
> whose behalf he may afterwards act as director. For present purposes,
> his position is the same as if he had sold his business to another indi-
> vidual and agreed to act on his behalf ... Whether the principal is a
> company or a natural person, someone acting on his behalf may incur
> personal liability in tort as well as imposing vicarious or attributed
> liability upon his principal. But in order to establish personal liability
> under the principle of *Hedley Byrne*, which requires the existence of a
> special relationship between plaintiff and tortfeasor, it is not sufficient
> that there should have been a special relationship with the principal.
> There must have been an assumption of responsibility such as to create
> a special relationship with the director or employee himself."[3]

---

[1] Under the Companies Act 2006, "director" includes any person occupying the position of
director, by whatever name called [s.250] and "shadow director", in relation to a company,
means a person in accordance with whose directions or instructions the directors of the
company are accustomed to act [s.251].
[2] *Salomon v Salomon & Co Ltd* [1897] A.C. 22. The position is unaltered by ss.172–177 of the
Companies Act 2006 which impose general duties on the directors of a company.
[3] per Lord Steyn at p.835.

In *Williams v Natural Life Health Foods Ltd & Mistlin*,[4] M was the managing director and principal shareholder in N Ltd. His wife was a nominal shareholder. Both were employed by N Ltd, with two others P and S, to franchise the concept of retail health food shops. M had run a health food shop successfully and this was taken over by N Ltd. M had all the experience of running a retail health food shop in the company whereas the other two employees had some experience in franchising. The claimants wished to open a health store under N Ltd's franchise. All their dealings were with P although M had played "a prominent part" in the pre-contract financial projections. The projections were significantly, and as was found by the trial judge, negligently, higher than could in fact be achieved. The claimants' shop traded at a loss for eighteen months and then ceased trading. Proceedings were originally issued against the company alone but M was joined as a defendant before trial. N Ltd was wound up and later dissolved, so the action proceeded to trial against M alone. Both at first instance and in the Court of Appeal, M was held to be liable to the claimants. The House of Lords disagreed on the facts. Lord Steyn encapsulated the test:

> "...a director of a contracting company may only be held liable where it is established by evidence that he assumed personal liability and that there was the necessary reliance."[5]

The necessary reliance is where the claimant could reasonably rely on the assumption of personal responsibility by the individual who performed the services on behalf of the company.

Ordinarily, no such situation will arise even where a one-man company relies on the expertise of its managing director. Although the House of Lords not only postulated circumstances in which this could arise but also considered earlier authorities where it had arisen, the facts of this case led them to conclude:

> "There was nothing in the circumstances to show that the plaintiffs could reasonably have looked to [M] for indemnification of any loss."

So, in civil law, although exceptions to it do exist, the general rule is vigorously applied to preserve the separation between the corporation, and those who control it or are employed by it.[6] This is the doctrine of the "corporate veil".

---

[4] *Williams v Natural Life Health Foods Ltd & Mistlin* [1998] 1 W.L.R. 830.
[5] At p.837.
[6] However, a director may be personally liable if he directed or procured the commission of a wrongful act. See, e.g. *Performing Right Society Ltd v Ciryl Theatrical Syndicate Ltd* [1924] 1 K.B. 1, 14, per Atkin L.J. and *C Evans & Sons Ltd v Spritebrand Ltd* [1985] 1 W.L.R. 317.

"LIFTING THE CORPORATE VEIL"

The corporate veil can be lifted in certain circumstances, but the civil courts **6.2** have done so almost only in actions in which fraud is alleged, and, but for the lifting of the veil of incorporation, would be impossible to thwart.[7] So, for example, where an ex-employee had contracted not to solicit his ex-employer's customers but formed a limited company which did so, the Court granted an injunction against both the limited company and the ex-employee.[8] In circumstances of fraud or where the corporation is a "mere facade to hide the true facts",[9] the criminal courts will also look behind the corporate structure to investigate an individual's liability.[10]

PERSONAL LIABILITY OF DIRECTOR, MANAGER OR OFFICER OF THE COMPANY—COMMON LAW

The veil of incorporation does not protect a company officer from criminal **6.3** liability, but equally such an officer will not ordinarily be criminally liable unless he himself has behaved culpably. In criminal law there is no parasitic liability of directors, so a director is not guilty of an offence simply because the corporation itself is guilty; a condition precedent to conviction of a director is some act (or omission) on his or her part. Where a director has himself acted criminally, it is no defence that he did so within the scope of his employment and was committing the crime on behalf of his employer.[11]

Where an individual, who may be a director, manager or other officer of the company, has committed a crime together with the company in which he plays a role, he may be joined as a co-defendant to proceedings. Thus, in *R. v Robert Millar (Contractors) Ltd*,[12] the managing director, who was a major shareholder in the company, knew an offence of driving with a dangerously defective tyre was about to be committed by a lorry driver employee. As a result of the defect, the tyre blew, causing a fatal accident in which six people died. The managing director and the limited company were both convicted of aiding, abetting, counselling and procuring the offence of

---

[7] *Creasey v Breachwood Motors Ltd* [1992] B.C.C. 638—in which no fraudulent intention was found but "an abuse of the corporate form". It has since been doubted as good law by the Court of Appeal in *Ord v Belhaven Pubs* [1998] B.C.C. 607.
[8] *Gilford Motor Co v Horne* [1933] Ch. 935.
[9] See Gore-Brown on Companies.
[10] See also *Restraint: "Lifting the Corporate Veil"* at Ch.9 below.
[11] See *Standard Chartered Bank v Pakistan National Shipping Corpn and Others (Nos 2 and 4)* [2003] 1 A.C. 959 HL per Lord Mustill at para.39.
[12] [1970] 2 Q.B. 54.

causing death by dangerous driving. Only the driver could be convicted as a principal.

Moreover, in two cases of common law "corporate" manslaughter,[13] directors were convicted and sentenced to terms of imprisonment. In *Kite & OLL Ltd*[14] the company was convicted of manslaughter together with its managing director (and effective owner of the company). The criminal disregard for safety of children on a school canoeing trip was the responsibility of both the individual and the corporation which ran the trip. In *Roy Bowles Transport Ltd*,[15] two of the directors were convicted of manslaughter after one of their employees (a lorry driver), repeatedly exceeded permitted hours and failed to hand in his tachograph charts. He fell asleep at the wheel killing two motorists in the subsequent crash. The driver admitted causing death by dangerous driving and was sentenced to 30 months' imprisonment. The directors were found to have criminally ignored (indeed encouraged) the excessive working hours of the driver and were given suspended sentences of imprisonment. The company itself was not prosecuted.

6.4   In principle, it is well established that a corporation can be jointly charged with its officers. Indeed, by virtue of the doctrine of identification, corporations are regularly fixed with liability for criminal acts or omissions by those individuals who can be described as the directing mind and will of the company.[16] In *JF Alford Transport Ltd*,[17] a prosecution was brought against a transport company, its managing director and transport manager, all of whom were charged with offences of aiding and abetting the making of a false entry on a record sheet contrary to the Transport Act 1968. The case concerned wholesale discrepancies between drivers' tachograph charts and the time sheets filled in by them, which documents were held in the defendants' offices. The drivers concerned had pleaded guilty to the substantive offences of making a false entry.[18] It was accepted that this "relatively small company", and the two individuals personally involved in the management of it could properly be prosecuted for the offences. In the event, the Court of Appeal quashed the convictions only on the basis of the inadequacy of the judge's direction in summing up on the necessary knowledge to be proved for aiding and abetting. The CA did not suggest that the company officers should not be convicted.

---

[13] Both these cases predated the Corporate Manslaughter and Corporate Homicide Act 2007, under which an individual, including an officer of the company, cannot be guilty of the offence of corporate manslaughter either as a principal or as a secondary party (by aiding, abetting, counselling or procuring the commission of the offence): s.18(1).

[14] *Independent*, December 9, 1994.

[15] *The Times*, December 11, 1999.

[16] See *Tesco Supermarkets Ltd v Nattrass* [1972] A.C. 153 and Ch.4 above.

[17] [1997] 2 Cr.App.R. 326.

[18] s.99(5) of the Transport Act 1968.

CONSPIRACY

There is no doubt that an indictment for a common law conspiracy to **6.5** defraud will lie against a limited company.[19] A limited company being a (legal) person can conspire with other persons both at common law and under statute. Where one of the co-conspirators is the managing director and effective owner of a company, the company can be prosecuted for conspiracy, provided that there are *other* conspirators, even if they be indicted as "persons unknown". In *R. v McDonnell*[20] a company and its managing director were indicted with offences of conspiracy to defraud; the director was, in reality, solely responsible for the acts of the company. In a preliminary ruling before trial, Nield J. held that the counts were bad[21]:

> "...in the particular circumstances here, where the sole responsible person in the company is the defendant himself, it would not be right to say that there were two persons or two minds. If it were otherwise, I feel that it would offend against the basic concept of a conspiracy, namely, an agreement of two or more to do an unlawful act, and I think it would be artificial to take the view that the company, although it is clearly a separate legal entity, can be regarded here as a separate person or a separate mind, in view of the admitted fact that the defendant acts alone so far as these companies are concerned."

Summarising the rule in a sentence, Nield J. stated:

> "...the true position is that a company and a director cannot be convicted of conspiracy when the only human being who is said to have broken the law or intended to do so is the one director..."

If it were otherwise a company director would be guilty of criminal conspiracy without ever agreeing with another person.

PERSONAL LIABILITY OF DIRECTOR, MANAGER OR OFFICER OF THE COMPANY: STATUTORY OFFENCES

Under s.1173(1) of the Companies Act 2006, "officer", in relation to a body **6.6** corporate, includes a director, manager or secretary, but in the context of statutory corporate liability, the courts have been careful, when interpreting statutory material, to have regard to the purpose of the legislation.[22] In

---

[19] *ICR Haulage Ltd* (1944) 30 Cr.App.R. 31. Following the enactment of the Fraud Act 2006, the Attorney-General issued guidance (January 9, 2007) to prosecuting authorities as to when it is appropriate to charge a common law conspiracy to defraud instead of a substantive offence under the 2006 Act.

[20] (1966) 50 Cr.App.R. 5.

[21] At p.16.

[22] See *Meridian Global Funds Management Asia Ltd v Securities Commission* [1995] 2 A.C. 5000.

Tesco Ltd v Nattrass,[23] for example, the store manager was held to be "another person", entitling the company to raise a defence under s.24(1) of the Trade Descriptions Act 1968. Within the company hierarchy the store manager was four tiers down from the Board of Directors. The House of Lords held that he was in no sense part of the directing mind of the company and he did not fall into the class of persons contemplated by s.20(1), the consent and connivance provision.

An early example of the purposive interpretation of the term "manager" occurred in *Gibson v Barton.*[24] The case supports the proposition that the courts look to the reality of a person's position within the corporation rather than his title. At the time, a company secretary had limited and specifically defined rights and duties. It concerned the liability to a penalty of "every director and manager of the company who shall knowingly and wilfully authorise or permit such default" in not forwarding an annual list of members to the Registrar of joint stock companies. The company was obliged to forward an annual list. There was no managing director, nor any provision in the articles of association for one to be appointed. Mr Gibson, the company secretary, was, however, acting as the manager of the company. He had called a general meeting of shareholders one year and indicated, two years later, that in certain circumstances he would feel compelled to call another; in fact none had been called. Blackburn J. put the issue thus[25]:

> "The first question raised is, whether there was evidence on which we could find, as a fact, that the appellant was 'manager' of the company. That involves two things: whether there was evidence that the appellant was a manager in any sense, and whether the sense in which he is shown to be a manager is a sense that would make him liable to the penalty under section 27 ... We have to say who is a manager. A manager would be, in ordinary talk, a person who has the management of the whole affairs of the company; not an agent who is to do a particular thing, or a servant who is to obey orders, but a person who is intrusted with power to transact the whole of the affairs of the company."

Later, having expressed the view that Mr Gibson was indeed in such a position although not legally appointed by the board of directors, he considered the second part of the test[26]:

> "The question, therefore, is whether a person who is thus a manager *de son tort*—a manager in his own wrong,—whether he can protect himself from the liability cast upon a manager under section 27 by saying 'I am not manager *de jure*'. I think he cannot. There are many instances in

---

[23] [1972] A.C. 153.
[24] [1875] L.R. 10 Q.B. 329.
[25] At p.356.
[26] At pp.337–8.

which a person who *de facto* exercises an office cannot defend himself by saying, when he is called upon to bear liablity in consequence of his wrong, 'I am not rightfully in the office, there is another man who may turn him out' ... The answer is ... you have usurped the office and must bear the liabilities".

It is apparent that the court was not treating "manager" as a term of art, but interpreting the statute in a practical way so as to give effect to the legislation. It was unnecessary to look to specific appointments made by the corporation to appreciate that a person could properly be described as a manager for the purposes of the statute being considered. Mr Gibson, although answering to the title of secretary, was in fact manager of the company.

An example which shows that the *context* is always important in inter- **6.7** preting statutory powers is to be found in *Registrar of Restrictive Trading Agreements v WH Smith & Son Ltd.*[27] This concerned the power[28] of the Registrar to order that a person be given notice requiring him to state whether he was a party to any restrictive trade agreement and, if so, to give particulars of it; and the further power that[29]:

> "Where notice under section 14 of this Act has been given to a body corporate, an order may be made under this section for the attendance and examination of any director, manager, secretary or other officer of that body corporate".[30]

Lord Denning MR held that "manager" and "other officer" should not be given an extended meaning:

> "The law of England abhors inquisitorial powers. It does not like to compel a man to testify against himself. It never wants him to incriminate himself or to be faced with interrogation against his will ... When Parliament thinks it right to give the power to administer questions, it should do so in clear terms specifying who is the person to be interrogated; just as it should make clear who is the person to be made guilty of a criminal offence."

In his concurring judgment, Megaw L.J. stated that the phrase "director, manager, secretary or other officer of that body corporate" was to be construed in accordance with the ordinary use of language which required that the words "of that body corporate" apply to each category of person identified. So, in interpreting the words "manager ... or other officer", a

---

[27] [1969] 3 All E.R. 1065 CA (Civ).
[28] s.14 Restrictive Trade Practices Act 1956.
[29] At p.1068.
[30] s.15(3) Restrictive Trade Practices Act 1956.

manager could only be so described if he was also an officer of the company.[31]

Re A Company[32] was a case on the other side of the line in determining who was "an officer of the company". This concerned the Director of Public Prosecution's powers pursuant to s.441(1) of the Companies Act 1948. The section states:

> "If ... there is shown to be reasonable cause to believe that any person has while an officer of a company, committed an offence in connection with the management of the company's affairs and that evidence of the commission of the offence is to be found in any books or papers of or under the control of the company an order may be made [to inspect the company's books or papers/ require an officer of the company to produce them]."

The facts were that a junior manager of a company sent false statements to company customers demanding payments of more than was due. A number of customers paid the inflated price without query, and as the company benefited, it was suspected of fraud. In order to obtain proof of the company's involvement, the DPP made an application under s.441. Lord Denning held that an "officer of a body corporate" includes a director, manager or secretary (see s.445). But he went on[33]:

> "Its meaning may depend on the context in which it is used and in this case on the whole phrase "while an officer of the company, committed an offence in connection with the management of the company's affairs". The officer here referred to is a person in a managerial situation in regard to the company's affairs. I would not restrict these words too closely. The general object of the Act is to enable the important officers of the State to get at the books of the company where there has been a fraud or wrongdoing. It seems to me that whenever anyone in a superior position in a company encourages directs or acquiesces in defrauding creditors, customers, shareholders, or the like, then there is an offence committed by an officer of the company in connection with the company's affairs."[34]

Templeman L.J. added that were it not intended to confer an "extensive and weighty power", the section would have, in practice, very little effect.

Another more recent example of the interpretation of "manager" is found in the case of *R. v Boal*.[35] Mr Boal was the assistant general manager of Foyles bookshop in Charing Cross Road, having worked as a senior sales

---

[31] At p.1071.
[32] [1980] 1 All E.R. 284.
[33] pp.286–7.
[34] Lord Denning apparently did not regard his view in this case as being in conflict with his earlier judgment although it was referred to in argument.
[35] (1992) 95 Cr.App.R. 272.

assistant for some 10 years. When the general manager was away on holiday, the local fire authority inspected the shop and found a number of serious breaches of the fire certificate. The company and Mr Boal were both indicted with offences against the Fire Precautions Act 1971. Criminal liability arose from s.23 of the Act:

> "Where an offence under this Act committed by a body corporate is proved ... to be attributable to any neglect on the part of any director, manager, secretary or other similar officer of the body corporate ... he as well as the body corporate shall be guilty of that offence..."

Each count on the indictment alleged that Mr Boal was "a manager" of Foyles. In fact he pleaded guilty, only appealing his sentence. The Court of Appeal itself queried whether he was truly a manager caught by the section and went on to hold that where a person was liable to be convicted of a criminal offence, the words of the section should be narrowly construed— i.e. the phrase "managing in a governing role" relates to the company itself, since Parliament intended:

> "to fix with criminal liability only those who are in a position of real authority, the decision-makers within the company who have both the power and responsibility to decide corporate policy and strategy. It is to catch those responsible for putting proper procedures in place; it is not meant to strike at underlings".[36]

R. v Boal indicates a reluctance on the part of the courts to accept any broadening of the concept of manager where a section creates a criminal offence. The authorities are explicable by reference to the purpose of the legislation. Where it is designed to fix criminal liability or to require compliance with an order for compulsory questioning, the courts have tended to construe the phrase narrowly. By contrast, where the purpose of the legislation is enforcement of a regulatory regime, for example production of company books to the Registrar[37] or notification of acquisition of a sizeable shareholding,[38] the definition has been interpreted less restrictively. As Templeman L.J. stated in *Re A Company*[39]:

> "section 441 does not convict anybody. It merely enables a judge of the High Court on the application of the experienced and responsible officials who are mentioned in the section to make quite sure that when there is a slightly unpleasant aroma hanging around somebody should be sent in to trace the source and find out what is going on."

---

[36] per Simon Browne J. at p.276.
[37] For example, in *Re A Company* [1980] 1 All E.R. 284.
[38] *Meridian Global Funds Management Asia Ltd v Securities Commission* [1995] 2 A.C. 500.
[39] [1980] 1 All E.R. 284, 288.

Where a statutory provision extends liability to a person purporting to act in the capacity of director, manager, secretary or other simial officer,[40] there is "liability not only on directors, but on those who, not being directors, act as if they were ..."[41]

CONSENT, CONNIVANCE AND NEGLECT

6.8 The phrase:

> "where an offence committed by a body corporate ... is proved to have been committed with the consent or connivance of [any director, manager, secretary or officer of the company]"

is commonly included in legislation which affects corporations. An example is s.18 of the Theft Act 1968[42]:

> *"Liability of company officers where a company has been guilty of obtaining property by deception, obtaining a pecuniary advantage by deception or false accounting*
>
> 18—(1) Where an offence committed by a body corporate under section 17 of this Act is proved to have been committed with the consent or connivance of any director, manager, secretary or other similar officer of the body corporate, or any person who was purporting to act in any such capacity, he as well as the body corporate shall be guilty of that offence, and shall be liable to be proceeded against and punished accordingly. (2) Where the affairs of a body corporate are managed by its members, this section shall apply in relation to the acts and defaults of a member in connection with his functions of management as if he were a director of the body corporate."

Despite the title of the section, it is probably unnecessary for the company itself to be prosecuted, as long as the offence is proved against it. So, if a corporation has been wound up before trial, or for some other reason has not been prosecuted, it would not be a bar to proceeding against appropriate individuals. It would, however, be a condition precedent to the conviction of an individual for the prosecution to prove the guilt of the corporation, including disproving any corporate defence such as due diligence.

Similar wording appears in many statutes across the spectrum of criminal and regulatory legislation. The purpose is to prosecute and punish not only

---

[40] e.g. s.171(4) Customs and Excise Management Act 1979.
[41] *Chaudhry v HM Revenue & Customs* [2007] EWHC 1805 (Admin).
[42] as amended by the Fraud Act 2006 (removing references to ss.15 and 16 which were abolished by that Act).

the corporation but those who are in control and hide behind the veil of incorporation.

Section 20 of the Trade Descriptions Act 1968 provides another example of a similar provision.

> "**20. Offences by corporations** (1) Where an offence under this Act which has been committed by a body corporate is proved to have been committed with the consent and connivance of, or to be attributable to any neglect on the part of, any director, manager, secretary or other similar officer of the body corporate, or any person who was purporting to act in any such capacity, he as well as the body corporate shall be guilty of that offence and shall be liable to be proceeded against and punished accordingly."

It is to be noted that the words consent *and* connivance are conjunctive in s.20 of the Trade Descriptions Act 1968. It would seem therefore that a greater burden falls on the Crown than would be the case where mere consent *or* connivance is required.

"Consent" may not require actual knowledge, but "connivance" connotes a higher degree of involvement. "Connivance" has been the subject of much case law in the context of divorce. In the grounds for divorce by reason of adultery, a husband would not be granted a divorce if he had connived in the adulterous behaviour of his wife:

> "Connivance implies that the husband has been accessory to the very offence on which his petition is founded, or at the least has *corruptly acquiesced* in its commission."[43]

"Neglect" has been defined as importing a "failure to do something which the person under the obligation knows or ought to know" should be done. "... 'Neglect' does not cover every case of failure but only that case where the person, acting consciously, omits to do that which he ought to do ..."[44] This case concerned a proviso to a will which provided that in order to benefit from a settlement, the potential beneficiary did not "neglect" to use the testator's surname within a year of entitlement. The beneficiary was unaware of the proviso. It was held that he had not neglected to fulfil the condition, since he could not comply with a condition of which he was ignorant.

In a first instance decision in the Crown Court, *R. v McMillan Aviation* **6.9** *Ltd & R. J. S. McMillan*,[45] the judge acceded to a submission that there was no case for a director to answer of neglect in relation to the sale of a car by his company with a false trade description contrary to s.20(1) of the Trade Descriptions Act 1968. The car in question displayed a false odometer

---

[43] *Churchman v Churchman* [1945] P. 44, 45 at 51, per Lord Merriman (*emphasis added*).
[44] *Re Hughes, Rea v Black* [1943] Ch.296 per Simonds J. at 298, 299.
[45] (1981) Crim.L.R. 785.

reading. The director had made no checks of the person the car was bought from. The judge held that "neglect" suggested some failure to do something that a person ought to have done. To prove that an offence was attributable to a director's neglect, the prosecution had to show from evidence either that he knew the trade description was false, in which case quite clearly he had a duty to prevent the offence, or that he had reasonable cause to suspect that the company was applying a false trade description, in which case he would have a duty as director to take steps to see if it was false or not; if he failed to do so he was guilty. This would not affect the company's guilt as s.1 of the Trade Descriptions Act 1968 imposes strict liability on a corporation.

Recently the Court of Appeal[46] stated in relation to s.37 HSWA 1974 that the correct question was whether or not a defendant *ought to have been aware* that a particular practice occurred, not whether he knew of the practice but turned a blind eye. Even if the officer was unaware of the practice, if by reason of the circumstances, he ought to have been put on inquiry, he would be guilty of "neglect". The Court expressed the view that Parliament intended consent, connivance and neglect to be distinct.

In some offences, liability for consent/connivance/neglect is extended to shareholders where a corporation is managed by its members. So, for example, s.20(2) of the Trade Descriptions Act 1958, s.14 of the Company Director's Disqualification Act 1986, or s.9(3) of the Knives Act 1997[47] extend the provisions to catch the shareholder who consents, connives or neglects his duty in the offence committed by the corporation, where it is managed by its members. Here again, the aim of the legislation is to ensure that individuals who manipulate corporate activities from behind the scenes are not immune from prosecution.

PARTICIPATION BY UNDISCHARGED BANKRUPT IN CORPORATE AFFAIRS

6.10 By s.11 of the Company Directors Disqualification Act 1986 it is an offence for an undischarged bankrupt without leave of the court to take part in or be concerned in the production, formation or management of a company. "Company" includes unregistered or foreign companies provided that the latter has an established place of business in Great Britain.[48] The offence is one of strict liability so it is no defence that the person did not believe he was a bankrupt or that he did not consider himself to be taking part in the

---

[46] *R. v P* unreported, July 11, 2007 CA.
[47] Penalising the marketing and publishing of material promoting the use of knives in a violent or combative manner.
[48] s.22 (interpretation) also gives definitions of directors, etc.

management of the company,[49] or indeed, that the bankruptcy was subsequently annulled.[50]

By s.13, if a person acts in contravention of a disqualification order or disqualification undertaking, he is liable on conviction on indictment to imprisonment for a maximum of two years or a fine or both; a body corporate may also be guilty of contravening a disqualification order or undertaking contrary to s.14, and if that corporate offence occurred with the consent or connivance of, or was attributable to any neglect on the part of any director, manager, secretary or similar officer, or anyone purporting to act in that capacity, he as well as the company is guilty of an offence. "Company" includes any company which may be wound up.[51]

The Company as Victim

There was some question as to whether a sole director and majority **6.11** shareholder could steal corporate assets from his own company: since he is the "directing mind and will" of the company, how could it be said that he acted (a) dishonestly, or (b) without the consent of the owner and thus fall within the definition of appropriating property? Not long after the Theft Act 1968 was passed (which statute was aimed, at least in part, at ridding the law of the technicalities of the Larceny Acts), it was decided that on appropriate facts, a partner could steal partnership property.[52] Edmund-Davies L.J. held that provided there be the basic ingredients of dishonesty, an intention permanently to deprive, and no claim of right made in good faith, one partner can steal partnership property "just as much as one person can commit the theft of property of another to whom he is a complete stranger".[53]

But what was the position with a corporation?[54] It had already been decided by the Court of Appeal in relation to conspiracy to cheat and defraud, that directors of the corporate victim could conspire with others dishonestly to take a risk with the company's assets in a manner known not to be in the best interests of the company and to be prejudicial to its minority shareholders.[55]

The question came to be decided by the Court of Appeal in *Att-Gen's Reference (No.2 of 1983)*.[56] The two defendants in the trial were charged with theft of funds from companies of which they were both directors and

---

[49] *R. v Dorling* [2003] 1 Cr.App.R. 9.
[50] *Inland Revenue v McEntaggart* [2007] B.C.C. 260 Ch D.
[51] s. 22(2)(b).
[52] *R. v Bonner* (1970) 54 Cr.App.R. 257.
[53] At p.266.
[54] *Moore v I Bresler* [1944] 1 K.B. 515.
[55] *R. v Sinclair* [1968] 1 W.L.R. 1246.
[56] [1984] 78 Cr.App.R. 131.

shareholders. At the end of the prosecution case the trial judge had ruled that there was no evidence upon which a jury could find either defendant to have acted dishonestly and stopped the trial. The Court of Appeal found that the judge was wrong. The defendants, who ran a number of businesses both together and separately with other members of their families, drew considerable and regular amounts of money from the company accounts for personal expenditure (including family travel, yachts, home improvements, antiques and couture clothes) which had nothing to do with the business of the respective companies.

6.12 All of their personal assets eventually found their way into their wives' names. The companies failed owing millions of pounds to creditors. Kerr L.J. decided the case according to first principles which can be summarised thus:

(a) a company is a separate legal entity from its directors and shareholders (*Salomon v Salomon Ltd*)[57];

(b) the defendants "were" the company in the sense that any offences committed by them in relation to the affairs of the company would be capable of being attributed to the company (*Tesco Super-markets Ltd v Nattrass*)[58];

(c) *Tesco v Nattrass* had no bearing on offences committed *against* the company;

(d) where the directors and shareholders had acted honestly in consenting to a transaction made in the operation of a solvent company, the liquidator could not subsequently set the transaction aside on the ground of fraud of the company, its shareholders or creditors; but, where the allegation is that they have acted dishonestly or illegally in relation to the company, the company will not be fixed with their knowledge, since it is the victim of the wrongdoing (*Belmont Finance Corporation Ltd v Williams Furniture Ltd (No.1)*[59]).

Dishonesty is always a matter for a jury to decide, so where all the ingredients of theft were present, the judge was wrong to stop the case after the prosecution had closed its case. Where a defendant seeks to rely on s.2(1)(b), Theft Act 1968,[60] the belief he holds must be "an honest belief in a true consent, honestly obtained knowing all the relevant circumstances". The consent of the company founded on the dishonesty of the director cannot be a true consent. However, in the particular circumstances of the case, s.2(1)(b) did not apply. Where the defence is that the director and

---

[57] [1897] A.C. 22.
[58] [1972] A.C. 153.
[59] [1979] Ch D 250.
[60] "a person's appropriation of property belonging to another is not to be regarded as dishonest ... if he appropriates the property in the belief that he would have the other's consent if the other knew of the appropriation and circumstances of it".

shareholders "are" the company, and their consent is the consent of the company, there is no room for a sensible interpretation of the word "other". The only conceivable defence would be under s.2(1)(a)—an honest belief "that he has in law the right to deprive the other (the company) of it (the property)". In ordinary language the issue for the jury would be: has the prosecution proved that the defendants did not honestly believe that they were entitled to withdraw and spend all the monies from the company's account? Whether or not an act was intra or ultra vires the company was highly relevant but not determinative.

This case illustrates the point that the courts will not allow a dishonest defendant to benefit from his position as the directing mind and will of the company by asserting that he had the consent of the corporation dishonestly to do acts detrimental to the company, its members and creditors. In other words, it will not be possible for an individual to hide behind the corporate identity on the one hand, and obtain his own "consent" to unlawful and dishonest conduct which is detrimental to the company on the other.

This case was followed in *Att-Gen of Hong Kong v Nai-Keung*,[61] decided **6.13** by the Privy Council. A director of a company which exported textiles had the company's authority to deal in its export quotas. Without the knowledge of the co-director and majority shareholder, he sold a large quantity of the quotas (which were valuable) to another textile company in which he had an interest. The price paid was a gross undervalue. Lord Bridge of Harwich summarised the law since the *Att-Gen's Reference (No.2 of 1983)*[62]:

> "So long as an agent is acting within the scope of his authority in selling the property of his principal, he is not assuming any rights of the owner, but merely exercising rights which the owner has conferred upon him. But an agent authorised to sell can have no authority to sell dishonestly against the owner's interest. Thus, for example, if an agent in purported exercise of his authority dishonestly sells the principal's property to a third party at an undervalue, he clearly exceeds his authority and thereby assumes the rights of the owner in a way which amounts to an appropriation under ... [the Theft Act 1968]".

The issue of whether sole directors and shareholders could steal from "their" company was again considered in *R. v Philippou*.[63] P and his co-director and shareholder X (who was too ill to stand trial) purchased a block of flats in Spain through their company S Co, by transferring money from its UK bank account to the vendor. They then put the block into the name of a Spanish company that they owned. S Co subsequently went into liquidation with debts in excess of £11 million. P and X were charged with theft of a *chose in action* belonging to S Co, namely a debt—the money

---

[61] [1987] 1 W.L.R. 1339.
[62] (1984) 78 Cr.App.R. 131.
[63] (1989) 89 Cr.App.R. 290.

transferred—owed by Barclays Bank Plc to S Co. It was argued there was no appropriation because the directors were the mind of S Co and so their instruction to the bank to transfer the money was the instruction of S Co. Accordingly, it had consented to the transfer. The Court of Appeal disagreed. O'Connor L.J. quoted at length from the *Att-Gen's Reference (No.2 of 1983)*. Even if the transfer instruction could not be said to have been adverse to the rights of the owner, there was another component. The court found that "the fact that the money was being used to put the blocks of flats into the pockets of the appellant and [X] through the Spanish company"[64] provided a foundation for the inference that the transaction was (i) dishonest; and (ii) done with an intention permanently to deprive S Co of its money; therefore the drawing from the bank was adverse to the rights of the company and thus an appropriation.

It is submitted that the present position is that a sole director and majority shareholder (or two individuals in the same position) can steal from their company. Even where they have the authority to act *as* the company, they can still act dishonestly in relation to it. If they so act, an appropriation can be inferred. The director cannot rely on the consent of the company where he has acted dishonestly. Appropriation, intention permanently to deprive and dishonesty are all matters of fact for the jury. It is clear that questions of dishonesty should not be withdrawn from the jury by a judge at the close of the prosecution case. These are supremely questions of fact, interpretation and degree which a jury is required and able to decide.

---

[64] At p.300.

Part III

CORPORATIONS AND CRIMINAL PROCEDURE

CHAPTER 7

JURISDICTION OVER CORPORATIONS

Most statutory criminal offences do not contain any reference to a cor- **7.1**
poration as a potential offender; ordinarily a provision creating a criminal
offence will describe the offender simply as "a person".

However, by the Interpretation Act 1978, Sch.1: "person includes a body
of persons corporate or unincorporate". By Sch.2, s.4(5):

> "The definition of 'person' so far as it includes bodies corporate,
> applies to any provision of any Act whenever passed relating to an
> offence punishable on indictment or on summary conviction".

How a corporation is fixed with liability is dealt with in detail elsewhere[1] but
may be narrowed down to the following: vicarious liability, strict liability,
and the doctrine of identification.

As a matter of common sense, there are offences which cannot be committed by a corporation for a variety of differing reasons.

The catalogue of criminal offences which a company cannot commit as **7.2**
principal is very small indeed[2]: certainly it includes murder[3] (because the
only lawful sentence, life imprisonment, can only be inflicted upon an
individual in his personal capacity) and bigamy (since a corporation cannot
marry one person, let alone more than one at a time), some driving offences,[4] incest, rape and some other sexual offences.

Although a company may be a criminal conspirator,[5] it cannot conspire
with its sole director because a conspiracy requires the agreement of two

---

[1] See Pt I.
[2] A corporation can be convicted of an offence punishable with a fine, see s.32 Magistrates
Courts Act 1980 and s.30 Powers of Criminal Courts Act 1973.
[3] And any other offence in respect of which the only sentence is one of imprisonment: *Hawke v
Hulton & Co* [1909] 2 K.B. 93. Until 1925 this included all felonies: see below.
[4] *Richmond upon Thames LBC v Pinn and Wheeler* (1988) 87 L.G.R. 659 DC.
[5] *R. v ICR Haulage* [1944] K.B. 551, 554.

89

separate minds; the sole director and the company are indistinguishable for this purpose.[6]

It is contended that there is no reason why, in an appropriate factual situation, a corporation should not be guilty as a secondary party; for example, a corporation procuring children for sexual services to adult males would be guilty at least of indecent assault as a secondary party; equally a corporation arranging marriages for men who are already married[7] would be guilty of bigamy as a secondary party.

7.3   It had been considered that perjury fell into the category of an offence that a corporation could not commit, since it could not be committed vicariously. However, in a civil case it has been held that evidence given by a director and general manager on behalf of a company may be treated as the evidence of the company, and that if false, both the individual and the corporation may be guilty of perjury. In *Odyssey Re (London) Ltd (formerly Sphere Drake Insurance Plc) & Another v OIC Run Off Ltd (formerly Orion Insurance Co Plc)*,[8] Nourse L.J. stated three "obvious propositions":

> "First, a company could not give evidence itself. Second, a person who gave evidence on behalf of a company did not do so as its agent. Third, there would be an unacceptable shortcoming in company law if evidence given on behalf of a company was incapable of being treated as the evidence of the company."

In deciding whether an earlier judgment based on perjured evidence of the director should be set aside as having been procured by fraud, he articulated the question for the court: for the purposes of the fraud of a party rule, did [the director] have the status necessary to make his evidence the evidence of [the company]? On the basis that he was the witness on whose evidence the success of the company's case relied, and he had been a "committed" member of the team deciding how the company's case was to be presented, it would be unjust not to treat his evidence as that of the company. This is a somewhat circular argument, and Buxton L.J. (dissenting) concluded that the factual basis for attributing the director's perjury to the company had not been established although he did not rule it out in principle.

It is, of course, always open to Parliament to indicate that "person" is not intended to apply to a corporation.[9] By way of example, the offence of insider dealing[10] may be committed only by "individuals" as opposed to "persons", a clear indication that corporations are excluded from liability as principals.

---

[6] *R. v McDonnell* [1966] 1 Q.B. 233.

[7] A corporation which keeps a brothel, however, commits an offence as a principal contrary to s.33 of the Sexual Offences Act 1956.

[8] *The Times*, March 17, 2000.

[9] See *Wills v Tozer* (1904) W.R. 74 Ch D; *The Pharmaceutical Society v London & Provincial Supply Association* (1880) 5 App. Cas. 857 HL.

[10] Criminal Justice Act 1993, Pt V.

Assuming that a corporation can in law be guilty of the offence and that there is territorial jurisdiction,[11] the courts of England and Wales have power to try companies registered in England and Wales. Moreover, provided it has a place of business in the United Kingdom, a foreign corporation (i.e. one that is not British, and does not therefore have its registered office in this country) can still be served by the delivery of a summons to its trading address or the place where it conducts its business.[12] If the corporation has no such address, it will still be capable of being served with the summons by virtue of arrangements made by the Secretary of State pursuant to s.2 of the Criminal Justice (International Co-operation) Act 1990.

TERRITORIAL JURISDICTION

General Rule

The normal rule is that the courts of England and Wales have jurisdiction **7.4** only over crimes committed in England and Wales:

> "There is a well established presumption that, in the absence of clear and specific words to the contrary, an 'offence-creating section' of an Act of Parliament ... was not intended to make conduct taking place outside the territorial jurisdiction of the Crown an offence triable in an English criminal court".[13]

Normally, a crime committed abroad will not be within the jurisdiction of the English courts; where both the actus reus and the mens rea are to be found together, as they are in most crimes, there will be little difficulty in establishing the place where the crime was committed. Confusion arises where the two are split: for example, in a case of fraud by misrepresentation,[14] the misrepresentation may be made out in one country, but the gain achieved in another.

This separation of elements may also be crucial to the jurisdiction of the courts in respect of a criminal conspiracy or attempt to commit a crime [see below 7.8–7.10], and is likely to arise more frequently where the defendant is a corporation rather than an individual, simply because corporations can be multi-national in management and operation.

Where the liability of a corporation for a crime depends upon the doctrine of identification, the geographic whereabouts of its controlling mind may be important to jurisdictional issues. In 1957 it was argued and accepted that

---

[11] See para.7.4 below.
[12] Magistrates' Courts Rules 1981, r.99(3).
[13] per Lord Diplock in *Air-India v Wiggins* (1980) 71 Cr.App.R. 213, 217.
[14] s.2 Fraud Act 2006.

"criminal jurisdiction rests on *locus* and the wrong, while civil jurisdiction rests on personal amenability to the jurisdiction and *locus* is generally immaterial".[15] At the time, the general principle of jurisdiction was that subject to overt statutory extensions, the criminal courts of England and Wales could only try crimes which occurred in England and Wales: "to aid in the preservation of the Queen's peace and the maintenance of law and order within the realm with which generally speaking, the criminal law is alone concerned"[16]. Since then, and following a number of conflicting decisions, the law of jurisdiction has wavered, caught between authority and a judicial desire for legislative change. The globalisation of modern life has led to the territorial basis for jurisdiction becoming increasingly outmoded.[17]

7.5   The general presumption is that a statute will not be construed as applying to foreigners in respect of acts done by them abroad. Both presumptions, according to Lords Diplock and Scarman are rebuttable.[18]

In these circumstances the courts have followed one of two distinct criteria although not always consistently.

(a) The "Last Act" or Terminatory Rule

7.6 This doctrine has been applied by the courts in many older cases. For an English criminal court to have jurisdiction "the act needed to complete the *actus reus* ... should take place within the jurisdiction".[19]

Another way of expressing the same rule is the "object" principle: where the object or gist of the crime is to commit an offence abroad, the English court will not have jurisdiction. Where, on the other hand, the object of the crime is to procure a result in England, the court will have jurisdiction. In *DPP v Stonehouse*,[20] S attempted by deception (by faking his death in America) to obtain insurance monies for his wife, who was not a party to the deception. Although S did no physical acts within the jurisdiction, his acts abroad had "natural and inevitable consequences" which would set in train the obtaining of the monies in England by her, had the deception in fact operated. According to Lord Diplock[21]:

> "The basis of the jurisdiction under the terminatory theory is not that the accused has done some physical act in England, but that his physical acts, wherever they were done, have caused the obtaining of the property in England from the person to whom it belonged".

---

[15] *Board of Trade v Owen* [1957] A.C. 602.
[16] [1957] A.C. 602 per Lord Tucker at p.625.
[17] per Lord Griffiths in *Liangsiriprasert v USA Government* (1991) 92 Cr.App.R. 77, 88.
[18] *Air India v Wiggins* above at p.217 and p.219 respectively.
[19] per Buxton L.J. in *R. v Manning* [1998] 2 Cr.App.R. 467 applied in *R. v Naini (Jamshid Hashemi)* [1999] 2 Cr.App.R. 398.
[20] (1977) 65 Cr.App.R. 192.
[21] At p.207.

Or, as Lord Keith put it: "The principle that an offence is committed if the effects of the act intentionally operate or exist within the jurisdiction".[22]

If, however, the conduct at which the statute is aimed has happened abroad, and has "finished" abroad, in the absence of clear and unambiguous statutory language to the contrary, the crime will not be triable in England and Wales. For example, in *Air India v Wiggins*,[23] the relevant offence was a prohibition on causing or permitting an animal to be carried by sea in a way which was likely to cause injury or unnecessary suffering to the animal. By the time that the defendant's aeroplane was in British territory it was clear that animals which had so suffered were already dead. The offence had terminated outside British territory. Thus, where the statute was silent on extra-territorial jurisdiction, the House of Lords held that the English court had no jurisdiction to hear the case.

The last case to follow this rule was *R. v Manning*[24], in which the Court of Appeal criticised an earlier decision of a differently constituted court which had followed the comity rule. In that case, the appellant ran a maritime insurance business from England. The prosecution case was that he obtained premiums from clients, but either failed to place the cover at all, or placed it only for a lesser percentage than instructed, or deceitfully placed the cover with unacceptable companies. A Greek shipping company issued cheques in Greece to pay him on receipt of the false cover notes. The Court of Appeal held that the last act theory remained binding as to jurisdiction and stated that *Smith (Wallace Duncan)* was wrongly decided (last act done in New York for deception in England).

(b) Comity Rule

This can broadly be defined as the rule that nations should co-exist in **7.7** harmony, with due deference given to each other's sovereignty and legal system.

> "The rules of international comity in my view do not call for more than that each sovereign state should refrain from punishing persons for their conduct within the territory for another sovereign state where all that conduct has had no harmful consequence within the territory of the state which imposes the punishment".[25]

Lord Diplock's view that statutes could be interpreted as having no territorial limit, but only being subject to the rules of comity, has been applied

---

[22] At p.231; see also *R. v McPherson & Watts* [1985] Crim.L.R. 508.
[23] (1980) 71 Cr.App.R. 213.
[24] [1998] 2 Cr.App.R. 461.
[25] per Lord Diplock in *Treacy v DPP* (1970) 55 Cr.App.R. 113, 140.

occasionally.[26] In *R. v Liangsiriprasert*, an appeal to the Privy Council from the Court of Appeal of Hong Kong, Lord Griffiths, giving judgment of their Lordships, made these observations:

> "Unfortunately in this century, crime has ceased to be largely local in origin and effect. Crime is now established on an international scale and the common law must face this new reality. Their Lordships can find nothing in precedent, comity or good sense that should inhibit the common law from regarding as justiciable in England inchoate crimes committed abroad which are intended to result in the commission of criminal offences in England."

(c) Conclusion

7.8 Since this line of authority, Buxton L.J. (in *Manning*[27]) has strongly criticised the idea that the comity theory has replaced the last act rule.

However, in *R. v Smith (Wallace Duncan) (No.4)*[28] the Court of Appeal has now clarified the vexed issue of jurisdiction. The Court concluded that there is jurisdiction in this country as long as the crime has "a substantial connection" with this jurisdiction. It noted that in relation to conspiracy, a broader approach had undoubtedly been adopted[29] than would follow on the application of the terminatory theory; it did not follow that the same process of development would not also be appropriate in cases involving offences of obtaining by deception.

As Griffiths L.J. said in *R. v Liangsiriprasert*[30]:

> "But why should an overt act be necessary to found jurisdiction? In the case of conspiracy in England the crime is complete once the agreement is made and no further overt act need be proved as an ingredient of the crime. The only purpose of looking for an overt act in England in the case of a conspiracy entered into abroad can be to establish the link between the conspiracy and England or possibly to show the conspiracy is continuing. But if this can be established by other evidence, for example the taping of conversations between the conspirators showing a firm agreement to commit the crime at some future date, it defeats the preventative purpose of the crime of conspiracy to have to wait until some overt act is performed in pursuance of the conspiracy."[31]

---

[26] e.g. in *DPP v Doot* (1973) 57 Cr.App.R. 600 by Lord Salmon at p.629, *Liangsiriprasert v USA Government* (1991) 92 Cr.App.R. 77 and *Smith (Wallace Duncan)* [1996] 2 Cr.App.R. 1.
[27] [1998] 2 Cr.App.R. 461.
[28] [2004] 2 Cr.App.R. 17.
[29] Crimianl Justice Act 1993 (which only came into force in 1999).
[30] (1991) 92 Cr.App.R. 77.
[31] At p.251.

It now appears conclusive that the only jurisdictional limitation is where there is no connection with this country and/or the rules of comity point away from the UK courts assuming jurisdiction.

EXTENSIONS OF JURISDICTION

Dishonesty, Forgery and Blackmail

The jurisdiction of the courts of England and Wales was substantially **7.9** altered by Part I of the Criminal Justice Act 1993 ("CJA 1993"). Although enacted in 1993, the CJA 1993 only came into force on June 1, 1999. Most of the cases cited above were decided before then and accordingly do not deal with the position under this part of the Act.

The Act divides offences into two broad groups, A and B, as follows:

Group A relates to: offences under the Theft Acts: theft, handling, obtaining etc by deception, false accounting, false statements by company directors etc; under the Forgery and Counterfeiting Act 1981 of forgery and counterfeiting; cheating the public revenue (a common law offence); offences under the Fraud Act 2006.[32]

Group B relates to: conspiracy to commit a Group A offence; conspiracy to defraud; attempt to commit a Group A offence; incitement to commit a Group A offence.

The courts will have jurisdiction to try a Group A case provided any one of the relevant events (i.e. any act or omission proof of which is required for conviction) took place in England and Wales.[33] The nationality of an individual (unless required for the specific offence) or his presence in England and Wales is irrelevant for Group A or B offences.[34] On a charge of conspiracy to commit a Group A offence or conspiracy to defraud, where a person became a party to the conspiracy is irrelevant, as is whether any act or omission occurred in England and Wales, unless the courts have extended jurisdiction under s.1A, Criminal Law Act 1977 (see below).[35] On a charge of attempting to commit a Group A offence, it is irrelevant whether the attempt was made or the attempt had an effect in England and Wales unless brought under s.1A of the Criminal Attempts Act 1981 (see below). In relation to both Group A and B offences, property is obtained in England

---

[32] Inserted by Sch.1 para.24(3) Fraud Act 2006.
[33] s.2.
[34] s.3(1) and s.3(4).
[35] s.3(2) and s.3(5), & para.7.12.

and Wales if it is despatched from or received at a place in England and Wales, and a communication of any information, instruction, request, demand, "or other matter", occurs in England and Wales if it is sent either to or from a place in England and Wales.[36]

Conspiracy

7.10 Under the CJA 1993, whether a person became a party to the conspiracy in England and Wales, or any act, omission or other event occurred in England and Wales it is immaterial to a conviction for a conspiracy to commit a Group A offence or a conspiracy to defraud, except insofar as s.1A of the Criminal Law Act 1977 is relevant (see below).

A person may be guilty of conspiracy to defraud if a party (or his agent) to the conspiracy did anything in England and Wales in respect of the agreement before it was formed; or, a party to the agreement became such in England and Wales (including through an agent); or, a party to it did or omitted to do anything in England and Wales in pursuance of the agreement, even if the fraud in view was not intended to take place in England and Wales (s.5(3)).

A defendant is guilty of conspiracy to defraud by s.5(3) only if the agreement would involve an act, omission or an event constituting an offence (defined as conduct punishable under law) in the foreign country where it was intended to take place (s.6(1)).

7.11 The jurisdiction of the courts to try conspiracy to commit offences outside the United Kingdom was extended by ss.5–8 of the Criminal Justice (Terrorism and Conspiracy Act 1998) which inserted s.14 into the Criminal Law Act 1977.

To bring a conspiracy to commit offences outside the UK within the ambit of s.1(1) of the Criminal Law Act 1977, the following conditions must be met[37]:

(a) the pursuit of the agreed course of conduct would involve an act by at least one of the parties or an event intended to take place outside the United Kingdom;

(b) the act or event constitutes an offence (defined as conduct punishable under law) in that other country;

(c) the agreement would be an offence under section 1(1) but for the fact that the result was intended not to take place outside the United Kingdom;

(d) a party (or his agent) to the agreement did anything in relation to the agreement before its formation, or did or omitted to do anything in England and Wales in pursuance of the agreement or a

---

[36] s.4.
[37] s.1A(1)–(5) Criminal Law Act 1977.

> party became a party to the agreement in England and Wales (either directly or through his agent).

Any act done by a message is done in England and Wales if it is sent or received there. Once these four conditions are met, the offence referred to is that which it would be but for the fact that it is not an offence triable in England and Wales.[38] It is immaterial whether the defendant is a British citizen at any time.[39] This section came into force on September 4, 1998; it is not retrospective.[40]

Attempts

It is immaterial to a conviction for an attempt to commit a Group A offence **7.12** whether the attempt was made in England and Wales or whether the attempt had an effect in England and Wales—except insofar as s.1A of the Criminal Attempts Act 1981 (concerning attempts to commit offences abroad) is relevant.

If an act is done in England and Wales and it would be more than merely preparatory to the commission of a Group A offence, but if completed, the offence would not be triable in England and Wales, what the person doing the act "had in view" shall be treated as an offence.

This section which was inserted by s.5(2) of the Criminal Justice Act 1993, came into force on June 1, 1999. It is not retrospective. Thus an attempt (as defined) in England and Wales to commit an offence abroad can now be triable in England and Wales, subject only to the offence "in view" being an offence (as defined[41]) under the law in force where at least part of it was intended to take place and also an offence in England and Wales.[42]

By s.1(1A) and (1B) of the Criminal Attempts Act 1981 this extended jurisdiction is specifically applied to misuse of computers in a similar fashion [see below—para.7.19].

Incitement

In cases of incitement to commit a Group A offence, jurisdiction is now **7.13** extended by s.1(3)(d) of the Criminal Justice Act 1993. A person may now be tried for incitement to commit a Group A offence if the incitement or part of it takes place in England and Wales and it would be triable but for the fact that what the person had in view was not an offence triable in England and Wales, as long as what he had in view would involve the

---

[38] s.1A(6) Criminal Law Act 1977.
[39] s.1A(12) Criminal Law Act 1977.
[40] s.1A(14) Criminal Law Act 1977.
[41] Conduct punishable under the law in force is an offence however described in that law.
[42] s.6 Criminal Justice Act 1993.

commission of an offence (as defined) under the law where at least part of it was intended to take place (ss.5 and 6). It is immaterial whether the accused is or was a British citizen (unless specified by statute) or was in England and Wales at any material time (s.3). Where an allegation of incitement to distribute indecent photos of children was done by a person within the jurisdiction, but the person incited was outside the jurisdiction, the courts of England and Wales had jurisdiction to try the case.[43]

EXTENSION OF JURISDICTION FOR SPECIFIC OFFENCES

7.14 What follows is not intended to be an exhaustive list of the circumstances in which the normal rules of jurisdiction are extended, but rather those which are most likely to affect corporations.

Aviation Offences

7.15 By s.92 of the Civil Aviation Act 1982, any act or omission taking place on board (i) a British-controlled aircraft, (ii) a foreign aircraft in flight elsewhere than in or over the United Kingdom, which would constitute an offence if it occurred in the United Kingdom and is not expressly or impliedly authorised by the relevant foreign law, may be tried in England and Wales. A British controlled aircraft is (a) one registered in the UK; or (b) an unregistered aircraft operated or owned by someone so qualified, and the operator or owner has his principal place of business in the UK; or (c) a foreign registered aircraft chartered to persons fulfilling the requirements of (b).

A foreign aircraft is only subject to the jurisdiction if the next landing is in the UK and the act or omission would constitute an offence in the country in which it is registered. In other words, if during a flight of a foreign aircraft an offence occurs outside British airspace, but which would be an offence in England and Wales as well as in the country in which it is registered, provided that the next landing is in the UK, the courts of England and Wales have jurisdiction. All proceedings require the Director of Public Prosecution's consent. Military aircraft are excluded.

Offences at Sea

7.16 The Crown Court has jurisdiction over offences committed within the Admiralty of England and Wales (s.46, Supreme Court Act 1981), i.e. offences committed within the territorial waters of the United Kingdom, or on board a British ship on the high seas or on board foreign ships within the territorial waters of Her Majesty's Dominions (Territorial Waters

---

[43] *R. v Tompkins* [2007] Crim.L.R. 235.

Jurisdiction Act 1878). "Ship" includes hovercraft. "Territorial waters" is defined in the Territorial Sea Act 1987, and also the Merchant Shipping Act 1995. A Secretary of State's consent is required to commence a prosecution.

Contraventions of restrictions on vessels in relation to safety zones around off shore installations are triable in England and Wales. These provisions apply specifically to corporations wherever incorporated (s.23, Petroleum Act 1987).

Seizing or exercising control of or endangering the safety of a fixed platform is triable in England and Wales (ss.10–11, Aviation & Maritime Security Act 1990).

The English courts have jurisdiction in respect of an offence of unlawfully **7.17** and intentionally destroying, damaging or seriously interfering with the operation of property used for the provision of maritime navigation facilities, or of intentionally communicating information which endangers the safe navigation of any ship which an accused knows to be false (s.12, Aviation & Maritime Security Act 1990).

The courts have jurisdiction over acts or omissions on or in the vicinity of an installation in territorial waters or parts of the Continental Shelf which would constitute an offence if in the United Kingdom (s.10, Petroleum Act 1998).

Channel Tunnel

There is a similar extension of jurisdiction for offences of damage to or **7.18** endangering the safety of the operation of the Channel Tunnel system (Channel Tunnel (Security) Order 1994 (SI 1994/570) under the Channel Tunnel Act 1987).

By the Customs and Excise Management Act 1979 and regulations thereunder, goods intended to be imported to, and in "control zones" in France and Belgium are to be treated as having been imported into England and Wales. Thus jurisdiction is extended onto the continent for these limited purposes.[44]

Computer Misuse

Under ss.1–4 of the Computer Misuse Act 1990, offences of gaining unau- **7.19** thorised access to computer material (with or without intent to commit or facilitate further offences)[45] or of making an unauthorised modification of

---

[44] Channel Tunnel (Customs & Excise) Order 1990 (SI 1990/2167) art.5.
[45] i.e. "hacking".

the contents of a computer, are triable in England and Wales wherever the acts occurred or the accused was, as long as there is a "significant link", as defined,[46] with England and Wales (ss.1–4, Computer Misuse Act 1990). Attempt, conspiracy and incitement to commit such offences are also triable subject to similar criteria (ss.6–7). It is immaterial whether the accused was a British citizen at the relevant time (s.9), but external law is relevant (s.8).

Revenue & Customs Offences

7.20　The offence of being knowingly concerned in the fraudulent evasion of the prohibition on importation of goods or of any duty on payable on the goods (s.170 Customs and Excise Management Act 1979) can be tried in England and Wales even if the defendant's act or omission is performed abroad, because the offence is a continuing one[47] and is not limited to the point of importation.[48] So, for example, if a corporation provided warehousing for illegal drugs in France prior to their importation to England, it would be liable to be tried in England.

European Union Tax Offences

7.21　A person who, in the United Kingdom, assists or induces conduct outside the United Kingdom which involves the commission of an offence involving tax or duty in another Member State may be tried in England and Wales (s.71, Criminal Justice Act 1993). This is broad enough to cover value added tax, agricultural levy frauds and diversion frauds in another Member State.

Manslaughter

7.22　Murder or manslaughter of a person (whether or not a British citizen) committed by a British subject on land outside the United Kingdom is triable in the courts of England and Wales. Section 28 provides that jurisdiction under the Corporate Manslaughter and Corporate Homicide Act 2007 is limited to the harm resulting in death being sustained anywhere in the UK, within its waters or on a UK registered ship, aircraft or hovercraft, or as a result of it being wrecked or suffering some "mishap"; in other words, jurisdiction is extended along the same lines as s.10 of the Offences Against the Person Act 1861.

---

[46] The accused was in England and Wales when he did the act causing the computer to perform the function, or the computer was in England and Wales when the accused secured or intended to secure unauthorised access (for s.1). Similarly for the unauthorised modification (for s.3).

[47] *R. v Martin & White* [1998] 2 Cr.App.R. 385 CA.

[48] *R. v Wall* (1974) 59 Cr.App.R. 58.

PROCEEDINGS AGAINST CORPORATE DEFENDANTS IN CRIMINAL COURTS

COMMENCEMENT OF PROCEEDINGS

Criminal proceedings are generally started by the laying of an information **8.1** or the issue of a summons/warrant or with an arrest. As a corporation cannot be arrested, proceedings commence with the laying of an information: unless so required by statute the information need not be in writing although in practice it normally will be. The laying of the information at the magistrates' court by the prosecution must be a deliberate act with a view to commencing a prosecution.[1] Unless a statute specifies a particular person or class of person who may do so, an information may be laid by anyone, including a corporation.

The information should contain a sufficient description of the specific offence charged and a reference to the section of the statute or provision creating the offence—r.100, Magistrates' Courts Rules 1981. It should state the name and address of the person charged.

The information must be laid at the court within any relevant limitation period. The justice[2] or the justice's clerk then performs a judicial function in issuing a summons, ensuring that it makes out an offence and is not defective. If it is defective, it will still be sufficient if it indicates the alleged wrongdoing and is capable of amendment, provided it relates to the same wrongdoing.[3]

---

[1] *Schiavo v Anderton* [1987] Q.B. 20.
[2] For the purpose of this work Justice of the Peace, lay magistrate, District Judge (formerly stipendiary magistrate) are interchangeable and refer to a magistrate.
[3] *Simpson v Roberts, The Times*, December 21, 1984.

LIMITATION ON PROCEEDINGS

8.2 Many of the offences which affect corporations are summary only and subject to a six month limitation (s.127, Magistrates' Courts Act 1980) unless the statute specifies a longer period. The information must be laid within six months of the time when the offence was committed. For a continuing offence, time starts to run from the last day of alleged offending. As long as the information is laid in time, the fact that the summons is issued outside the six month period is not fatal to proceedings.

At common law there is no time limit on the commencement of criminal proceedings, in the absence of statutory limitation to the contrary. There is no time limit for indictable offences, even if the trial in fact occurs in the magistrates' court.

INSTITUTION OF PROCEEDINGS REQUIRING PARTICULAR CONSENTS

8.3 Where a statutory provision requires the consent of the Attorney-General or the Director of Public Prosecutions to be obtained before proceedings are commenced, the absence of such consent will be fatal- they will be a nullity.[4] Most criminal proceedings will be instituted by or on behalf of the Director of Public Prosecutions. Some offences affecting corporations require specific consent and must be instituted by a particular person. What follows is a list of those offences requiring consent most likely to affect corporations.

8.4

Type of Offence	Statute	Consent	Instituted by
Customs & Excise offences	s.145 Customs & Excise Management Act 1979	Commissioners of Revenue & Customs /Director of RCPO	Commenced in name of officer
Contempt of court (strict liability)	s.7 Contempt of Court Act 1981	Attorney-General	Attorney-General or court having jurisdiction to deal with it
Companies Act	ss.448, 450 & 451	Secretary of State or Director of Public Prosecutions	
Corruption of agent	s.2 Prevention of Corruption Act 1906	Attorney-General	
Defamatory libel	s.8 Law of Libel Amendment Act 1888	Attorney-General	

[4] *R. v Angel* (1987) 52 Cr.App.R. 280.

Some health & safety at work offences	ss.38–9 Health & Safety At Work Act 1974	Director of Public Prosecutions/ Inspector of Environment Agency	Inspector
Certain public health offences	s.298 Public Health Act 1936	Attorney- General	Person aggrieved/ council or body whose function it is to enforce provisions
Insider dealing	s.61 Criminal Justice Act 1993 s.402 FSMA 2000	Secretary of State, Director of Public Prosecutions, Financial Services Authority	
Market-rigging	s.401 Financial Services & Management Act 2000	Financial Services Authority, or the Secretary of State or Director of Public Prosecutions	
Money laundering	s.402 FSMA 2000 Money Laundering Regulations 2007	Financial Services Authority	
Official Secrets offences	ss.9 & 10 Official Secrets Act 1989	Attorney-General, Director of Public Prosecutions (for s.4(2) material)	
Obscene publications & obscene broadcasting publications	s3A Obscene Publications Act 1959 s.4 Broadcasting Act 1990 Sch. 15	Director of Public Prosecutions Director of Public Prosecutions	
Acts intended or likely to stir up racial hatred, racially inflammatory material	s.27 Public Order Act 1986 Pt III	Attorney-General	
Terrorism offences	s.117 Terrorism Act 2000	Director of Public Prosecutions or, if related to a country other than the United Kingdom, Attorney-General	

Weights & measures offences	s.83 Weights & Measures Act 1985	Local weights & measures authority or the chief officer of police	
Any offence once the corporation is wound up or a provisional liquidator appointed	s.130 Insolvency Act 1986	No proceedings may be continued or instituted without leave of the court dealing with the winding up	

ISSUE OF SUMMONS

8.5   Since 2003, lay magistrates have had jurisdiction over cases in England and Wales regardless of where the crime was committed or the defendant resides.[5] Each summons must only allege one offence.

Once the magistrate, or his clerk, has issued a summons from the information, it must be served on the accused. The information and/or summons can be amended, (even after the six month period) to allege a different offence if the same factual wrongdoing is targeted and it is in the interests of justice.[6] Where an information failed to make it clear which of a number of offences under s.15(1) of the Food Safety Act 1990 was alleged, the information could not be amended to refer to the "same wrongdoing" because a particular factual scenario had not originally been alleged.[7]

Where the summons is defective, the accused who appears should be informed of the defect so that he has the opportunity to waive or take any objection. Defects in respect of the date and place of the offence, and the name of the defendant have all been held to be curable.[8] Substitution of a different defendant is, however, not permissible. The real question for the magistrates when considering an application to amend the summons is whether there would be prejudice to the accused: if none, or very slight, the amendment should be allowed. If, however, the accused would face a significantly more serious charge, or the amendment would result in an inevitable adjournment, which would in itself defeat the purpose of the six month limitation rule, the court should be slow to allow an amendment.[9]

A magistrate can issue a series of summonses relating to the same information—but the information must be laid within the limitation period,

---

[5] s.43 Courts Act 2003.

[6] *R. v Scunthorpe Justices Ex p. McPhee & Gallagher, The Times,* March 10, 1998, 162 J.P. 213.

[7] *Ward v London Borough of Barking & Dagenham* [1999] Crim.L.R. 920.

[8] *Allan v Wiseman* [1975] Crim.L.R. 37.

[9] *R. v Scunthorpe Justices Ex p. McPhee & Gallagher* above; *R. v Sheffield Stipendiary Magistrate Ex p. DPP, Independent* (CS) November 27, 2000.

otherwise the proceedings will be out of time and invalid even though there was no prejudice to the accused.[10]

SERVICE OF THE SUMMONS

A summons requires the attendance of the accused at a particular court on a **8.6** particular day to answer an information. The summons may be served by delivering it or sending it by post (or probably by fax) to the registered office of the corporation in the UK, or if there is no registered office in the UK, any place in the UK where the corporation trades or conducts its business.[11] Even though there are different legal systems throughout the United Kingdom, provisions permit the service of summonses throughout the different countries.[12] A summons may be issued even though the accused is outside the UK and may be served by post or by another method where the address is unknown or postal service cannot be effected in accordance with the Crime (International Co-operation) Act 2003.[13]

An accused must have a reasonable opportunity to attend.

SUMMONSING THE WRONG DEFENDANT

Although a summons can usually be amended to correct mistakes, sum- **8.7** monsing the wrong defendant may be fatal to the proceedings. This is particularly so if the defendant is a corporation, since amending the summons to change the name may be a substitution of the accused, not just an insignificant or merely technical alteration.

Where a person attends voluntarily, that will cure the defect of process or service, unless the attendance is only to draw attention to the defect.[14] If a litigant waives any objection to the defect, or agrees to the amendment, or answers the charge, the proceedings are valid and the case may continue. But where the wrong person is summonsed, the defect cannot be cured because it is a defence to the charge. An information and summons served on a differently named defendant at the address cannot be amended by substituting the name of another corporation. In *Marco (Croydon) Ltd v Metropolitan Police*,[15] the Divisional Court held that where the wrong defendant was summonsed for a Highways Act 1980 offence, albeit at the

---

[10] *R. v Network Sites Ltd Ex p. London Borough of Havering* [1997] Crim.L.R. 595.
[11] r.4.1(2) Criminal Procedure Rules 2005; SI 2005 No.384.
[12] s.39 Criminal Law Act 1977; s.126, Magistrates' Courts Act 1980; Criminal Justice and Public Order Act 1994, Pt X.
[13] ss.3 and 4.
[14] *Pearks Gunston & Tee Ltd v Richardson* [1902] 1 K.B. 91; *Dixon v Wells* (1890) 25 Q.B.D. 249.
[15] [1983] Crim.L.R. 395 and followed in *Sainsbury's Supermarkets Ltd v HM Courts (South West Region, Devon and Cornwall Area)* [2006] EWCA 1749 Admin.

correct address, and within the same group of companies, the magistrates were wrong to allow the amendment because the wrong legal person was initially before the court. The company which had in fact been summonsed appeared (by counsel), but when the magistrates allowed the amendment, they granted counsel an adjournment to ascertain whether he was representing the company the prosecution had meant to summons. Thus it was clear that the company had not yet appeared before them. Had the company been served at its registered address but with a typing error in its name, it is uncertain whether amendment could properly be made by the court: an error in its name may quite conceivably be a summons to a totally different defendant against whom there is no case at all. This was different from the situation where the person who was intended to receive the summons did receive it and knew it was for him, although he was misnamed. In *Allan v Wiseman*[16] the surname on the summons was Loach. No-one attended; the case was proved against the person named on the summons and a warrant for his arrest was issued. It was executed on the arrest of the defendant, Allan, whom the prosecution had always intended to summons. The different name was unexplained, and allowing the prosecution application, the magistrates amended the name in the proceedings to that of the man produced before them (Allan) and sentenced him. It was not suggested that Allan was not involved in the offence, so no injustice was done. Amendment could be made at any time until the proceedings were concluded and were ongoing until sentence had been passed. The defendant never sought to challenge the propriety of the summons until he had in fact been sentenced. Submission to the jurisdiction of the court is thus crucial.

The court may not substitute the corporation's name for that of the company secretary—again they are different persons in law.[17]

REPRESENTATION AT COURT

8.8 A corporation will appear before the magistrates court either by a representative as defined, or, more usually, by a legal representative. A representative as defined by s.33(6) of the Criminal Justice Act 1925 means:

> "A person duly appointed by the corporation to represent it for the purpose of doing any act or thing which the representative of a corporation is by this section authorised to do ... a representative ... need not be appointed under the seal of the corporation, and a statement in writing purporting to be signed by a managing director of the corporation, or by any person ... having, or being one of the persons having, the management of the affairs of the corporation, to the effect

---

[16] [1975] Crim.L.R. 37.
[17] *City of Oxford Tramway Co v Sankey* (1890) 54 J.P. 564, 106.

that the person named in the statement has been appointed as the representative of the corporation for the purposes of this section, shall be admissible without further proof as prima facie evidence that that person has been so appointed."

Such a representative may enter a plea of "guilty" or "not guilty", either in writing or in person, and may apply to dismiss the charge, consent or object to summary trial or elect crown court trial. A director or secretary of the corporation may notify or intimate a guilty plea, where the procedure allows for a hearing in the absence of the defendant.

Schedule 3 of the Magistrates' Courts Act 1980[18] sets out provisions relating to representation and presence of a corporation in the magistrates court.

Schedule 3:

1. (1) A magistrates' court may commit a corporation for trial by an order in writing empowering the prosecutor to prefer a bill of indictment in respect of the offence named in the order.

   (2) An order under this paragraph shall not prohibit the inclusion in the bill of indictment of counts that under section 2 of the Administration of Justice (Miscellaneous Provisions) Act 1933 may be included in the bill in substitution for, or in addition to, counts charging the offence named in the order.

2. A representative may on behalf of a corporation—

   (a) make before examining justices such representations as could be made by an accused who is not a corporation;

   (b) consent to the corporation being tried summarily;

   (c) enter a plea of guilty or not guilty on the trial by a magistrates' court of an information.

3. (1) Where a representative appears, any requirement of this Act that anything shall be done in the presence of the accused, or shall be read or said to the accused, shall be construed as a requirement that that thing shall be done in the presence of the representative or read or said to the representative.

   (2) Where a representative does not appear, any such requirement, and any requirement that the consent of the accused shall be obtained for summary trial, shall not apply.

4. (1) Notification or intimation for the purposes of subsection (2) and (3) of section 12 above may be given on behalf of a corporation by a director or the secretary of the corporation, and those subsections shall apply in relation to a notification or intimation purporting to be so given as they apply to a notification or intimation purporting to be given by an individual accused.

---

[18] As amended by the Criminal Justice Act 1991, s.25 and the Criminal Procedure and Investigations Act 1996, Sch.1.

(2)   In this paragraph "director", in relation to a corporation which is established by or under any enactment for the purpose of carrying on under national ownership any industry or part of an industry or undertaking and whose affairs are managed by the members thereof, means a member of that corporation.

5.   *(Repealed).*

6.   Subject to the preceding provisions of this Schedule, the provisions of this Act relating to the inquiry into, and trial of, indictable offences shall apply to a corporation as they apply to an adult.

7.   Where a corporation and an individual who has attained the age of 17 are jointly charged before a magistrates' court with an offence triable either way, the court shall not try either of the accused summarily unless each of them consents to be so tried.

8.   Subsection (6) of section 33 of the Criminal Justice Act 1925 shall apply to a representative for the purposes of this Schedule as it applies to a representative for the purposes of that section.

CATEGORISATION OF OFFENCES BY TRIAL VENUE

8.9 Criminal cases brought against corporations will fall into one of the following categories:

(a)   summary only;
(b)   triable either way;
(c)   indictable only;
(d)   serious fraud cases.

Each category of offence has its own separate procedure:

(a)   summary only offences can only be tried at the Magistrates' Court;

(b)   offences triable either way may be tried at the Magistrates' Court or committed to the Crown Court for trial, either by order of the Magistrates' Court or at the request of the defence;

(c)   indictable only offences are immediately sent to the Crown Court by section 51 Crime and Disorder Act 1998: there is no committal either on the indictable only offence or any offence which is triable either way or summarily and which appears to the court to be related to the indictable only offence; if summary only, it must be punishable with imprisonment or disqualification from driving;

(d)   serious frauds are transferred to the Crown Court for management at that court.

Each procedure is dealt with separately below.

SUMMARY ONLY OFFENCES

If the corporation does not by its representative enter a plea, a not guilty **8.10** plea is entered and the prosecution must prove the case by the calling of evidence.

If the corporation is convicted, the magistrates will hear antecedents and mitigation and then proceed to sentence [see below, Ch.10: Sentencing Corporate Defendants].

There are circumstances in which a number of different allegations may be tried together. A summons may contain a number of separate informations or charges. It is for the magistrates to decide if it is in the interests of justice and fair to try them together. Similarly, where a number of defendants appear together at court, whether in the same or separate informations, it is for the magistrates to decide on the same criteria, whether to try them all together. Where all parties consent, it is likely that the justice of the case will demand a joint trial, but even in the absence of such consent, the magistrates must decide on joinder or severance of allegations and/or defendants in the interests of justice and fairness.

OFFENCES TRIABLE EITHER WAY

The corporation is asked to indicate by its representative whether it intends **8.11** to plead guilty or not guilty ("plea before venue" procedure). The court is obliged to explain that if a guilty plea is entered it shall proceed to hear the case as if it were a summary matter, but that if it is of the opinion, having heard the case, that its sentencing powers are inadequate, it may commit the case for sentence to the Crown Court—Magistrates' Courts Act 1980, s.17A.

The representative then enters the plea. If the plea is "guilty", the prosecution will open the facts and any antecedents of the corporation; the representative will mitigate and the court will either sentence the corporation or commit it for sentence to the Crown Court.

If the representative indicates a not guilty plea, or no plea is indicated, the court will then proceed to "mode of trial". Representations may be made by the prosecution and defence as to where the trial should be heard (ss.18–19, Magistrates' Courts Act 1980). The court will then consider the most suitable venue for the trial. Having heard representations, if the court is satisfied that the case is suitable for summary trial it will say so. The defendant is asked to indicate whether it consents to summary trial or wishes to elect trial by jury. If the representative does consent, the trial will be heard in the magistrates court. If not, the matter will be committed to the Crown Court.

Tactically, the principal advantage of a magistrates' court trial is that the **8.12** sentence is likely to be lower because the magistrates' court is limited to lower maximum financial penalties than the Crown Court can impose. In addition, the costs incurred are likely to be lower. The advantages of a Crown Court trial are often said to be the common sense of the jury and the separation of issues of law (decided by the judge) from issues of facts (decided by the jury). In a summary trial the magistrates decide all issues of law, admissibility and fact.

It is possible for the prosecution to withdraw or substitute a summary only charge for a charge where the defendant has elected trial by jury: it will not be an abuse of the process unless the substituted charge is inappropriate and the prosecution has acted in bad faith, or there is unfairness or prejudice to the defendant by the substitution.

If the court decides the matter is not suitable for summary trial, the case will be committed to the Crown Court irrespective of the wishes of the defendant.

Where the corporation is jointly charged with another defendant, if it considers the matter suitable for summary trial, the court may not take into account the likelihood that one would elect trial, in order to avoid separate trials.[19] But by s.7, Sch.3 of the Magistrates' Courts Act 1980, the court shall not try either the individual or the corporation summarily unless both agree. Nor can the court revert, part way through a summary trial, to a committal to avoid separate trials.[20]

COMMITTAL PROCEEDINGS

8.13 The purpose of committal proceedings was originally to provide a winnowing process to ensure that no one against whom there was not a prima facie case should stand trial. The procedure now only applies to "either way" offences where the magistrates have declined jurisdiction or the defendant has elected trial by jury. There are two possible modes of committal—with or without consideration of the evidence:

(a) Section 6(2) Magistrates' Courts Act 1980: "paper committal". This is by far the most common type of committal. Where the defendant is represented and accepts that there is sufficient evidence to found a case on the charge against it, there is no consideration of the evidence. The case will be committed to the appropriate Crown Court and the parties will be given the date of the first Plea and Directions hearing. Once committed, the case is no longer within the jurisdiction of the magistrates' court.

(b) Section 6(1) Magistrates' Courts Act: "Old-style committal".

---

[19] *Nicholls v Brentwood JJ.* [1992] 1 A.C. 1; *Wigan JJ. Ex p. Layland* [1995] Crim.L.R. 892.
[20] *Bradford Magistrates Court Ex p. Grant* [1999] Crim.L.R. 324.

All committals used to involve a consideration of the sufficiency of the evidence against the defendant on the charge. Now this type of committal is a rarity and is limited to a consideration of the evidence as it appears in the statements and exhibits forming the committal bundle; no "live" witnesses are called or cross-examined. The prosecution may open the case by summarising the evidence to the magistrates, after which the statements will be read or summarised (if there is no dispute and they are lengthy or repetitive), and the exhibits produced. After the evidence has been fully presented, the defence makes submissions. If the court finds that there is insufficient evidence to call for an answer from the defendant, it will not commit the case for trial. If the court concludes there is a case to answer, it must commit to the Crown Court.

VOLUNTARY BILL OF INDICTMENT

8.14 Should the magistrates refuse to commit, the prosecution may apply to the High Court for a voluntary bill of indictment to try and recommence proceedings which will, if the application is successful, go directly to the Crown Court.[21] This method can also be used, in unusual circumstances, quickly to bring a defendant against whom the magistrates have never considered a charge to the Crown Court. It is commonly used to join a co-defendant against whom proceedings are still at a very early stage (e.g. through avoiding arrest or due to a later extradition), with a defendant whose case has already been committed for trial.

The procedure governing applications is set out in Consolidated Criminal Practice Direction IV.35.[22] The judge "to whom application for consent to the preferment of a voluntary bill is made ... may invite oral submissions from either party, or accede to a request for an opportunity to make such oral submissions, if the judge considers it necessary or desirable to receive such oral submissions in order to make a sound and fair decision on the application. Any such oral submissions should be made on notice to the other party, who should be allowed to attend."[23]

It is made explicit in the Practice Direction that "The preferment of a voluntary bill is an exceptional procedure. Consent should only be granted where good reason to depart from the normal procedure is clearly shown and only where the interests of justice, rather than considerations of administrative convenience, require it."[24]

The prosecution in seeking the preferment of a voluntary bill must demonstrate that the tribunal "was obviously wrong or unreasonable".[25]

---

[21] s.2 Administration of Justice (Miscellaneous Provisions) Act 1933.
[22] Practice Direction (Voluntary Bill) [1999] 2 Cr.App.R. 442.
[23] CCPD IV.35.6.
[24] CCPD IV.35.3.
[25] *R. v Davenport* [2005] EWHC 2828 per Pitchers J. at paras 18–24.

The High Court judge is required to scrutinise the prosecution evidence in a similar fashion to the magistrates' court.

INDICTABLE-ONLY OFFENCES

8.15 Section 51 of the Crime and Disorder Act 1998 abolished committals for all indictable only offences whatever the date of the offence alleged. At the first appearance in the magistrates' court, the court must forthwith "send" the case to the Crown Court for trial. The magistrates' send the offence(s) triable only on indictment and "any either-way or summary offence with which he is charged which ... is related to the indictable-only offence and if summary only, is punishable with imprisonment or disqualification from driving".[26] The description of "adult" provided by s.51(12)(a), currently includes a corporation. A co-defendant on a related either-way offence may be caught by s.51(3). Thus a corporation charged jointly with an adult who faces a related indictable-only offence will find itself subject to this procedure. A related either-way offence is one that could be joined in the same indictment as the indictable-only offence.[27] A related summary offence is one arising out of circumstances which are the same as or connected to those giving rise to the indictable-only offence.[28]

Under the s.51 procedure, once in the Crown Court, a defendant can challenge (on notice) the sufficiency of the evidence on any charge before he is arraigned, at a dismissal hearing. If the prosecution have failed to show sufficient evidence which could properly be left to a jury, the judge hearing the application shall dismiss the charge and quash any count relating to it. A judge may allow oral evidence to be given if it is in the interests of justice, so the procedure is wider than the current committal proceedings. If one of a number of charges is dismissed, it can be resurrected by a voluntary bill, so the prosecution cannot obtain further evidence of the dismissed charge and then seek to add it to an indictment except via the High Court.[29] Alternatively, instead of obtaining a voluntary bill, the prosecution may start the proceedings again by re-charging or laying a new information. The procedure just described would then be repeated. There may be an application to stay for abuse of process if the second proceedings are simply a duplication of the first on the same material, but it may be appropriate when the prosecution is able to present an evidentially improved case.

After conviction on the indictable-only offence (whether following a plea of guilty or a trial) the related summary offence shall be put to the defendant. If a "guilty" plea is indicated the court shall sentence, as the

---

[26] s.51(1) and s.51(11) Crime and Disorder Act 1998.
[27] s.51(12)(c).
[28] s.51(12)(d).
[29] Sch.3 reg.2.

magistrates could have. If a "not guilty" plea is indicated, and the prosecution wishes to proceed on the summary offence, it will be remitted to the magistrates' court. Should the prosecution decide it is not in the interests of justice to proceed, it must inform the court that it does not wish to present evidence in relation to the charge and the Crown Court shall dismiss it.[30]

Where, as a result of a successful application to dismiss or for any other **8.16** reason, no indictable-only offence remains on the indictment, the Crown Court must go through the "plea before venue" procedure, as if it were a magistrates' court.[31] In the absence of a guilty plea, it must consider whether the matter is more suitable for summary trial; the same procedures and choices follow as outlined above. The defendant will then either be remitted for trial to the magistrates' court or tried by the Crown Court.[32] However, despite the wording of the Act, it has been held that a Crown Court has power to deal with a summary only offence which is related to an either way offence, after the indictable only offence has been disposed of.[33] This seems explicable only as a matter of convenience. Where the prosecution is brought by the Attorney-General, Solicitor General or Director of Public Prosecutions and he applies for the trial to be on indictment, the Crown Court has no discretion but must retain jurisdiction and proceed to trial.[34]

Preliminary Hearing

When a case is sent to the Crown Court under s.51 of the Crime and **8.17** Disorder Act 1998, a preliminary hearing will be listed no later than 28 days thereafter. At this hearing an indication of plea may be given. The prosecution must serve the evidence in the case within 70 days.[35] If the prosecution is unable to do so within this time, application may be made to the court for an extension.[36] Should the prosecution fail either to serve the evidence or apply in time for an extension, the proceedings are not a nullity. There is power to extend the time limit retrospectively.[37] The date for the Plea and Directions Hearing will be set at the preliminary hearing.

---

[30] Sch.3 reg.6.
[31] Failure to follow the "plea before venue" procedure in the Crown Court does not render the indictment a nullity: *R. v Ashton and others* [2006] EWCA Crim 794.
[32] Sch.3 regs 7–11.
[33] *R. v Nembhard, The Times*, February 22, 2002.
[34] Sch.3 reg. 12.
[35] Crime and Disorder Act 1998 (Service of Prosecution Evidence) Regulations 2005 (S.I. 2005/ 902), reg.2 for a defendant on bail.
[36] ibid. reg.3.
[37] *Fehily v Governor of Wandsworth Prison, The Times*, July 18, 2002, DC.

Transfer of Serious Fraud Cases

8.18 If a person has been charged with an indictable offence, and in the opinion of a designated authority the evidence of an offence charged (a) would be sufficient for the person charged to be committed for trial and (b) reveals a case of fraud of such seriousness and complexity that it is appropriate that the management of the case should be taken over by the Crown Court without delay, then, provided notice of transfer certifying such an opinion of the designated authority was given to the court within the required time, the functions of the magistrates' court cease (with certain exceptions) and the matter is transferred to the Crown Court.[38]

The designated authorities are the Director of Public Prosecutions, the Director of the Serious Fraud Office, the Commissioners of Revenue & Excise and the Secretary of State.[39]

The Notice of Transfer immediately takes the case to the Crown Court. As with the dismissal hearing procedures under s.51, Crime and Disorder Act 1998 (above), the Crown Court may, on notice, hear an application to dismiss the charge because of insufficiency of evidence. Such an application must be made prior to arraignment. The court may take into account any written or oral statement tendered by the defendant in support of its application to dismiss.[40] If he considers it in the interests of justice, the judge may allow oral evidence to be given. Thus, in cases of serious fraud and indictable only offences, a defendant has the opportunity (subject to notice and judicial leave) to call/cross-examine witnesses, reversing to some degree the limitation on submissions of no case to answer before arraignment, to which "either way" offences are now subject.[41]

Preparatory Hearings

8.19 Once the Crown Court is seized of the matter and after any application to dismiss, it may order a preparatory hearing where "the evidence on an indictment reveals a fraud of such seriousness or complexity that substantial benefits are like to accrue from" such a hearing.

Arraignment takes place at the start of the hearing, which is deemed to be the beginning of the trial.[42] The same judge who hears the preparatory hearings must also try the case, save in exceptional circumstances—thus emphasising that it is all part of the trial process.

The purpose of the hearing(s) is to identify issues for the jury and help

---

[38] ss.4–5 Criminal Justice Act 1987.
[39] s.4(2) Criminal Justice Act 1987.
[40] s.6 Criminal Justice Act 1987 and (SI 1988/1695) rr.2–7.
[41] *R. v X* [1989] Crim.L.R. 726.
[42] s.8 Criminal Justice Act 1967.

them to understand them; to expedite the hearing before the jury; to help the judge manage the trial.[43]

At or before the preparatory hearing, the judge may determine questions of law and admissibility, order a prosecution case statement setting out its case, order draft admissions to be served on the defence, and give directions likely to assist the smooth running of the trial. He may also order the defendant to reply to the Case Statement and draft admissions indicating areas of disagreement and challenge.[44]

This procedure is designed to ensure the jury trial runs as smoothly as possible.

PREPARATORY HEARINGS IN LONG OR COMPLEX CASES

Provision is also made for similar preparatory hearings to be held in long or **8.20** complex cases where it appears to the judge that "substantial benefits are likely to accrue from a hearing" before the jury is sworn in order to (a) identify issues which are likely to be material to the verdict of the jury; (b) assist their comprehension of any such issues; (c) expedite the proceedings before the jury; (d) assist the judge's management of the trial.[45]

The wording of the statute follows very closely that relating to preparatory hearings in serious fraud cases and the decisions in respect of one piece of legislation will be persuasive in respect of the other. In order for the 1996 legislation to bite, the judge must declare the case to be one of such complexity or length that a preparatory hearing would be of substantial benefit: it is not possible for the procedure to be adopted as a matter of convenience part-way through proceedings. Nor can it be adopted in order, for example, that an interlocutory ruling would become susceptible, pre-trial, to appeal, as rulings made on such hearings are.[46] The parameters of and procedures to be adopted in preparatory hearings are now covered by the House of Lords in *R. v H.*[47]

INTERLOCUTORY APPEALS

An appeal lies to the Court of Appeal from any ruling of a judge under **8.21** s.31(3): questions of admissibility of evidence or law (which includes rulings under s.78, PACE 1984,[48] and a ruling on the ambit of the indictment,[49]) but

---

[43] s.7 Criminal Justice Act 1967.
[44] ss.9 and 9A Criminal Justice Act 1967.
[45] Pt III Criminal Procedure and Investigations Act 1996 (CPIA 1996).
[46] s.35 CPIA 1996.
[47] [2007] 2 Cr.App.R. 6.
[48] *R. v R* [2000] 5 *Archbold* News 1.
[49] *R. v G, The Times*, March 30, 2001.

only with the leave of the judge or the Court of Appeal. The preparatory hearing may continue pending an appeal, but no jury may be sworn. The Court of Appeal has deprecated Crown Courts adopting the preparatory hearing procedure to obtain a ruling on a point of law in cases that in reality are neither long nor complex.[50] The procedure is exceptional and should only be used in exceptional cases.

The preparatory hearing may be adjourned or proceed pending appeal. Once the appeal process has been exhausted, either by an appellate judgment or by abandonment of the appeal, the jury may be empanelled.[51] A strict and speedy timetable is provided by rules under both statutes, since these appeals must be heard expeditiously so as not to hold up unduly the progress of the trial.

---

[50] *R. v Rudolph Alps* [2001] EWCA Crim 218.
[51] s.9(11) Criminal Justice Act 1987, ss.35–36 (CPIA) 1996.

CHAPTER 9

RESTRAINT AND CONFISCATION ORDERS

THE CRIMINAL CONFISCATION REGIME

Part 2 of the Proceeds of Crime Act 2002 (PoCA) came into force on March **9.1** 24, 2003[1] and applies to any offence committed on or after March 24, 2003. Offences committed before, and offences which began before but continue after that date are subject to the relevant pre-existing regime.[2] The 2002 Act provides for distinct criminal and civil proceedings. There is no reason in principle why the criminal confiscation regime should not apply to a corporate defendant. Although the term "criminal lifestyle"[3] is not apt to describe a legal person, it is submitted that the provisions apply to any convicted defendant, natural or legal.[4] However, if a corporation were to be convicted of an acquisitive crime, it would almost inevitably be on the basis that one or more individuals used the corporate structure as a vehicle for the crime. If so, and if such a person had also been convicted, it is likely that the corporate assets would be treated as those of the natural defendant, and it would be against him or her that a confiscation order would ultimately be made.

In *Re H and others*,[5] Rose L.J. made it clear that people should not be permitted to escape confiscation by adopting the corporate mantle. Although it would not usually be worthwhile prosecuting the company as well as the human actors (given the complexities of the corporate "mind and will"), in such circumstances, it will be appropriate for the courts to "lift the corporate veil" and treat the property of the corporate vehicle as belonging to the human defendant. That said, there will be cases where the court is

---

[1] Proceeds of Crime Act 2002 (Commencement No.5, Transitional Provisions, Savings and Amendment) Order 2003, (SI 2003/333) (c.20).
[2] Part VI of the Criminal Justice Act 1988; Drug Trafficking Act 1994.
[3] PoCA 2002, ss.6 and 10, Pt 2; Sch.2 (4 and 5 in Scotland and Northern Ireland respectively).
[4] See ss.5 & 11 of the Interpretation Act 1978.
[5] [1996] 2 All E.R. 391, 401.

asked to make a confiscation order against a corporate defendant, the only distinction being that the court cannot impose a term of imprisonment to be served in default of payment.

RESTRAINT ORDERS UNDER PART 2 OF THE PROCEEDS OF CRIME ACT 2002

9.2 Under Part 2 of the Proceeds of Crime Act jurisdiction for making restraint orders in respect of any offences committed on or after March 24, 2003 has been transferred to the Crown Court.[6] Application may be made at a very early stage, provided only that an "investigation" has been initiated.[7] The prosecution does not need to have charged or even anticipated charging any person; indeed, there need be no prosecution in contemplation. There is only a duty on the investigating officers to "investigate" and determine whether or not a crime has been committed.

A restraint order may be made provided the court is persuaded, on the balance of probabilities that the person has "benefited from criminal conduct". Section 76 defines both "benefit" and "criminal conduct" very broadly; for the purposes of s.40(2)(a) it is irrelevant where or when the offence took place.

The application will normally be made ex parte to a judge in chambers.[8] Where company assets are restrained, the order, together with a copy of the applicant's witness statement, must be served on the company affected. When considering an ex parte application, the court should be alive to the possibility that the company may be able to establish that it has a legitimate existence as a legal person carrying on lawful business; only if the company has been used as a vehicle for the defendant's alleged crime should a restraint order over the company's assets be made. If the position is unclear, the court can make the order last only until a fixed date when the parties may make representations as to the continuance or discharge of the order.

If granted, a restraint order has the effect of freezing property for the purpose of making it available to satisfy any confiscation order that may be made. Plainly, even if a criminal prosecution does follow, it will not always result in conviction. Between a restraint order being made and the determination of a subsequent trial, it is likely that many months will have passed.

9.3 The only protection available to a defendant subject to restraint is to apply to discharge the order if "within a reasonable time proceedings for the offence are not started".[9] The defendant is left without an effective remedy

---

[6] s.41(1) PoCA.
[7] s.40(2)(a).
[8] s.42(1)(b).
[9] s.42(7).

where the practical effect of the order might be considerable. Unlike a freezing injunction[10] (formerly called a *Mareva* injunction) which has a similar effect, the applicant does not have to give a cross-undertaking in damages.[11]

Where an application for a restraint order is made only after a person is charged,[12] the order will be discharged on the conclusion of proceedings including any re-trial.[13] No compensation is available under s.72 for any loss attributable to the restraint order.

A restraint order prohibits "any specified person" from dealing with any realisable property held by him. On application, the court may make such order as it believes appropriate for the purpose of ensuring that the restraint order is effective.[14] The defendant will be prohibited from dealing with his assets, which really means doing anything with them unless expressly sanctioned by the order itself. Typically, the court will order the defendant to provide information as to the extent and whereabouts of his assets (a disclosure order).[15] Failure to comply with such an order will be punished as a contempt of court. Given that restraint and receivership orders can bear heavily upon the individuals involved and may leave a defendant who is ultimately acquitted with substantially depleted assets, the court should, in deciding whether initially to make, vary or discharge, such orders, weigh up the balance of competing interests with the greatest of care.[16]

The court has a discretion to vary the terms of a restraint order, but it is a narrow discretion which *must* be exercised in accordance with s.69(2) which contains the legislative "steer". Section 41(4) precludes the courts from varying an order to release funds to a defendant or the recipient of any "tainted gift"[17] for legal expenses in relation to "offences in respect of which the restraint order is made". However, provision is made for such a person to have access to public funds from the Legal Services Commission for any proceedings in the Crown Court. By s.41(3) the court has express discretion to make provision "in particular" for the following exceptions:

(a) for reasonable living expenses;
(b) to enable any person to carry on any trade, profession or occupation;
(c) other exemptions subject to any conditions imposed.

The applicant for a restraint order may ask the court[18] to appoint a **9.4** management receiver over the defendant's realisable property. This will

---

[10] See CPR r.21.1.
[11] CPR Pt 25; Practice Direction 25A, para.5.1.
[12] s.40(3).
[13] s.42(6).
[14] s.41(7).
[15] s.357, Pt 8.
[16] *Hughes v Commissioners for Customs and Excise* [2003] 1 W.L.R. 177, 194 para.60.
[17] s.41(4).
[18] Under s.48.

commonly happen where the court making the order has "lifted the corporate veil" and restrained assets held in the name of the company controlled by the defendant. The receiver is empowered to receive and manage the property for the time being.[19] If the defendant is convicted, the receiver may be appointed by the court to enforce any confiscation order that is made. Moreover, s.45 provides a power to enable a constable or a Customs officer to seize any realisable property subject to a restraint order in order to prevent it from being removed from the jurisdiction. It is submitted that this power should only be exercised where there is evidence to suggest that the asset is at risk of "disappearing".

A management receiver may be given extensive powers by the court by s.49(2) and (3) including power to take possession of property[20] and to manage or otherwise deal with property.[21]

In order to exercise his functions, the receiver may be authorised to: hold property; enter into contracts; sue and be sued; employ agents; execute powers of attorney, deeds or other instruments; take any other steps the court thinks appropriate.[22] A receiver may recover his remuneration and expenses from assets under his control without violating the property rights of the defendant protected under art.1 of the First Protocol to the European Convention of Human Rights.[23] The basis upon which a receiver is remunerated is set out in CPR Part 60.6.

A question that commonly arises in receivership cases is: "does the receiver have power to settle the trading debts of a company subject to restraint?" In *Re X (Restraint Orders:Variation)*[24] a CJA restraint order was made against X and a receiver appointed over Y Ltd, a company controlled by X. The receiver was asked by Z Ltd to meet what were said to be trading debts owed by Y Ltd. Z Ltd applied for a variation of the restraint order to permit payment by the receiver of the sum said to be due. The judge concluded that it was plain from the wording of Part VI of the CJA that the court was empowered to sanction the payment of trade creditors from restrained funds. However, there was a clear distinction to be drawn between the position pre- and post-conviction. Pre-conviction there is a presumption of innocence; the defendant might be acquitted and a confiscation order might never be made. The Crown does not have priority over other creditors. A balance has to be struck between, on the one hand, preserving the worth of the defendant's property against the possibility that he may be convicted, and on the other hand allowing him in the meantime to continue with the ordinary course of his life.[25] However if the restrained

---

[19] s.49(2).
[20] s.49(2)(a).
[21] s.49(2)(b).
[22] By s.49(4).
[23] *Hughes & Connor v Commissioners for Customs and Excise* [2003] 1 W.L.R. 177, 194 para.59.
[24] [2004] EWHC 861 (Admin).
[25] per Simon Brown L.J. in *Re P (Restraint Order: Sale of Assets)* [2000] 1 W.L.R. 473.

person is convicted, a confiscation order will be made and no account should be taken of any obligations of the convicted person which conflict with the obligation to satisfy the order.

Re X was a case under the CJA; the position under the Proceeds of Crime **9.5** Act 2002 is not identical because the "legislative steer" contained in s.69(2) narrows the discretion of the courts. Under the 2002 Act, the restrictions apply pre as well as post conviction (s.69(2)(b)). Moreover, s.69(2)(c) requires the court to take no account of any obligations of the defendant (or even 'suspect', as a restraint order may be obtained pre-charge) which conflicts with the object of satisfying "any confiscation order". In *SFO v Lexi Holdings Plc (In Administration)* [2008] EWCA Crim 1443, the Court of Appeal considered the position under the old Acts (Criminal Justice Act 1988/Drug Trafficking Act 1994) and the 2002 Act, concluding that the changes had withdrawn all but the narrowest discretion to permit unsecured creditors to seek payment of debts from restrained funds:

> "The statutory provisions have changed significantly since the pre-2002 Act legislation and *In re X* would be decided differently today. Unless there is no conflict with the object of satisfying any confiscation order that has been or may be made, a restraint order should not be varied so as to allow for the payment of a debt to an unsecured creditor."

It is submitted that the position will depend upon the terms of the restraint order and the purpose for which the receiver has been appointed. If the order permits a company controlled by the defendant to trade, albeit under the management of a receiver,[26] it can be inferred that settlement of trading debts may be permitted provided the receiver is satisfied that the debt is genuine (and not itself part of the criminal conduct alleged). Where a management receiver is appointed with the powers in under s.41(3), the Crown Court will seek to control carefully the amounts involved; the purpose of the power is only to allow a defendant, in person or through a corporate vehicle, to carry on his trade or business and thereby avoid a depreciation of his business assets so they can be available to satisfy any confiscation order that may be made.

Once a confiscation order has been made but is neither satisfied nor subject to appeal,[27] the Crown Court may appoint an enforcement receiver[28] (inter alia) to realise the property[29] and give him the attendant powers[30] necessary for him to do so. Again, any person holding an interest in the property is entitled to a reasonable opportunity to make representations to the court.[31] This means, for example, that where the receiver wishes to sell

---

[26] see s.41(3)(b).
[27] s.50(1).
[28] s.50(2).
[29] s.51(2)(c).
[30] ss.51(3) and (4).
[31] s.51(8).

property, anyone else with an interest in the property has a right to make representations before the Court makes any order for sale. Moreover, any person affected by action proposed or taken by a receiver may apply to the Crown Court for directions[32] or to vary or discharge the order.[33]

Where there is a dispute as to any interest in property, the receiver may apply to the court for a declaration and an order for sale; the party claiming an interest will seek the discharge from the order of the disputed property. Findings made during the confiscation proceedings are not determinative of the interest of a third party even if he or she was called as a witness in the confiscation hearing.[34] A receiver appointed under ss.48, 50 or 52 is not liable to any person in respect of any loss or damage resulting from the action except so far as the loss or damage is caused by negligence.

In the event that a defendant is acquitted at trial, or the conviction is quashed on appeal, the costs of the receivership are nevertheless met from the receivership.[35] The receiver has a lien over the assets in the receivership for the payment of his costs.[36]

"LIFTING THE CORPORATE VEIL"

9.6 Whilst technically a corporation may have a confiscation order made against it and may be the subject of a restraint order pending trial, in practice the assets of a company will usually become the subject of criminal proceedings as a result of the misconduct of a natural person who is alleged to have used the corporate personality for his criminal purposes. Where a person has used the corporate structure as a device or facade to carry on or conceal his criminal activities, the court can "lift the corporate veil" and treat the assets of the corporation as the property of the defendant.[37] However, the court will only do so where the corporation is used to avoid or conceal liability for criminal activities (e.g. fraud[38]). In *Adams v Cape Industries*, Slade L.J. said that[39]:

> "...the court is not free to disregard the principle of *Salomon v A. Salomon & Co Ltd* merely because it concludes that justice so requires."

A company duly formed and registered is a separate legal entity and must be treated like any other independent person with its own rights and liabilities distinct from those of its shareholders; it makes no difference whether, as

---

[32] s.62(3).
[33] s.63(2).
[34] *Re Norris* [2001] 1 W.L.R. 1388 HL.
[35] *Hughes and Connor v Commissioners for Customs & Excise* [2003] 1 W.L.R. 177.
[36] See *Re Andrews* [1999] 1 W.L.R. 1236.
[37] *Re H & Others (Restraint Order)* [1996] 2 All E.R. 391, 401 per Rose L.J.
[38] See, e.g. *Gencor ACP Ltd v Dalby* [2000] 2 B.C.L.C. 734.
[39] [1990] Ch D 433 at 542; [1991] 1 All E.R. 929, 1024.

was the position in *Salomon v Salomon & Co Ltd*, the company is controlled by a single person. However, the fact that a company is separate in law does not mean that the status, identity or conduct of the person or persons who control it is irrelevant; where it is relevant, the court may go beind the mere status of the company as a separate legal entity to establish who directs and controls its activities.[40] In *Daimler Co Ltd v Continental Tyre & Rubber Co (Great Britain) Ltd*[41] a majority of their Lordships considered the fact that the shareholders were all Germans living in Germany at a time when Britain was at war with that country was relevant because if the defendant company (Daimler) had settled an admitted trading debt, it would have been trading with the enemy. Although the company could neither be "friend nor enemy", the enemy character of the shareholders was very material to the question of whether the persons in de facto control of the company were taking instruction from the enemy.[42]

Nevertheless, the court will not pierce the corporate veil simply on the ground of impropriety:

> "Companies are often involved in improprieties. But it would make undue inroads into the principle of *Salomon's* case if an impropriety not linked to the use of the company to avoid or conceal liability for that impropriety was enough".[43]

To justify lifting the corporate veil, it is necessary to show that the company was used as a device or facade to conceal the true facts and so avoid or conceal the liability of specific individuals. In *Re H*,[44] the evidence suggested that the defendants controlled the companies; that the companies had been used for the evasion of excise duty on a large scale; that the defendants treated the companies as carrying on the family business and that the defendants had benefited from company assets (cash). In the circumstances, it was entirely appropriate to lift the corporate veil and treat the assets of the company as though held by the defendants. The courts should not permit those profiting from crime to escape the confiscation of their ill-gotten gains by adopting the corporate mantle.[45] Where a company is used as a vehicle for fraud, the corporate veil should be lifted.[46]

However, the distinction is sometimes a fine one: in *R. v Gokal*,[47] the defendant conducted a fraud the effect of which was to prop up the family company ("Gulf") using money fraudulently obtained from BCCI. Without those funds (approximately £548 million), Gulf would have been insolvent.

---

[40] *Merchandise Transport Ltd v BTC* [1962] 2 Q.B. 173 CA per Dankwerts L.J. at 206.
[41] [1916] 2 AC 307 HL.
[42] per Lord Parker at 345.
[43] per Sir Andrew Morritt V.C. *Trustor AB v Smallbone (No.2)* Ch D 1185.
[44] [1996] 2 All E.R. 391.
[45] *Crown Prosecution Service v Comptons of Brighton Ltd and others* [2002] EWCA Civ 1720 para.18.
[46] *R. v Dimsey and Allen* [2000] 1 Cr.App.R.(S.) 497.
[47] May 7, 1997 Central Criminal Court transcript T 950223.

The prosecution applied for confiscation; the court was asked to "pierce the corporate veil" and treat the funds obtained by the company as those of the defendant on the basis that Gulf had been used as a "device or facade to conceal" Gokal's crime. Buxton J. refused to do so. He found that Gulf had obtained the funds through the fraud of Gokal; the money became the company's property, not the property of the defendant. Although the company had obtained money as a result of fraud, it was not used as a device to conceal the fraud. In effect, Gokal had divested himself of any interest in the money so it was not appropriate to pierce the corporate veil so as to treat funds in which he no longer had any interest as if they belonged to him.

9.7 Where a company does carry on legitimate business in addition to engaging in (allegedly) fraudulent transactions, the prosecution should be cautious when applying for a restraint order since the effect of the order may be to close the business down.[48] Even if a company has been used in the commission of a crime, it does not follow that its separate status should be ignored or that it should be treated as indivisible from the individual defendants for all purposes, or as being incapable of having entered into legitimate legal relations with third parties.[49] In such circumstances, under the terms of the order, the court should permit the person restrained to deal with his assets in the ordinary course of business.[50] Where a company was not set up as a sham in the first place and it was only deployed for the purpose of the (human) defendant's fraud some time later, it will be appropriate to lift the veil if it is shown that the company was used by the defendant at some point to carry out or conceal his fraud.[51] The real question is whether assets of the company can be treated as assets of the defendant. If there is intermingling of a criminal's realisable assets with funds obtained on a result of the company's legitimate business activities, the court can lift the corporate veil:

> "There would obviously be a very considerable lacuna in the ability of the Act to achieve its objective if in principle, because such a company was not a one mans band or wholly criminal in its origin, funding or activities, assets held in it could not be subject to receivership or restraint order provisions."[52]

Although the phrase "lifting (or 'piercing') the corporate veil" is familiar to lawyers, it should not appear in the body of a restraint order;[53] the order should, in clear terms, prohibit the company as well as the defendant from dealing with its property.

---

[48] *Re G* (2001) Unreported, Case No.110/01 per Stanley Burton J. at para.14.
[49] per Clarke L.J., *Crown Prosecution Service v Comptons of Brighton Ltd*, [2002] EWCA Civ 1720 at para.22.
[50] See s.41(3)(b).
[51] *R. v Omar* [2004] EWCA Crim 2320, per Scott Baker L.J.
[52] *Re D* [2006] EWHC Admin 254 per Ousley J.
[53] See *Re K* [2005] EWCA Crim 619; *Re G*, (2001) unreported, Case No. 110/01 at para.12.

SENTENCING CORPORATE DEFENDANTS

GENERAL SENTENCING PRINCIPLES

The overarching objects of sentencing are set out in s.142 of the Criminal **10.1** Justice Act 2003:

"Purposes of sentencing

(1) Any court dealing with an offender in respect of his offence must have regard to the following purposes of sentencing—

(a) the punishment of offenders,
(b) the reduction of crime (including its reduction by deterrence),
(c) the reform and rehabilitation of offenders,
(d) the protection of the public, and
(e) the making of reparation by offenders to persons affected by their offences."

Although some doubt remains about the applicability of (c) to companies, these tenets can all apply to a corporate defendant as well as to an individual. When sentencing, a court is obliged to take into account the principles set out above.

In addition the court must have regard to the principle of parity of sentence between defendants. So where for example there is equal guilt between defendants but one pleads guilty and the other contests the matter, there should be appropriate discount for the defendant pleading guilty.

"the approach ...[should be]... would right-thinking members of the public, with full knowledge of all the relevant facts and circumstances, learning of ...[the disparity in sentences]... consider that something had gone wrong with the administration of justice."[1]

In addition the Sentencing Guideline Council has now given guidance in relation to reducing a sentence in order to reflect a plea of guilty. The stage at which the plea is made will affect the amount of credit given. It recommends that a discount of one-third is appropriate where a defendant pleads guilty "at the first reasonable opportunity" (be that in the Magistrates' Court or at the PCMH, depending on the case) and that a reduction of 10 per cent is appropriate where the defendant pleads guilty just before trial or at the door of the court. Where a plea of guilty is entered part way through the trial it may well be that no discount is attracted at all.[2] Of course, theses discounts are easily seen in terms of reduction in the length of a custodial sentence but they are equally applicable in principle to the level of fines. Where a company could have expected a fine of £x after a trial, depending on the stage which a guilty plea is entered, the court must give an appropriate level of discount of say £x – 10 per cent. The court is now urged to indicate what the sentence would have been but for the guilty plea, so it should be capable of analysis.

FACTUAL BASIS OF SENTENCE

10.2 Once convicted, whether by a guilty plea or after a trial, a corporate defendant faces the same sentencing procedure as an individual. After a trial, it is for the sentencing tribunal to determine the factual basis on which to sentence according to the evidence heard during the trial. Where there has been a trial it is in the interests of justice for the same tribunal (whether magistrates or the judge in a jury trial) to sentence the defendant. It is where a defendant pleads guilty to a charge, that a factual issue between the parties as to the basis for sentence is most likely to arise. In either situation, the factual basis of sentence must have an evidential foundation true to the verdicts in the case. For example, where a corporation is convicted of a number of Health & Safety at Work Act offences by a jury in the Crown Court, but acquitted on others, those on which it has been acquitted must not be brought to bear in sentence. The seriousness of those of which it has been convicted is a matter for the judge to determine.

When entering a guilty plea, the defendant may indicate the basis upon which it accepts liability. Where that basis is different from the prosecution case, the court is obliged to determine whether that difference would affect the sentence. If satisfied that the difference is immaterial or minor, the court should sentence according to the defendant's version of the facts. If, on the

---

[1] *R. v Fawcett* (1983) 5 Cr.App.R.(S.) 158, 161 per Lawton L.J.
[2] *http://www.sentencing-guidelines.gov.uk* in respect of all sentences after July 23, 2007.

other hand, the version put forward by the defendant is "manifestly false" or "wholly implausible" the tribunal may reject it without hearing evidence. Where there is a material factual dispute (i.e. one which *would* make a difference to sentence) the judge will need to hear evidence to resolve the dispute—a "Newton hearing".[3] It is most important, particularly when setting the level of a fine for example, to establish the criminality of the defendant's conduct: in *R. v Tropical Express Ltd*,[4] a malicious manager had presented a consignment of toxic, flammable and explosive goods for passage by air in contravention of the Air Navigation (Dangerous Goods) Regulations 1994. The corporation pleaded guilty to the strict liability offence although the manager had maliciously delivered the items in revenge after he had been reported to Customs & Excise for smuggling cigarettes in a multimillion pound evasion fraud by the sole director and shareholder of the company. The court held that it was entitled to take account of all the circumstances; as the company having behaved absolutely properly, what would normally be a very substantial fine was reduced to one of £5,000. If the defence put forward mitigation, which does not contradict the prosecution case but puts a gloss on it, it may either do so by submission alone or evidence.

TAKING OFFENCES INTO CONSIDERATION

A defendant may ask the court to take into consideration when sentencing **10.3** it, other offences of a similar character which it admits and which would not otherwise be before the court. This procedure obviates the need for separate proceedings in respect of the other offences. The court will not pass separate sentences for the offences taken into consideration, but those other "admitted" offences will be reflected in the global sentence passed by the court. Provisions exist empowering the court to make compensation orders[5] and restitution orders[6] in respect of the other "admitted" offences. This procedure (which has no statutory foundation) has the considerable advantage to the defence of bringing those other matters to an end. The admitted offences cannot be separately prosecuted, and will usually result in a lower overall sentence than would have been the case had they been separately prosecuted. The advantage to the prosecuting authority is that it is spared the trouble and expense of bringing additional proceedings and proving additional allegations.

This method of a defendant accepting liability for other offences should not be followed where: it is in the public interest for a trial to be held (e.g. of

---

[3] *R. v Newton* (1983) 77 Cr.App.R. 13.
[4] [2002] 1 Cr.App.R.(S.) 27.
[5] s.130 Powers of Criminal Courts (Sentencing) Act 2000 ("PCC(S)A 2000") and see Compensation Orders below.
[6] s.148 PCC(S)A 2000 and see Restitution Orders below.

a serious offence); or where the sentencing court has no jurisdiction to try the admitted offence (e.g. a summary only offence in the Crown Court).[7]

SENTENCING VENUE

10.4 There is a number of ways in which a corporate defendant may find itself appearing for sentence: summary only offences must be sentenced by the magistrates' court except in circumstances which are unlikely to apply to a corporation[8]; having pleaded guilty or been found guilty at the magistrates' court, that court may sentence or commit to the Crown Court for sentence; having pleaded guilty or been found guilty at the Crown Court, sentence will follow.[9] A magistrates' court may commit a defendant for sentence for an either way offence where, after a trial or a plea of guilty to another offence, the court is of the opinion that the offence or combination of the offence and one or more associated offences is so serious that greater punishment should be inflicted than the court has power to impose.[10] The court may also commit a defendant on an indication of a guilty plea to an either way offence where the court takes a similar view of the level of punishment required, or where it is committed with another offence to the Crown Court.[11] Once at the Crown Court, the defendant may be dealt with in any way in which it could have been sentenced on conviction on indictment.[12] The magistrates can commit for sentence at any stage up to the passing of sentence.

Magistrates' and Crown Courts have the same range of sentencing options for corporate defendants. In a magistrates' court the maximum fine for summary offences is £5,000 unless the statute provides for a greater amount (e.g. Health and Safety at Work Act 1974 maximum fine in the magistrates' court is £20,000).[13]

TYPES OF DISPOSAL

10.5 It goes almost without saying that a corporation cannot be imprisoned. At present, corporate defendants can be sentenced[14] in the following ways:

---

[7] *R. v Simons* (1953) 37 Cr.App.R. 120.

[8] s.41 Criminal Justice Act 1988.

[9] s.3 PCC(S)A 2000. By s.3(5) this procedure applies to a corporation.

[10] s.3 PCC(S)A 2000.

[11] s.4 PCC(S)A 2000.

[12] s.5 PCC(S)A 2000.

[13] For numerous offences under the Companies Act 1985 a multiple of the maximum fine may be applied for second or subsequent offences [see Ch.14: Companies Act Offences, below].

[14] A corporate defendant can be made the subject of a confiscation order in addition to any sentence passed—see Ch.10: Sentencing.

- Fine.
- Compensation order.
- Restitution order.
- Absolute or conditional discharge.
- Deferred sentence.
- Remedial orders.
- Publicity orders (in Corporate Manslaughter only).
- Forfeiture.
- Financial reporting orders.
- Directors' disqualification orders.

FINES

General Principles

Every crime of which a corporation can be convicted can be punished by a **10.6** fine.[15] Fines are by far and away the most common type of sentence passed on a corporate defendant. Before fixing the amount of the fine the court must take into account the seriousness of the offence[16] and the financial circumstances of the offender.[17] The means of the offender may increase as well as reduce the level of the fine.[18] A plea of guilty will almost always provide some mitigation in the level of the fine imposed.

Means of the Offender

The means of the offender, and particularly a corporate defendant, are **10.7** relevant to the level of fine imposed by a court, but the court in *F Howe & Son (Engineers) Ltd*[19] did not accept that the fine should bear any specific relationship to the turnover or net profit of the defendant.[20] The court stated:

> "The objective of prosecutions for health and safety offences in the work place is to achieve a safe environment for those who work there and for other members of the public who may be affected. A fine needs to be large enough to bring that message home where the Defendant is a company not only to those who manage it but to its shareholders."[21]

---

[15] s.163 CJA 2003.
[16] s.164(2) CJA 2003.
[17] s.164 (3) CJA 2003.
[18] s.164(4) CJA 2003.
[19] [1999] 2 Cr.App.R.(S.) 37.
[20] ibid. at 43.
[21] ibid. at 44.

In *R. v Jarvis Facilities Ltd*[22] Hedley J. indicated that where there was a conflict between achieving consistency of sentence and ensuring that a fine was commensurate with the means of the offender, it was the means of the offender which should have priority. Having quoted the passage from *F Howe & Sons* above, he commented:

"It will be seen at once that this gives rise to real difficulty both in achieving consistency of sentence and in ensuring that some proportion is maintained between the quantum of the fine and the gravity of the specific case given that offending companies may have vast disparities of economic strength. A fine that may hardly touch a multi-national might put a small company out of business yet their offence may have been the same. Consistency of level of fine may not therefore be a primary aim of sentencing in these cases."

In *R. v Balfour Beatty Rail Infrastructure Ltd*[23] the prosecution that followed the Hatfield Rail crash that caused the death of four passengers and injuries to 102 others, Lord Phillips' remarks[24] explain the objective of a fine:

"Section 3 of the 1974 Act requires positive steps to be taken by all concerned in the operation of the business of a company to ensure that the company's activities involve the minimum risk, both to employees and to third parties. Knowledge that breach of this duty can result in a fine of sufficient size to impact on shareholders will provide a powerful incentive for management to comply with this duty. This is not to say that the fine must always be large enough to affect dividends or share price. But the fine must reflect both the degree of fault and the consequences so as to raise appropriate concern on the part of shareholders at what has occurred. Such an approach will satisfy the requirement that the sentence should act as a deterrent. It will also satisfy the requirement, which will rightly be reflected by public opinion, that a company should be punished for culpable failure to pay due regard for safety, and for the consequences of that failure."

The relevance of the financial state of the company was reiterated in a case concerning breaching of a safety zone and consequent collision with a gas installation in the North Sea by a fishing boat.[25] A £40,000 fine was reduced to £15,000 on appeal; describing the finances of the company as being "in a parlous state". Kay L.J. stated :

"In fixing the fine in cases such as this amongst the features the court has to have regard to are the level of culpability, the financial circumstances of the defendant and the consequences and potential

---

[22] [2005] EWCA Crim 1409.
[23] [2006] EWCA Crim 1586.
[24] at para.42.
[25] *R. v Armana Ltd* [2004] EWCA Crim 1069.

consequences to others of the breach of safety which the court is examining..."

Matters in mitigation included: the financial consequences of the matter to the defendant (such as increased insurance premiums, loss of revenue and repair costs incurred), the overall financial position of the company and the very low level of fault in what was a strict liability offence. When considering the level of penalty the court must also look at the totality of financial orders made, including any costs order.[26] However, the fact that a corporate defendant may take a number of years to pay a fine does not necessarily mean it is excessive. In *R. v Rollco Screw & Rivet Co Ltd*[27] Lord Bingham C.J. stated:

> "With a personal defendant with a fine hanging over him, there are arguments for keeping the period of that continuing punishment within bounds. It appears to us that those arguments are much weaker (if indeed they apply at all) when one is considering a corporate defendant. There is not the same sense of anxiety as is liable to afflict an individual, and it appears to us to be acceptable on proper facts and in appropriate circumstances for a fine to be payable by a company over a substantially longer period than might be appropriate in the case of an individual."

In that case the court reduced the totality of the financial orders from £70,000 to £60,000 by limiting the order for costs to £10,000. The period for payment was reduced from six years, five months to five years, seven months. It was said that a large sum over a long period might assist the company's cash flow and help it survive difficult trading conditions.

In the case of *R. v Yorkshire Sheeting & Insulation Ltd*,[28] allowing an appeal against sentence based to some extent on disparity, the Court of Appeal took into account the fact that a costs order apportioned between the two defendants should not be altered in amount, and reduced the level of fine payable by the Appellant company to take practical heed of the extra costs burden.

Levels of Fine

10.8 In the magistrates' court there is a standard scale of fines. Many statutes express the maximum penalty for an offence as "not exceeding" a particular level.

---

[26] See Costs below.
[27] [1999] 2 Cr.App.R.(S.) 436.
[28] [2003] EWCA Crim 458.

Level on the scale	Maximum fine
1	£200
2	£500
3	£1000
4	£2500
5	£5000[29]

In addition, certain statutes impose maximum fines expressly for offences tried summarily. For example, the Health & Safety at Work Act 1974 (as amended) "HSWA"; empowers the magistrates' court to impose a maximum fine of £20,000 for breach of the duties under ss.2–6 of the Act.

The level of fines has grown considerably in the last few years. The most serious health and safety prosecutions have repeatedly resulted in fines of millions of pounds even after a plea of guilty. Great Western Trains were fined £1.5 million in respect of the Southall rail disaster in which seven people died in 1997, after a guilty plea to s.3 of the HSWA. Since then in a Scottish case, *R. v Transco*, a gas company, was fined £15 million for very serious breaches of health and safety legislation and, in England, following the Hatfield rail disaster which led to the deaths of four passengers and the injury of 102 in 2000, Balfour Beatty was fined £7.5 million (reduced on appeal from £10 million).[30]

Relevant Sentencing Features

10.9 Scott Baker J. identified various factors in HSWA prosecutions which would be relevant to sentence:

> (i)   in assessing the gravity of the breach the court should look at how far short of the "reasonably practicable" standard the company fell.
>
> (ii)   whether the breach was an isolated incident or committed over a period of time.
>
> (iii)   whether the breach resulted from the company deliberately running a risk in order to save money or with a view to profit.
>
> (iv)   a fatality would usually be an aggravating feature.
>
> (v)   the degree of risk and extent of the danger created by the offence.
>
> (vi)   the company's resources and the effect of the fine on the business.

Mitigating features included:

> (i)   a prompt admission of guilt and an early plea of guilty;

---

[29] s.37 Criminal Justice Act 1982 as amended by the CJA 1991.
[30] *R. v Balfour Beatty Rail Infrastructure Services Ltd* [2006] EWCA Crim 1586.

(ii) the taking of steps to remedy deficiencies drawn to the company's attention;

(iii) a good safety record and/or no previous convictions or warnings.

Aggravating features included:

(i) a failure to heed warnings;

(ii) a deliberate breach of the health and safety legislation with a view to profit.

Further guidance as to the best practice to be adopted in such sentencing hearings was provided by the Court of Appeal in *R. v Friskies Petcare (UK) Ltd.*[31] The prosecution should set out in documentary form the facts of the case and the aggravating features. The document should be served on the court and the defence. In the event of a guilty plea, the defence should submit a similar document outlining mitigating features. Following this procedure will: (i) enable the court to determine whether there is an agreed basis of plea, and if not, whether a *Newton* hearing is necessary; and (ii) clarify the basis on which sentence is passed. In *Friskies Petcare (UK) Ltd,* the HSE did not put forward as an aggravating feature the fact that the defendant had put profit before safety, but the judge specifically found that to be the case. A fine of £600,000 was reduced to £250,000 on appeal.

Although these features are specific to HSWA prosecutions, and the remarks were made for guidance in an area where it was generally considered that fines were far too low, it is submitted that they provide assistance generally in setting the level of financial penalties for corporate defendants.

Fines at the top end of the scale are now imposed frequently by the courts, **10.10** indicating intolerance of safety breaches, but taking into account the size and profitability of the defendant corporation. That said, there is at present no legislation requiring a case of statutory breaches resulting in death to be tried in the Crown Court.[32] Accordingly, where an offence is dealt with in the magistrates' court, the fine will necessarily be limited to the summary maximum even if there has been a fatality.

Where the brunt of the fine may fall on the general public or reduce the funds available for safety improvements, the courts have typically imposed lower penalties, although still sufficient to mark disapproval of the defendant's method of operating. However, an overarching principle seems to emerge that courts are entitled to take a more severe view of breaches of health and safety where there is a significant public element; as the Court of Appeal observed in *Jarvis*[33]:

---

[31] [2000] 2 Cr.App.R.(S.) 401.
[32] Although see the remarks of Scott Baker J. in *R. v Howe & Sons (Engineers)*, above.
[33] [2005] EWCA Crim 1409 para.11.

"This is so particularly in cases (like the railway) where public safety is entrusted to companies in the work that they do and where the general public simply has to trust in the competence and efficiency of such companies. Moreover where the failures are such that (as here) it is fortuitous that the risks thereby generated were not greater in the sense that these failures could have happened anywhere, the court is entitled to take account of that as well. Accordingly in our view, public service cases will often be treated more seriously than those in which the breaches are confined within the private sector even where there is comparability between gravity of breach and economic strength of defendant."

At the other end of the scale there will be cases where the corporate defendant is not criminally culpable in any meaningful sense. Where a defendant is convicted of a strict liability offence it may not even have acted negligently. It may, at one extreme, be the victim of the blameworthy behaviour for which it must accept liability.[34] Such circumstances will neither deter a prosecution nor prevent a conviction but the court will take them into account in sentencing. In *St Margaret's Trust Ltd*[35] other defendants had fraudulently conspired to induce the defendant finance company to advance more than it was lawfully permitted to. The company executed a transaction prohibited by a postwar hire-purchase Order, although it had acted quite innocently throughout. Whereas the defendants convicted of the conspiracy were morally to blame and fined £50 on each charge, *St Margaret's Trust Ltd* was fined £5 on each. The company appealed against conviction on the basis that it had acted entirely innocently. The Court of Appeal found the offence to be one of strict liability.[36] Donovan J. giving the judgment of the court stated[37]:

"There would be little point in enacting that no one should breach the defences against a flood, and at the same time excusing anyone who did it innocently ... It is true that Parliament has prescribed imprisonment as one of the punishments that may be inflicted for a breach of the Order, and this circumstance is urged in support of the appellants' argument that Parliament intended to punish only the guilty. We think it is the better view that, having regard to the gravity of the issues, Parliament intended the prohibition to be absolute, leaving the court to use its powers to inflict nominal punishment or none at all in appropriate cases ... But if Parliament enacts a certain thing shall not be done, it is not necessarily an excuse to say: 'I carry on my business in such a way that I may do this thing unwittingly and therefore should

---

[34] See, e.g. *R v. Tropical Express Ltd*, above.
[35] [1958] A.C. 183.
[36] Hire-Purchase and Credit Sale Agreements (Control) Order 1956 art.1.
[37] At pp.190–191.

suffer no penalty if I transgress'. The answer in some cases is that the importance of not doing what is prohibited is such that the method of business must be re-arranged so as to give the necessary knowledge."

(2) Compensation Orders

Compensation orders may be made in addition to or instead of other sentencing options.[38] Such an order may be made: **10.11**

> "For any personal injury, loss or damage resulting from that offence or any other offence which is taken into consideration by the court in determining sentence"

or

> "for funeral expenses or bereavement in respect of a death resulting from any such offence".[39]

Compensation orders should only be made where the position is clear, not only in relation to liability and causation,[40] but also to the amount which should be either agreed, proved or capable of being assessed.[41] A compensation order may be made even though the loss or damage in question is not actionable in civil law or against the defendant. In *R. v Chappell*,[42] the defendant was a director of a company who was convicted of recklessly completing VAT returns with the result that the company paid less VAT than it should have done. Before trial the company had been dissolved and so could not be pursued for the underpayment. However, the judge was entitled to make a compensation order which had the effect of making the defendant pay the sums owed by the company to the Commissioners for Customs and Excise, even though the debt was the company's and not his.

Compensation may be awarded for emotional distress,[43] for example, from a misdescription in a brochure resulting in a holiday which did not have the promised facilities. It may also be ordered where the person who suffered the loss has died.[44]

In the magistrates' court, compensation is limited to £5,000 per offence. Offences taken into consideration may also attract an order not exceeding the difference between the maximum amount possible for all the offences of

---

[38] s.130(1) PCC(S)A 2000 which replaces similar legislation under the Powers of Criminal Courts Act 1973, s.35.

[39] Other than a death due to an accident arising out of the presence of a motor vehicle on a road.

[40] Where the loss can "fairly be said to result from the offence"—*Rowlston v Kenny* (1982) 4 Cr.App.R.(S.) 85; *R. v Vivian* 68 Cr.App.R. 53.

[41] s.130(4) PCC(S)A 2000.

[42] (1984) 6 Cr.App.R.(S.) 214.

[43] *R. v Thomson Holidays Ltd* (1974) 58 Cr.App.R. 429.

[44] *Holt v DPP* [1996] 2 Cr.App.R.(S.) 314.

which a defendant has been convicted and that actually already ordered to be paid.[45] There are special rules for motor accidents.[46]

10.12   Compensation may be ordered having regard to assets which are lawful and nothing to do with criminal conduct. The purpose of such an order is to compensate the loser.[47]

A compensation order may include a sum to reflect loss of interest as long as the method for calculation of it is not unduly complicated.[48] The order need not even be a precisely calculated sum since the legislation gives the court some discretion (for example, on what rate of interest to apply) but, as a general rule, where the amount of compensation is relatively large, the time between the damage and the sentencing hearing is a long one[49] and there is no doubt that the defendant can pay, the sentencing judge is quite entitled to make such an order rather than leave the claim to be litigated in the civil courts.

(3) Restitution Orders

10.13   A restitution order[50] may be made where goods have been stolen and a person is convicted of any offence with reference to the theft or a person is convicted of any other offence, but any offence with reference to the theft is taken into consideration in sentencing.

A restitution order may be made either:

(a)   by ordering anyone having control or possession of the stolen goods to restore them to anyone entitled to recover them from him; or

(b)   on the application of a person who is entitled to recover from the person convicted any goods representing the stolen goods (being the proceeds of disposal or realisation of them), by ordering that those goods be transferred or delivered to the applicant; or

(c)   by ordering the payment of a sum of money, out of monies taken from his possession on his apprehension, not being greater than the value of the stolen goods to a person who, if the goods were in the possession of the convicted person would be entitled to recover them from him.[51]

Such an order may only be made in accordance with the evidence given or admissions made[52] and, like compensation orders, only in clear and

---

[45] s.131 PCC(S)A 2000.
[46] s.130(6) PCC(S)A 2000 and the provisions relating to the Motor Insurers' Bureau.
[47] *R. v Copley* (1979) 1 Cr.App.R.(S.) 55.
[48] *R. v Schofield* (1978) 67 Cr.App.R. 282.
[49] In *R. v Schofield*, the time lapse was one of approximately four years.
[50] ss.148 & 149 PCCA(S)A 2000.
[51] ibid.
[52] *R. v Church* (1971) 55 Cr.App.R. 65.

uncomplicated circumstances.[53] Where there was any possibility that third parties who could not intervene in proceedings may be prejudiced, or there were complex questions of ownership, no order should be made:

> "On the other hand, in appropriate cases where the evidence is clear, it is important that the court should make proper use of the power to order restitution since this can frequently avoid unnecessary expense and delay in the victim receiving the return of his property".[54]

The order, however made up, should only be for the value of the items actually stolen and not recovered—so that if a stolen item is recovered, the court should not then make a restitution order for the value of the goods.[55]

(4) Absolute and Conditional Discharge

The court may absolutely or conditionally discharge a defendant, in **10.14** appropriate cases where "having regard to the circumstances including the nature of the offence and the character of the offender . . . it is inexpedient to inflict punishment". An absolute discharge may be used where there has been a technical breach of a statute. A conditional discharge, which may operate for up to three years, is a discharge subject to the condition that the defendant commits no offence during the requisite period.[56] Subject to that, the discharge shall not be deemed to be a conviction for any purpose other than in the original proceedings (or, if in breach by virtue of another offence during the period, for those purposes also).[57] A fine may not be combined with a discharge.[58]

Discharges are relatively rare in practice. Even in a case[59] where a corporation was convicted as a result of malicious acts by a disgruntled employee taking revenge for being dismissed, the court did not consider that the imposition of a discharge was appropriate. Despite an exemplary record, the plea of guilty and the "wholly exceptional" nature of the case, in allowing an appeal from a fine of £20,000 and prosecution costs of £18,000, the Court of Appeal declined (without giving reasons) to discharge the corporation. Although the fine was reduced to £5,000 and orders were made for the defendant corporation to pay the prosecution's costs after taxation. The mitigating circumstances in this case would seem to justify a discharge but, as a matter of principle it will seldom be appropriate for the courts to impose a discharge where a defendant is to be sentenced for a strict liability

---

[53] *R. v Ferguson* (1970) 54 Cr.App.R. 410.
[54] *R. v Calcutt & Varty* (1985) 7 Cr.App.R.(S.) 385.
[55] *R. v Parker* (1970) 54 Cr.App.R. 339.
[56] s.12 PCC(S)A 2000.
[57] s.14 *ibid.*
[58] *R. v Sanck* (1990–91) 12 Cr.App.R.(S.) 155.
[59] *R. v Tropical Express Ltd* [2002] 1 Cr.App.R.(S.) 115.

offence; to do so would undermine the public policy in the scheme of regulatory offences and vitiate the intention of the Legislature.

In creating a strict liability offence, Parliament recognises that convictions may occur even though the defendant is not morally culpable. It would undermine the legislative intent for the courts to impose a discharge in such a case. The justification for strict liability offences has been considered by the courts on many occasions. As early as 1902, Channel J. observed:

> "But there are exceptions to this rule in the case of quasi-criminal offences, as they may be termed, that is to say, where certain acts are forbidden by law under a penalty, possibly even under a personal penalty, such as imprisonment, at any rate in default of payment of a fine; and the reason for this is, that the Legislature has thought it so important to prevent the particular act from being committed that it absolutely forbids it to be done; and if it is done the offender is liable to a penalty whether he had any mens rea or not, and whether or not he intended to commit a breach of the law. Where the act is of this character then the master, who, in fact, has done the forbidden thing through his servant, is responsible and is liable to a penalty. There is no reason why he should not be, because the very object of the legislature was to forbid the thing absolutely."[60]

In *Sweet v Parsley*,[61] Lord Diplock explained the policy considerations that lie behind strict liability offences by reference to the hazardous consequences to members of the public:

> "But where the subject matter of a statute is the regulation of a particular activity involving potential danger to public health, safety or morals, in which citizens have a choice whether they participate or not, the court may feel driven to infer an intention of Parliament to impose, by penal sanctions, a higher duty of care on those who choose to participate and to place on them an obligation to take whatever measures may be necessary to prevent the prohibited act, without regard to those considerations of cost or business practicability which play a part in the determination of what would be required of them in order to fulfil the ordinary common law duty of care."

Perhaps the most explicit acknowledgement of the need for the courts to reflect, when sentencing, Parliament's intention in giving effect to regulatory offences, comes from the judgment of Devlin J. in *Reynolds v GH Austin & Sons Ltd*[62]:

> "It may seem, on the face of it, hard that a man should be fined, and, indeed, made subject to imprisonment, for an offence which he did not

---

[60] *Pearks, Gunston & Tee Ltd v Ward* [1902] 2 K.B. 1, 11.
[61] (1969) 53 Cr.App.R. 221, 236.
[62] [1951] 2 K.B. 135, 149.

know that he was committing. But there is no doubt that the legislature has for certain purposes found that hard measure to be necessary in the public interest. The moral justification behind such laws is admirably expressed in a sentence by Dean Roscoe Pound in his book 'The Spirit of the Common Law', at p. 52: see The Law Quarterly Review, vol. 64, p. 176. 'Such statutes', he says, 'are not meant to punish the vicious will but to put pressure upon the thoughtless and inefficient to do their whole duty in the interest of public health or safety or morals.' Thus a man may be made responsible for the acts of his servants, or even for defects in his business arrangements, because it can fairly be said that by such sanctions citizens are induced to keep themselves and their organizations up to the mark. Although, in one sense, the citizen is being punished for the sins of others, it can be said that, if he had been more alert to see that the law was observed, the sin might not have been committed."

Accordingly, the absence of fault is not, itself, a justification for a discharge. The defendant has been convicted because the forbidden event has occurred. To discharge a defendant does nothing to discourage the adoption of safer or better practice needed to protect the public from risk.

In *R. v British Steel Plc*[63] the company sought leave to appeal against a £100 fine on the basis that the correct sentence was an absolute discharge. The company was prosecuted under s.3(1) of HSWA 1974. The defendant engaged two sub-contracted labourers to reposition a steel platform, supervised by a section engineer employed by British Steel. Unbeknownst to the section engineer who had not supervised their work, the two labourers cut the platform free of practically all supports without first securing it. One of the men stepped onto the platform which collapsed and fell onto the other, killing him. Steyn L.J. dealt with the application for leave to appeal against sentence thus[64]:

"The judge imposed a fine of £100. He viewed the offence as a technical one. In urging us to grant leave to appeal against sentence, counsel for British Steel plc submitted that the judge should have imposed an absolute discharge. We disagree. It was a highly dangerous operation. A man was killed. Mr Crabb [the section engineer] was negligent. In these circumstances, the fine of £100 was derisory. In our view, a substantial fine was required but, unfortunately, it is beyond our power to increase the fine."

---

[63] [1995] 1 W.L.R. 1356.
[64] At p.1364.

(5) Deferred Sentence

10.15 Rather than deal with the offender immediately, sentence may be deferred. Unusual in the case of an individual defendant, in practice the power has not been used to the knowledge of the authors in the case of a corporate defendant.

(6) Remedial Orders

10.16 Some statutes in the regulatory field enable the courts to order remedial work to be done as a sentencing option. One such example is s.42 of the HSWA 1974:

> "(1) where a person is convicted of an offence under any of the relevant statutory provisions in respect of any matters which appear to the court to be matters which it is in his power to remedy, the court may, in addition to or instead of imposing any punishment, order him, within such time as may be fixed by the order, to take such steps as may be specified in the order for remedying the said matters."

The remedial order can be imposed alone or together with any other punishment available. Whilst the time for complying with the order runs, the person subject to the order shall not be liable under any statutory provision in respect of the matters to be remedied.[65] The time for complying with the order may be extended upon application by any party including the person subject to the order.[66] Failing to comply with a remedial order is itself an offence[67] which carries a maximum fine of £20,000 (and/or six months' imprisonment) in the magistrates' court, or an unlimited fine or two years' imprisonment on indictment.[68]

Although this power has been available to court for a considerable period of time it has been little used. It is a specific sentencing option in the Corporate Manslaughter and Corporate Homicide Act 2007. The Centre for Corporate Accountability has suggested it is "unlikely [to] be a useful sentence since the regulatory body should already have used its powers after the death to force through improvements. A similar (though slightly narrower) remedy order exists under the health and safety law—and it is almost never used."

This type of provision has a positive function in two respects: first, it enables sentencing to be a constructive measure, aimed at improving the working systems of a defendant who has committed a crime; secondly, it allows the court to oversee the progress made in compliance with the

---

[65] s.42(3) HSWA 1974.
[66] s.42(2).
[67] s.33(1)(o).
[68] s.33(2)(A).

remedial order, and to enforce it with the ultimate sanction that non-compliance will lead to the commission of another, quite separate criminal offence with draconian sentencing powers.

(7) Publicity Order

By s.10 of the Corporate Manslaughter and Corporate Homicide Act 2007[69] **10.17** on conviction for an offence of corporate manslaughter or homicide a defendant may be ordered to publicise the fact and details of its conviction and any sentence imposed. The Act enables a court to specify the manner and timing of the publicity, having consulted with such regulatory bodies as the court considers appropriate and heard from the prosecution and defence. Non-compliance with the order is itself an indictable offence punishable with an unlimited fine.

(8) Finanical reporting orders

By s.76 of the Serious Organised Crime and Police Act 2005, where a court **10.18** is dealing with a person convicted of an offence set out in subs.(3) it may impose a financial reporting order. A person subject to the order must make a report setting out particulars of his financial affairs as directed accompanied by such documentation as specified. The order can last for as long as five years. The categories of offences are fraud and other dishonesty offences, bribery offences, money laundering and funding terrorism and tax evasion offences.

(9) Forfeiture Orders

Forfeiture may generally be ordered as a result of conviction of any prop- **10.19** erty lawfully seized from the defendant, or which was in his control at the time when the summons was issued (or he was apprehended) for the offence, if the court is satisfied that it has been used for "the purpose of committing or facilitating the commission of, any offence or was intended by him to be used for that purpose".[70] Forfeiture may also be ordered in respect of an offence to be taken into consideration.[71] It can be ordered in addition to any other sentence or order including a conditional discharge.[72] It operates so as to deprive the defendant of any right in the property (although it does not deprive a third party of his right). The realisation of the property in police hands may be ordered to be used to pay compensation to any person. The

---

[69] In force April 6, 2008.
[70] s.143 PCC(S)A 2000.
[71] s.143(2).
[72] s.12(7).

court may make such an order, only if it would have made a compensation order and did not do so because of the defendant's apparent inability to pay.[73] Forfeiture orders should, like compensation and restitution orders only be made in clear, simple cases; particular care should be taken where issues over the ownership of the property may arise.[74] Real property does not fall within the section,[75] so, for example, office or warehouse premises could not be forfeited under this power. Forfeiture orders will not in general violate Protocol 1 of the ECHR, firstly because the right to "quiet enjoyment of property" is expressly qualified, and secondly, because third party rights are respected subject to determination by the court on application by that party.[76]

(10) Disqualification of Company Directors

10.20 The disqualification of a person from acting as a director is an order which can be imposed on a corporate defendant as well as an individual. The circumstances in which a disqualification may be imposed are varied. A person convicted of an indictable offence (whether tried in the magistrates' or Crown court) in connection with the promotion, formation, management or liquidation of a company, with the receivership of a company's property or with his being an administrative receiver of a company, may be disqualified.[77] The offence need not be specifically aimed at corporations; it could be, for example, an offence of obtaining by deception,[78] or insider dealing. The phrase "in connection with the management of a company" has been interpreted as meaning that "the indictable offence must have some relevant factual connection with the management of the company".[79] So, where defendants were convicted of a missing trader VAT fraud through their otherwise genuine companies acting as "buffers", disqualification orders (of 8 and 4 years respectively) should have been imposed.[80] The scope is deliberately broad so that those using corporations to commit criminal offences can be prevented from doing so for a defined period.

The disqualification will prohibit the person from being a director of a company, or acting as a receiver of a company's property or, being concerned (whether directly or indirectly) or taking part in the promotion

---

[73] s.145.
[74] *R. v Troth* (1980) 71 Cr.App.R. 1.
[75] *R. v Khan* [1982] 4 Cr.App.R.(S.) 298.
[76] See Corporations and Human Rights; art.1, First Protocol 12.72.
[77] s.2 Company Directors Disqualification Act 1986 ("CDDA 1986"). This power is discretionary. In the Chancery Division disqualification is mandatory if the court finds the person guilty of conduct which makes him unfit to be concerned in the management of a company—s.6.
[78] e.g. *R. v Corbin* (1984) 6 Cr.App.R.(S.) 17.
[79] *R. v Goodman* (1993) 14 Cr.App.R.(S.) 147 per Staughton L.J.
[80] *Att-Gen's Reference (Nos 88 of 2006)* (*R. v Meehan*) [2007] 2 Cr.App.R.(S.) 28.

formation or management of a company, or acting as an insolvency practitioner.[81] The disqualified person may apply to the court during the currency of the disqualification for leave to act in a particular way. It is a general disqualification, prohibiting a number of different activities: it is wrong for the court to specify only particular activities.[82]

In the magistrates' court the maximum period of disqualification is five years; in the Crown Court it is 15 years. The top bracket of 10–15 years is reserved for particularly serious cases including where a defendant has already been disqualified; the middle bracket of 6–10 years should apply to serious cases which do not merit the top bracket and the minimum bracket of 2–5 years should be applied where the case is not very serious.[83]

The aim of disqualification is to protect the public, but it is a punishment **10.21** nonetheless. It is thus inappropriate to disqualify a person whom the court has thought it right to conditionally discharge.[84] It has been held to be inappropriate to disqualify a person and also to order him to pay compensation where his ability to pay depnded on his running a new business, since the making of the disqualification order was likely to hamper the ability to meet the compensation order.[85] The court should be mindful of the fact that a disqualification may very significantly restrict the employment that a person subject to it may legally undertake during the currency of the order.

A disqualification order may be made against a corporate defendant, and is appropriate where, as a director of another corporation, it has committed a criminal offence.

In a case decided in the Chancery Division, two individuals and their nominee Jersey companies were all disqualified from being directors.[86] The Jersey companies failed as directors and, having found as a matter of law that corporations which were directors could be disqualified under the Company Directors Disqualification Act 1986 and could be treated in the same way as individual directors, Jacob J. gave reasons for disqualifying a corporation:

> "As a matter of practice there may be a useful purpose in being able to disqualify companies as well as the individuals behind them. It means that one of the tools used by people who are unfit to be company directors can themselves be attacked. It may be in some cases this would have advantages in relation to costs. There may be a host of

---

[81] s.1 CDDA.
[82] *R. v Ward & Howarth, The Times*, August 10, 2001.
[83] See *Re Sevenoaks Stationery (Retail) Ltd* [1991] Ch D 164; *R. v Millard* (1994) 15 Cr.App.R.(S.) 445, 448.
[84] *R. v Young (S.K.)* (1990) 12 Cr.App.R.(S.) 262.
[85] *R. v Holmes* (1992) 13 Cr.App.R.(S.) 29 where the compensation order was revoked on appeal, the disqualification order remained.
[86] *Official Receiver v Brady* [1999] B.C.C. 258.

other advantages. You may not be able to find the individuals behind the controlling director."

The companies were each disqualified for the maximum 15 years. There is no reason why the power to disqualify a corporation could not equally be used in criminal cases, although there is no reported cases of such an order.

SENTENCING CORPORATE DEFENDANTS IN OTHER JURISDICTIONS

10.22 Before publicity orders were introduced by s.9 of the Corporate Manslaughter and Corporate Homicide Act 2007, there was in the United Kingdom the no penalty specifically tailored to corporate defendants. Some other jurisdictions, however, have fashioned such penalties. The US Federal Courts have the power to "imprison" corporations by restraining them from doing certain specified acts or behaving in particular ways. Indeed, it is possible, where a corporation has been set up for an illegal purpose, for the courts compulsorily to wind it up. Other methods of punishment include corporate probation[87] through which the court requires changes to corporate processes and decision-making which are externally monitored. The advantage is that the judicial system has some influence over the structure of a corporation that has offended. Were this power to be introduced in the United Kingdom a whole new type of "probation service" would need to be put in place. It is arguable that the regulatory agencies in the United Kingdom are moving towards that role in certain specific spheres which affect corporations (e.g. Financial Services Agency).

One criticism of the financial penalties meted out in this country is the general inadequacy of fines either to reflect the seriousness of the result of the offending behaviour (for example death of an employee) or to have any real impact on the future conduct of the defendant. In Australia provision is made for a corporation convicted of an offence to incur a financial penalty up to five times the maximum amount capable of being imposed on an individual, to reflect the different considerations in sentencing a corporation.[88] In European anti-trust laws penalties may be imposed of up to 10 per cent of the previous year's global turnover of the corporate defendant.[89]

In the UK, under the Competition Act 1998, administrative penalties, (not criminal sentences), can be imposed for infringements of the prohibition on anti-competitive agreements and the abuse of a dominant position. They are designed both as a penalty and a deterrent. The Director General of Fair Trading can impose a penalty of up to 10 per cent of the UK turnover of the relevant corporation. Guidelines published on the criteria to be used when setting the level of penalty indicate that the starting point is a

---

[87] Sentencing Reform Act 1984 in the United States; also Canada.
[88] Australian Commonwealth Crimes Act 1914.
[89] EEC Council Reg, art.15(2).

percentage of the relevant turnover; adjustments should then be made for aggravating and mitigating features. It is noteworthy that those in a cartel who come forward first and positively assist the OFT will be immune from fines and others may receive up to a 50 per cent discount.[90]

In the United States corporations are vicariously liable for the offences of their employees. The level of fine imposed will be reduced by up to 90 per cent where a company shows that it has not only co-operated with the authorities and responded positively to a regime of self-regulation, but also reported its own breaches.[91]

Academics have canvassed for some time the prospect of "equity" fines.[92] **10.23** These would be levied by raising a new block of stock instead of cash. The argument that ordinary fines penalise employees and customers rather than shareholders would then be addressed because the equity fine dilutes the stock-holding without removing cash from the business. The shareholders who benefit from the profits to be made from limited liability corporations would thus bear the brunt of its offending behaviour. They, more than the employees, have the influence to effect changes in the corporate structure (both through selling their shareholding and voting in meetings). It is argued, therefore, that the shareholders should be principally affected by the sentence passed on a corporation which offends the law.

---

[90] OFT Press Release No.31/99 (10.8.99). And see The Enterprise Act 2002 (not in force at the time of writing).

[91] US Sentencing Guidelines manual, Ch.8 para.8A1.2; Federal Principles of Prosecution of Corporations, Department of Justice 1999.

[92] See Celia Wells, *Corporations & Criminal Responsibility*, 2nd edn (Oxford, Oxford University Press, 2001).

COSTS

The court has power to order all or part of the costs of either party in a **11.1** criminal case to be paid and may order payment from a variety of sources: the other party, central funds or occasionally from a legal representative or individual. The court's power to order costs is discretionary. Guidance on the awarding of costs can be found in Practice Direction (Crime: Costs in Criminal Proceedings).[1] The following costs orders may be made: Defendants' Costs, Prosecution Costs, Costs Against Legal Representatives; each of these is discussed below.

DEFENDANTS' COSTS

FROM CENTRAL FUNDS

A magistrates' court may order the defendants' costs to be paid from central **11.2** funds (a defendants' costs order), where

(a) an information is not proceeded with, either by withdrawal,[2] stay,[3] discontinuance,[4] or the prosecution offers no evidence,[5] or having heard the evidence; the information is dismissed.[6]
(b) the magistrates, as examining justices, do not commit a charge for trial.[7]

A Crown Court may make a defendant's costs order, to include costs in the magistrates' court, where the defendant has not been tried for or has been

---

[1] [2004] 2 All E.R. 1070.
[2] *R. v Bolton JJ. Ex p. Wildish* (1983) 147 J.P. 309.
[3] *Patel v Blakey* (1987) 151 J.P. 532 where the summons was laid out of time.
[4] *DPP v Denning and Pearce* [1991] 2 Q.B. 532.
[5] Prosecution of Offences Act 1985, s.16(1)(a).
[6] s.16(1)(b) Prosecution of Offences Act 1985.
[7] s.16(1)(c) Prosecution of Offences Act 1985.

dealt with in the Practice Direction.[21] There is no provision for interest to be paid from central funds, nor for expenses not directly incurred.

It does not necessarily follow that a person who is not convicted will be awarded his costs. In the exercise of its discretion the court may take into account the whole of the circumstances. The discretion is exercisable by the tribunal dealing with the case.

Where a case is stopped, there is an acquittal, or a successful appeal, and a defendants' costs order should be made "unless there are positive reasons for not doing so, as where, for example, the defendants' own conduct has brought suspicion on himself and has misled the prosecution into thinking that the case against him is stronger than it is".[22] For example, where there was a case to answer but it was oppressive to continue on grounds of ill health, the court might not make a costs order, regardless of whether a not guilty verdict was entered. Equally, where a defendant embarked upon a course of conduct which even a single telephone call to the relevant professional body would have revealed to be illegal, and a prosecution followed, the court, in its discretion, could properly find that it would be wrong to use public funds to protect him from the consequences of his failure to enquire.[23] Where a defendant had contributed to confusion over the correct name to be put on a summons by failing to identify itself accurately, and a prosecution failed as a result of summonsing the wrong defendant, the Divisional Court declined to make a defendant's costs order.[24]

11.6   The mere rehearsal of the prosecution allegation cannot form the basis of a finding against the defendant, in the absence of independent evidence to support the assertion, since is untried.[25] Where the court is not minded to grant a defendant his costs or a part of them, it must indicate the reason why.[26]

The 1991 Practice Direction was amended in 1999[27] by the deletion of para.2.2(b) which had until then allowed a court to make a defendant's costs order in circumstances where:

> "there is ample evidence to support a conviction but the defendant is acquitted on a technicality which has no merit."

Bingham L.J. considered the altered position in a costs case the following year[28] saying (at para.10):

---

[21] [2004] 2 All E.R.
[22] Practice Direction [2004] 2 All E.R. 1070 as above at II.2.1. See *Berkshire County Council v Olympic Holidays Ltd* [1994] 158 J.P. 421 DC.
[23] *R. v Spens, Independent*, March 18, 1992.
[24] *Mulvenna v Aldi Stores GmbH* (1995) 159 J.P. 717 DC.
[25] *Mooney v Cardiff Magistrates' Court* 164 J.P. 220 DC.
[26] Practice Direction II 2.1.
[27] By Practice Direction (Crime: Defence Costs) [1999] 1 W.L.R. 1832.
[28] *South West Surrey Magistrates' Court Ex p. Wayne James* CO/4302/97 April 18, 2000.

"I draw attention to the amendment, however, in order to make plain that this is sensitive territory. The deletion was made in order that courts should not decline to make costs orders in situations where a denial of such an order would undermine the presumption of innocence and so infringe the requirements of the European Convention on Human Rights."

Lord Bingham stated the principle in clear terms (at para.12):

"It is important to remind oneself of the general rule, which is that a defendant is entitled to a defendant's costs order *prima facie* if proceedings against him have been discontinued [as they were in the instant case]. The exception to the rule is narrowly drawn in order to respect the presumption of innocence which is both a fundamental principle of the common law and a right guaranteed by the Convention. The exception reflects the common sense view that if a defendant misleads the state into initiating proceedings against him as, for example, by making a spurious confession or advancing a demonstrably fraudulent alibi, he should not then be entitled to reimbursement by the state when in due course the proceedings against him collapse."

The jurisprudence of the ECtHR makes it clear that art.6(2) of the Convention does not confer on a person "charged with a criminal offence" a right to reimbursement of his legal costs where proceedings against him are discontinued.[29] However, there may be occasions where such a refusal amounts in substance to a determination of guilt of the former accused without his having been proved guilty or where the case has been discontinued, without his having had the opportunity to exercise his right to defend the proceedings. The ECtHR has said that the presumption of innocence will be violated where, following discontinuance or formal acquittal, a judicial decision concerning him reflects an opinion that he is guilty. This may be so in the absence of any such finding, if the reasoning suggests that the court regarded the accused as guilty.[30]

Costs cases decided before the amendment of the 1991 Practice Direction should be read subject to the ECtHR and recent English court decisions. Significantly, the latest practice direction indicates that a costs order should not be made in favour of a defendant where "there are positive reasons for not doing so. For example, where the defendant's own conduct has brought suspicion on himself and has misled the prosecution into thinking that the case against him was stronger than it was..."[31]

---

[29] *Leutscher v The Netherlands* 24 E.H.R.R. 181, 29.
[30] *Minelli v Switzerland* 5 E.H.R.R. 544, 37, an example of an order that interfered with the presumption of innocence and see *Barrington v Preston Crown Court* [2001] EWHC Admin 599.
[31] Practice Direction II.2.1.

DEFENDANT'S COSTS FROM THE PROSECUTION

11.7 The defendant's costs may be ordered directly against the prosecution, as opposed to from central funds. Such an order is made where there has been some sort of bad practice or inefficiency on the part of the prosecution. It achieves not only a compensatory purpose but also a disciplinary one.[32] So, where a court is satisfied that costs have been incurred in respect of the proceedings by one of the parties "as a result of any unnecessary or improper act or omission by, or on behalf of, any party to the proceedings", the court may, after hearing the parties, order that all or part of the costs so incurred by that party shall be paid to him by the other party".[33] "Improper" has been explained in these circumstances as "intended to cover an act or omission which would not have occurred if the party concerned had conducted his case properly".[34] The costs ordered must have been incurred by the party *as a result* of the other party's improper or unnecessary behaviour.[35] There must be evidence (either admitted or proved) to that effect—the judge can not *assume* all costs were so incurred.[36]

PROSECUTION COSTS

FROM CENTRAL FUNDS

11.8 There is no power to make an order for costs from central funds in favour of a public authority, a person acting on behalf of one or an official appointed by such an authority. A private prosecutor may recover costs from central funds in respect of an indictable offence in any court and in respect of a summary offence only in the Divisional Court or the House of Lords. The amount is that which the court considers reasonably sufficient to compensate the prosecutor for any expenses properly incurred by him in the proceedings.[37] Any application should be supported by a detailed breakdown of the costs sought.

The court order will include costs properly incurred in the lower court for an indictable offence unless, for good reason, the court directs that such costs are not included in the order.[38] The private prosecutor must apply for the costs from central funds and the application should be granted except where there is good reason for not doing so (e.g. where the prosecution

---

[32] Practice Direction (Costs in Criminal Proceedings) [1993] Cr.App.R. 89 per Lord Lane C.J. in the foreword, now in the 2004 Practice Direction (Costs in Criminal Proceedings) at VII.1.

[33] VII.1.

[34] per Nolan L.J. in *DPP v Denning* 94 Cr.App.R. 272.

[35] This power applies equally to orders made against the prosecution or the defence.

[36] *R. v Wood Green Crown Court Ex p. DPP* [1993] 1 W.L.R. 723.

[37] Prosecution of Offences Act 1985, s.17(1) and (2).

[38] Practice Direction (Crime: Costs in Criminal Proceedings) above at 1.5.

should not have been commenced or continued). So, a private prosecutor may recover costs from central funds even if the accused is acquitted.

AGAINST A DEFENDANT

Where a person is convicted at the magistrates' court or Crown Court, or **11.9** the Crown Court dismisses an appeal from the magistrates court or the Court of Appeal dismisses an appeal or leave to appeal to the Court of Appeal or the House of Lords, the court may order the accused to pay such costs as it considers just and reasonable to the prosecutor.[39]

In a case with several convicted defendants, it will usually be appropriate when making an order for costs to look to see what would be a reasonable estimate of the costs if each defendant were tried alone.[40] Where one (or more) defendant could pay costs and another could not, it would normally be appropriate to divide the costs by the number of defendants; if (as in *R. v Ronson and Parnes*) two out of three defendants were in a position to pay costs, they should only be required to pay one third of the total costs each. However, this is not an inflexible rule. Where one defendant is the principal offender it may be appropriate for him to bear a larger share of or even pay all of the costs. In *R. v Harrison*,[41] the appellant was the principal offender; he was the proprietor of the business and he alone stood to gain financially from the offending (car "clocking"). In the circumstances, although his son was also a defendant, it was just and reasonable that he (father) should pay the full costs of the prosecution. On the conviction of a company together with its employees, it may well be appropriate for the corporate defendant to bear more of the costs on the ground that it was the true beneficiary of the crime, and may have encouraged it. This principle was approved by the Court of Appeal in *R. v Fresha Bakeries Ltd and Harvestime Ltd*[42] Mantell L.J. said:

> "If the sentencing court concludes that any particular defendant amongst a number of defendants is more responsible than the others for the criminal conduct which has led to their conviction then it may be appropriate to order that defendant to pay a greater share of the costs than he would have had to pay if he had been tried alone. We are of the opinion that the judge was entitled to conclude that the corporate defendants bore a greater responsibility than the individual defendants for the overall breaches of the Act that led to the prosecution of them all."

---

[39] Prosecution of Offences Act 1985, s.18.
[40] *R. v Ronson and Parnes* (1992) 13 Cr.App.R.(S.) 153.
[41] (1993) 14 Cr.App.R.(S.) 419.
[42] [2002] EWCA Crim 1451.

Indeed, it has recently been held that even where a costs order was made against a convicted defendant, but the court was precluded from making such an order against an acquitted defendant, it was not in breach of the equivalent of art.6 ECHR.[43]

11.10   Prosecution costs may cover the investigation which preceded the prosecution, including costs which were incurred before it modified and reduced its case.[44] The cost of preparing the prosecution can be claimed by a local authority, even though the people investigating the case were employees acting within their ordinary employment.[45] In *R. v Associated Octel Co Ltd (Costs)*, the Court of Appeal observed that a detailed schedule of costs should be served on the defence sufficiently early to be considered by them. The defence should then give notice to the prosecution and the court clearly setting out their objections. This is particularly important as costs must be for a specified sum and cannot be taxed.

The costs must be for a fixed amount.[46] Costs are enforceable in the magistrates' court.[47]

An order for costs should not be made where a defendant cannot satisfy the order within a reasonable period.[48] Costs orders must not be determined in isolation; a court must first consider confiscation (where appropriate) and the imposition of a fine. A court must not impose a costs order which would wrongly restrict the ability of a defendant to satisfy a confiscation order[49] or to meet the appropriate financial penalty. These orders should be given priority by the court; the public has a greater moral interest in the appropriate level of punishment being set than in recouping the costs of the prosecution from the defendant.[50]

11.11   It has been held that an order for the payment of costs should not be grossly disproportionate to a fine imposed. Where the total sum of the fine and costs was greater than a defendant could be expected to pay, the fine should take priority and the costs reduced accordingly.[51] A guilty plea and the stage at which it is indicated are relevant considerations in assessing the amount of costs a defendant should be ordered to pay.[52]

Where a court makes a confiscation order, it is wrong also to order the defendant to pay the prosecutor's costs except where the defendant has the means to pay both. In *R. v Threapleton*[53] the Crown Court judge ordered the

---

[43] *Att-Gen for Gibrlater v Shimidzu (Bellarque intervening)* [2005] 1 W.L.R. 3335 PC.
[44] *R. v Associated Octel Co Ltd (Costs)* (1997) 1 Cr.App.R.(S.) 435.
[45] *Neville v Gardner Merchant Ltd* (1984) 148 J.P. 23.
[46] Prosecution of Offences Act, 1985, s.18.
[47] Administration of Justice Act 1970, Sch.9 Pt I.
[48] But see *R. v Rollco Screw & Rivet Co Ltd* [1999] 2 Cr.App.R.(S.) 436 in Levels of Fine, para.10.8 above.
[49] *R. v Threapleton* [2001] EWCA Crim 2892.
[50] A private prosecutor may apply for its costs from central funds.
[51] *R. v Northallerton Magistrates' Court Ex p. Dove* [2000] 1 Cr.App.R.(S.) 136 DC.
[52] *R. v Matthews* (1979) 1 Cr.App.R.(S.) 346; *R. v Maher* [1983] Q.B. 784.
[53] [2001] EWCA Crim 2892.

defendant to pay £15,000 costs and then made a confiscation order of £15,000. The Court of Appeal held that the costs order was wrong in principle. The court is obliged to determine confiscation before sentence (s.71(1) of the Criminal Justice Act 1988; "CJA 1988"); by s.72(5) of the CJA 1988, before imposing a fine or order for costs, the court must take account of the confiscation order it has made. Stanley Burnton J. (giving the judgment of the court) observed:

> "Those requirements are not merely formal; they are intended to ensure that the determination of the amount payable under the confiscation order has priority over, in this case, an order for the payment of costs. The amount payable under the confiscation order depended on the realisable property of the defendant (or 'the amount that might be realised at the time the order [was] made' (s.71(6)), and the effect of the statutory procedure is that the property should not have been depleted by an order for costs when the determinations required for the making of a confiscation order are made."

Where a defendant has sufficient assets to satisfy both, confiscation and costs orders may be made but if not, confiscation is given statutory priority. The position is the same under the Proceeds of Crime Act 2002.[54] In practice, confiscation is regularly pursued at the expense of making a costs order in favour of the Crown.

Where the prosecution and defence disagreed markedly on the estimated length of trial, the judge being unable to decide which estimate was correct, it was proper to divide the total costs of trial between all defendants and order each capable of paying, to pay his own share.[55]

CORPORATION FUNDING LEGAL COSTS OF INDIVIDUALS

In the context of corporate prosecutions it is commonplace for the costs of a **11.12** director or other employee to be met by his employer. If such a defendant would, in principle, be awarded his costs from central funds, will the taxing master allow the claim when, in fact, it is his employer rather than he, who is primarily liable for the costs? The wording of the statute refers to the costs order being made "in favour of the accused".[56] There is, however, a line of authority which suggests that, where the costs of defending a criminal accusation are in fact borne by another person and not the accused, the court may still make a defendants' costs order. In *R. v Miller & Glennie*,[57] the legal costs of the defence of the acquitted defendant were paid by his

---

[54] See s.13.
[55] *R. v Ronson & Parnes* (1992) 13 Cr.App.R.(S.) 153.
[56] s.16 Prosecution of Offences Act 1985.
[57] (1984) 78 Cr.App.R. 71. The relevant statute was the Powers of Criminal Courts Act 1973.

employer. The taxing authority (upheld by the taxing master), held that, as he was supported by his employers, there was no realistic prospect of his having to bear any costs at all and thus no costs had been incurred by him. On appeal to the High Court, Lloyd J. rejected the submission that "costs incurred by" meant "costs paid by".[58] If the reality was that the accused instructed the solicitors, and that, if his employer failed to pay the solicitor, the accused would be liable, the costs were incurred *by him*. In the absence of an express agreement that under no circumstances would he be liable for the costs, the costs remained incurred by him.

Similarly where, in a civil case, an individual appealed to the Court of Appeal, and he was supported by the Automobile Association, who agreed to indemnify him for the costs of the appeal, it was held that in law the party to an appeal was responsible for the costs, so that they were "incurred by him".[59] Had the appeal been lost and the unsuccessful litigant been ordered to pay the costs, it would be he, and not the AA, who would be liable. It now appears to be settled law that a third party may, through a defendants' costs order, claw back costs incurred "by the accused". In *R. v Jain*,[60] it appears from the very brief report, that where an accused's appeal had been funded by his mother, he having been adjudged bankrupt following the conviction, the court could make an order for a specified sum—"of such amount as the court considers reasonably sufficient to compensate him for any expenses properly incurred by him", to his mother, even though s.16(1)–(5) appears to contemplate that the only person in respect of whom a defendant's costs order can be made is "a defendant".

The important questions are (i) is the accused instructing the lawyers whose costs are under consideration, and (ii) is there an agreement that the accused will under no circumstances be liable to the lawyers for the costs? If the first question is answered "yes" and the second "no", the court can make the order specifically to a third party in circumstances where the defendants' costs order would otherwise not go to the person who actually incurred the costs(e.g. in *R. v Jain* above any award of costs would have gone to the trustee in bankruptcy).

---

[58] At p.75.

[59] *Lewis v Averay (No.2)* [1973] 1 W.L.R. 510—a civil case concerned with similar wording under the Legal Aid Act 1974.

[60] *The Times*, December 10, 1987.

Part IV

CORPORATIONS AND HUMAN RIGHTS

CHAPTER 12

CORPORATIONS AND THE EUROPEAN CONVENTION ON HUMAN RIGHTS

INTRODUCTION

From the conception of a corporation as a legal person, corporations have **12.1**
enjoyed legal rights and privileges in domestic law. These have been supplemented by European/International provisions in accordance with the
UK's treaty obligations and are generally uncontroversial. To what extent,
though, should corporations enjoy fundamental rights and freedoms that
are intrinsically human in nature, such as the rights guaranteed by the
European Convention on Human Rights? To the extent that the economic
aspects of civil and political rights are protected, the position is relatively
straightforward, but in the field of criminal law, should a corporate defendant be in any different position from a natural person?

It is beyond doubt that the Convention applies to the legal fiction that is a
corporation.[1] Whether it makes any logical sense for "human" rights to
apply to a legal person is another matter. It might well have been argued
that, being distinct from its human directors and managers, a corporation
should not be able to avail itself of rights which are intrinsically individualistic and personal—"human". To do so, the argument would run, is to
ignore the very essence of corporate identity and liability, as well as the real
reason for and effect of the rights encapsulated in the ECHR. As will be
seen, however, this distinction, has not been adopted, and has had no place
in the application of the principles upon which European and English
decisions have been based. In numerous reported cases it has been taken for
granted that art.6 applies to corporations and has not even been raised as an
issue. It is, moreover, clear that other articles, such as art.10 (freedom of
expression) and art.1 of the First Protocol (right to property) also apply to
corporations.

---

[1] See, e.g. art.1 of the First Protocol.

159

CHAPTER 12

THE EUROPEAN CONVENTION ON HUMAN RIGHTS

12.2   The European Convention on Human Rights[2] (ECHR) was drafted on the mandate of the newly formed Council of Europe in response to the atrocities of the Second World War. The aim of the Council was to establish a code of minimum standards which could be implemented into domestic law and enforced in international law to protect against the derogation of individual rights which occurs once a democratic society curtails basic freedoms. The Convention was adopted by the Member States of the Council of Europe in 1950 and ratified by the United Kingdom in 1951. It was finally brought into English law by the enactment of the Human Rights Act 1998.

The Convention provides no definition of the terms "company" or "corporation", nor does it state that the word "person" is to be construed as including "a body of persons corporate or unincorporated".[3] Given the Convention's origins, it is not surprising that the draftsmen did not have corporations in mind. That said, the Convention does explicitly recognise and protect corporate rights in relation to the enjoyment of private property: art.1(1) of the First Protocol (adopted March 20, 1952) applies to "every natural and legal person".

Under the Human Rights Act it is unlawful for any public authority, including a court or tribunal, to act in a manner which is incompatible with a Convention right.[4] Accordingly, Convention rights have priority over any common law rule; primary legislation must be read if possible in a manner which is compatible with Convention rights.[5]

12.3   By s.7(1) a person who claims that a public authority (including a court or tribunal) has acted (or proposes to act) in a way which is made unlawful by s.6(1) may bring proceedings against the authority[6] or rely on the Convention right or rights concerned in any legal proceedings, but only if he is (or would be) a victim of the unlawful act.[7] "Victim" is defined by art.34 of the Convention and includes "any person, non-governmental organisation or group of individuals". The term "non-governmental organisation" has been held by the Court to include a corporation[8]; the ECtHR has held that a company can bring a complaint[9] as can a minority share holder.[10]

---

[2] The European Convention for the Protection of Human Rights and Fundamental Freedoms (1950) (Cmd. 8964).
[3] cf. ss.5 & 11 and Sch.1 of the Interpretation Act 1978.
[4] s.6 HRA 1998.
[5] s.3(1) HRA 1998.
[6] s.7(1)(a) HRA 1998.
[7] s.7(1)(b) HRA 1998.
[8] *Sunday Times v UK* (1979/1980) 2 E.H.R.R. 245 was the Court's first encounter with a corporate applicant.
[9] *Pine Valley Developments Ltd & Others v Ireland* [1993] 16 E.H.R.R. 379.
[10] *Neves e Silva v Portugal* (1991) 13 E.H.R.R. 535.

GENERAL PRINCIPLES

1. Margin of Appreciation

The ECtHR recognises that national authorities, including the courts, have **12.4** a discretion in interpreting their legislation in terms of the convention rights and in assessing any interference with them. This reflects the continued recognition of the sovereignty of the Member States and the right of Member States to legislate as sovereign nations, whilst the Convention provides a framework outside which they may not go. This is referred to as the "margin of appreciation"; it is a doctrine of restrained review, reflecting the primary role which the national authorities (courts included) are intended to perform in human rights protection.[11] The doctrine is subject to supervision by the ECtHR. In summarising the status of the margin of appreciation, Lord Hope (in *R. v DPP Ex p. Kebilene & Others*) stated[12]:

> "This doctrine is an integral part of the supervisory jurisdiction which is exercised over state conduct by the international court. By conceding a margin of appreciation to each national system, the court has recognised that the Convention, as a living system, does not need to be applied uniformly by all states but may vary in its application according to local needs and conditions. This technique is not available to the national courts when they are considering Convention issues arising within their own countries. But in the hands of the national courts also the Convention should be seen as an expression of fundamental principles rather than as a set of mere rules. The questions which the courts will have to decide in the application of these principles will involve questions of balance between competing interests and issues of proportionality."

Although weight must be given to Parliament's legislative policy, the courts are qualified to determine whether, by a criminal statute, Parliament has adopted a legislative scheme which makes an excessive inroad into the right to a fair trial.[13]

In *A v Secretary of State for the Home Department; X v Same*,[14] the House of Lords emphasised that the role of judges in interpreting and applying the law "is universally recognised as a cardinal feature of the modern democratic state, a cornerstone of the rule of law itself."[15]

---

[11] See *Handyside v UK* (1976) 1 E.H.R.R. 737 in which the national court's decision was upheld in pursuance of this doctrine.

[12] [2000] 2 A.C. 326, 380.

[13] *R. v A (No.2)* [2002] 1 A.C. 45 in which the House of Lords declared s.41 of the Youth Justice and Criminal Evidence Act 1999 incompatible with the right to a fair trial because it rendered inadmissible evidence which might be relevant to the issue of consent on a charge of rape.

[14] [2005] 2 A.C. 68.

[15] [2005] 2 A.C. 68 per Lord Bingham at para.42.

2. Compatibility

12.5 Primary and secondary legislation must be read so as to be compatible with the Convention rights so far as is possible (s.3(1), HRA 1998); the interpretative obligation is a "strong one".[16] So, for example, some statutes which unequivocally put a "legal burden" on a defendant to prove something, have been "read down" so as to impose only an evidential burden.[17] Insofar as a piece of legislation *cannot* be read so as to be compatible with Convention rights, the legislation or part of it must be the subject of a "declaration of incompatibility". However a declaration of incompatibility is a measure of last resort and must be avoided unless it is plainly impossible to do so.[18]

3. Proportionality

12.6 The jurisprudence of the ECtHR has brought a new concept into English law: is the restriction of a Convention right *proportionate* to the legitimate aim pursued? The question is one of balance: is the measure a proportionate response to the legitimate aim in a democracy, or does it go beyond what is necessary to achieve that objective?[19] The court "must determine whether a fair balance was struck between the demands of the general interests of the community and the requirements of the protection of the individual's fundamental rights".[20] It may be seen that in the context of any interference with Convention rights, proportionality is a key to the legality of measures taken.[21] However where a right is absolute, such as the defendant's right to a fair trial pursuant to art.6(1), no such evaluation takes place; if the trial is unfair to the accused there is no question of, for example, a balancing exercise in favour of the victim, or the interest that a democracy has in a guilty person being convicted. Infringement of a particular right may nevertheless not result in a breach of art.6; that will be a matter of interpretation, as will be seen below. For example, forfeiture of an aeroplane (and its subsequent release subject to payment), whilst being an exceptional measure to bring about security improvements by an airline, was a proportionate response in the circumstances, to the public interest in combating international drug trafficking.[22]

---

[16] *R. v A (No.2)* [2002] 1 A.C. 45 HL per Lord Steyn.
[17] See, e.g. *R. v Lambert* [2002] 2 A.C. 545.
[18] *R. v A (No.2)* [2002] 1 A.C. 45 HL per Lord Steyn at para.44.
[19] See *Handyside v UK* (1976) 1 E.H.R.R. 737.
[20] *Sporrong & Lonnroth v Sweden* (1983) 5 E.H.R.R. 35, 69.
[21] For a review of the principles see *International Transport Roth GmbH v Home Secretary* [2002] EWCA Civ 158.
[22] see *Air Canada v UK* (1995) 20 E.H.R.R. 150.

ARTICLE 6

RIGHT TO A FAIR TRIAL

1. In the determination of his civil rights and obligations or of any **12.7** criminal charge against him, everyone is entitled to a fair and public hearing within a reasonable time by an independent and impartial tribunal established by law. Judgment shall be pronounced publicly but the press and public may be excluded from all or part of the trial in the interest of morals, public order or national security in a democratic society, where the interests of juveniles or the protection of the private life of the parties so require, or to the extent strictly necessary in the opinion of the court in special circumstances where publicity would prejudice the interests of justice.

2. Everyone charged with a criminal offence shall be presumed innocent until proved guilty according to law.

3. Everyone charged with a criminal offence has the following minimum rights:

    a. to be informed promptly, in a language which he understands and in detail, of the nature and cause of the accusation against him;

    b. to have adequate time and facilities for the preparation of his defence;

    c. to defend himself in person or through legal assistance of his own choosing or, if he has not sufficient means to pay for legal assistance, to be given it free when the interests of justice so require;

    d. to examine or have examined witnesses against him and to obtain the attendance and examination of witnesses on his behalf under the same conditions as witnesses against him;

    e. to have the free assistance of an interpreter if he cannot understand or speak the language used in court.

Fairness is a constantly evolving concept that may require the adequacy of procedures once deemed to be fair to be re-assessed.[23] The right to a fair trial is absolute, but the constituent rights are themselves not absolute; limited qualification of those rights may be acceptable if reasonably directed towards "a clear and proper public objective" and if representing no greater qualification than the situation called for.[24]

---

[23] *R. v H* [2004] 2 A.C. 134 HL at para.11.
[24] *Brown v Stott* [2003] 1 A.C. 681 PC per Lord Bingham.

THE DEFINITION OF A CRIMINAL CHARGE

12.8 Although art.6 also applies to civil rights, it is most stringently applied to criminal proceedings, providing an absolute right to a fair trial of a criminal charge. It is therefore crucial to know how "a criminal charge" has been defined. The ECtHR has an "autonomous" approach to defining a criminal charge (i.e. it provides its own definition).

There are three general criteria which the ECtHR has applied (following the case of *Engel v Netherlands*)[25]:

   (i)   domestic classification: if the contracting state classifies an offence as criminal, that is decisive. However, the reverse does not apply; since a contracting state cannot be allowed to defeat the Convention merely by the way it chooses to categorise a matter;

   (ii) the nature of the offence; whether there is a punitive or deterrent (as opposed to compensatory) element to the process is relevant, as is the enforcing body's powers;

   (iii) the severity of the penalty: generally, a primary liability to a sentence of imprisonment will give rise to the conclusion that a matter is criminal. As will be seen, however, this is only a starting point. Where a sentence of imprisonment may be imposed in default, e.g. of payment of a fine, that does not necessarily bring it within the definition of a criminal charge.[26]

If the applicable domestic law treats the proceedings as criminal, this will be decisive, but where the proceedings are treated as non-criminal by the domestic authorities, that classification is no more than a starting point. In determining whether the proceedings are criminal the ECtHR will consider their "true nature". The following are examples of situations which have been held to involve a criminal charge:

   (a)   where a penalty under competition law could amount to 5 per cent of the annual turnover of a firm and/or up to FF 5 million, the penalties were deterrent in nature and thus the infringements were criminal charges—*Societé Stenuit v France*[27];

   (b) where customs officers had powers of search and seizure of documents to obtain particulars of overseas assets, proceedings for further disclosure in which penalties were imposed for an offence of failing to provide further documentation were criminal. The court noted that although the proceedings were separate from

---

[25] (1979–80) 1 E.H.R.R. 647.

[26] *Engel v Netherlands* 1 E.H.R.R. 647 at para.82. See *Phillips v UK* [2001] C.L.R. 817 where the ECtHR held that the mere fact that a sentence of imprisonment was imposed in default of satisfaction of a confiscation order did not entitle a defendant to rely on art.6 rights.

[27] (1992) 14 E.H.R.R. 509.

a criminal charge on indictment, they constituted necessary pre-liminaries to them[28];

(c) The requirement to provide documents, on pain of a penalty for failure to do so, is a criminal charge—*JB v Switzerland.*[29] In tax evasion proceedings, following a request to a tax payer to provide documents to the authorities, despite admitting a failure to declare all his income, he refused to submit the documents and was fined a total of SF 3,000. (The taxpayer had compromised the tax liability proceedings themselves by paying SF 21,625 and this was not an area of complaint or part of the decision of the ECtHR.) The fact that the documents the taxpayer was being compelled to produce might provide evidence which could have been used against him in tax evasion proceedings (violating the privilege against self-incri-mination) was the foundation for the argument that his right to a fair trial[30] based on the privilege against self-incrimination was breached.[31]

(d) The imposition of a fixed penalty under s.32 of the Immigration and Asylum Act 1999 in respect of the clandestine transportation of illegal immigrants into the UK is a criminal charge and incompatible with Art.6 rights insofar as there was no opportunity to mitigate the penalty.[32]

(e) Proceedings in connection with an assessment to a penalty under the Finance Acts 1985 and 1994 and the Value Added Tax Act 1994 in respect of the dishonest evasion of VAT[33] amounted to a criminal charge.

(f) infringement of competition law leading to substantial penalties.[34]

The following situations have been held *not* to constitute a criminal **12.9** charge:

(a) Where a company, not *itself* the subject of a criminal prosecution, had property forfeited because of proceedings triggered by the arrest and criminal convictions of a third party for smuggling the property into the UK, the proceedings in which the issue of return of the forfeited property was to be decided were administrative and not criminal.[35]

(b) Being required to provide evidence in proceedings to inquire into alleged illegal practices was not a criminal charge. Although

---

[28] *Funke v France* (1993) 16 E.H.R.R. 297 at paras 50–55.
[29] (2001) Crim.L.R. 748.
[30] Applicable because it is a criminal charge.
[31] See below for: Corporations and the privilege against self-incrimination.
[32] *International Transport Roth GmbH v Home Secretary* [2002] EWCA Civ 158.
[33] *Georgiou (t/a Marios Chippery) v UK* [2001] S.T.C 80 ECtHR.
[34] *Office of Fair Trading v D* [2003] EWHC 1042 (Comm) per Morison J. at para.6.
[35] *Allgemeine Gold und Silberscheideanstalt v UK* (1987) 9 E.H.R.R. 1. See below for Protocol 1—protection of property.

recommendations may be made by the Inquiry, no offence and no penalty were involved although there was a power to order costs.[36] A public inquiry is a proper mechanism in a democratic society for investigating matters of major public importance and is not "proceedings the privilege against relating to a criminal charge". Moreover, in conducting the inquiry, the Tribunal had not interfered with any of the applicants' civil rights. The company and its director argued that the fact of the Tribunal investigating its business practices would damage their business reputation;

(c) Where, after warnings from H.M. Customs, the applicants' aircraft was seized as liable to forfeiture when cannabis resin was found on board by Customs officers, but released on payment of £50,000, the powers of seizure did not involve the determination of a "criminal charge": the payment of £50,000 for the release of a very valuable aircraft was not a criminal penalty; there was no "criminal" provision or suggestion or threat of criminal proceedings against the applicant.[37]

(d) Proceedings to disqualify a company director from so acting without leave of the court, were not a determination of a criminal charge.[38] Similarly, proceedings in which objection was taken to the applicant's appointment as Chief Executive of an insurance company pursuant to the Insurance Companies Act 1982 by which it is required that he be a "fit and proper person", were civil.[39]

(e) Confiscation proceedings following conviction and sentence are not the determination of a criminal charge[40];

(f) Proceedings for a civil recovery order under Part 5 of the Proceeds of Crime Act 2002 were not for a criminal charge.[41]

(g) Proceedings for failure to comply with the requirement to deliver company accounts and documents to the Company Registrar were civil in nature.[42]

(h) Disciplinary proceedings instituted by the Financial Services Authority.[43]

[36] *Goodman International & Goodman v Ireland*, 16 E.H.R.R. C.D. 26.
[37] *Air Canada v UK*, 20 E.H.R.R. 150.
[38] *Official Receiver v Stern* [2000] 1 W.L.R. 2230.
[39] *X v UK* 5 E.H.R.R. 273.
[40] *R. v Benjafield; R. v Rezvi* [2003] 1 A.C. 1099 HL.
[41] *R. v Director of the Assets Recovery Agency v He and Chen* [2004] EWHC 3021 Admin.
[42] *R. (POW Trust) v Chief Executive and Registrar of Companies* [2004] B.C.C. 268.
[43] *R. (on the application of Fleurose) v Securities and Futures Authority Ltd* [2001] EWCA Civ 2015.

THE PRESUMPTION OF INNOCENCE AND REVERSE BURDENS

At common law the prosecution has the burden of proving every element of **12.10** the offence. As Viscount Sankey L.C. memorably declared in *Woolmington v DPP*[44]

> "Throughout the web of the English criminal law, one golden thread is always to be seen, that it is the duty of the prosecution to prove the prisoner's guilt."

However, the "golden thread" was subject to what Viscount Sankey referred to as "statutory exceptions". Parliament had by 1935 already enacted a great deal of legislation which in a variety of ways alleviated the burden on the prosecution to prove every element and instead imposed a burden on the accused to prove his defence. Many of the statutory criminal offences which place some burden on the defendant are regulatory in nature, but not all can be so characterised. Ashworth and Blake[45] found 219 examples of legal burdens or presumptions operating against the defendant among 540 offences triable in the Crown Court (so, by definition, serious offences), i.e. no fewer than 40 per cent.

The vast majority of regulatory offences are only triable summarily; most of these impose some burden on the defendant; in addition, s.101 of the Magistrates' Courts Act 1980 provides that:

> "Where the defendant to an information or complaint relies for his defence on any exception, exemption, proviso, excuse or qualification, whether or not it accompanies the description of the offence or matter of complaint in the enactment creating the offence or on which the complaint is founded, the burden of proving the exception, exemption, proviso, excuse or qualification shall be on him; and this notwithstanding that the information or complaint contains an allegation negativing the exception, exemption, proviso, excuse or qualification."

The impact of the legislation has been to erode the "Woolmington principle" to such an extent as very nearly to make a rule of the exception.

STRICT LIABILITY

Separate from but linked to the reversal of the burden of proof is the issue of **12.11** mens rea for criminal offences. At common law, mens rea is a necessary element of every criminal offence and must be proved by the prosecution. Many regulatory offences impose strict liability simpliciter, or strict liability subject to a defence of due diligence which the defendant must prove to

---

[44] [1935] A.C. 462, 481.
[45] *The Presumption of Innocence in English Criminal Law* [1996] Crim.L.R. 306.

avoid conviction. According to the Ashworth and Blake survey, 123 of the indictable offences examined had at least one strict liability element and 121 more were strict liability subject to a due diligence defence. On indictment, virtually all of those 244 offences carried a maximum prison sentence of more than six months.[46] Although the courts have been obliged to uphold the will of Parliament and its legislation, the presumption in favour of mens rea is strong. As Lord Goddard C.J. said:

> "...it is of the utmost importance for the protection of the liberty of the subject that a court should always bear in mind that, unless a statute, either clearly or by necessary implication, rules out mens rea as a constituent part of a crime, the court should not find a man guilty of an offence against the criminal law unless he has a guilty mind."[47]

This principle applies to statutory offences unless Parliament has clearly indicated to the contrary.[48]

Historically, the courts have been obliged to give effect to legislation which derogated from the "golden thread". This dilution of principle has long caused concern. In 1972, the Criminal Law Revision Committee noted[49]:

> "...We are strongly of the opinion that, both in principle and for the sake of clarity and convenience in practice, burdens on the defence should be evidential only."

The courts' approach to the presumption was summarised by Dyson L.J. in *R. v Muhamad*[50] in this way:

1. There is a presumption of law that mens rea is required before a person can be guilty of a criminal offence;
2. The presumption is particularly strong where the offence is "truly criminal" in character[51];
3. The presumption applies to statutory offences and can be displaced if this is clearly or by necessary implication the effect of the statute;

---

[46] The Presumption of Innocence in English Criminal Law, [1996] Crim.L.R. 306, 313.
[47] *Brend v Wood* [1946] L.T. 306, 307.
[48] *B. v DPP* [2000] 2 A.C. 428, 460 C–D, per Lord Nicholls.
[49] Eleventh Report Evidence (General) Cmnd 4991 of 1972; at para.140.
[50] [2002] EWCA Crim 1856.
[51] The distinction between "truly criminal" and "quasi criminal" offences is not entirely helpful. As Lord Atkin remarked:

> "The domain of criminal jurisprudence can only be ascertained by examining what acts may at any particular period be declared to be crimes by the state, and the only common nature they will be found to possess is that they are prohibited by the state and that those who commit them are punished": *Proprietary Articles Trade Association v A.G. for Canada* [1931] A.C. 310.

4.   The only situation in which the presumption can be displaced is where the statute is concerned with an issue of social concern and public safety is such an issue;

5.   Even where a statute is concerned with such an issue, the presumption of mens rea stands unless it can be shown that the creation of strict liability will be effective to promote the objects of the statute by encouraging greater vigilance to prevent the occurrence of the prohibited act.

Although the presumption of innocence in criminal proceedings is guaranteed by art.6(2), strict liability offences do not necessarily violate the Convention. In *Salabiaku v France*,[52] the ECtHR pointed out that:

"... in principle, the Contracting States may, under certain conditions, penalise a simple or objective fact as such, irrespective of whether it results from criminal intent or from negligence. Examples of such may be found in the laws of the Contracting States."

Article 6 as a whole is concerned essentially with procedural guarantees to ensure that there is a fair trial, not with the substantive elements of the offence with which the person has been charged; it is a matter for the contracting states to define the essential elements of the offence with which the person has been charged.

In *R. v G*[53] the Court of Appeal had to consider the offence of rape of a child under 13, contrary to s.5 of the Sexual Offences Act 2003, a strict liability offence. Drawing from the reasoning in *Salabiaku*, the Court said (at para.33):

"An absolute offence may subject a defendant to conviction in circumstances where he has done nothing blameworthy. Prosecution for such an offence and the imposition of sanctions under it may well infringe articles of the Convention other than article 6. The legislation will not, however, render the trial under which it is enforced unfair, let alone infringe the presumption of innocence under article 6(2)."

This view was endorsed by Lord Hope in the House of Lords[54]; he concluded that art.6(2) does not proscribe offences of strict liability, so long as the prosecution bears the burden of proof of all the elements that constitute the offence.

---

[52] (1991) 13 E.H.R.R. 379 at para.42.
[53] [2006] EWCA Crim 821; [2006] 1 W.L.R. 2052.
[54] *R. v G* [2008] UKHL 37.

LEGAL AND EVIDENTIAL BURDENS ON THE DEFENDANT

12.12 A distinction must be drawn between a legal and an evidential burden. A legal or persuasive burden places the burden of proving the particular facts on the accused; the standard to which he must prove them is on the balance of probabilities (hence the "persuasive burden"). The burden of proof is reversed by removing it from the prosecution and transferring it to the accused. An evidential burden merely requires the accused to raise as an issue on the evidence the particular matter; if he does so it is then for the prosecution to prove its case beyond reasonable doubt in the normal way. The evidential burden has been described by Professor Glanville Williams as the burden of introducing evidence in support of his case.[55]

Where the statute imposes a legal or persuasive burden on the defence, the accused has the burden of proving the particular matter, on the balance of probabilities; the matter must be taken as proved against the accused unless he does so. A persuasive burden requires the accused to prove a fact which is essential to the determination of his innocence.

The Impact of the Human Rights Act 1998

12.13 Until the enactment of the Human Rights Act 1998 ("HRA"), the only check on Parliament's right to impose a legal burden on the accused in any particular legislation was political. By creating offences of strict liability without a defence of due diligence, mens rea was sidestepped entirely. Parliament remains sovereign, but legislation must now be approached from the perspective of constitutional and human rights law. Primary legislation must be read and given effect in a manner which is compatible with Convention rights, so far as it is possible to do so.[56] This has had a dramatic impact on the lawfulness of statutory reverse burdens.

Article 6(2) provides that:

> "Everyone charged with a criminal offence shall be presumed innocent until proved guilty according to law".

Although framed in absolute terms, Convention case law shows that art.6(2) is not regarded as imposing an absolute prohibition on reverse burden clauses. Article 6(2) certainly does not prohibit rules which transfer an evidential burden to the accused, provided the usual burden of proving guilt remains on the prosecution.[57] However, any incursion into the presumption of innocence must be: (i) justified; (ii) no broader than necessary; and (iii) a

---

[55] The phrase "evidential burden" has itself been regarded as inapposite, certainly if phrased as an "evidential burden of proof": *Jayasena v The Queen* [1970] A.C. 618, 624, per Lord Devlin.

[56] s.3(1).

[57] *Lingens & Leitgens v Austria* (1982) 4 E.H.R.R. 373, 384.

proportionate measure confined within reasonable limits in relation to the legitimate legislative aim.

Strict liability offences have been explained on the basis that Parliament **12.14** regarded it as so important that the act be prevented that it absolutely prohibited it being done. Where the proscribed event happens, the person responsible is guilty; no mens rea is required. The harshness of strict liability is sometimes mitigated where the statute provides a defence, e.g. of due diligence. It is thus reasonable to put the burden of proving that defence on the defendant. The prosecution still has to prove its case (to the criminal standard), but the statutory provision gives a defendant a "get out of jail card".

The justification for the imposition of strict liability in regulatory offences **12.15** is the protection of the public in areas such as health and safety, but the same reasoning does not apply to offences which are truly criminal. There is a substantial public interest in the reduction of serious crime, yet there is no suggestion that such offences should depend on strict liability or that there should be a legal burden on the accused to prove an essential ingredient of the offence charged.[58] This point was made by the South African Constitutional Court[59]:

> "There is a paradox at the heart of all criminal procedure in that the more serious the crime and the greater the public interest in securing convictions of the guilty, the more important do constitutional protections of the accused become. The starting point of any balancing enquiry where constitutional rights are concerned must be that the public interest in ensuring that innocent people are not convicted and subjected to ignomiy and heavy sentences massively outweighs the public interest in ensuring that a particular criminal is brought to book ... Hence the presumption of innocence, which serves not only to protect a particular individual on trial, but to maintain public confidence in the enduring integrity and security of the legal system. Reference to the prevalence and severity of a certain crime therefore does not add anything new or special to the balancing exercise. The perniciousness of the offence is one of the givens, against which the presumption of innocence is pitted from the beginning, not a new element to be put into the scales as part of a justificatory balancing exercise. If this were not so, the ubiquity and ugliness argument could

---

[58] Following the decision of the House of Lords in *R. v Director of Public Prosecutions, Ex p. Kebilene* [2000] 2 A.C. 326, the Terrorism Act 2000 was enacted. Although it contains several provisions which say it shall be a defence for a person charged with an offence to prove something, by s.118(2):

> "If the person adduces evidence which is sufficient to raise an issue with respect to the matter the court or jury shall assume that the defence is satisfied unless the prosecution proves beyond a reasonable doubt that it is not.".

[59] *State v Coetzee* [1997] 2 LRG 593, 677 per Sacks J. para.220.

be used in relation to murder, rape, car-jacking, housebreaking, drug-smuggling, corruption ... the list is unfortunately almost endless, and nothing would be left of the presumption of innocence, save, perhaps, for its relic status as a doughty defender of rights in the most trivial cases."

The threat posed to the public cannot justify a departure from fairness. In the case of *R. v Lambert*,[60] a drug trafficking case, Lord Clyde said[61]:

"Of course trafficking in controlled drugs is a notorious social evil, but if any error is to be made in the weighing of the scales of justice, it should be to the effect that the guilty should go free rather than an innocent person should be wrongly convicted."

Most offences of strict liability are punished by sentences at the lower end of the scale. This factor is itself relied upon as counterbalancing strict liability. But virtually all such offences triable on indictment carry a maximum sentence of imprisonment of more than six months. In *Sweet v Parsley*,[62] Lord Reid said:

"In the first place a stigma still attaches to any person convicted of a truly criminal offence, and the more serious or more disgraceful the offence, the greater the stigma."

The imposition on the defendant of a legal burden of proof has been considered several times since the coming into force of the HRA. In *R. v Director of Public Prosecutions Ex p. Kebilene and Others*,[63] the House of Lords allowed an appeal by the Director of Public Prosecutions against the decision of the Divisional Court that he had acted unlawfully in deciding to proceed with the prosecution of the defendants for offences under s.16A of the Prevention of Terrorism Act 1989.[64] By s.16A(1):

"A person is guilty of an offence if he has any article in his possession in circumstances giving rise to a reasonable suspicion that the article is in his possession for a purpose connected with the commission, preparation or investigation of acts of terrorism to which this section applies."

By s.16A(3) it was a defence for a person so charged to prove that the offending article was not in his possession for a terrorist purpose [as mentioned in subs.1].

In the Divisional Court, Lord Bingham considered that s.16A breached the presumption of innocence "in a blatant and obvious way". Although the appeal before their Lordships did not in fact turn on the compatibility of

---

[60] [2002] 2 A.C. 545.
[61] ibid. at 156.
[62] [1969] 2 W.L.R. 470, 474; [1969] 1 All E.R. 347.
[63] [2000] 2 A.C. 326.
[64] Now replaced by the Terrorism Act 2000.

s.16A with art.6(2), Lord Hope did not regard such a finding of incompatibility as inevitable. As he said[65]:

> "It is not immediately obvious that it would be imposing an unreasonable burden on an accused who was in possession of articles from which an inference of involvement in terrorism could be drawn to provide an explanation for his possession of them which could displace that inference."

and[66]:

> "... as a matter of general principle, a fair balance must be struck between the demands of the general interests of the community and the protection of the fundamental rights of the individual."[67]

In the case of *R. v Lambert*,[68] the House of Lords[69] considered s.28 of the **12.16** Misuse of Drugs Act 1971. L was seen alighting from a train at Runcorn station holding an envelope. He was met by a man; they shook hands and went out to the car park. A minute or two later, he walked back into the station, alone. The envelope was gone but he was now holding a bag. He was arrested. The bag contained two kilos of cocaine worth about £140,000. The judge directed the jury that the prosecution only had to prove that there was cocaine in the bag, and that Lambert had, and knew he had, the bag in his possession. The prosecution did not have to prove he knew there was cocaine in the bag, rather the burden was on him to prove that he did not know the bag contained a controlled drug. This was an orthodox direction to the jury at the time of the trial.

By s.5(2) of the Misuse of Drugs Act it is an offence "for a person to have a controlled drug in his possession" and by s.5(3) it is an offence for a person to have a controlled drug in his possession with intent to supply it to another ...". Section 28(3)(b)(i) provides a defence if the defendant proves that he neither believed, nor suspected nor had reason to suspect that the substance or product in question was a controlled drug.

Almost 20 years earlier, Lord Scarman had described the statutory offence under s.5(1) as:

> "... an absolute one in the sense that the prosecution establish it by proving possession without authority. Section 28 provides for certain defences which, if they are to succeed, the defendant must prove on the balance of probabilities".[70]

---

[65] At p.387.
[66] At p.384.
[67] See also *Sporrong and Lonnroth v Sweden* (1983) 5 E.H.R.R. 35, 69.
[68] [2002] 2 A.C. 545.
[69] Lords Slynn, Steyn, Hope, Clyde and Hutton.
[70] *R. v Boyesen* [1982] A.C. 768, 773.

In *Lambert*, Lord Clyde said[71]:

> "Section 28 provides an escape for the defence by adding a qualification to the strict operation of the definition of possession. It affords a defence to an accused person where no defence had previously existed under earlier legislation (*R. v Ashton-Rickard* [1978] 1 W.L.R. 37, 43)".

After L had been convicted but before the case went to the House of Lords, the HRA came into force. Their Lordships concluded (by a majority) that the HRA did not operate retrospectively so as to enable him to rely on art.6(2), and the appeal was dismissed. However, the House did consider whether the reverse burden in s.28 violated the presumption of innocence, concluding, by a majority, that it did.

12.17 Each of the speeches acknowledged that in a constitutional democracy, limited inroads on the presumption of innocence may be justified; in *Salabiaku v France*[72] the ECtHR observed that:

> "Presumptions of fact or of law operate in every legal system. Clearly the Convention does not prohibit such presumptions in principle. It does, however, require Contracting States to remain within certain limits in this respect as regards criminal law.
>
> Article 6(2) does not therefore regard presumptions of fact or of law provided for in the criminal law with indifference. It requires States to confine them within reasonable limits which take into account the importance of what is at stake and maintain the rights of the defence."[73]

The prosecution argued that s.5(1) made unlawful the possession of drugs *simpliciter*, thus making the defendant responsible for ensuring that he did not take into his possession items which, in fact, contained drugs. Lord Steyn rejected this argument, pointing out that the maximum sentence that could be imposed for this offence was life imprisonment. In reality the gravamen of the offence was the *knowing* possession of drugs. The offence could not be characterised as one of strict liability subject to a defence of due diligence; in reality "knowledge" was an essential element of the offence, and since the burden of proving lack of knowledge lay on the defendant, s.28 derogated from the presumption of innocence.

The distinction between constituent elements of the crime and matters which the defendant must prove "will sometimes be unprincipled and arbitrary"[74]; a true constituent element can easily be removed from the definition of the crime and cast as a defensive issue. So, "knowledge" is not part of the definition of the offence, rather the Act casts the burden of disproving knowledge on the accused. Despite the wording of s.5, their

---

[71] [2002] 2 A.C. 545, 128.
[72] (1991) 13 E.H.R.R. 379, 388.
[73] ibid. at 28.
[74] per Lord Steyn, at 517, para.35.

Lordships all regarded "knowledge" as an essential ingredient of s.5 of the Misuse of Drugs Act. Lord Steyn[75] made it clear that:

"[It] is necessary to concentrate not on technicalities and niceties of language, but rather on matters of substance."

For Lord Steyn, the presumption of innocence was not respected by legislation that excluded mens rea from the definition of the offence, even if it permitted a defendant who could prove lack of mens rea to be acquitted. Knowledge was an essential element of criminality and so to place on the defendant the burden of proving he did not have such knowledge was an unjustified violation of the presumption of innocence. He referred to a decision of the Canadian Supreme Court which reached the same conclusion. The argument that the constitutional presumption of innocence only applied to elements of the offence and not excuses was rejected; Lord Dickson C.J. observed[76]:

"The real concern is not whether the accused must disprove an element or prove an excuse, but that an accused may be convicted while a reasonable doubt exists. When that possibility exists, there is a breach of the presumption of innocence. The exact characterisation of a factor as an essential element, a collateral factor, an excuse, or a defence should not affect the analysis of the presumption of innocence. It is the final effect of a provision on the verdict that is decisive. If an accused is required to prove some fact on the balance of probabilities to avoid conviction, the provision violates the presumption of innocence because it permits a conviction in spite of a reasonable doubt in the mind of the trier of fact as to the guilt of the accused."

The problem identified by the Canadian court is that if legislation places a legal burden on the accused to disprove any element of the offence, he can be convicted even if, the jury is as sure as not of that element. The majority of their Lordships in *Lambert* were concerned that in such a grave case a defendant might in practise be convicted even though the jury were 50 per cent sure that he did not know the package contained drugs. To put it another way, wherever a legal burden is imposed on the accused, the court is obliged to convict even if the defendant's account is as likely to be true as not. Within the context of a regulatory offence, a defendant would be liable to conviction if the judge of the facts was 50 per cent satisfied that he had exercised due diligence. It does not matter how the element is characterised, what matters is that if the defendant does not make the jury more sure than not, he must be convicted. Were the burden on the prosecution throughout to prove that element, the defendant would be acquitted if the jury were left in such a state of uncertainty.

---

[75] per Lord Steyn, at 571, para.35.
[76] *R. v Whyte* (1988) 51 D.L.R. 4th 481, 493.

12.18   Lord Hutton also rejected the argument that the protection of art.6(2) was excluded simply by reference to the wording of the offence creating section:

> "...the Crown cannot rebut an argument based on a violation of Article 6(2) by simply contending that the Government of the United Kingdom is entitled 'to define the constituent elements of the ... offence', and that a violation of Article 6(2) is avoided because the 1971 Act makes absence of knowledge of being in possession of a controlled drug a defence rather than making knowledge an ingredient of the offence which the prosecution has to prove."[77]

Of course, earlier cases on the effect of ss.5(1) and 28(1) of the Misuse of Drugs Act[78] did not consider the reverse burden in terms of the Convention because it was inapplicable. Before 1998, Parliament was free to legislate in whatever form it chose; as Ashworth & Blake put it,[79] although the presumption of innocence was:

> "enshrined in common law, Parliament could ignore it whenever it pleased and for whatever reasons, good or bad. In a system based on parliamentary supremacy, there is no arguing with that".

Lord Hutton's approach to criminal statutes has been followed by the courts in other cases, the most recent general exposition being by the House of Lords in the case of *Sheldrake v DPP*.[80] Lord Bingham of Cornhill stated the test to be applied in these terms:

> "The task of the court is never to decide whether a reverse burden should be imposed on a defendant, but always to assess whether a burden enacted by Parliament unjustifiably infringes the presumption of innocence."[81]

He continued in relation to the specific burden on the defendant in the offence of being in charge of a vehicle when unfit through drink or drugs:

> "It may not be very profitable to debate whether section 5(2) infringes the presumption of innocence. It may be assumed that it does. Plainly the provision is directed to a legitimate object: the prevention of death, injury and damage caused by unfit drivers. Does the provision meet the tests of acceptability identified in the Strasbourg jurisprudence? In my view it plainly does. I do not regard the burden placed on the defendant as beyond reasonable limits or in any way arbitrary. It is not objectionable to criminalise a defendant's conduct in these circumstances

---

[77] [2002] 2 A.C. 545 para.185.
[78] See, e.g. *R. v McNamara* (1988) 87 Cr.App.R. 246; *R. v Boyesen* [1982] A.C. 768.
[79] The Presumption of Innocence in English Criminal Law [1996] Crim.L.R. 306.
[80] [2005] 1 A.C. 264.
[81] at para.31.

without requiring a prosecutor to prove criminal intent. The defendant has a full opportunity to show that there was no likelihood of his driving, a matter so closely conditioned by his own knowledge and state of mind at the material time as to make it much more appropriate for him to prove on the balance of probabilities that he would not have been likely to drive than for the prosecutor to prove, beyond reasonable doubt, that he would. I do not think that imposition of a legal burden went beyond what was necessary."[82]

According to Lord Bingham, the crucial question is whether the imposition of a legal burden on a defendant in the particular situation is a proportionate and justifiable legislative response to an undoubted problem. Even in anti-terrorism legislation, although security considerations carry weight, they do not absolve a state of its duty to ensure that basic standards of fairness are observed.[83]

Now that the Convention is part of domestic law, the courts are obliged to interpret legislation in a way which is compatible with the HRA. Although Parliament remains sovereign, legislation which imposes a legal burden on the accused must be compatible with the Convention.[84] Even if the prosecution can demonstrate an objective justification for a transfer of the burden of proof, the principle of proportionality requires the courts to decide whether the legislative means of achieving the objective are not greater than necessary. The burden of proving that it is proportionate is on the prosecution.

Under the HRA the court is "the guardian of human rights".[85] It must judge whether a statutory scheme is fair. In order to do so:

"the court must determine whether a fair balance was struck between the demands of the general interests of the community and the requirement of the protection of the individual's fundamental rights. The search for this balance is inherent in the whole of the Convention . . ."[86]

Whether a statutory provision is arbitrary or oppressive is a question of balance depending upon:

"Whether: (i) the legislative objective is sufficiently important to justify limiting a fundamental right; (ii) the measures designed to meet the legislative objectives are rationally connected to it; and (iii) the means

---

[82] At para.41.
[83] At para.51.
[84] *Sheldrake v DPP* provides an example of a post-HRA criminal offence (s.11 Terrorism Act 2000) which casts a legal burden on the accused. Lord Bingham indicated that in the circumstances the reverse burden was compatible with HRA responsibilities [paras 53 & 54.
[85] per Simon Brown L.J. in *International Transport Roth Gmbh v Secretary of State for the Home Department* [2002] EWCA Civ 158, 167.
[86] *Sporrong & Lonnroth v Sweden* (1983) 5 E.H.R.R. 35, 52.

used to impair the right or freedom are no more than is necessary to accomplish the objective."[87]

Although balancing those interests is necessary, there is an irreducible minimum of Convention rights, including of course, "... the fundamental and absolute right to a fair trial"[88]:

"The only balancing permitted is in respect of what the concept of a fair trial entails: ... here account must be taken of the familiar triangulation of interest of the accused, the victim and society."[89]

Any impairment or modification of the rights of the accused must not only be no more than necessary for the attainment of the objective sought "in the public interest", but also must not impose an excessive burden on the accused.[90]

So, in *Lambert*, the majority considered that the *legal* burden imposed by s.28 was not a proportionate response; the imposition of an *evidential* burden would achieve Parliament's objective without violating the presumption of innocence.[91] Their Lordships decided that s.28 could be "read down" (pursuant to s.3 HRA 1998) or as Lord Hope put it "translated into compatible language"[92] so as to impose no more than an evidential burden on the accused; the word "prove" should be read as "adduce sufficient evidence" to raise a reasonable doubt. By this device, the section became compatible with the Convention.

REVERSE BURDENS IN REGULATORY OFFENCES

12.19 It follows that the imposition of a reverse burden does not necessarily involve a violation of the Convention. As the art.6(2) right is not absolute or unqualified,[93] the test to be applied is whether the modification or limitation

---

[87] per Lord Clyde in *De Freitas v Permanent Secretary of Ministry of Agriculture, Fisheries, Lands and Housing* [1999] 1 A.C. 69, 80 PC.

[88] per Lord Hope in *Brown v Stott* [2001] 2 All E.R. 97; [2001] 2 W.L.R. 817, 851.

[89] per Lord Steyn in *R. v A (No.2)* [2001] U.K.H.L. 25; [2002] 1 A.C. 45; [2001] 2 W.L.R. 1546, 1560.

[90] See *James v UK* (1986) 8 E.H.R.R. 123.

[91] In support of this observation, Lord Steyn referred to a number of decisions from cognate legal systems. *R. v Oslin* [1993] 4 S.C.R. 595; *State v Manamela* [2000] 5 L.R.C. 65. In that case the majority held (at para.49) that:

"... the State has failed, in our view, to discharge the onus of establishing that the extent of the limitation is reasonable and justifiable and that the relation between the limitation and its purpose is proportionate. It equally failed to establish that no less restrictive means were available to Parliament in order to achieve the purpose. The imposition of an evidential burden on the accused would equally serve ... the prosecution."

Lord Clyde regarded *Hardy v Ireland* App. 23456/94 as support for the same proposition.

[92] [2002] 2 A.C. 545, para.91.

[93] per Lord Clyde at para.88.

of that right pursues a legitimate aim and whether it satisfies the principle of proportionality.[94] Provided it is a proportionate response to a legitimate aim, a "contracting State may penalise a simple or objective fact as such, irrespective of whether it arises from criminal intent or from negligence".[95] It is necessary to look not only at the form of the legislation, but also its substance and effect.[96] What is decisive is the substance and reality of the language creating the offence rather than its form.[97]

In *Lambert*, Lord Steyn made it clear that he regarded as different in principle the narrow exception of "... offences arising under enactments which prohibit the doing of an act save in specified circumstances or by persons of specified classes or with specified qualifications or with the licence or permission of specified authorities".[98] Such offences are unlikely to be found to be incompatible with art.6(2).

Whenever confronted with a provision which unambiguously imposes a reverse legal burden, the courts will have to conduct the balancing exercise described above. Strict liability may be acceptable in the case of statutory offences which are concerned to regulate the conduct of some particular activity in the public interest. The promotion of health and safety and the avoidance of pollution are examples of the purposes to be served by such controls.[99]

In 1990, the ECtHR considered an application concerning a statutory **12.20** provision making a company director guilty of an offence committed by the company "unless he proves that the offence was committed without his knowledge".[1] The Commission declared the application inadmissible, concluding that the presumption was rebuttable and reasonable:

> "The Commission notes that in the present case the legislation provides that a director of a company is presumed guilty of an offence committed by the company unless he proves that the offence was committed without his knowledge and that he exercised all due diligence to prevent the commission of the offence. The applicant was therefore provided under the legislation with the possibility of exculpating himself. The Commission does not consider that the conditions, which required the applicant to prove that he had no actual knowledge of the offence and he was not negligent in his duties as an officer of a company, were ... contradictory or imposed an irrebuttable presumption. The Commission further finds that the Maltese courts enjoyed a genuine freedom of assessment in this area and that there is no indication that art.13 of the

---

[94] See *Ashingdane v UK* (1985) 7 E.H.R.R. 528.

[95] See *Salabiaku* (1991) 13 E.H.R.R. 379, para.27.

[96] *X v UK* App. No. 5124/71, July 1972.

[97] *Att-Gen of Hong Kong v Lee Kwong Kut* [1993] A.C. 951, 968.

[98] *R. v Edwards* [1975] Q.B. 27; *R. v Hunt* [1987] A.C. 352, s.101 of the Magistrates' Courts Act 1980.

[99] [1991] 1 A.C. 69 per Lord Clyde at para.154.

[1] *Att-Gen v Malta* App. No. 16641/90 (December 10, 1990 unreported).

1975 Act was applied to the applicant in a manner incompatible with the presumption of innocence."

Whether or not a section offends art.6(2) depends, amongst other things, upon whether the presumption is confined within reasonable limits, taking into account the importance of what is at stake.

The following questions can be used to test the compatibility of a legal burden imposed on the accused:

(a) Is the presumption directed towards a clear and proper public objective?

(b) Is the creation of the presumption a reasonable measure for Parliament to take and is there a reasonable relationship of proportionality between the means employed and the aim sought to be realised? In assessing this question it is necessary to assess whether a fair balance has been struck between the general interest of the community and the personal rights of the individual.[2] Where the presumption is justified in the public interest, the difficulty of proving knowledge is one of the factors that may render the remedy proportional.[3]

In argument before their Lordships in the case of *Ex p. Kebilene*,[4] David Pannick Q.C., counsel for the Director of Public Prosecutions, proposed the following questions as a tool to consider where the balance lies between the interests of the community and the interests of the accused:

"1. What does the prosecution have to prove in order to transfer the onus to defendant?

2. What is the burden on the accused—does it relate to something which is likely to be difficult for him to prove, or does it relate to something which is likely to be within his knowledge or to which he readily has access?

3. What is the nature of the threat faced by society which the provision is designed to combat?"

The courts have the task of arbitrating between the competing interests. As Lord Hope said in that case[5]:

"There is also the question of balance, as to the interests of the individual against those of society. The Convention jurisdiction and that which is to be found from the cases decided in other jurisdictions suggests that account may legitimately be taken, in striking the right balance, of the problems which the legislation is designed to address."

---

[2] *Brown v Stott* [2001] 2 All E.R. 97 per Lord Hope.
[3] This test was articulated by Lord Hutton in *Lambert* [2002] 2 A.C. 545 at para.190.
[4] *Ex p. Kebilene* [1999] 3 W.L.R. 972, 988 per Lord Hope.
[5] At p.326.

There cannot be a simple definitive rule as to whether a burden or pre- **12.21** sumption will violate the Convention or not. Lord Hope said in *Ex p. Kebilene*:

"...this is not an exact science. The provisions vary so widely in their detail as to what prosecutors must prove before the onus shifts and their effect on the presumption of innocence depends so much on circumstances."[6]

It is submitted that this margin is entirely consistent with the nature of Convention rights. Clayton and Tomlinson point out[7]:

"Convention rights are expressed in broad and open textured language. This means that when construing the Human Rights Act, it will be appropriate and inevitable that the English courts should put these broad concepts in context by reflecting domestic legal and cultural values and traditions. Precisely because the Commission and the court recognise an interpretative obligation to respect the primacy of domestic states in interpreting the scope and content of rights, the English courts will be afforded *a margin of appreciation* in developing a human rights jurisprudence to meet domestic conditions."

In determining whether a "fair balance" has been struck by the legislation, a factor to which the court must have regard is the deference to be paid to "the democratically accountable legislature" acting within its "discretionary area of judgment".[8] The court's role is one of review. Parliament, not the court, is charged with the primary responsibility for deciding as a matter of policy what should be the constituent elements of a criminal offence. As Lord Nicholls stated in the House of Lords:

"The court will reach a different conclusion from the legislature only when it is apparent the legislature has attached insufficient importance to the fundamental right of an individual to be presumed innocent until proved guilty."[9]

Is, then, a particular regulatory offence likely to be regarded as Convention compliant? What is clear is that the courts will proceed on a case-by-case basis; the variety of such offences is too great for there to be any hard rule to determine compatibility with confidence. Already courts and judges have disagreed, sometimes over the same provision.

In *R. v Carass*,[10] the defendant was charged with concealment of the debts **12.22** of a company in anticipation of a winding up contrary to s.206(1)(a) of the Insolvency Act 1986. By that section, when a company is wound up, an

---

[6] [1999] 3 W.L.R. 972, 380.
[7] "*The Law of Human Rights*", para.6.37.
[8] per Lord Bingham in *Brown v Stott* [2001] 2 W.L.R. 817, 835.
[9] *R. v Johnstone* [2003] UKHL 28, [2003] 1 W.L.R. 1736, para.51.
[10] [2002] 1 W.L.R. 1714.

officer of the company is deemed to have committed an offence if he has concealed any part of the property of the company. It is a defence for a person charged under para.(1)(a) to prove that he had no intention to defraud.[11]

The Crown argued that it had to prove that there had been deliberate concealment of a debt before the burden of proof shifted to the defence. Since "concealment" involved deliberate activity, it was not unfair then to require a defendant to prove he had no intention to defraud. The Court of Appeal rejected this argument: an intention to defraud was an important element of the offence.[12]

Within a few months, a differently constituted Court of Appeal considered[13] s.352 of the Insolvency Act 1986, which provides that a person is not guilty of an offence under s.354:

"...if he proves that, at the time of the conduct constituting the offence, he had no intent to defraud or to conceal the state of his affairs."

As Auld L.J. noted, s.206(4) and s.354 of the Insolvency Act:

"...were sufficiently similar in form and purpose ... to make both the context and the reasoning of *Carass* indistinguishable".[14]

and accordingly, the appeal was allowed. However, the judge did not regard the imposition of a legal burden in the circumstances as a violation of art.6(2)[15]:

"The position of the bankrupt is quite different to that of citizens who are not. When a person becomes bankrupt he is taken to be aware of the duties imposed upon him by the 1986 Act. The bankrupt must make full disclosure of all material facts in order to protect the rights of his creditors. Why should it be unreasonable to require a person who has deliberately concealed a debt in circumstances where he knows he was obliged to disclose it, to prove that he did not intend to defraud or to conceal the state of affairs?"

But for the fact that it was bound by the decision in *Carass*, the court would have held that the burden of proof in s.354 was a legal one and did not violate art.6(2). These decisions were both reviewed by the Court of Appeal in a consolidated reference before a 5 judge court presided over by the Lord Chief Justice, Lord Woolf.[16]

12.23   The Court considered the legislative history, policy and scheme of the

---

[11] See para.15.9.
[12] See the commentary to this decision by Professor Birch—[2002] Crim.L.R. 316.
[13] *R. v Anthony Daniel* [2002] EWCA Crim 959.
[14] [2002] EWCA Crim 959, para.25.
[15] At para.31.
[16] *Att-Gen's Reference (No.1 of 2004)* [2004] 2 Cr.App.R. 424.

Insolvency Act 1986 and the particular position of an officer of an insolvent company, concluding:

> "In our judgment, these considerations will normally justify the imposition on the defendant, who is proved to have deliberately acted in a manner that gives rise to an inference that he sought to defraud his creditors, of the burden of proving, on the balance of probabilities, that he did not intend to do so."

The Court did not follow the decision in *Carass* which it regarded as impliedly overruled by the decision in *R. v Johnstone*.[17] In *Sheldrake v DPP* Lord Bingham endorsed this approach, stating that *Carass* was wrongly decided.[18]

The combined effect of ss.3(1) and 33(1) of the Health and Safety at Work Act 1974 ("HSWA") is to make it an offence for an employer to fail to discharge the duty to conduct his undertaking in such a way as to ensure, so far as is reasonably practicable, that persons not in his employment who may be affected thereby are not exposed to risks to their health and safety. By s.40 it shall be for the accused to prove that it was not reasonably practicable to do more than was in fact done to satisfy the duty. In *R. v Davies*[19] the Court of Appeal held that the imposition of a legal burden on the defendant is not incompatible with art.6(2) of the Convention; it is justified, necessary and proportionate. The Court pointed out that in the field of health and safety, the EEC (as it then was) had accepted that it could be appropriate to impose absolute duties on employers. Article 5.1 of Council Directive 89/391/EEC requires member states to provide that:

> "The employer should have a duty to ensure the safety and health of workers in every aspect related to their work."

Member States may, but need not, provide a due diligence defence. Section 1 HSWA states that the provisions of the Act should have effect:

> "with a view to securing the health, safety and welfare of persons at work and protecting persons other than persons at work against risks to health and safety."

The Act gave effect to the recommendations of the Robens Report[20] that employers be encouraged to be safety conscious so as to prevent accidents. These were all factors taken into account by the court.

The HSWA is regulatory in character and a necessary measure in the face **12.24** of an average of 700 fatal injuries and 200,000 major non-fatal injuries suffered at work every year. That the obligation is on employers (who will

---

[17] [2003] 1 W.L.R. 1736 HL.
[18] [2005] 1 A.C. 264, para.33.
[19] [2002] EWCA Crim 2949; Tuckey L.J., Douglas Brown J. and H.H.J. Gordon.
[20] 1972, Cmd 5034.

often be corporations) had a material bearing on the compatibility of the provision. Unlike "unengaged and disinterested members of the public", those subject to the provisions of the HSWA (and upon whom the burden of persuasion is imposed by s.40):

> "... have chosen to engage in work or commercial activity (probably for gain) and are in charge of it ... and in choosing to operate in a regulated sphere of activity they must be taken to have accepted the regulatory controls that go with it."[21]

The characterisation of the regulatory scheme in this way echoes the approach of Auld L.J. in *R. v Anthony Daniel* where he was considering provisions of the Insolvency Act 1986.[22]

Other factors that influenced the Court in *Davies* included: the recognition that ordinarily it would not be difficult for the accused to prove the facts relied on in support of the defence as they would be within the knowledge of the defendant; that if there were only an evidential burden on the accused, enforcement might become impossible; and that none of the offences created by ss.2 to 7 and 33(1) of the Act carries a sentence of imprisonment.

12.25 A reverse burden included in an offence which is "truly criminal" is more likely to violate the Convention than if the offence is regulatory.[23] Certainly Lord Clyde[24] thought that:

> "A strict responsibility may be acceptable in the case of statutory offences which are concerned to regulate the conduct of some particular activity in the public interest. The requirement to have a licence in order to carry on certain kinds of activity is an obvious example. The promotion of health and safety and the avoidance of pollution are among the purposes to be served by such controls. These kinds of cases may properly be seen as not truly criminal. Many may be relatively trivial and only involve a monetary penalty. Many may carry with them no real disgrace or infamy."

As has been shown, in *Davies v Health and Safety Executive*,[25] the court concluded that the Health and Safety at Work Act was regulatory legislation. The court referred to the judgment of Cory J. in a Canadian case, *R. v Wholesale Travel Group*,[26] as explaining the rationale for the distinction. Cory J. said:[27]

---

[21] [2002] EWCA Crim 2949, para.25.
[22] See also *R. v Muhamad* [2003] Q.B. 1031 CA.
[23] But see *R. v G* [2008] UKHL 37.
[24] *R. v Lambert* [2002] 2 A.C. 545, para.154.
[25] [2002] EWCA Crim 2949.
[26] (1991) 3 S.L.R. 154.
[27] At pp.219–220.

"The objective of regulatory legislation is to protect the public or broad segments of the public (such as employees, common consumers and motorists to name but a few) from the potentially adverse effects of otherwise lawful activity. Regulatory legislation involves the shift of emphasis from the protection of individual interests and the deterrence and punishment of acts involving moral fault to the protection of public and societal interests. While criminal offences are usually designed to condemn and punish past, inherently wrongful conduct, regulatory measures are generally directed to the prevention of future harm through the enforcement of minimum standards of conduct and care."

Those who choose to carry on a regulated activity are in a different position from the general public because "they have chosen to engage in the regulated activity ... and in doing so placed themselves in a responsible relationship to the public generally and must accept the consequences of that responsibility ... Those persons who enter a regulated field are in the best position to control the harm which may result and they should therefore be held responsible for it."[28] The reversal of the burden of proof takes into account that fact.[29]

In cases decided since the coming into force of the HRA, regulatory provisions imposing a legal burden on the defendant have usually (but not always) been upheld. Regulated activity is frequently conducted by corporations. Without a legal burden cast on the defendant to prove, for example, due diligence, the prosecution would have real difficulty in showing that a company had failed to act with due diligence.

When considering a reverse legal burden imposed by statute the court **12.26** must determine: "the quality of any deference owed by the courts to the legislature"; the degree of deference owed must depend upon "where the impugned measure lies within the scheme of things".[30] The question of deference was considered by Lord Hope in *Ex p. Kebilene*[31]:

"In this area difficult choices may have to be made by the executive or the legislature between the rights of the individual and the needs of society. In some circumstances it will be appropriate for the courts to recognise that there is an area of judgment within which the judiciary will defer, on democratic grounds, to the considered opinion of the elected body or person whose act or decision is said to be incompatible with the Convention."

---

[28] At p.228.
[29] per Tuckey L.J. in *Davies v Health and Safety Executive*, [2002] EWCA Crim 2949 at para.25.
[30] per Laws L.J. in *International Transport Co GmbH v Secretary of State for the Home Department* [2002] EWCA Civ 158, paras 76–77.
[31] [2000] 2 A.C. 326, 380 E–G.

In *Brown v Stott*,[32] Lord Bingham explained the tension between individual rights and legislative sovereignty in this way:

> "Judicial recognition and assertion of the human rights defined in the
> Convention is not a substitute for the processes of democratic gov-
> ernment but a complement to them. While a national court does not
> accord the margin of appreciation recognised by the European Court as
> a supra-national court, it will give weight to the decisions of a repre-
> sentative legislature and a democratic government within the discre-
> tionary area of judgment accorded to those bodies..."

Although only the ECtHR can accord to domestic courts a "margin of
appreciation",[33] the national courts may accord to the decisions of national
legislatures some deference "where the context justifies it".[34]

12.27   In considering regulatory schemes, the courts should accord a degree of
deference to the legislative steps taken to safeguard the public from the
potentially adverse effects of regulated activity. As Lord Woolf said in *Att-
Gen of Hong Kong v Lee Kwong-kut*[35]:

> "In order to maintain the balance between the individual and the
> society as a whole, rigid and inflexible standards should not be imposed
> on the legislature's attempts to resolve the difficult and intransigent
> problems with which society is faced when seeking to deal with serious
> crime."

The factors that inform the categorising of an offence as prescriptive
("truly" criminal) or regulatory are the scale of punishment and the extent
to which social obloquy attaches to it. In *Sweet v Parsley*,[36] Lord Reid said:

> "In the first place a stigma still attaches to any person convicted of a
> truly criminal offence, and the more serious or more disgraceful the
> offence, the greater the stigma".[37]

In *Lambert*, the fact that the maximum sentence on conviction for an
offence contrary to s.5 of the Misuse of Drugs Act 1971 was life imprisonment was an important consideration in determining whether the legal
burden on the defendant was a proportionate response by the State to drug
trafficking. A legal burden imposed on the defendant in a regulatory offence
is likely to be upheld even where a substantial sentence may be imposed. By
way of example, s.92 of the Trade Marks Act 1994 carries a maximum

---

[32] [2001] 2 W.L.R. 817, 834–835.
[33] Which recognises that national institutions are better placed than international courts to
evaluate local needs and conditions.
[34] per Lord Steyn, *Brown v Stott* [2001] 2 W.L.R. 817, 842. See also *Att-Gen's Reference (No.4
of 2002)* [2003] EWCA Crim 762.
[35] [1993] A.C. 951, 975; this dictum was approved by Lord Nicholls in *R. v Johnstone* [2003]
UKHL 28, para.51.
[36] [1970] A.C. 132.
[37] At p.149.

sentence of 10 years' imprisonment. In *Sliney v London Borough of Havering*,[38] Rose L.J. thought that given the nature of the offence:

"... the moral obloquy involved will normally be likely to be rather less than what have been styled 'truly criminal' cases."[39]

As to the maximum sentence, the court "did not think it unprincipled also to have regard to the reality of the matter: which is that most cases under s.92 are brought in the magistrates' court and of those, the majority result in a fine." The respondents adduced statistical evidence showing that between 1998 and 2000 custodial sentences were imposed in fewer than 10 per cent of all cases, both in the Crown and magistrates' courts. However, another division of the Court of Appeal had earlier arrived at the opposite conclusion; the offence "carrying with it a sentence of up to 10 years imprisonment was one which rendered it important to give adequate protection to the defendant."[40] The House of Lords has now decided that the persuasive burden imposed upon the accused by the s.92(5) defence is compatible with art.6(2).[41]

What is clear is that the more serious the punishment which may flow from conviction, the more compelling must be the reasons justifying placing a persuasive burden on the accused.[42] Lord Bingham had described the Road Traffic Offences Act 1988 as a regulatory regime[43]:

"All who own or drive motor cars know that by doing so they subject themselves to a regulatory regime which does not apply to members of the public who do neither. Section 172 of the 1988 Act forms part of that regulatory regime. This regime is imposed not because owning or driving cars is a privilege or indulgence granted by the state but because the possession and use of cars (like for example shotguns, the possession of which is very regulated) are recognised to have the potential to cause grave injury."

It can be argued that any criminal offence whether prescriptive or regulatory is serious and certainly can become so depending on the facts in issue. A prosecution under s.3 of the Health and Safety at Work Act may involve a workplace death, or equally something quite trivial. The seriousness of the result is not determinative of the offence being criminal or quasi criminal.

The principle of proportionality requires the court to consider whether **12.28** there is a "pressing necessity to impose a legal rather than an evidential

---

[38] [2002] EWCA Crim 2558.
[39] At para.48.4.
[40] *R. v Johnstone* [2002] EWCA Crim 194, para.81 per Tuckey L.J.
[41] per Lord Nicholls in *R. v Johnstone* above at para.54.
[42] [2002] EWCA Crim 194 at para.50.
[43] *Brown v Stott* [2001] 2 All E.R. 97, 116 endorsed by the Grand Chamber in *Francis and O'Halloran v UK*, *The Times*, July 13, 2007, ECtHR.

burden on the accused."[44] The onus on the state seeking to persuade the court that a legal burden is necessary in any case is a heavy one.[45] In *Grundy & Co Excavations Ltd v The Forestry Commission*,[46] the question was posed in this way:

> "In order to show that a legal burden is proportionate the Commission must show that it was necessary, not merely reasonable."[47]

Linked to this is the extent to which the matters the accused is required to prove are "peculiarly within his knowledge" (see, e.g. *Sliney* or *Att-Gen's Reference (No.1 of 2004)*). This is the subject of David Pannick's second question.[48] It is particularly likely to be the case where the accused must prove for example that he was licensed to do the act,[49] or where the accused has to prove due diligence.

Whether a matter is "peculiarly within [the accused's] knowledge" is not dispositive of the question whether a reverse burden is a "necessary and proportionate measure". An accused's knowledge is an element of many criminal offences which the prosecution has the burden of proving. It will seldom be a "necessity" for a provision to impose a legal burden on the accused to prove his lack of knowledge.[50]

Although reverse burdens may be upheld by the courts, it is now clear that, as the ECtHR said in *Salabiaku*[51] at para.28, presumptions of fact or law are not regarded with indifference. It will always be necessary for the prosecution to demonstrate that a particular presumption is no more than a necessary, justified and proportionate response to a real social harm.

PRIVILEGE AGAINST SELF-INCRIMINATION

12.29 There is no doubt that any person (natural or legal) prosecuted for a criminal offence is entitled to a fair trial. What is less clear is whether *all* the privileges enjoyed by a human defendant and held to be constituent elements of a fair trial apply, *mutatis mutandis*, to a corporate defendant. Is the common law privilege against self-incrimination to be enjoyed equally by a natural and a legal person.

The privilege against self-incrimination at common law developed as a judicial reaction to the perogative courts of the sixteenth and seventeenth centuries, and as such, predates by several hundred years any modern

---

[44] *R. v Lambert* [2002] 2 A.C. 545, para.37.
[45] per Rose L.J. in *Sliney v London Borough of Havering* [2002] EWCA Crim 2558, para.47.
[46] [2003] EWHC Admin 272 per Clarke L.J.
[47] At para.63.
[48] See para.12.26 above.
[49] See *Grundy* [2003] EWHC Admin 272.
[50] cf. *Torbay Council v Singh*, [1999] 2 Cr.App.R. 451, 455; *Sliney v London Borough of Havering* [2002] EWCA Crim 2558, paras 48.2 and 48.3.
[51] *Salabiaku v France* (1988) E.H.R.R. 378.

notions of corporate liability. The privilege is the corollary of the requirement that the prosecution proves its case without resort to evidence
obtained through methods of coercion or in defiance of the will of the
accused.[52] Even when such practices were abandoned, the privilege was
retained in both criminal and civil proceedings because "it discourages the ill
treatment of a suspect and ... the production of dubious confessions".[53]

Although corporations have no body to oppress nor will to overbear, the
courts have not distinguished between natural and legal persons in this
context. In civil proceedings, the entitlement of corporations to assert the
privilege has not been doubted.[54] Interestingly, in a decision of the European
Court of Justice (ECJ) in relation to Community competition law,[55] the
Court observed that the domestic law of Member States granted such a right
only to natural persons charged in criminal proceedings. No similar right
was accorded to legal persons in relation to infringement of regulations,
particularly in the commercial sphere. However, this distinction is not one
that has been acknowledged by the domestic courts or the ECtHR,[56]
although as discussed below, other Commonwealth jurisdictions have dismissed corporate claims to what is in essence a "flesh and bone
protection".[57]

It is noteworthy, that where the proceedings in question are not of a
criminal nature (according to the Convention criteria), compulsory questioning can be a proper and fair procedure. Even in *Saunders v UK*,[58] the
case before the ECtHR related only to the use of evidence from compulsory
questioning obtained in a D.T.I. inquiry in subsequent *criminal* proceedings,
and no complaint was made of the compulsory procedure in the inquiry.
The court noted[59]:

"While an administrative investigation is capable of involving the
determination of a 'criminal charge' in the light of the court's case law
concerning the autonomous meaning of this concept, it has not been
suggested in the pleadings before the court that art.6(1) was applicable
to the proceedings conducted by the Inspectors or that these proceedings themselves involved the determination of a criminal charge within
the meaning of that provision. In this respect the court recalls its

[52] *Serves v France* (1999) 28 E.H.R.R. 265, 40.
[53] *Istel v Tully* [1993] A.C. 45, 53.
[54] See *Triplex Safetyglass Co Ltd v Lancegaye Safetyglass (1934) Ltd* [1939] 2 K.B. 395; *Rio Tinto Zinc Corp v Westinghouse Electric Co* [1978] A.C. 547; *Rank Film Distribution Ltd v Video Information Exchange* [1982] A.C. 380; but c.f *Kensington International Ltd v Congo and others* [2007] EWHC 1632 (Comm). See paras 12.44 to 48 below.
[55] *Orkem SA v Commission of the European Community* Case 374/87 [1989] ECR 3283 at paras 28 & 29.
[56] And see *PVC Cartel II* [1999] 5 CMLR 303, 449.
[57] *British Columbia Securities v Branch* [1995] 2 S.C.R. 3, 39 and see paras 12.44–12.48 below.
[58] (1997) 23 E.H.R.R. 313.
[59] At para.57.

judgment in *Fayed v UK*[60] where it held that the functions performed by the Inspectors under section 432(2) of the Companies Act 1985 were essentially investigative in nature and that they did not adjudicate either in form or in substance. Their purpose was to ascertain and record facts which might subsequently be used as the basis for action by other competent authorities—prosecuting, regulatory, disciplinary or even legislative. As stated in that case, a requirement that such a preparatory investigation should be subject to the guarantees of a judicial procedure as set forth in Article 6(1) would in practice unduly hamper the effective regulation in the public interest of complex financial and commercial activities."

The subsequent use of the compulsorily obtained answers in a criminal trial is now subject at the very least to s.76 and s.78 Police & Criminal Evidence Act 1984 (PACE) and it is most unlikely that such answers would now be admissible since they offend the principle that the prosecution should prove its case without the accused having to provide, against his will, evidence of his own guilt. Moreover, where statute has abrogated the privilege against self-incrimination, the use to which answers given as a result of compulsory questioning may be put has been restricted by further legislation (see Sch.3 of the Youth Justice and Criminal Evidence Act 1999). The judgment of the majority of the Court in *Saunders v UK* outlined the principle in these terms[61]:

"The Court recalls that, although not specifically mentioned in Article 6 of the Convention, the right to silence and the right not to incriminate oneself, are generally recognised international standards which lie at the heart of the notion of a fair procedure under Article 6. Their rationale lies, inter alia, in the protection of the accused against improper compulsion by the authorities thereby contributing to the avoidance of miscarriages of justice and to the fulfilment of the aims of Article 6. The right not to incriminate oneself, in particular, pre-supposes that the prosecution in a criminal case seek to prove their case against the accused without resort to evidence obtained through methods of coercion or oppression in defiance of the will of the accused. In this sense the right is closely linked to the presumption of innocence contained in Article 6(2) of the Convention.

The right not to incriminate oneself is primarily concerned, however, with respecting the will of an accused person to remain silent. As commonly understood in the legal systems of the Contracting Parties to the Convention and elsewhere, it does not extend to the use in criminal proceedings of material which may be obtained from the accused through the use of compulsory powers but which has an existence

---

[60] (1994) 18 E.H.R.R. 393.
[61] (1997) 23 E.H.R.R. 313, paras 68–69.

independent of the will of the suspect such as, inter alia, documents acquired pursuant to a warrant, breath, blood and urine samples and bodily tissue for the purpose of DNA testing."

As a result of the decision of the ECtHR in the *Saunders* case, many statutory provisions which compel the giving of information have expressly prohibited the use by the prosecution of such material in subsequent criminal proceedings, e.g. s.447(8A) and (8B) Companies Act 1985, s.174 Financial Services and Markets Act 2000, s.433 of the Insolvency Act 1986 and s.360 of the Proceeds of Crime Act 2002. No distinction is made between corporate and natural persons. These statutory prohibitions echo the earlier Attorney General's Guidelines[62] as to the use that could be made of answers given under compulsion in an administrative or regulatory procedure, in subsequent criminal proceedings. The Guidelines advocated a general prohibition on use in a criminal trial, save to permit the prosecution to prove the breach of a statutory duty to provide answers where a person under that duty failed so to do. Examples of such limited use are to be found in *R. v Kearns*,[63] in which the Court of Appeal held that such a provision did not violate a person's right to a fair trial pursuant to art.6,[64] and in *R. v Allen*[65]; in which a taxpayer who was prosecuted for furnishing a false declaration of assets under compulsion, had not been compelled to incriminate himself about an earlier offence, but had committed the offence itself.

In *Att-Gen's Reference (No.7 of 2000)*,[66] a further gloss was put on the privilege against self-incrimination and art.6(2). That case concerned the prosecution of a bankrupt for an offence of materially contributing to or increasing the extent of his insolvency by gambling in the two years before his bankruptcy contrary to s.362(1)(a) of the Insolvency Act 1986. Pursuant to his obligations under the Insolvency Act 1986, he had been required to deliver up to the Official Receiver in his bankruptcy documents, books, papers and records of his affairs and in particular those relating to his gambling activities. Had he refused to deliver up as required he would have been in contempt of court and punishable with up to two years' imprisonment. It was that material which the Crown had wished to rely on at trial and which the Judge had ruled inadmissible under s.78 PACE 1984.[67]

---

[62] Issued in February 1998.
[63] [2002] EWCA Crim 748.
[64] See further Derivative Use, para.12.36 below.
[65] [2002] 1 A.C. 509 and endorsed by the ECtHR in *Allen v UK* [2003] Crim.L.R. 280.
[66] [2001] 2 Cr.App.R. 286.
[67] s.78 of the PACE 1984 reads:

"In any proceedings the court may refuse to allow evidence on which the prosecution proposes to rely to be given if it appears to the court that, having regard to all the circumstances including the circumstances in which the evidence was obtained, the admission of the evidence would have such an adverse effect on the fairness of the proceedings that the court ought not to admit it.".

The judge directed verdicts of not guilty to be entered. The Attorney General referred the point of law for the opinion of the Court of Appeal. The Court of Appeal,[68] reviewing the authorities, differentiated between words spoken and documents, or, as Justice La Forest stated in the Canadian case of *Thomson Newspapers Ltd v Director of Investigation & Research*,[69] "evidence the accused has been compelled to create (the compelled testimony), and the independently existing evidence he or she has been forced to assist in locating, identifying or explaining (evidence derived from compelled testimony)".

12.30   The court held that the privilege against self-incrimination is not absolute, but subject to statutory in-roads. The judge had been wrong to conclude that the subsequent use by the prosecution of compulsorily delivered documents (subject to a contempt sanction) violated the bankrupt's rights under art.6. Insofar as the decisions in *Funke v France* and *Saunders v UK* were incompatible, the Court of Appeal preferred *Saunders v UK*, in which the distinction between compelled statements of the accused and items which had a life separate from the will of the accused, was made. This does not just cover documents seized under warrant, i.e. without assistance from the accused, but all documents, however obtained[70] Thus, for example, where an officer of a corporation is duty bound to deliver documentation to a liquidator, and those documents reveal evidence of a criminal offence by the officer or the corporation, the likely position at a subsequent criminal trial is that the evidence of those documents will be admissible, subject to the exercise of judicial discretion to exclude under s.78 PACE 1984. Justice La Forest[71] found no difficulty in differentiating between documents compelled to be produced and compulsorily obtained answers from an accused:

> "The difference between evidence which the accused has been forced to create (the compelled testimony) and the independently existing evidence he or she has been forced to assist in locating, identifying or explaining (evidence derived from compelled testimony), will be readily discernible".

Indeed, it is apparent that the judge went further, dealing with derivative use from compelled testimony.[72]

In *R. v Hertfordshire County Council Ex p. Green Environment Industries Ltd*[73] ("GEI Ltd"), Lord Hoffmann dealt with the right of a local authority in an environmental protection case to require compulsory answers by a

---

[68] Rose L.J. delivered the judgment.
[69] (1990) 54 C.C.C. 417, 508 Supreme Court of Canada.
[70] In *L v UK* [2000] 2 F.L.R. 322; and see *Att-Gen's Reference (No.7 of 2000)* [2001] Cr. App.R. 286.
[71] *Thomson Newspapers Ltd v Director of Investigation & Research* (1990) 54 C.C.C. 417, Supreme Court of Canada.
[72] For "Derivative Use", see para.12.36 below.
[73] [2000] 2 W.L.R. 373 HL.

company suspected of offences relating to the unlicensed storing of waste, whilst refusing to give undertakings that it would not use those answers against the company in a subsequent prosecution. Pursuant to s.71(2) of the Environmental Protection Act 1990, the local authority served on GEI Ltd and its sole director a notice requiring them to furnish particulars of the suppliers and transporters of waste to GEI Ltd's sites, a list of employees and details of any other sites it used. The penalty for the offence of failing to comply with the notice was a penalty of a fine and/or up to two years' imprisonment. GEI Ltd refused to supply the information unless the local authority undertook not to use the answers against it in any subsequent prosecution. The local authority refused to give such an undertaking.

GEI Ltd did not comply with the notice and was prosecuted for the failure. By way of judicial review, the company challenged the validity of the notice. Confirming the decisions of the Divisional Court and the Court of Appeal, the House of Lords held that the notice was valid. The purpose of the legislation was to ensure so far as possible that the public's health was not put at risk by the waste disposal. The vast majority of the information sought by the Local Authority pursuant to the notice ought already to have been available because documentation concerning waste transfers was required to be kept pursuant to regulations. In this case GEI Ltd had not got the transfer notes available for inspection. In other words, the notice was necessary because of quite separate lapses by the company. The notice was a proportionate response to the very serious risks to the public that environmental omissions or error might create.

Of prime importance was the fact that the request did not form even a **12.31** preliminary part of any criminal proceedings. Nor was there any question of potential abuse of interrogatory powers over a person accused or charged with a crime. The company (and its director) could answer on advice and at its leisure.

Crucially, the requirement to provide information could not prejudice the fairness of a criminal trial: the company had not provided any information to be used in that trial; if it had, the trial judge would have had to consider the fairness of admitting the evidence pursuant to s.78 PACE 1984. The question for the court, on analysis, was the legality of the procedure which required GEI Ltd to give information/answers. Their Lordships relied on the European Court's decision in *Saunders v UK*, which in no way criticised this method of gleaning information for investigative or administrative purposes. The question of the fairness of criminal proceedings in which the prosecution seeks to make use of compulsorily obtained answers is treated as a quite separate matter. One of the safeguards for a defendant is the discretion of the court to exclude otherwise admissible evidence which would be unfair.

It is worthy of note that in the *GEI Ltd* case, quite separately, the company and director were prosecuted for breach of the section prohibiting the unlicensed keeping of waste on land. On arraignment they pleaded guilty—

thus no use was made, either of compulsory answers, or the failure to provide the information in the substantive criminal proceedings.

12.32   In *R. v Director of Serious Fraud Office Ex p. Smith*,[74] the Director of the Serious Fraud Office ("SFO") served a notice on S requiring him to answer questions to her, just before he was charged in criminal proceedings. The penalty for refusing to answer was a fine or imprisonment. The House of Lords held that the powers of the SFO to question did not cease on charge but allowed the Director to compel S to answer questions without being cautioned. It was not concerned with the admissibility of those answers at trial, nor whether in fact they were voluntary (which they plainly were not, on the face of it).

It had been thought after *Saunders* and the *GEI Ltd* case that the use which could be made of "compelled testimony" was limited to administrative, disciplinary, or investigative proceedings. However, the law appears to have been modified as a result a decision of the Privy Council in the Scottish case of *Brown v Stott*.[75] The discussed, B, was arrested for stealing a bottle of gin from a shop. The arresting officer formed the view that she had been drinking. He asked her how she had come to the store. She said she had travelled by car and pointed to a nearby vehicle which she said was hers. The Defendant was required, by s.172 of the Road Traffic Act 1988 to divulge who had been driving the car in which she had arrived at the scene of the crime. Her answer was an admission that she had driven there. She was subsequently breathalysed and, the test being positive, was prosecuted for "drink-driving". Had she failed to name the driver she would have committed an offence carrying a penalty of up to £1,000 and discretionary disqualification from driving. Their Lordships held that the requirement to answer a simple question, the answer to which did not necessarily in itself incriminate the person required to answer, was an entirely proportionate statutory response to the legitimate aim of road safety. It was clearly envisaged that use would be made of the required response under s.172 in subsequent criminal proceedings under Scots law. However, this did not answer the question of the fairness of the criminal proceedings which included the compulsory response: quite apart from the question of proportionality, there were safeguards in place (including the burden and standard of proof) and the need in Scots law for corroboration of the defendant's admission and:

> "All the usual protections against unreliable evidence and evidence obtained by oppression or other improper means remain in place. I think, therefore, that it is reasonable to conclude that the limited modification which section 172(2)(a) makes, in pursuance of a legitimate aim in the public interest, to the right to silence and the right not

---

[74] (1992) 95 Cr.App.R. 191.
[75] [2001] 2 W.L.R. 817.

to incriminate oneself is compatible with the right of the accused to a fair trial. I would hold that a fair balance has been achieved between these competing interests".[76]

Although the decision in this case represents an apparent departure from previous case law dealing with the privilege against self-incrimination, it could be said that, as to the point in issue, namely, the identity of the driver of a vehicle, the decision is consistent with the presumption that the keeper of a vehicle is its driver at a given moment. In Belgium and France, for example, the presumption exists in law, but can be rebutted by the keeper providing evidence to the contrary. The interest to corporations and their officers lies in the point that, even where the very purpose of a compulsorily obtained answer is to get from the potential suspect evidence necessary for a successful prosecution, the Privy Council has emphasised that it cannot be assumed that an application (under s.78 PACE 1984) to exclude such evidence will be successful. This case represents an important departure from the principle embodied in *Saunders v UK*, which had been regarded as authority for the almost inevitable exclusion of compulsorily obtained evidence.

12.33 *Saunders v UK* was followed in *IJL, GMR & AKP v UK*,[77] which concerned Mr Saunders's co-defendants in the Guinness trial. The ECtHR held that the defendants' right to a fair trial had been denied by the use of compulsorily obtained answers which they had given in the earlier DTI inquiry. The court clarified any doubt that may have been lurking about compulsory questioning itself:

"The applicants are not correct in their assertion that a legal requirement for an individual to give information demanded by an administrative body necessarily infringes Article 6 of the Convention.

The court considers that whether or not information obtained under compulsory powers by such a body violates the right to a fair hearing must be seen from the standpoint of the use made of that information at the trial".[78]

It is submitted that this approach accords both with common sense and the spirit of the Convention; it is the subsequent *use* made of the information at a criminal trial which will be of paramount interest.

The decision in *Brown v Stott* sits uneasily, it is said,[79] with two European cases. In *Heaney & McGuinness v Ireland*,[80] the ECtHR held that an offence of refusing to give an account of one's movements to the police contrary to the Offences Against the State Act 1939 which was punishable with

---

[76] per Lord Hope of Craighead at p.855.
[77] [2001] Crim.L.R. 133.
[78] At p.134.
[79] See commentary in [2001] Crim.L.R. 134.
[80] [2001] Crim.L.R. 481.

imprisonment, violated art.6(1) of the Convention. The second, *JB v Switzerland*[81] concerned the refusal of JB, in tax evasion proceedings, to submit documents requested by the District Tax Commission, although he had admitted failing to declare various taxable investments. During the period covered by the requests, the District Tax Commission informed JB of the assessed tax plus interest. There were three separate disciplinary fines for the failure to submit the documents totalling SF 3,000 in addition to payment of the assessed taxes. The tax evasion proceedings themselves were compromised by the payment of a fine of SF 20,000. The fine related to the years 1981/2–1995/6; all pending proceedings, including those concerning the disciplinary fines were cancelled and the fine already paid was deducted. The ECtHR held that there was a violation of art.6(1) which applied both because of the level of the fines and their punitive nature; the proceedings were thus characterised as criminal. The authorities were trying to compel JB to provide documents which would indicate his income and therefore his liability to tax. It could not be excluded that the documents would provide evidence which could have been used against JB in the tax evasion proceedings.

12.34   The court held that the documents, which in the earlier cases can be seen to have been treated as "independent" of the person compelled to deliver them up, were not so categorised here.

The right not to incriminate oneself in particular presupposes that the authorities seek to prove their case without resort to evidence obtained through methods of coercion or oppression in defiance of the will of the "person charged". The court found that documents providing information as to his income in order to assess his taxes did not have "an existence independent of the person concerned" unlike a tachograph, blood or urine. The logic behind this decision seems to be that, in order to deliver up the document, the requirement to produce it operates on the person asked "in defiance of his will"; why this may not equally be the case where a person is required to provide an intimate sample is not explained. However, it is always crucial to have regard to the particular piece of legislation, the wrong it is seeking to address and the penalty for disobedience.

In *JR v Dimsey; R. v Allen*,[82] *JB v Switzerland* was cited in argument by the appellant (taxpayer) who claimed that his right to a fair trial had been violated because he had been compelled by the Revenue to provide information about his tax affairs which were being investigated with a view to possible prosecution. In the event, he was charged with cheating the public revenue; he gave false information by deliberately omitting items from the Schedule of Assets he was obliged to provide. Moreover, the appellant was induced, it was argued, to produce the information on the strength of an implicit assurance that if he made full disclosure, criminal proceedings

---

[81] [2001] Crim.L.R. 748 and ECHR App. no. 31827/96.
[82] [2002] 1 A.C. 509.

would not be instituted against him ("the Hansard procedure"). The appellant had, it was alleged by the Crown, deliberately omitted from the Schedule which he eventually provided his beneficial interest in shares issued in off-shore companies. Lord Hutton referred to the judgment of the ECtHR in the *Saunders* case and then stated[83]:

" ... the present case is one which relates to the obligation of a citizen to pay taxes and to his duty not to cheat the revenue. It is self-evident that the payment of taxes, fixed by the legislature, is essential for the functioning of any democratic state. It is also self-evident that to ensure the due payment of taxes the state must have power to require its citizens to inform it of the amount of their annual income, and to have sanctions available to enforce the provision of that information..."

His Lordship then referred to ss.8(1) and 93 of the Taxes Management Act 1970, and to the notice that appears on the tax return sent to every individual taxpayer which requires the taxpayer to "Give details of all your income and capital gains ... Please remember that there are penalties for supplying false information." He then went on[84]:

"It is clearly permissible for a state to enact such provisions and there could be no substance in an argument that there is a violation of article 6(1) if the revenue prosecuted a citizen for cheating the revenue by furnishing a standard tax return containing false information. Similarly in the present case, viewed against the background that the state, for the purpose of collecting tax, is entitled to require a citizen to inform it of his income and to enforce penalties for failure to do so, the section 20(1) notice [under the 1970 Act] requiring information cannot constitute a violation of the right against self-incrimination."

Although *JB v Switzerland* was not specifically cited by Lord Hutton, he observed that the Convention point had been fully argued, so it is safe to assume that he had it in mind when delivering his opinion. In this case, as in *Brown v Stott*, use was properly made of compelled answers. Accordingly, there is no blanket prohibition on subsequent use of evidence obtained as a result of compulsory questioning. The admissibility of that evidence will depend on the circumstances giving rise to the compulsion. The correctness of this reasoning was subsequently confirmed by the ECtHR on the basis that the prosecution for making a false declaration "was not an example of forced self-incrimination about an offence which had previously been committed; it was the offence itself".[85]

There is no principle that prohibits statements obtained under compulsory powers being passed from one law enforcement authority to another,

---

[83] At p.538.
[84] At p.543.
[85] *Allen v UK* [2003] Crim.L.R. 280 ECtHR.

nor is there any obligation to provide the maker of the statement with notice that this may be done.[86]

12.35   The position is even less clear where an individual director is required to answer questions concerning corporate affairs, and the defendant in subsequent criminal proceedings is the corporation. Does the privilege against self incrimination apply also to an individual questioned in administrative or investigatory proceedings in his position as an officer of the company so as to protect the company—an entirely separate legal entity—by excluding that evidence under s.78 PACE 1984? That question was left unanswered by the House of Lords in *Rio Tinto Zinc Corp v Westinghouse Electric Co.*[87]

Lord Hoffmann described the right to silence and the privilege against self-incrimination as:

> "... prophylactic rules designed to inhibit abuse of power by investigatory authorities and to preserve the fairness of the trial by preventing the eliciting of confessions which may have doubtful probative value."[88]

And what of the delivery up of company documents? Whether these will be held to have "an existence independent of the [corporate] person concerned" remains to be seen. It is logical to suggest that they must do, but the inconstant, and at times contradictory, decisions of both the English and European courts invite speculation and uncertainty. The decision of the ECtHR in *Shannon v UK*[89] appears to have qualified earlier decisions of the Court (including *Saunders v UK*) in making the following important observations:

   i.   although generally speaking, art.6 does not apply during the investigative stage, the possibility of prosecution is sufficient to engage the protection against self-incrimination;
   ii. the possibility that compulsorily obtained material may be passed to prosecutors, in circumstances where the maker has not been eliminated as a suspect, may violate art.6;
   iii. the "*Saunders* exception" (documents produced as opposed to answers given) was not, on the facts of the case, sufficient to ensure compliance with art.6.

However, the Court did not suggest it had departed from the general reasoning in *Saunders* and this decision should not be taken as an indication that compulsory questioning within the confines of an investigation under, for example, the Companies Act 1985, nor the compelled production of documents and other data which has an existence independent of any questioning, is incompatible with art.6.

---

[86] *R. (Kent Pharmaceuticals Ltd) v Director of Serious Fraud Office* [2005] 1 W.L.R. 1302 CA (Civ).
[87] [1978] A.C. 547; see also *Sonangol v Lundquist* [1991] 2 Q.B. 310.
[88] *R. v Hertfordshire County Council Ex p. Green Environmental Industries* above at p.419C.
[89] App. No.6563/03 October 4, 2005.

In *Jalloh v Germany* [90] the Grand Chamber of the ECtHR indicated that in examining whether evidence obtained by resort to compulsory powers has "extinguished the very essence of the privilege against self-incrimination" the court will have regard to the following elements:

the nature and degree of the compulsion;
the existence of any relevant safeguards in the procedures; and
the use to which any material so obtained is put.

It is fair to say that the English courts have given a stricter meaning to and interpretation of the privilege against self-incrimination than Strasbourg [91] so it is likely that a corporate defendant in the English criminal courts will have to show very good grounds for excluding documents which were compulsorily obtained in separate administrative or investigative proceedings.

DERIVATIVE USE

The issue for the ECtHR in *Saunders v UK* [92] and *IJL, GMR & AKP v UK* [93] **12.36** was not the propriety of compelling answers in administrative proceedings, but using the answers as evidence in a criminal trial to convict the compelled person of a criminal offence.

The effect of the decision in *Saunders v UK* was to establish what might be termed a "use immunity" protecting a defendant from having evidence of answers compulsorily obtained used against him in a criminal trial. What is less clear is whether there is any protection against the use by a prosecuting authority of any *revelations* made by a person during the course of such compulsory questioning—is there a "derivative" use immunity?

As Justice La Forest observed in the *Thomson Newspapers case*, [94] on analysis, compelled testimony and evidence derived from it are two quite distinct matters:

"The compelled testimony is evidence that simply would not have existed independently of the exercise of the power to compel it, it is in this sense evidence which could have been obtained *only* from the accused.

By contrast, evidence derived from compelled testimony is, by *definition*, evidence that existed independently of the compelled testimony. Although such evidence may have gone undetected or unappreciated in the absence of compelled clues, going undetected or unappreciated is not the same thing as non-existence. The mere fact that the derivative

---

[90] (2007) 44 E.H.R.R. 32 667, 101.
[91] See e.g. *C Plc v P* [2007] EWCA Civ 493.
[92] (1997) 23 E.H.R.R. 313.
[93] [2001] Crim.L.R. 133.
[94] (1990) 54 C.C.C. 417.

evidence existed independently of the compelled testimony means that it *could* have been found by some other means, however low the probability of such discovery may have been".

There is a difference between a person being compelled to make a statement that incriminates him and being compelled to produce documents that may have the effect of incriminating him. Historically, the anxiety of the courts as to the former was that without a privilege against self-incrimination there would be nothing the courts could do "to discourage the ill-treatment of a suspect or the production of dubious confessions".[95]

12.37 Different considerations apply so far as documents are concerned. As Lord Griffiths pointed out in the context of a civil case:

> "I can for myself see no argument in favour of the privilege against producing documents the contents of which may go to show that the holder has committed a criminal offence. The contents of the document will speak for itself and there is no risk of the false confession which underlies the privilege against having to answer questions that may incriminate the speaker."[96]

At common law, evidence of facts discovered in the course of an inadmissible confession could be adduced provided the evidence could be called without reference to the confession from which it derived.[97] The admissibility of such facts is now governed by s.76(4)–(6) Police and Criminal Evidence Act 1984 which retains the common law position. Accordingly, "the fruit of the poisoned tree" is not inadmissible per se.

However, unless there exists some independent link between the defendant, the crime and the material in question, its discovery and existence might be irrelevant.[98]

12.38 Where however the revelation resulting from compelled questioning leads a prosecuting authority to material (e.g. details of a bank account) which on its face discloses evidence of an offence by that person, the material will be relevant and thus prima facie admissible because it is independent of the compelled answers.

The decision of the House of Lords in *R. v Hertfordshire County Council Ex p. Green Environment Industries Ltd*[99] did not turn on "derivative use". However, had it done so, Lord Cooke observed that a reference to the ECtHR might well have been appropriate:

> "Such issues are the subject of much and difficult case-law in various jurisdictions, and at the present stage, the jurisprudence of the European Courts may leave the matter unclear."

---

[95] per Lord Templeman, *AT & T Istel Ltd v Tully* [1993] A.C. 45, 53B.
[96] ibid. at 57.
[97] *R. v Warwickshall* (1783) 1 Leach 291; *R. v Berriman* (1854) 6 Cox 388.
[98] [1991] 2 A.C. 212 PC.
[99] [2000] 2 A.C. 412, 426.

The lack of clarity identified by Lord Cooke is exemplified in two conflicting decisions on similar facts, judgments being given within two months of each other. In March 2001 the Court of Appeal gave judgment in *Att-Gen's Reference (No.7 of 2000)*.[1]

12.39 The defendant was a bankrupt. He had completed Form B40.1, a preliminary questionnaire in his bankruptcy. The form made clear that he was required to answer the questions posed and to do so truthfully. He admitted to losing money through betting or gambling. Subsequently, the Official Receiver demanded from him the delivery up of various documents (cheque stubs, betting slips, bank statements etc) pursuant to s.291 Insolvency Act 1986. By s.291(6) of that Act, a bankrupt who fails to comply with such a demand commits an offence punishable with up to two years' imprisonment. The defendant complied with the demand. A prosecution was brought against him under s.362 of the Act[2] relying on the documents produced by the defendant.

It was successfully argued at his trial that the documents were inadmissible. The judge ruled that the documents obtained by the Official Receiver were inadmissible and that their admission would give rise to a violation of art.6. He directed a verdict of not guilty.

12.40 The point of law referred by the Attorney-General for the opinion of the Court of Appeal was whether the use by the prosecution of the documents delivered up under compulsion violated the defendant's rights under art.6 of the Convention.

Giving the opinion of the Court, Rose L.J. conducted a thorough review of the domestic and European authorities. The Court of Appeal noted that in *Saunders v UK* the European Court concluded that the privilege did not extend to the use in criminal proceedings of material which may be obtained from the accused through the use of compulsory powers but which has an existence independent of the will of the suspect.[3]

The court referred to the *Thomson Newspapers Ltd* case and adopted Justice La Forest's reasoning[4]:

> "The fact that derivative evidence exists independently of the compelled testimony means, as I have explained, that it could also have been discovered independently of any reliance on the compelled testimony. It also means that its quality as evidence does not depend on its past connection with the compelled testimony. Its relevance to the issues with which the subsequent trial is concerned, as well as the weight it is accorded by the trier of fact, are matters that can be determined

---

[1] [2001] 2 Cr.App.R. 19.
[2] s.362(1): The bankrupt is guilty of an offence if he has—(a) in the two years before petition, materially contributed to, or increased the extent of, his insolvency by gambling or by rash and hazardous speculations, or (b) in the initial period, lost any part of his property by gambling or by rash and hazardous speculations.
[3] (1997) 23 E.H.R.R. 33, para.68.
[4] At p.295.

independently of any consideration of its connection with the testimony of the accused".

Applying his reasoning, the Court of Appeal found that the documents in question would be admissible as a matter of law subject to the trial judge's discretion to exclude the evidence under s.78 PACE 1984.

In *JB v Switzerland*[5] the ECtHR came to the conclusion on a factually similar scenario, that the Swiss tax authorities had violated the art.6 rights of a taxpayer by seeking to compel from him documents relevant to his tax assessment. The documents had a dual purpose: firstly, for the calculation of his tax liability; but secondly, to provide evidence which could be used by the prosecution in tax evasion proceedings. Although not strictly a derivative use case, because the taxpayer refused to *produce* the documents (and, in consequence, was fined) it plainly has great significance on this topic. If the competent authority is not permitted to sanction an individual who refuses to comply, when required to produce documents which may incriminate him in separate criminal proceedings, it would be inconsistent to permit the authority to make use of documents in separate criminal proceedings where a compelled person *has* produced the required documents.

12.41   There was no analysis by the court in *JB v Switzerland* of the qualification to the privilege identified by the ECtHR in *Saunders v UK* as regards "material which has an existence independent of the will of the suspect" although it must follow that the court did not regard the material in question as falling into that category.

These apparently conflicting decisions were considered in *R. v Kearns*.[6] The appellant refused to answer questions asked of him by the Official Receiver ("OR") in respect of his bankruptcy and was prosecuted under s.354(3)(a) Insolvency Act 1986 for the strict liability offence of failing to account to the OR for the loss of any substantial part of his property during the relevant period. The judge rejected the argument that s.354(3)(a) violated the bankrupt's right to remain silent and his right not to incriminate himself, whereupon he pleaded guilty. He appealed.

The Court of Appeal reviewed the European and English decisions including: *Saunders v UK, JB v Switzerland, Heaney and McGuiness v Ireland, R. v Hertfordshire County Council Ex p. Green Environment Industries Ltd, Brown v Stott* and *Att-Gen's Reference (No.7 of 2000)*. One of the conclusions the court reached[7] was:

"There is a distinction between the compulsory production of documents or other material which had an existence independent of the will of the suspect or accused person and statements that he has had to make under compulsion. In the former case there was no infringement

---

[5] For the facts see para.12.33 above.
[6] [2002] EWCA Crim.748.
[7] At para.53(4).

of the right to silence and the right not to incriminate oneself. In the latter case there could be depending on the circumstances."

In the event the court decided that Mr Kearn's rights were not violated **12.42** and the appeal was dismissed.

In *Kearns*, the Court of Appeal appeared to treat *JB v Switzerland* as turning on its particular facts, and did not regard it as inconsistent with *Saunders* or the cases that followed it. Both *Saunders* and *JB v Switzerland* were considered by the Grand Chamber of the ECtHR in *Jalloh v Germany*[8] a case concerning evidence of drugs swallowed by the defendant whose existence was established by the forcible application of an emetic (via a tube inserted through his nostril) which caused him to vomit up a package containing cocaine. The Court observed that:[9]

> "the right not to incriminate oneself is primarily concerned with respecting the will of an accused person to remain silent. As commonly understood in the legal systems of the contracting parties to the Convention and elsewhere, it does not extend to the use in criminal proceedings of material which may be obtained from the accused through the use of compulsory powers but which has an existence independent of the will of the suspect, such as, inter alia, documents acquired pursuant to a warrant, breath, blood, urine, hair or voice samples and bodily tissues for the purposes of DNA testing."

The principles derived from both the earlier cases were affirmed without analysis of their apparent inconsistency.

In a case decided by the Court of Final Appeal of Hong Kong,[10] a claim to "a derivative use immunity" was rejected. Information compulsorily given to the Financial Secretary could be provided to the prosecuting authority as part of its investigation into serious fraud. The power to compel the production of documents came from s.143 of the Companies Ordinance; s.145(3A) abrogated the privilege against self-incrimination and replaced it with a limited direct use prohibition, by which questions and answers obtained in the course of an inspection could not be given as evidence in criminal proceedings against the person giving the answers. The court was satisfied that there was no free-standing common law concept of derivative use immunity, independent of the privilege against self-incrimination. The immunity provided by art.11(2)(g) of the Hong Kong Bill of Rights was only a "testimonial immunity", namely the right "not to be compelled to testify against himself or to confess guilt". The derivative use of compulsorily obtained materials could be justified if it was a proportionate response to a serious social problem; combatting corporate fraud was a major problem calling for strong regulation. A fair balance had been struck between the

---

[8] (2007) 44 E.H.R.R. 32, 667, para 102
[9] at para.102.
[10] *H.K.S.A.R. v Lee Ming Tee and Another* [2001] 1 H.K.L.R.D. 599.

general interests of the community in realising the legislative aim and the protection of the fundamental rights of the individual.

12.43   All that can be said at this point is that there is no case known to the authors which has expressly acknowledged a derivative use immunity although, of course, there are instances, like that in *Jalloh v Germany* (above) where the use of evidence obtained under lawful compulsory powers have infringed the right to a fair trial under art.6(1).[11] On the strength of the English authorities at least, it is submitted that the doctrine is unlikely to establish a firm footing. At present, neither corporations, nor their officers can demand from an inquiring authority any immunity against the subsequent use of material to be provided, before complying with a requirement to answer questions or produce documents in investigative, administrative or regulatory proceedings.

CORPORATIONS AND SELF INCRIMINATION

12.44 The privilege against self-incrimination is intrinsically human and justified on the ground of human frailty. Why then, should a corporation be entitled to rely on the privilege? The common law world is split on the question. The courts in England and New Zealand the courts have held that a corporation can invoke the privilege, but in Canada, Australia and the United States, the contrary view obtains.

The House of Lords has held that the privilege applies to a corporate entity.[12] However, there was little more than a cursory examination of the issue in that case because it was assumed, without argument, that an earlier decision of the Court of Appeal[13] represented the correct statement of law.

12.45   In fact, the earlier decision in *Triplex* appears to have been little more than an adoption of the reasoning of the Canadian court in *Webster v Solloway Mills & Co (No.2)*,[14] in which it was held that whilst a company cannot suffer the physical pains of conviction, criminal sanction can result in other grave consequences, such as the effect on a company's reputation and members.

More recently, the correctness of the position has been doubted. In *AT & T Istel v Tully*,[15] the extension of the privilege to corporations was strongly criticised. Lord Templeman said:

---

[11] For reference to the position in other common law jurisdictions, see *"The Coming of Derivative Use Immunity"* Jonathan Caplan Q.C., (2002) Journal of Criminal Law p.273.
[12] *Rio Tinto Zinc Corporation v Westinghouse Electric Corporation* [1978] A.C. 547.
[13] *Triplex Safety Glass Co Ltd v Lancegaye Safety Glass (1934) Ltd* [1939] 2 K.B. 395.
[14] [1931] 1 D.L.R. 831.
[15] [1993] A.C. 45.

"...in my opinion the privilege can only be justified on two grounds, first that it discourages the ill-treatment of a suspect and secondly that it discourages the production of dubious confessions."[16]

In Canada, at common law, a corporation could rely on the privilege,[17] but since the enactment of the Canadian Charter of Rights and Freedoms (1982) the Supreme Court has held that s.11(c) only affords the privilege to witnesses; since a corporation cannot be a witness, it cannot claim the privilege.[18] This position has since been confirmed by the Supreme Court in *British Columbia Securities v Branch*,[19] as Justices Sopinka and Iacobucci explained[20]:

"We do not believe that a right against self-incrimination can be applied to artificial entities in any meaningful way. It is the *self*-conscriptive effect of compulsion which the Charter guards against. This is a flesh and bone protection which cannot be easily extended to corporations."

In New Zealand, on the other hand, following the decision of the Court of Appeal in *New Zealand Apple and Pear Marketing Board v Master & Sons*[21] it is clear that corporations can claim privilege against self-incrimination. The extension of the principle to companies was justified on the foundation that (a) as corporations could be convicted on the basis of the acts, omissions and statements of their officers and agents, there was no policy reason why the privilege should not be so extended; and (b) as corporate status could cover small family businesses, it would be unfair to prevent such entities claiming the privilege against self-incrimination.

In Australia, the matter was carefully examined by the High Court in a **12.46** pollution case, *Environmental Protection Authority v Caltex Refining Company Ltd.*[22] In 1990, Caltex was charged with 11 offences contrary to the Clean Waters Act 1970 and the State Pollution Control Commission Act 1970. As a consequence of these charges the company was served with notices[23] requiring the production of various business documents. In the lower court, Caltex successfully resisted the production orders arguing, inter alia, that they were entitled to claim privilege against self-incrimination.

EPA, the appellant, argued that the right to silence is a human right based on the desire of the courts to guard against ill-treatment of suspects and the coercion of evidence. Since a corporation is not so vulnerable, it should not

---

[16] At 53B.
[17] See, e.g. *Webster v Solloway Mills & Co [No.2]* [1931] IDL 831.
[18] *R. v Amway Corporation* (1989) 56 D.L.R. (4th) 309.
[19] [1995] 2 S.C.R. 3.
[20] ibid. at para.39.
[21] [1986] 1 N.Z.L.R. 191.
[22] (1992–1993) 178 C.L.R. 477.
[23] Under a power conferred by s.29(2)(a) of the Clean Waters Act 1970 and also pursuant to a rule of court.

be permitted to claim the privilege. Moreover, incorporation is a benefit conferred by the state which carries with it public responsibilities including, where appropriate, an obligation to reveal company documents to regulatory authorities. The appellant also argued that the privilege against self-incrimination essentially attached to oral testimony: a person could not be compelled to provide from his own mouth evidence which incriminated him. However, documentary evidence has an existence independent of a witness. A person does not incriminate himself when ordered to produce documents, albeit that they may incriminate him.

For Caltex it was argued that the privilege against self-incrimination is an integral part of "due process", an aspect of the right to silence and the presumption of innocence, and as such enjoyed by all defendants, natural or legal. Although a corporation cannot be tortured or imprisoned, it can be adversely affected by criminal sanctions.

12.47   By a majority, the High Court held that Caltex could be compelled to comply with the production orders obtained by the EPA. Although the court still had to guard against tainted evidence, a corporation was not entitled to that protection.

The court concluded that the privilege represented a key element in maintaining a fair balance between individuals and the state. The government is required to leave the subject alone (unless good cause can be shown) and to bear the entire burden of proving any charge against him. A dominant rationale for the privilege is a desire to prevent the affront to personal dignity and privacy which self-incrimination represents. Personal dignity is a peculiarly human right. However, the fair balance between the state and other parties impacts differently as regards natural and legal persons.

Justices Mason and Toohey pointed out that corporations enjoy many advantages as a result of incorporation but also had to accept responsibilities including an obligation to comply with the regulatory regime applicable to the area of industry or commerce within which they operate. Moreover, the nature of much corporate crime is complex and, without the compelled production of company records and other documents, would be undetectable.[24] There was a clear public interest in ensuring that hazardous industrial processes were closely monitored to prevent, for example, pollution. To this end, Parliament had enacted regimes of regulation aimed at securing public health and safety etc. As Justices Mason and Toohey stated:

> "... the necessity for these provisions demonstrates beyond any doubt that the shield of privilege as applied to corporations is a formidable obstacle to the ascertainment of the true facts in the realm of corporate activities."[25]

---

[24] A very similar argument was developed by Tuckey L.J. in respect of the reverse burden imposed on the defendant by s.3 of the Health and Safety at Work Act 1974; see *Davies v Health & Safety Executive* [2002] EWCA Crim 2949 above.

[25] (1992–1993) 178 C.L.R. 477, 504.

Application of Other Convention Rights to Corporations

Breach of a Convention right will not necessarily lead to a violation of **12.48** art.6(1), unless the right is absolute. Rather, the breach will provide an entry point for the argument that there cannot be a fair trial. There are numerous European decisions which illustrate this proposition:

> "While Article 6 of the Convention guarantees the right to a fair trial, it does not lay down any rules on the admissibility of evidence as such, which is therefore primarily a matter for regulation under national law. The court cannot exclude as a matter of principle and in the abstract that unlawfully obtained evidence of the present kind may be admissible. It has only to ascertain whether Mr Schenk's trial as a whole was fair".[26]

Whereas a finding that a defendant cannot have a fair trial is an absolute answer to any charge, even where he may overwhelmingly be shown to be guilty, violations of qualified rights will be a factor for the court to evaluate in deciding, for example, whether there has been a breach of art.6(1).

Certain human rights will impact on corporations in the criminal process, particularly art.7, art.10 (freedom of expression), and the First Protocol art.1.

Article 7

> (1) "No one shall be held guilty of any criminal offence on account of **12.49** any act or omission which did not constitute a criminal offence under national or international law at the time when it was committed. Nor shall a heavier penalty be imposed than the one that was applicable at the time the criminal offence was committed".

Article 7 only applies to criminal proceedings which may result in conviction and sentence. It certainly applies to corporations.[27] It has been interpreted broadly as providing two essential rights: (i) no retroactivity, and (ii) certainty in defining an offence/penalty.

> "Article 7(1) of the Convention is not confined to prohibiting the retrospective application of the criminal law to an accused's disadvantage. It also embodies, more generally, the principle that only the law can define a crime and prescribe a penalty and the principle that the criminal law must not be extensively construed to an accused's

---

[26] *Schenk v Switzerland* (1991) 13 E.H.R.R. 242, 265 para.46.
[27] See, e.g. *X Ltd & Y v UK* 28 D.R. 77 (1982); *Sunday Times (No.1) v UK* (1979) 2 E.H.R.R. 245.

detriment for instance by analogy; it follows from this that an offence must be clearly defined in law".[28]

No Retroactivity

12.50 This prohibits the retroactive application of legislation so as to make criminal conduct which, when it occurred, was not so categorised. It applies equally to the common law. A distinction must be drawn between legislative changes in the law (which could not be retroactively applied) and explaining the correctness of a ruling by reference to case law which post-dated the instant decision.[29]

In *X Ltd & Y v UK*,[30] the boundaries of retroactivity as they affect case law were elaborated thus:

> "In the area of the criminal law it is excluded, by virtue of art.7(1) of the Convention, that any acts not previously punishable should be held by the courts to entail criminal liability, or that existing offences should be extended to cover facts which previously clearly did not constitute a criminal offence. This implies that constituent elements of an offence such as e.g. the particular form of culpability required for its completion may not be essentially changed, at least not to the detriment of the accused, by the case law of the courts. On the other hand it is not objectionable that the existing elements of the offence are clarified and adapted to new circumstances which can reasonably be brought under the original concept of the offence."

Certainty

12.51 It is a principle of the Convention that citizens must be able to understand clearly whether they are committing an offence in the sense that it is clearly defined. A person should be able to ascertain the law in order to regulate his conduct so as to avoid breaking it. The law need not be clear solely on the words of a statute, but by reference to case law as well.

In *Kokkinakis v Greece*,[31] the applicant was convicted of an offence of proselytism, he being a Jehovah's Witness and, as found by the national court, trying to convert a woman with Greek Orthodox beliefs. The ECtHR held by eight votes to one that art.7 was not breached.[32] In explaining the majority decision, the court noted:

---

[28] *Kokkinakis v Greece* (1994) 17 E.H.R.R. 397, para.52.
[29] See *X v UK* 3 D.R. 1975.
[30] (1982) 28 D.R. 77.
[31] (1994) 17 E.H.R.R. 397.
[32] Although there was a breach of art.9.

"...that the wording of many statutes is not absolutely precise. The need to avoid excessive rigidity and to keep pace with changing circumstances means that many laws are inevitably couched in terms which, to a greater or lesser extent, are vague. Criminal law provisions on proselytism fall within this category. The interpretation and application of such enactments depend on practice.

In this instance there existed a body of settled national case law. This case law, which had been published and was accessible, supplemented the letter of section 4 and was such as to enable Mr Kokkinakis to regulate his conduct in the matter."[33]

It has been a feature of applications to the ECtHR alleging breaches of other Convention rights that the particular provision be "prescribed by law". Thus, in seeking to apply, for example, art.10 (freedom of expression) in cases of contempt of court, the courts have taken into consideration the accessibility and precision of the law in question. In *Sunday Times (No.1) v UK*[34] which concerned a newspaper article written about the thalidomide settlement that was then being negotiated between the manufacturers, distillers and the families of the afflicted children, the ECtHR encapsulated the level of certainty required[35]:

"Even if the Court does have certain doubts concerning the precision with which that principle[36] was formulated at the relevant time, it considers that the applicants were able to foresee, to a degree that was reasonable in the circumstances, a risk that publication of the draft article might fall foul of the principle."

Notwithstanding art.7, a corporation (just as any individual) is taken to know the law which affects its operations and can never plead ignorance of it as a defence.

FREEDOM OF EXPRESSION

Article 10

Everyone has the right to freedom of expression. This right shall include **12.52** freedom to hold opinions and to receive and impart information and ideas without interference by public authority and regardless of frontiers. This article does not prevent States from requiring the licensing of broadcasting, television or cinema enterprises.

The exercise of these freedoms, since it carries with it duties and

---

[33] At para.40.
[34] (1981) 3 E.H.R.R. 317.
[35] 2 E.H.R.R. 245, para.52, see also para.49.
[36] "The prejudgment principle" in contempt proceedings.

responsibilities, may be subject to such formalities, conditions, restrictions or penalties as are prescribed by law and are necessary in a democratic society, in the interests of national security, territorial integrity or public safety, for the prevention of disorder or crime, for the protection of health or morals, for the protection of the reputation or rights of others, for preventing the disclosure of information received in confidence, or for maintaining the authority and impartiality of the judiciary.

In *Handyside v UK*,[37] the owner of a publishing firm (H) was prosecuted and convicted under the Obscene Publications Acts 1959 and 1964 for having in his possession obscene books for publication for gain. The particular books were freely available in other areas of Europe, Northern Ireland, the Isle of Man, the Channel Islands and Scotland, as well as other parts of England and Wales. In holding that the restriction on the right to freedom of expression was "necessary in a democratic society ... for the protection of ... morals" the ECtHR emphasised that it was:

> "not possible to find in the domestic law of the various contracting States a uniform European conception of morals. The view taken by their respective laws of the requirements of morals varies from time to time and from place to place, especially in our era which is characterised by a rapid and far-reaching evolution of opinions on the subject. By reason of their direct and continuous contact with the vital forces of their countries, State authorities are in principle in a better position than the international judge to give an opinion on the exact content of these requirements as well as on the 'necessity' of a 'restriction' or 'penalty' intended to meet them. The Court notes at this juncture that, whilst the adjective 'necessary' within the meaning of Article 10(2) is not synonymous with 'indispensable', neither has it the flexibility of such expressions as 'admissible', 'ordinary', 'useful', 'reasonable' or 'desirable'. Nevertheless it is for the national authorities to make the initial assessment of the reality of the pressing social need implied by the notion of 'necessity' in this context."

It is important to observe that: (i) the "margin of appreciation" is of particular importance in this field, and (ii) this is a swift-moving area. It is a fundamental principle of construction that the Convention is to be treated as "a living instrument which must be interpreted in the light of present day conditions".[38] Thus what is an acceptable restriction to a right at one time may well not be acceptable as time moves on. On the particular facts of *Handyside*, it is submitted it would be most unlikely that the same result would follow if the case were decided today. The ECtHR is not bound by precedent in the same way as the domestic courts.

---

[37] (1976) 1 E.H.R.R. 737.
[38] *Tyrer v UK* (1978) 2 E.H.R.R. 1 at para.31; *Airey v Ireland* (1979–80) 2 E.H.R.R. 305, para.26.

Article 10 has also been invoked in challenging contempt of court proceedings which media corporations occasionally face. The right to report facts, and the protection of journalists' sources are two areas affected by the Convention. A balancing of rights and duties of the various interests of the parties and general good is at the heart of these decisions.

In *Goodwin v UK*[39] a journalist refused to disclose the identity of the person who had provided him with confidential financial information about a company, Tetra Ltd. The journalist telephoned Tetra to check the information. Tetra obtained an injunction stating that if the confidential corporate plan (of which there were only eight copies all marked "Strictly Confidential") were to be made public, the company would face a crisis of confidence which could lead to liquidation and many consequent redundancies for its workforce. The plan was almost certainly stolen. The court ordered Goodwin to disclose his source in order to help the company discover who had leaked the information and to prevent further leaks. It was held that there was a continuing threat to Tetra. When Goodwin refused to disclose his source, he was held in contempt of court and fined £5,000. He appealed to ECtHR which concluded that in considering the proportionality of the order to disclose the source, the legitimate aims of Tetra Ltd in (1) limiting dissemination of the material (already achieved by way of injunction), and (2) discovering who the inside source was in order to take action against him, were outweighed by the public interest in protecting the journalist's source in a democratic society. The ECtHR held that the order of disclosure of a source would only be lawful where there was "an overriding requirement in the public interest to disclose".[40] In other words, the general rule was *against* disclosure. The applicant's right to freedom of expression under art.10 had been breached, because, the ECtHR held, the disclosure was not "necessary in a democratic society".

12.53 This approach was considered by the House of Lords in the case of *Ashworth Hospital Authority v MGN Ltd.*[41] Lord Phillips put the test for the domestic court thus:

> "The 'necessary' involves a single exercise in which the court considers not merely whether, on the facts of the particular case, disclosure of the source is necessary to achieve the legitimate aim, but more significantly, where the achievement of the legitimate aim on the facts of the case is so important that it overrides the public interest in protecting journalistic sources in order to ensure free communication of information to and through the press".[42]

---

[39] 22 E.H.R.R. 123.
[40] ibid. at para.39.
[41] [2001] 1 W.L.R. 515.
[42] At para.90.

In *Ashworth Hospital Authority v MGN Ltd*,[43] an article was published in the defendant's newspaper concerning medical details of Ian Brady, a convicted murderer, who was on hunger strike. The information had been supplied to MGN Ltd through an intermediary who had been paid by them. It was probable that the information had been supplied by an employee of Ashworth Hospital Authority in breach of his duty of confidentiality under his contract of employment. In a civil action, MGN Ltd were ordered to serve a witness statement on the authority explaining how they had came to have the information and identifying any person involved. MGN Ltd appealed against the order for disclosure of the journalist's sources under the Contempt of Court Act 1981 relying on art.10. The House of Lords held, dismissing the appeal, that in the particular case disclosure of the source was a necessary and proportionate response because of the essential need for the integrity and confidentiality of the Authority's records.

Similarly, in *Financial Times Ltd v Interbrew SA*,[44] the English courts ordered disclosure of a journalist's source, where a brewing company's confidential report about a possible takeover bid of another brewer came into the hands of various newspapers. The report was allegedly falsified. The newspapers published articles based on the report and the share value of both brewing companies was significantly affected. The Court of Appeal held that the following elements were important:

1. What is "necessary" within section 10 must also be "necessary in a democratic society" within article 10(2) which is one in which press sources are properly protected;
2. Any invasion of that protection must meet a pressing social need, not merely an individual one;
3. There must be no less invasive alternative available;
4. There is a direct logical relationship between the disclosure of the source and the interests of justice;
5. The disclosure is a limitation on the right to freedom of expression, not a negation of it;
6. Whether disclosure is a proportionate response is a "value judgment ... a synthesis of what has been established as legally relevant in fact and in law".[45]

12.54 The Court of Appeal held that in the particular circumstances one of the relevant factors was the purpose (but *not* the motive) of the source. If it was a maleficent purpose "calculated to do harm", the public interest in protecting the source was not as great, and was "not sufficient to withstand the countervailing public interest in letting Interbrew seek justice in the courts

---

[43] [2002] 1 W.L.R. 2033.
[44] [2002] EWCA Civ 274.
[45] per Sedley L.J. at para.53.

against the source".[46] It is at least arguable that the source's purpose is generally irrelevant to the balancing exercise. Whether a person is high-minded or not will not necessarily affect the public interest in the publication of the material he provides; the confidentiality of a source is, after all, of general importance to the public in the same way as the anonymity of an informant. The public interest in a source's protection is a matter of principle and should not usually be affected by the particular details of the case.

Article 10 is self-evidently aimed at protecting the free flow of information which is crucial to a democratic society. The English courts have considered the criteria set out in the European case law and in both *Interbrew* and *Ashworth* have found that the balance of what is necessary in a democratic society has come down in favour of disclosure of the source, limiting the art.10 right accordingly.

FIRST PROTOCOL ARTICLE 1

The First Protocol was adopted by the Member States of Europe in March **12.55** 1952 and ratified by the United Kingdom in November 1952. Section 1 of the Human Rights Act 1998 defines Convention rights as including Articles 1–3 of the First Protocol.

Article 1: Protection of Property:

> "Every natural or legal person is entitled to the peaceful enjoyment of his possessions. No one shall be deprived of his possessions except in the public interest and subject to the conditions provided for by law and by the general principles of international law. The preceding provisions shall not, however, in any way impair the right of a State to enforce such laws as it deems necessary to control the use of property in accordance with the general interest or to secure the payment of taxes or other contributions or penalties."

This entitlement to non-interference with property specifically applies to corporations ("every natural or *legal* person ..."). It is not an absolute right, but limited by, amongst other things, the public interest. It comprises three distinct but connected rules[47]:

(a)   an entitlement to the peaceful enjoyment of property;
(b)   no deprivation of that save lawfully and in the public interest;
(c)   a Contracting State is entitled to control the use of property in particular circumstances, broadly for the general interest or to uphold or give effect to fiscal legislation.

Any interference must be proportionate:

---

[46] At para.55.
[47] *Air Canada v UK* (1995) 20 E.H.R.R. 150.

"There must be a reasonable relationship of proportionality between the means employed and the aim sought to be realised by any measure depriving a person of his possessions."[48]

In *Air Canada v UK* it was held that temporary forfeiture (pending payment of a £50,000 fine) of the applicants' aeroplane was a "control of the use of property", but was proportionate as a response to widespread drug trafficking through the applicants' airline which occurred despite warnings given to the airline to improve security.[49] In *Allgemaine Gold-Und Silberscheideanstalt v UK*,[50] prohibition on importation was "a control of the use of property". It was compatible with art.1 of the First Protocol because the measure taken was a proportionate response to the legitimate aim sought. It was held, moreover, that where there was an administrative procedure to determine the issue of return of forfeited goods, the proceedings were sufficient to protect an innocent owner and to comply with the First Protocol, provided the owner of the property had a fair opportunity to be heard. The forfeiture proceedings did not constitute a criminal charge. Such proceedings were subject to judicial review which was held to be an adequate safeguard for the owner.

Damage to reputation which can be quantified in economic terms can be an interference with the enjoyment of property. In order for this to be established, the claim must be substantiated by evidence.[51]

---

[48] *Holy Monasteries v Greece* (1995) 20 E.H.R.R. 1, para.4.
[49] See above at 12.8: The Definition of a Criminal Charge.
[50] (1986) 9 E.H.R.R. 1.
[51] *Goodman International and Goodman v Ireland* (1993) 16 E.H.R.R. C.D. 27 in which the Commission found the allegation of a violation of Protocol 1 art.1 "manifestly ill-founded", for lack of evidence.

Part V

SPECIFIC OFFENCES

CHAPTER 13

CORPORATE MANSLAUGHTER

More than any other aspect of corporate criminal liability, it has been the **13.1** apparent inability of the criminal law adequately to punish those perceived as being responsible for corporate deaths that has provoked the most controversy. After discussing how to amend the law (if at all) for more than a decade, Parliament finally responded to the deficiencies of the common law by enacting the Corporate Manslaughter and Corporate Homicide Act 2007 and abolishing the offence of gross negligence manslaughter so far as it applies to corporations. The Act received Royal assent on July 26, 2007 and came into force on April 6, 2008, creating a new offence with the title "corporate manslaughter" ("corporate homicide" in Scotland).

The Act had a lengthy gestation with numerous complications, but its birth has been welcomed. Whether it will achieve the objectives and provide a more effective means of accountability for very serious management failings causing death remains to be seen. In particular, there is concern that the new offence too closely follows the contours of gross negligence manslaughter, replicating the very shortcomings that the new legislation was intended to overcome. The Act needs to be considered in the context of the controversies that inspired its conception and for this reason it is useful to consider first the development of common law offence.

HISTORICAL POSITION

It had not been considered possible to indict a corporation for the common **13.2** law offence of manslaughter. Judicial objections were procedural (e.g. requiring the presence in court of a defendant), historical (e.g. a corporation could not commit a felony[1]) and pragmatic—where the only sentence was corporal, such as death or imprisonment, a corporation could not be

---

[1] *R. v Cory Brothers & Co Ltd* [1927] 1 K.B. 810.

indicted because it was not susceptible to the sentence that could be passed.[2]

There has actually been no legal or procedural impediment to the prosecution of a corporation for manslaughter since 1925,[3] but as late as 1990 it was argued (in the prosecution that followed the Herald of Free Enterprise ferry disaster) that since the definition of homicide was "the killing of one human being by another human being" the offence could not be committed by a corporation.[4] This argument failed; the trial judge, Turner J., held that in principle a corporation could be indicted for and convicted of manslaughter. However, the judge ruled that there was no case to answer after the close of the prosecution case.

Corporations responsible for work-related deaths have, of course, been successfully prosecuted under various statutory provisions such as the Health and Safety at Work Act 1974, the Road Traffic Act 1988 and the Merchant Shipping Act 1988.[5] Sentences have in some notable cases been very substantial,[6] nevertheless the perception is that regulatory offences do not sufficiently reflect the public concern about work-related death.

13.3 Until the ruling by Turner J., there was no reported case in which it had been expressly held that a corporation could be convicted of the common law offence of manslaughter. No doubt the lack of precedent discouraged prosecutions, but practical considerations also played a significant part. The Health and Safety Executive ("HSE") has a statutory duty to investigate any work-related death. The HSE openly adopts a compliance strategy; it favours advising and assisting companies to ensure good health and safety practice. Even in cases of work-related death, the HSE only brings a prosecution in approximately 20 per cent of cases.[7] Between 1996 and 2006, 2721 workers and 4312 members of the public were killed in work-related or public incidents in the United Kingdom.[8] The HSE claims that the majority of workplace deaths are preventable and considers that the deterrent effect of criminal prosecutions can play an important part in reducing risks to health and safety arising from work activity. This encouragement is diluted

---

[2] per Stable J, *R. v ICR Haulage Ltd* [1944] 1 K.B. 551, 553.

[3] s.33(3) Criminal Justice Act 1925.

[4] *R. v P&O European Ferries (Dover) Ltd* (1991) 93 Cr.App.R. 72, 84.

[5] See, e.g. *R. v Robert Millar (Contractors) Ltd & Robert Millar* [1970] 2 Q.B. 233 where the company was charged with counselling and procuring the offence of causing death by dangerous driving committed by its driver. The Court of Appeal held that the corporation and the managing director, having instructed their employee to drive a lorry knowing that it had a dangerously defective tyre were both guilty of counselling and procuring the dangerous driving.

[6] For example, in August 2005 Transco was fined £15 million in the High Court of Justiciary for breaching health and safety laws, leading to an explosion that killed a family of four in Glasgow, and in March 2007, Network Rail was fined £4 million for offences arising out of the Paddington rail disaster.

[7] See D.Bergman, *The Case for Corporate Responsibility*, (Disaster Action, 2000).

[8] Although the latter figure includes acts of suicide and trespass on the railway system which make up approximately two thirds of the overall figure HSE:Statistics of fatal injuries.

if in the most serious cases there is no conviction or the sentence passed is very low.[9]

The HSE had no legal authority to bring a prosecution for the common law offence of manslaughter and before 1998 the HSE and CPS did not even coordinate their investigations.[10] After an inquiry by the HSE into a work-related death, the file could be handed over to the CPS for it to consider whether to bring a prosecution but between 1992 and 1998 that only occurred in 59 cases. Of those, the CPS brought 18 prosecutions for manslaughter, almost all against individual defendants.[11]

The greatest obstacles to prosecuting a corporation for manslaughter were legal and evidential. As discussed below, the legal foundation of corporate liability was the doctrine of identification. In all but cases involving very small companies, the evidential difficulty of proving gross negligence on the part of an individual who could be identified with the corporation proved insurmountable. Sufficient fault on the part of a person who can be identified with a corporation, and which would fix it with criminal responsibility for a death, is by no means the same as serious fault on the part of a corporation.

THE HERALD OF FREE ENTERPRISE PROSECUTION

On March 6, 1987 the Herald of Free Enterprise, a roll-on/roll-off ferry, set **13.4** sail from Zeebrugge bound for Dover with her bow doors open and trimmed by the head, i.e. with her nose down. Within a few minutes of leaving port, millions of gallons of sea water entered the vehicle deck through the open doors, causing the vessel to list and then capsize just outside Zeebrugge harbour with the loss of nearly 200 lives.

A formal investigation was held under s.55 of the Merchant Shipping Act 1970; in his report Sheen J. concluded:

> "There appears to have been a lack of thought about the way in which the Herald ought to have been organised for the Dover/Zeebrugge run. All concerned in management, from the members of the Board of Directors down to the junior superintendents, were guilty of fault in that all must be regarded as sharing responsibility for the failure of management. From top to bottom the body corporate was infected with the disease of sloppiness."

Shutting the doors was the responsibility of the assistant bosun who was asleep in his bunk when the Herald set sail. Checking that the doors were shut was the responsibility of the Chief Officer; he failed to check. From the

---

[9] see Ch.10: Sentencing.
[10] *Work-Related Deaths; a Protocol for Liaison* (2003); *https://www.hse.gov.uk.*
[11] Figures from the Centre for Corporate Accountability 1999.

bridge it was not possible for the Master to see whether the bow doors were open or shut. In the event, Sheen J. found that the capsize of the "Herald of Free Enterprise" was caused or contributed to by the fault of three employees of low rank and the company "at all levels from the Board of Directors through the managers of the Marine Department down to the junior superintendents".

There was an inquest. The coroner decided that even if a corporation could be convicted of manslaughter in principle:

> "the acts of the company would have to be those of an individual (and I should have said an individual director) who was himself guilty of unlawful killing. I made it clear there was no *prima facie* evidence that any of the three relevant directors had done any act or been guilty of any omission which could be said to be a direct or substantial cause of the capsize and that therefore the question of corporate manslaughter did not in any event arise."

The coroner also rejected the principle of aggregation as a basis for liability, i.e. the cumulative effect of a number of different negligent acts by different persons, so as to amount, in total, to gross negligence.

13.5   In the judicial review of the coroner's ruling,[12] Bingham L.J. concluded that a company could be convicted of the common law offence of manslaughter, the basis of such liability being the doctrine of identification: "the *mens rea* and the *actus reus* of manslaughter should be established not against those who acted for or in the name of the company but against those who were to be identified as the embodiment of the company itself".

Rejecting the argument that liability could be established by aggregating fault Bingham L.J. said: "A case against a personal defendant cannot be fortified by evidence against another defendant. The case against a corporation can only be made by evidence properly addressed to showing guilt on the part of the corporation as such".

Despite the discouraging conclusions of the coroner and Bingham L.J., the decision was taken to prosecute the owner of the Herald of Free Enterprise, (by that time P&O European Ferries (Dover) Ltd) and various individuals, including the Master of the ship. Before a jury was sworn, the company argued that, as a matter of law, it could not be guilty of the offence of manslaughter.[13] The judge, Turner J., held that: (i) a manslaughter charge could lie against a corporation, and (ii) where a person who is the embodiment of a corporation and is acting for the purposes of the corporation causes the death (by act or omission), the corporation as well as that person may also be found guilty of manslaughter.

13.6   However, at the close of the prosecution case the judge acceded to submissions made on behalf of the corporation and directors that there was

---

[12] *R. v HM Coroner for East Kent Ex p. Spooner* (1989) 88 Cr.App.R. 10.
[13] *R. v P&O European Ferries (Dover) Ltd* (1991) 93 Cr.App.R. 72 (C.C.C.).

insufficient evidence against them and so no case to answer and directed their acquittal. The prosecution then offered no evidence against the individual officers and crew of the vessel.

GROSS NEGLIGENCE MANSLAUGHTER

At the time of the Herald of Free Enterprise prosecution, liability for **13.7** involuntary manslaughter was founded on the concept of recklessness,[14] but in the case of *R. v Adomako*,[15] it was held by the House of Lords that involuntary manslaughter could be proved by gross negligence. Lord Mackay stated[16]:

> "The ordinary principles of the law of negligence apply to ascertain whether or not the defendant has been in breach of a duty of care towards the victim who has died. If such breach of duty is established the next question is whether that breach of duty caused the death of the victim. If so, the jury must go on to consider whether that breach of duty should be characterised as gross negligence and therefore a crime. This will depend on the seriousness of the breach of duty committed by the defendant in all the circumstances in which the defendant was placed when it occurred."

Corporate liability required proof of gross breach of the duty of care by an individual acting as the directing or controlling mind of the corporation. However, the officers of a company do not owe a duty of care to any third party simply by reason of their office.[17] Equally unless an officer assumes a duty in respect of health and safety duties, he does not owe any general duty of care in respect of the company's statutory responsibilities.[18] A duty of care may arise where an officer has expressly procured or authorised the particular act resulting in death, but some nexus between the death and the individual acting as the directing or controlling mind of the corporation is necessary.

In the case of a very small company of the "one-man band" type, there may be no difficulty in proving that there was gross negligence by an individual attributable to the corporation because of his control over it. However, in a typical corporation, responsibility for its day-to-day operation is likely to be highly devolved; proving sufficiently proximate fault on the part of a director, or other such person, so as to be identified with the corporation, will normally be impossible. The more distant the board of directors and other senior management with sufficient authority to be

---

[14] As defined in the cases of *R. v Caldwell* [1982] A.C. 341 and *R. v Lawrence* [1982] A.C. 510.
[15] (1994) 99 Cr.App.R. 362; the case concerned a grossly incompetent anaesthetist.
[16] At p.369.
[17] *Williams and another v Natural Life Health Foods Ltd and another* [1998] 2 All E.R. 577.
[18] *Huckerby v Elliot* [1970] 1 All E.R. 189 DC; *R. v P and another* [2007] All E.R. (D) 173 (Jul).

identified with the corporation, the less likely it is that any such person will have played any part whatsoever in events leading up to an unlawful homicide. Unless such an individual has himself been grossly negligent with the result that death was caused, the corporation cannot be guilty. This is born out by the statistics. Since 1992 there have been some 34 prosecutions for gross negligence manslaughter against corporate defendants, but only seven convictions, each which has been in a case involving a very small company.[19]

The first of these was mounted following the Lyme Bay canoeing tragedy in which four school children died in March 1993.[20] The defendant, OLL Ltd, was essentially a one-man band, run by its managing director, K. There was no difficulty in fixing the corporation with K's criminality as he was the embodiment of the company; once the prosecution had proved the ingredients of manslaughter against him, as he was the directing or controlling mind of the corporation, it was identified with him. Ognall J., sentencing K to three years' imprisonment, commented that he was more interested "in sales than in safety". The company was fined a mere £60,000.

ATTORNEY-GENERAL'S REFERENCE (NO.2 OF 1999)

13.8 The approach of Turner J. at first instance in the Herald of Free Enterprise case was later approved by the Court of Appeal following the unsuccessful prosecution of Great Western Trains ("GWT") for manslaughter.

On September 19, 1997 a high speed passenger train (HST) operated by GWT collided with a freight train as it neared the end of its journey to London from Swansea. Seven passengers were killed, 151 people were injured, 36 seriously. The train had a very experienced driver, but no second driver. It was fitted with two safety devices each of which was designed to prevent the HST passing through a red signal without stopping. Each device operated independently of the other and of the driver. One (the Automatic Warning System) had been deliberately switched off the night before the crash because it was not operating properly and engineers had been unable to locate the fault. The other (the Automatic Train Protection) was also switched off. Had either device been switched on, it would have operated to stop the train as each was designed to do. The driver knew that neither was operating.

Travelling at an average speed of 116mph, the HST passed two signals,

---

[19] *Kite & OLL Ltd, Independent*, December 9, 1994, *R. v Jackson Transport (Ossett) Ltd*, Health & Safety At Work November 1996 at p.4; English Bros Ltd (2001); Dennis Clothier & Sons (2002); Telgard Hardwood (UK) Ltd (2003); Nationwide Heating services Ltd (2004); Keymark Services Ltd (2004). See *http://www.corporateaccountability.org/manslaughter/cases/convictions.htm*.

[20] ibid.

and collided with the freight train (which was being properly driven and in accordance with the signals which were correctly operating).

The prosecution alleged that the causes of the collision were: (1) the **13.9** driver's failure to observe or heed the two signals which warned of the red danger signal ahead; and (2) GWT's manner of operating the HST by causing or permitting the HST to be in service with the safety systems switched off and with just one man in the cab. The prosecution asserted that GWT owed a duty of care for the safety of its passengers, in respect of which it was in grossly negligent breach.

The defence submission, accepted by the trial judge, Scott Baker J., was that the only method of fixing criminal liability on GWT was to apply the doctrine of identification, in other words by proving the case of gross negligence against one or more specific individuals who could be identified with or as the corporation itself.

The questions posed by the Attorney-General for the Court of Appeal[21] were:

1. Can a defendant be properly convicted of manslaughter by gross negligence in the absence of evidence as to that defendant's state of mind?
2. Can a non-human defendant be convicted of the crime of manslaughter by gross negligence in the absence of evidence establishing the guilty of an identified human individual for the same crime?

The court answered the first question "Yes"—although such evidence may be relevant when assessing whether negligence was gross and therefore criminal, evidence of the state of mind of a defendant was not a pre-requisite to a conviction for gross negligence manslaughter.

The court answered the second question "No". The authorities made the **13.10** law plain:

"Unless an identified individual's conduct, characterisable as gross criminal negligence, can be attributed to the company, the company is not, in the present state of the common law, liable for manslaughter".[22]

The Court of Appeal expressly referred to the conclusions of the Law Commission Report No.237 "Legislating the Criminal Code Involuntary Manslaughter" in which the Commission concluded that a corporation's liability for manslaughter was solely based upon the doctrine of identification. Recommending legislation in order to clarify and indeed extend the law of manslaughter, the Commission produced a draft Bill by which it

[21] *Att-Gen's Reference (No.2 of 1999)* [2000] 2 Cr.App.R. 207.
[22] As above.

proposed to confer corporate liability for death based on management failure without invoking the principle of identification.

REFORM OF "CORPORATE MANSLAUGHTER"

13.11 The Law Commission Report No.237 "Legislating the Criminal Code Involuntary Manslaughter" was published in 1996; it followed an earlier Report on the Criminal Code and a consultation paper—Criminal Law: Involuntary Manslaughter (1994) Consultation Paper No.135. The Commission consulted a wide range of interested organisations and individuals, as well as receiving advice from academics and practitioners. It concluded that it was necessary to devise a specific corporate offence broadly corresponding to a proposed individual offence of killing by gross carelessness. The offence would be committed only where the corporation's conduct in causing death fell *far below* what could reasonably be expected, but the corporate offence would *not* require that the risk be obvious, nor that the defendant be capable of appreciating the risk. A death would be regarded as having been caused by the conduct of a corporation if it was caused by a failure in the way in which the corporation's activities were managed or organised, to ensure the health and safety of persons employed in or affected by those activities.[23] The concept of "management failure" would obviate the need to prove the requisite fault of an individual identified as the directing mind of the company. Management failure which was a cause of death, would be sufficient for corporate liability to be established even if the immediate cause was the act or omission of an individual.[24]

The Law Commission proposed that the offence would be capable of commission by any corporation, however and wherever incorporated, other than a corporation sole,[25] but it should not be capable of commission by an individual, even as a secondary party.[26]

The Government's response to the Law Commission's Report No.237 was generally positive,[27] but hardly prompt.[28] In 2000 it produced a Consultation Paper[29] endorsing the proposal for a new offence. There was then yet more delay until in March 2005, the Government published a

---

[23] Law Commission Report No.237 para.8.35.

[24] para.8.39.

[25] para.8.53.

[26] para.8.58.

[27] There had been a commitment in the Labour Party manifesto in 1997 to reform the law of corporate manslaughter.

[28] In Great Western Trains (1999) Scott Baker J. observed:

> "There is little purpose in the Law Commission making recommendations if they are to be allowed to lie for years on the shelf gathering dust ... It has remained notoriously difficult for the Crown to establish manslaughter against a corporation".

[29] Home Office, *Reforming the Law on Involuntary Manslaughter: the Government's Proposals* (2000).

substantially revised draft Corporate Manslaughter Bill.[30] Significantly, the Bill abandoned the concept of "management failure". The new offence would only be committed by an organisation if the way in which its activities were managed or organised caused a death and amounted to a gross breach of duty of care owed to the deceased in negligence; how the activities were managed or organised by senior management must be a substantial element of the gross breach. The problems inherent in the common law offence had crept back into the draft Bill. The Joint Committee of the Home Affairs and Work and Pensions Committees of the House of Commons recommended in its report on the Bill a return to the Law Commission's original proposals[31] following which a draft Bill was introduced in the House of Commons on July 20, 2006.[32] After a considerable amount of wrangling between the Commons and the Lords, the new Act finally received Royal Assent on July 26, 2007 and came into force on April 6, 2008.[33]

THE CORPORATE MANSLAUGHTER AND CORPORATE HOMICIDE ACT 2007

By s.1, the Act creates a new offence called corporate manslaughter[34] **13.12** (corporate homicide in Scotland[35]) and abolishes the common law offence of manslaughter by gross negligence in respect of its application to corporations.[36] Rather than being contingent on the guilt of one or more *individuals*, liability for the new offence depends on a finding of gross negligence in the way in which the activities of the organisation are run. In summary, the offence is committed where an organisation owes a duty to take reasonable care for a person's safety and the way in which activities of the organisation have been managed or organised amounts to a gross breach of that duty and causes the person's death. How the activities were managed or organised by senior management must be a substantial element of the gross breach.[37] The new offence is quite different from the existing statutory offence under, e.g.

---

[30] Home Office, *Corporate Manslaughter: the Government's Draft Bill for Reform*, Cm6497 (2005).
[31] *First Joint Report from the Home Affairs and Work and Pensions Committees* Session 2005–06. (HC 540 i–iii).
[32] *Corporate Manslaughter and Homicide Bill* (Bill 220).
[33] The Ministry of Justice has published "A Guide to the Corporate Manslaughter and Corporate Homicide Act 2007".
[34] s.1(5)(a).
[35] s.1(5)(b).
[36] s.20 (the abolition common law offence of manslaughter by gross negligence in respect of its application to corporations) does not affect liability, investigation, legal proceedings or penalty for or in respect of an offence committed wholly or partly before April 6, 2008: s.27(4). An offence is committed wholly or partly before the commencement of s.20 if any of the conduct or events alleged to constitute the offence occurred before that commencement (s.27(5)).
[37] Explanatory Notes to Corporate Manslaughter And Corporate Homicide Act 2007.

the Health and Safety at Work Act. As the title demonstrates, the harmful result (death) is the fundamental element of the offence. Instead of a failure to take all reasonable precautions and practicable measures being sufficient for conviction, under the new Act, the prosecution must prove gross breach of a relevant duty of care, defined as conduct that falls far below what can reasonably be expected of the organisation in the circumstances. The burden remains on the prosecution throughout; there is no "due diligence" defence to be proved by the defendant.

Sections 1(1) and (3) provide:

(1) An organisation to which this section applies is guilty of an offence if the way in which its activities are managed or organised—

(a) causes a person's death, and

(b) amounts to a gross breach of a relevant duty of care owed by the organisation to the deceased.

(3) An organisation is guilty of an offence under this section only if the way in which its activities are managed or organised by its senior management is a substantial element in the breach referred to in subs.(1).

The offence will be committed by a corporation[38] (or other organisation covered by the Act[39]) where:

i. it owed the deceased a duty of care and

ii. the way in which its activities were managed or organised:

• caused his death;

• amounts to a gross breach of a relevant duty of care; and

iii. the way in which its activities were managed or organised by its senior management was a substantial element in the breach.

Jurisdiction

13.13 A prosecution for the new offence (which may be tried only on indictment[40]) requires the consent of the Director of Public Prosecutions[41]. By s.28, the Act extends to England and Wales, Scotland and Northern Ireland; there is jurisdiction to prosecute if the harm resulting in death occurs in the United Kingdom or:

---

[38] A corporation is an "organisation" for the purposes of the Act: s.1(2)(a). A "corporation" does not include a corporation sole, but includes any body corporate wherever incorporated (s.25).

[39] see s.1(2) and Sch.1.

[40] s.1(6).

[41] s.17.

(a)   within the seaward limits of the territorial sea adjacent to the United Kingdom;

(b)   on a ship registered under Part 2 of the Merchant Shipping Act 1995 (c.21);

(c)   on a British-controlled aircraft as defined in section 92 of the Civil Aviation Act 1982 (c.16);

(d)   on a British-controlled hovercraft within the meaning of that section as applied in relation to hovercraft by virtue of provision made under the Hovercraft Act 1968 (c.59);

(e)   in any place to which an Order in Council under section 10(1) of the Petroleum Act 1998 (c.17) applies (criminal jurisdiction in relation to offshore activities).

In most cases, the harm and the fatal consequence will coincide geographically, but even if the death actually occurs abroad, the courts will still have jurisdiction provided the *harm* that caused it occurred in the United Kingdom (or as set out above). Moreover, provided the harm that caused the death occurred in the United Kingdom, it is irrelevant where the organisation or its senior management is located. The new offence applies to all companies and other corporate bodies operating in the United Kingdom, wherever incorporated. However, the parent company of a subsidiary cannot be convicted of the new offence where it was the subsidiary that caused the death in breach of a relevant duty of care.

Relevant Duty of Care

The offence can only be committed if the organisation owed the deceased *a* **13.14** *relevant duty* of care. Section 2 provides categories of "relevant duty of care" under the law of negligence:

(a)   a duty owed to its employees or to other persons working for the organisation or performing services for it;

(b)   a duty owed as occupier of premises;

(c)   a duty owed in connection with—

   (i)   the supply by the organisation of goods or services (whether for consideration or not),

   (ii)   the carrying on by the organisation of any construction or maintenance operations,

   (iii)   the carrying on by the organisation of any other activity on a commercial basis, or

   (iv)   the use or keeping by the organisation of any plant, vehicle or other thing;

   . . .

It is for the prosecution to prove that the particular organisation owed a duty of care to the deceased; this is a question of law for the judge "who must make any findings of fact necessary to decide that question" [s.2(5)].[42] This reflects the heavily legal nature of the tests relating to the existence of a duty of care in the law of negligence and spares a jury from having to wrestle with the three stage test set out by Lord Bridge in *Caparo Industries Plc v Dickman*[43] which involves: forseeability of damage, a relationship of "proximity" and a situation such that it is "fair, just and reasonable" for the law to impose a duty of care.[44] For that sensible approach, it may be that thanks are due to Lord Justice Judge, President of the Queen's Bench Division, who gave evidence before the Joint Committee of the Home Affairs and Work and Pensions Committees. As to who should decide whether the particular organisation owed a duty of care he said:

> "The issue [the duty of care in the law of negligence] has gone to the House of Lords for decision very many times in the past ten years. I was very troubled about the possible consequences. However, if you make this a question of law for the judge, depending on whatever facts he has to find ... I do not think it presents a problem."

The question of whether a duty of care is owed to the deceased may be controversial in respect of some organisations, but so far as corporations are concerned, the existence of a duty of care will usually involve settled principles of law.[45]

A corporation may owe a duty of care to the deceased in any of four broad categories: employment; occupying premises; supplying goods or services, or other commercial activity. The aim is to include the sort of activities typically pursued by companies and other corporate bodies. By s.2(6), in determining whether a duty of care exists, the judge must disregard:

> (a) any rule of the common law that has the effect of preventing a duty of care from being owed by one person to another by reason

---

[42] For example, if considering whether a corporation owes a duty of care as employer, the judge will need to decide whether the victim was an employee of the corporation.

[43] [1990] 1 All E.R. 568 HL.

[44] Lord Bridge stated:

> "...in addition to the forseeability of damage, necessary ingredients in any situation giving rise to a duty of care are that there should exist between the party owing the duty and the party to whom it is owed a relationship characterised by the law as one of 'proximity' or 'neighbourhood' and that the situation should be one in which the court considers it fair, just and reasonable that the law should impose a duty of a given scope upon the one party for the benefit of the other." [1990] 1 All E.R. 568 HL at 574.

[45] Moreover, where the harm sustained is physical, Lord Bridge's third stage is not engaged: *Alcock v Chief Constable of South Yorkshire* [1992] 1 A.C. 310, 396.

of the fact that they are jointly engaged in unlawful conduct (*ex turpi causa*)[46];

(b) any such rule that has the effect of preventing a duty of care from being owed to a person by reason of his acceptance of a risk of harm. (*volenti non fit injuria*)

Employers: Section 2(1)(a)

The duty of care owed by an employer will include an employer's duty to **13.15** provide a safe system of work and a safe working environment for its employees. A duty of care may also be owed by the organisation to those who are not formally employed by it but whose work it is able to control or direct, contractors for example.[47] The offence does not impose new duties of care not currently owed.[48]

The term employee is defined by s.25 as: "... an individual who works under a contract of employment or apprenticeship (whether express or implied and, if express, whether oral or in writing), and related expressions are to be construed accordingly;" Whether there is a contract of employment is a mixed question of fact and law.[49] The issue is not always an easy one to resolve, indeed it has proved "elusive".[50] Under the Act, it is a question of law to be decided by the judge[51].

Occupiers of premises: Section 2(1)(b)

This covers an organisation's responsibilities to ensure, for example, that **13.16** buildings it occupies are kept in a safe condition. As regards the duties owed by an organisation under the law of negligence as occupier of premises, s.25 defines the term "premises" as including "land, buildings and moveable structures". Section 2(7) expressly declares that "the law of negligence" includes:

(a) in relation to England and Wales, the Occupiers' Liability Act 1957 (c.31), the Defective Premises Act 1972 (c.35) and the Occupiers' Liability Act 1984 (c.3);

---

[46] In *R. v Wacker* [2003] 2 Cr.App.R. 22; it was unsuccessfully argued in respect of the common law manslaughter offence that no duty of care could exist where the defendant and the victim were jointly engaged in an illegal act ("people smuggling").

[47] These people are covered by the phrase: "other persons working for the organisation or performing services for it"; s.2(1)(a).

[48] The Corporate Manslaughter and Corporate Homicide Act [HL 19], Explanatory Notes para.22.

[49] *Carmichael v National Power Plc* [1999] ICR 1226 HL.

[50] In *Lee Ting Sang v Chung Chi-Keung* [1990] 2 A.C. 374, 382, Lord Griffiths said despairingly: "... despite a plethora of authorities the courts have not been able to devise a single test that will conclusively point to the distinction in all cases".

[51] s.2(5).

Under the Occupiers' Liability Act 1957 an "occupier" owes a "common duty of care" to "lawful visitors" which includes invitees, licensees, contractors and "those who enter the premises for any purpose in the exercise of a right conferred by law".[52] The "common duty of care" is a duty to take such care as in all the circumstances of the case is reasonable to see that the visitor will be reasonably safe in using the premises for the purposes for which he is invited or permitted by the occupier to be there.[53] Under the Occupiers' Liability Act 1984 the occupier of premises also owes a duty to "persons other than his visitors ... to take such care as is reasonable in all the circumstances to see that he does not suffer injury on the premises by reason of the danger concerned" provided that: he is aware of the danger or has reasonable grounds to believe it exists; he knows or has reasonable grounds to believe that the other is in the vicinity of the danger concerned or that he may come into the vicinity of the danger (whether the other has lawful authority for being in that vicinity or not); and the risk is one against which, in all the circumstances of the case, he may reasonably be expected to offer the other some protection.[54] It is for the judge to determine whether, on the facts as he finds them, the particular organisation owed a relevant duty of care to the deceased on account of its occupation of and control over the premises in question.

Duties owed in connection with other activities: Section 2(1)(c)

(a) The supply of goods and services:

13.17 This will include duties owed by organisations to their customers and will cover, for example, duties owed by transport providers to their passengers and by retailers for the safety of their products. The duty of care owed in negligence in respect of the supply of goods is narrower than the protection provided by consumer legislation (e.g. the Sale of Goods Act 1979). A duty of care is owed by the provider of a service to a person who might reasonably forseeably suffer physical harm through the performance of the particular service.

(b) carrying on by the organisation of any construction or maintenance operations

13.18 By s.2(7), "construction or maintenance operations" means operations of any of the following descriptions—

---

[52] ss.2(1), 2(6), 3 and 5 Occupiers' Liability Act 1957.
[53] s.2(2) Occupiers' Liability Act 1957.
[54] ss.1(1)(a), 1(3) and 1(4) Occupiers' Liability Act 1984.

(a) construction, installation, alteration, extension, improvement, repair, maintenance, decoration, cleaning, demolition or dismantling of—

(i) any building or structure,
(ii) anything else that forms, or is to form, part of the land, or
(iii) any plant, vehicle or other thing;

(b) operations that form an integral part of, or are preparatory to, or are for rendering complete, any operations within paragraph (a);

As may be seen, duties of care may be owed under more than one heading in respect of the same operation. So, where a company is engaged in construction or repair it will owe a duty under that head as well as under the supply of a service head and because it is operating commercially (see below).

(c) carrying on any other activity on a commercial basis

This provision is intended to apply to other commercial operations per- **13.19** formed by companies not engaged in the supply of goods or services etc, such as farming or mining. It is hard to envisage any corporation not caught by this provision.

Causation and Breach

Having established that the particular organisation owed a duty of care to **13.20** the deceased, the next element of the offence to be proved is that:

i. the way in which its activities were managed or organised:

• caused his death;
• amounts to a gross breach of a relevant duty of care; and

iii. the way in which its activities were managed or organised by its senior management was a substantial element in the breach.

The usual principles of causation in the criminal law will apply to determine the question of causation. This means that the management failure need not have been the sole cause of death provided it was *a* cause.[55] Intervening acts may break the chain of causation in certain circumstances. Although the Law Commission and the Joint Committee of the Home Affairs and Work and Pensions Committees considered it desirable to include an express provision to make it clear that management failure may be *a* cause of death,

---

[55] The Corporate Manslaughter and Corporate Homicide Act, Explanatory Notes para. 15.

even if the *immediate* cause is the act or omission of an individual, the Act has eschewed this approach.[56]

The phrase "the way its activities are managed or organised" came from the Law Commission Report 237 (para.8.35) and focuses on the failings of the company rather than on the acts or omissions of an individual within it. The Commissioners considered that the proposed offence should be based upon the common law duty of care owed by an employer to provide a safe system of work and thus avoided the problem of identifying blameworthy conduct on the part of an individual or group of individuals of sufficient seniority to attribute to the company. The word "way" is likely to be interpreted to include an omission if, for example, the particular organisation omitted to take proper care to ensure the health and safety of persons employed in or affected by its activities. It was certainly the view of the Law Commission that liability for the offence could be proved by omission—an omission to maintain a proper system. There is no need to prove that the way the organisation managed or organised its activities was unlawful, only that it was a substantial cause of death. The Government has indicated that the sort of factors that might be considered will range from questions about the systems of work used by employees, their level of training and the adequacy of equipment, to issues of immediate supervision and middle management, to questions about the organisation's strategic approach to health and safety and its arrangements for risk assessing, monitoring and auditing its processes.[57]

Gross Breach

13.21 Once the prosecution proves (i) that the particular organisation owed a relevant duty of care to the deceased, and (ii) that the way its activities were managed or organised was a cause of the person's death, it is for the jury to decide whether "the way in which its activities were managed or organised amounts to a gross breach of a relevant duty of care".[58] A gross breach is

---

[56] Apparently the Government considered that such words were unnecessary following the clarification on the law of causation provided by the House of Lords in: *Environment Agency (formerly National Rivers Authority) v Empress Cars (Artillery) Ltd* [1999] 2 A.C. 22. Giving the only speech, Lord Hoffmann explained that a common sense answer cannot be given to a question of causation for the purpose of attributing responsibility under some rule without knowing the scope of the rule. "Does the rule impose a duty which requires one to guard against, or makes one responsible for, the deliberate acts of third persons. If so, it will be correct to say, when loss is caused by the act of such a third person, that it was caused by the breach of duty." (at 486). Human intervention will only be regarded as "breaking the chain of causation' if that intervention can fairly be regarded as something extraordinary.

[57] "Guide to the Corporate Manslaughter and Corporate Homicide Act 2007", Ministry of Justice, p.12.

[58] s.8(1).

defined as conduct that falls far below what can reasonably be expected of the organisation in the circumstances[59]. In deciding whether there has been a gross breach, the jury *must* consider whether the organisation failed to comply with relevant health and safety legislation and, if so, how serious that failure was and how much of a risk of death it posed[60]. The jury *may* also consider any relevant health and safety guidance and the extent to which the "corporate culture" ("attitudes, policies, systems or accepted practices within the organisation") encouraged or led to a tolerance of health and safety breach[61]. Health and safety guidance means "any code, guidance, manual or similar publication that is concerned with health and safety matters and is made or issued (under a statutory provision or otherwise) by an authority with responsibility for the enforcement of health and safety legislation".[62] The jury will need to decide what was reasonably to be expected of the particular organisation, and whether the way in which its activities were managed or organised fell far below that standard. The jury are not prevented by s.8 from having regard to any *other* matters they consider relevant.[63]

It is submitted that it is appropriate for the offence to require proof of a *gross* breach of the duty of care owed to the deceased. The new offence is a grave crime in which the resultant harm (death) is an element of the offence. The higher degree of fault required will ensure that the new offence will be targeted at only the most serious management failings. Not every work-related death is the result of gross negligence; the offences under the Health and Safety Act (where all that need be proved is breach of a relevant rule) will continue to apply in all but the most serious cases. The high threshold of gross negligence serves to reinforce this hierarchy.

Senior Management Failure

Crucially, a corporation will only be guilty of corporate manslaughter if the **13.22** way in which its activities were managed or organised by its *senior management* was a *substantial* element in the breach[64]. This aspect of the Act has provoked controversy. The main weakness of the common law offence was the need to prove that an individual "directing mind" of the corporation was himself guilty of the offence. The Law Commission Report and the draft Bill produced in 2000 required the more general "management failure". "*Senior* management failure" was introduced for the first time in the 2005 Bill.

---

[59] s.1(4)(b).
[60] s.8(2).
[61] s.8(3).
[62] s.8(5).
[63] s.8(4).
[64] s.1(3).

Does the need to prove that "senior management failure" was "a substantial element in the breach" reproduce the same old problems by focusing on individuals at particular level as opposed to systemic fault? The Government does not think so. According to the Introduction to the draft Bill, the object of this limitation was to ensure that the offence was targeted at failings in strategic management of an organisation's activities, rather than failings at relatively junior levels.[65] In the Guidance notes[66] the Government acknowledged that the old law "failed to provide proper accountability and justice for victims"; the new offence by contrast "allows an organisation's liability to be assessed on a wider basis, providing a more effective means of accountability for very serious management failings across the organisation". According to the Guide (which is non-statutory) "the Act does not require the prosecution to prove specific failings on the part of individual senior managers. It will be sufficient for a jury to consider that the senior management of the organisation collectively were not taking adequate care, and this was a substantial part of the organisation's failure".[67]

In contrast to the common law, the new offence permits aggregation of the actions and culpability of several individuals. "Senior management" in relation to an organisation is defined[68] as:

"the persons who play a significant role in—

(i)   the making of decisions about how the whole or a substantial part of its activities are to be managed or organised, or

(ii) the actual managing or organising of the whole or a substantial part of those activities."

This definition of "senior management" is intended to be wider than the concept of "directing mind" of a company at common law[69] The Guide explains what is meant by "senior management" as follows:

"These are the people who make significant decisions about the organisation, or substantial parts of it. This includes both those carrying out headquarters' functions (for example, central financial or strategic roles or with central responsibility for, for example, health and safety) as well as those in senior operational management roles.

Exactly who is a member of an organisation's senior management will depend on the nature and scale of an operation's activities. Apart from directors and similar senior management positions, roles likely to be

---

[65] para.28, *Corporate Manslaughter: the Government's Draft Bill for Reform*, Cm6497 (2005).

[66] "Guide to the Corporate Manslaughter and Corporate Homicide Act 2007", Ministry of Justice, p.3.

[67] p.14.

[68] in s.1(4)(c).

[69] See the discussion of *Tesco Supermarkets v Natrass* at Ch.4.10–4.19.

under consideration include regional managers in national organisations and the managers of different operational divisions"[70]

What is the purpose of this extra element? It is necessary to prove that the way in which the organisation's activities were managed or organised: (i) caused the death; and (ii) amounts to a gross breach of a relevant duty of care. Those requirements already mark out the offence as more serious than the offences under the Health and Safety at Work Act. The further ingredient of "senior management failure" adds an unnecessary element which is likely to be difficult to prove in practice. Although management failure need not be the sole cause of death, the prosecution will have to prove that "but for" the management failure (including the substantial element attributable to senior management), the death would not have occurred.[71] If the purpose of the legislation is to provide effective accountability for very serious management failings causing death, it is difficult to see how this will be achieved by requiring the prosecution to prove that *senior* management failure was a *significant* element in the breach. On the contrary, it can be argued that the inclusion of this ingredient means that the new offence entails little more than a broadening out of the identification doctrine to permit aggregation of the conduct of several senior managers.[72] The definition of "senior management" is likely to lead to arguments about a person's status within the corporate hierarchy. Worryingly, this ingredient will inevitably favour large corporations with highly devolved day-to-day operations; proving that the way in which its activities were managed or organised by its senior management was a substantial element in the breach may be impossible. By contrast, as with the common law offence, it will not be difficult to prove against a small corporation where the only management comes within the statutory definition.

The concern expressed by the Joint Committee of the Home Affairs and **13.23** Work and Pensions Committees that, by virtue this ingredient, organisations would be discouraged from prioritising health and safety by delegating those responsibilities to junior management, is perhaps exaggerated. These responsibilities are a central part of corporate governance and are firmly placed on senior management.[73] Under the Companies Act 2006, directors have a duty to promote the success of the company for the benefit of its members; there is a duty on any company listed on the LSE to report on the

---

[70] p.13.
[71] "Guide to the Corporate Manslaughter and Corporate Homicide Act 2007", Ministry of Justice, p.14.
[72] *First Joint Report from the Home Affairs and Work and Pensions Committees* Session 2005–06. (HC 540 i), p.38.
[73] By way of example, the Turnbull Guidance (*Revised Turnbull Guidance on Internal Control*; 2005), endorsed by the London Stock Exchange, requires senior directors to be responsible for managing risk and requires companies to have robust systems of internal control, covering not just "narrow" financial risks but also risks relating to the environment, business reputation and health and safety.

company's environmental and social activities. An important aspect of the responsibility of a board of directors is to protect the workforce and safeguard those who might be adversely affected by the company's activities so as to enhance shareholder value. In the event of conviction for an offence under the Act, as part of the sentence, the court can make a publicity order which would require the organisation to publicise details of the case.[74] Such publicity is unlikely to enhance the share price. Preventing work-related injury and deaths is now regarded as a major factor in corporate governance which cannot be ignored by senior management. In October 2007 the Institute of Directors and the Health and Safety Commission jointly produced guidance entitled "Leading health and safety: leadership actions for directors and board members".[75] The guidance states that "the board should set the direction for effective health and safety management ... All board members should take the lead in ensuring the communication of health and safety duties and benefits throughout the organisation." Against this backdrop senior management is obliged to treat health and safety as a core element of corporate governance. The Government has indicated that the Act is concerned with the way an activity is being organised or managed; failures by senior managers to manage health and safety adequately may include the inappropriate delegation of health and safety issues, which, in the event of a death, may leave a company vulnerable to a corporate manslaughter prosecution.[76]

Liability of Individuals

13.24 An individual cannot be guilty of corporate manslaughter either as a principal, because it can only be committed by an organisation to which the Act applies (see above), or as a secondary party by aiding, abetting, counselling or procuring the commission of the offence [s.18(1)]. In its report in 1996, the Law Commission considered that the corporate offence should not be capable of commission by an individual, even as a secondary party.[77] The Government was initially opposed to this restriction but, by the time the draft Bill was published in 2005, the Law Commission recommendation had been accepted.[78]

---

[74] see below at para.13.29.
[75] available at *http://www.hse.gov.uk/pubns/indg417.pdf*.
[76] "Guide to the Corporate Manslaughter and Corporate Homicide Act 2007", Ministry of Justice, p.14.
[77] Law Commission Report No.237 para.8.58; cl.4(4) of the Commissions draft Bill Provided: "No individual shall be convicted of aiding, abetting, counselling or procuring an offence under this section but without prejudice to an individual being guilty of any other offence in respect of the death in question".
[78] It not known whether the Government changed its mind as a result of lobbying by the CBI and IoD, but both organisations strongly opposed any individual liablity under the Act: see CBI Response to the Home Office Consultation Document: Corporate Manslaughter, the Government's Draft Bill (CBI, June 17, 2005); and Corporate Manslaughter Report (IoD Press Office, December 19, 2005).

This U-turn was the subject of sharp criticism:

> "Where there is an offence, you expect liability in the primary case to be on the person who committed it, and the secondary liability to be on someone who aids and abets. But not in this Bill; Clause 16 expunges all notion of secondary liability from the Bill's grasp. Anyone who aids, abets, counsels or procures the offence established by Clause 1 has a complete immunity under Clause 16. It has never yet been explained precisely why this should be so."[79]

This immunity has been criticised by academics: "... experience with enforcement of health and safety legislation suggests that individual directors shelter behind the firm and are not sufficiently deterred by a prosecution of the company"[80]; put another way: "unless individuals are also prosecuted, the punishment of corporations is of little relevance".[81] In manslaughter prosecutions under the common law, individuals were frequently in the dock beside the corporation; this was almost inevitable given that "a non-human defendant could not be convicted of the crime of manslaughter by gross negligence in the absence of evidence establishing the guilty of an identified human individual for the same crime".[82] In principle an individual can still be prosecuted for gross negligence manslaughter but given the different tests of liability that there would be, a joint trial would be unsatisfactorily complicated. However, if an HSWA offence is committed with the consent, connivance or neglect of an officer of the company, he, as well as the company, can be prosecuted.[83] If a corporation is prosecuted for corporate manslaughter, it may also be charged with health and safety offences arising out of the same circumstances and the jury may return verdicts on each charge; this indicates the level of seriousness of the breach of duty.[84]

SENTENCING

13.25 An organisation which is guilty of corporate manslaughter is liable on a conviction to a fine.[85] Additionally, the court may impose: (i) a remedial order; and/or a publicity order. The Sentencing Guidelines Council has asked the Sentencing Advisory Panel to provide advice on sentencing for corporate manslaughter. The Panel sought the opinion of a wide range of organisations. Guidelines are likely to be published in the autumn of 2008 both for corporate manslaughter and for breaches of health and safety law which result in death.

---

[79] Professor Lord Wedderburn of Charlton Q.C. HL Deb., col 539 (February 5, 2007).
[80] Prof C.Wells, "Corporations: Culture, Risk and Criminal Liability" [1993] Crim.L.R. 551.
[81] Prof. P. Glazebrook, "A Better Way of Convicting Businesses of Avoidable deaths and Injuries" [2002] C.L.J. 405.
[82] *Att-Gen's Reference (No.2 of 1999)* [2000] 2 Cr.App.R. 207 per Rose L.J. at 217.
[83] s.37 HSWA 1974.
[84] s.19.
[85] s.1(6).

Fines

13.26 There maximum fine is unlimited.[86] Corporate manslaughter is an extremely serious offence, reserved for the very worst cases of corporate mismanagement leading to death.[87] Where a corporation is convicted, the sentencing judge must reflect in the size of any fine imposed, the serious concern at the loss of life, the high degree of fault that must be proved, and, in particular, the fact that the offence is more serious than those under the Health and Safety at Work Act, even though the result of the harm (the death of a person) is the same. In the context of health and safety, the objective of the fine imposed should be to achieve a safe environment for the public and bring that message home, not only to those who manage a corporate defendant, but also to shareholders. The HSE claims that the majority of workplace deaths are preventable and considers that the deterrent effect of criminal prosecutions can play an important part in reducing risks to health and safety arising from work activity. Deterrence, both general and individual, should also be the main aim of sentencing for corporate manslaughter, so any fine is likely to be very substantial. In *R. v Balfour Beatty Rail Infrastructure Services Ltd*[88] the trial judge Mr Justice Mackay, imposed a fine of £10 million following the company's conviction on a count under s.3 of the HSWA following the Hatfield rail crash in which 4 people were called and more than 100 were injured. On appeal the Court approved the judge's approach.[89] Lord Phillips C.J. addressed the size of a fine in terms of the influence on shareholders:

> "Knowledge that breach of this duty can result in a fine of sufficient size to impact upon shareholders will provide a powerful incentive for management to comply with this duty. This is not to say that the fine must always be large enough to affect dividends or share price. But the fine must reflect both the degree of fault and the consequences so as to raise appropriate concerns on the part of shareholders as to what has occurred. Such an approach will satisfy the requirement that the sentence should act as a deterrent."[90]

In the past, the level of fines did not adequately reflect the gravity of the consequences in the case of a work-related death. Since the guidance given by the court of Appeal in *R. v F. Howe & Co (Engineers) Ltd*,[91] it is apparent that this trend has been reversed. Nevertheless according to recent research the average fine imposed on a company convicted in a case of work-related death is less than one percent of gross profits. The

---

[86] General principles relevant to fines are discussed in Ch.10.
[87] "Guide to the Corporate Manslaughter and Corporate Homicide Act 2007", Ministry of Justice, p.13.
[88] [2007] 1 Cr.App.R.(S.) 65.
[89] The judge distilled the guidance provided by the case law into 13 propositions; at para 22.
[90] [2007] 1 Cr.App.R.(S.) 65 at para.42.
[91] [1999] 2 Cr.App.R(S.) 37.

Consultation Paper prepared by the Sentencing Advisory Panel suggested consistency of approach could be achieved by calculating the level of fine by reference to the larger of either annual turnover or gross profit[92] This assumes that a fine expressed as a percentage of average annual turnover (the range proposed by the Panel is between 2.5 and 10 per cent) would have an equal impact on all sizes of organisation.[93] However, as the courts have repeatedly said, consistency of sentencing is truly achieved by applying existing principles (as set out in *Friskies*) to the facts of the case and to each corporate defendant. Were percentage of turnover or profit to be adopted by courts, the results would be a very significant increase in the level of fines. By way of example, in a Scottish case, Transco was fined £15 million after admitting breaches of safety regulations that led to the deaths of four members of the same family. The fine represented about 5 per cent of the company's after-tax profits and less than 1 per cent of annual turnover. Had the 2.5 and 10 per cent range been used, the fine would have been a minimum of £37.5 million.

Following the advice given by the Court of Appeal in *R. v Friskies Petcare (UK) Ltd*,[94] the prosecution should before sentence serve a document setting out the facts of the case and any aggravating factors.

Aggravating factors include: **13.27**

Factors relating to the harm

- More than one person killed as a result of the offence; in *R. v Balfour Beatty Rail Infrastructure Services Ltd*[95] the court stated that more than one death must be regarded as more serious.
- Serious injury caused as well as death

Factors relating to culpability

- was the death the result of an isolated breach of duty, several breaches occurring at around the same time or breaches that took place over a period of time.[96]
- Was the breach the result of a deliberate act; see *R. v Connolly* where the braking system had been disabled and then concealed by the defendant.[97]
- Failing to act upon advice, cautions or warnings from a regulatory authority, or similar incidents having occurred before.
- Failure to heed warnings over safety from employees. By way of example, in the prosecution after the Lyme Bay disaster, it

---

[92] Consistency is not necessarily a primary aim of sentencing in this area of law: *R. v Jarvis* [2005] EWCA Crim 1409, para.7.
[93] Sentencing Advisory Panel, Consultation Paper, November 2007, paras 58–63.
[94] [2000] 2 Cr.App.R.(S.) 401.
[95] [2007] 1 Cr.App.R(S.) 65.
[96] *R. v Howe and Sons (Engineers) Ltd* [1999] 2 Cr.App.R.(S.) 37.
[97] [2007] EWCA Crim 790.

transpired that staff had resigned in protest at poor safety standards, but still nothing was done. The following year, four children died during a canoeing trip organised by the company.

- Offender carrying out operations without an appropriate licence.
- Action or lack of action prompted by financial or other inappropriate motives; in the case of Keymark Services, a haulage company required its drivers grossly to exceed their permitted driving hours (and tamper with the tachograph equipment to cover up the breaches) to increase profits. A driver fell asleep at the wheel and crashed his lorry, killing himself and two other motorists.
- Corporate culture encouraging or producing tolerance of breach of duty.

Mitigating Factors include:

- Breach due to employee acting outwith authority; given that a jury can only convict if sure that the death was caused by the way in which the company's activities were managed or organised, the fact that the proximate cause of death was fault on the part of an individual is unlikely to have much weight as mitigation. The organisation should take all reasonably practicable steps to ensure that staff are properly trained so they do not stray beyond that authority.
- Prompt co-operation with the relevant authorities;
- Good previous safety record; it may have less value in a corporate manslaughter case given the gravity of the harm and the fact that there cannot be a conviction unless there has been a gross breach of a relevant duty of care that would not have occurred without senior management failure.

Remedial Orders

13.28 The new Act gives the court power to make an order[98] requiring the convicted organisation to remedy:

    (a)   the breach that caused the death ("the relevant breach");

    (b)   any matter that appears to the court to have resulted from the relevant breach and to have been a cause of death; and

    (c)   any deficiency, as regards health and safety matters, in the organisation's policies, systems or practices of which the relevant breach appears to the court to be an indication.

The Law Commission recommended that the court be given the power to make a remedial order in the event of conviction to remedy any

---

[98] s.9(1).

consequences of management failure if it appears to have been a cause of death.[99] Such orders could be made if the organisation has failed to respond to other interventions (itself an aggravating factor). A remedial order can only be made on an application by the prosecution specifying the terms of the proposed order and hearing any evidence called on behalf of the parties[1] and consulting the relevant regulatory body.[2] Failure to comply with a remedial order within the time permitted is an offence punishable on indictment by an unlimited fine.[3]

Remedial orders are already available under the Health and Safety at Work Act[4] although in practice they have seldom been made; this is usually because, by the time of sentence, measures have often already been taken to remedy the problems leading to the breach of the Act. A remedial order has a positive function in two respects: firstly, it enables sentencing to be a constructive measure, aimed at improving the working systems of a defendant who has committed a crime; secondly, it allows the court to oversee the progress made in compliance with the remedial order, and to enforce it with the sanction that non-compliance will lead to the commission of a separate criminal offence with robust sentencing powers.

It is not expected that this measure will often be used for the same reasons as set out above.

Publicity orders

Section 10 of the Act introduces an entirely new sentencing power[5]; on **13.29** conviction for an offence of corporate manslaughter, a defendant may be ordered to publicise the fact and details of its conviction and any sentence imposed. A court may specify the manner and timing of the publicity, having consulted with such regulatory bodies as the court considers appropriate and heard from the prosecution and defence. Non-compliance with the order is itself an indictable offence punishable with an unlimited fine. A publicity order is considered by the Government to be a deterrent in its own right because where one is made, it is likely to affect the reputation of the organisation. Where a publicity order is made, the court will specify the nature of the publication(s) in which the advertisement is to be placed including local and national newspapers, trade journals and websites.

---

[99] For example where management failure related to inadequate training of staff and monitoring of risk.
[1] s.9(2).
[2] s.9(3).
[3] s.9(5).
[4] s.42 HSWA 1974.
[5] Similar powers already exist in other jurisdictions: Canada, the United States and Australia.

CHAPTER 14

COMPANIES ACT OFFENCES

Being creatures of statute, corporations must abide by the rules which **14.1**
dictate and limit their conduct; these are numerous and complex. Quite
apart from the general statutes which impose criminal liability on any
person, whether natural or legal, a corporation has to operate within the
parameters provided by the Companies Acts[1] during its life-time, and the
Insolvency Act 1986 (as amended) in relation to its demise. The framework
is designed to ensure transparency and honesty, as well as consistency, in
corporate operations and accounting, so that an outsider, a potential
investor or creditor can properly assess the health of the company. Extensive
investigative powers are provided by the legislation in order that the relevant
authorities can gain access to company documents and records.[2] The
criminal sanctions are the means by which the legislation compels both the
errant corporation and the individuals behind it to comply. They are now
mostly contained in the Companies Act 2006, but numerous offences remain
in the Companies Act 1985, and many of the offences which have been

---

[1] The expression "the Companies Acts" is defined in s.2 of the 2006 Act as Pts 1 to 39 and 45 to
47 of [the 2006] Act (so far as they apply for the purposes of Pts 1 to 39), Pt 2 (community
interest companies (ss.26–63)) of the Companies (Audit, Investigations and Community
Enterprise) Act 2004, and the provisions of the Companies Act 1985 and the Companies
Consolidation (Consequential Provisions) Act 1985 that remain in force.
[2] For example, s.447 Companies Act 1985 enables the Secretary of State to require a company
to produce such documents as may be specified or to provide information and s.448 gives
powers of entry and search of premises where it is believed (on reasonable grounds) there are
any documents production of which has been required but which have not been produced.
Section 1132 of the 2006 Act confers a new power on the Director of Public Prosecutions (in
England and Wales), the Secretary of State or a chief officer of police, where there is reasonable cause to believe that an officer of a company has committed an offence in connection
with the management of the company's affairs and that evidence thereof is to be found in any
"documents" (which includes information recorded in any form) in the possession or control
of the company, to apply to a High Court judge for an order authorising the person named
within it to inspect the documents in question, or to require the company secretary or other
officer to produce the documents: s.1132(5).

replaced by provisions in the 2006 Act have been amended.[3] The 2006 Act repeals and restates most of the Companies Act 1985. It is the largest Act ever to be passed by Parliament.[4] It began as a piece of amending legislation, but ended up as a consolidating statute.[5] The original document that started the consultation process in 1998 suggested that the development of company law in the 20th century had come mostly from a series of reactions to "scandals and mischiefs" resulting in a "patchwork of legislation that is immensely complex and seriously out of date". The reforms reflect the recommendations of the Company Law Review which reported in July 2001.[6]

The Explanatory Notes to the original Bill state that the general principle underpinning criminal liability under the Companies Acts is that the company will not be liable for an offence if the victims are merely the company itself or its members, whereas the company should be potentially liable for an offence where other persons or entities are included amongst the victims; all the offences in the Bill (now the Act) and those remaining in the Companies Act 1985 have been reviewed in the light of this principle.

14.2 The range of offences under the Companies Acts is extensive, the great majority being regulatory in nature. They range from venial summary offences punishable by a level 2 fine (currently £500) and extend to offences of dishonesty, such as fraudulent trading—s.993 (formerly s.458 of the Companies Act 1985) for which the maximum penalty upon conviction on indictment is now 10 years' imprisonment, or a fine, or both.[7] Moreover, in addition to the offences created by the 2006 Act,[8] various sections confer power on the Secretary of State to make regulations which create offences.[9] In this chapter it is not possible to do more than highlight a few of the criminal offences in the 2006 Act,[10] but all of the offences are set out in tabular form[11] in Appendix A which indicates:

---

[3] s.1124 Companies Act 2006 gives effect to Sch.3 which amends surviving provisions of the 1985 Act relating to offences. The amended provisions are ss.444, 448 to 451, 453A and 455.

[4] The Act, which is in 47 parts (1300 sections) and has 16 schedules, received Royal Assent on November 8, 2006.

[5] Beginning as the Company Law Reform Bill (Bill No.190) and changing to the Companies Bill (renumbered as Bill No.218) along the way.

[6] See White Papers "Modernising Company Law" (Cmd 5553, 1aII, 2002) and "Company Law Reform" (Cmd 6456, 2005).

[7] Fraudulent trading is covered in detail in Ch.17, below.

[8] See Pt 36, ss.1121–1133.

[9] For example, in Pt 15, s.468 confers a general power on the Secretary of State to make further provision about company accounts and reports, which may amend that part of the Act and may create offences corresponding to those in which an offence is created by an existing provision (the maximum penalty being no greater than already provided for under the existing provision).

[10] Unless otherwise indicated, all references are to the 2006 Act

[11] Unhelpfully, the 2006 Act has no equivalent of Sch.24 which was a table containing all of the offences under the 1985 Act; however, Tables of Origins and Destinations were published with it, making it possible to track changes from previous Companies Acts: http://www. opsi.gov.uk/acts/en2006/ukpagen_20060046_origins_en.pdf.

(a)   the section of the Act;
(b)   the nature of the offence;
(c)   where the offence can be tried[12] and the maximum punishment(s); and
(d)   the derivation of the offence (where applicable).

Some offences attract a "daily default fine" upon summary conviction; this term is explained by s.1125 which states that an offender will be liable on a second or subsequent summary conviction to a fine not exceeding the amount specified for each day on which a contravention continued. Section 1133 makes clear that Part 36 of the 2006 Act does not apply to offences committed before the commencement of the relevant provisions.

GENERAL PROVISIONS

Since a corporation must be operated by its officers (usually, but not always **14.3** individuals) the offences under the Companies Acts can be committed by an officer where he or she is in default. Section 1121[13] provides that, in the event of contravention of an enactment in relation to a company, an offence is committed by every officer who is in default. The section defines "officer" as including: "any director, manager or secretary and any person who is to be treated as an officer of the company for the purposes of the provision in question"[14]; and provides that an officer is "in default" if "he authorises or permits, participates in, or fails to take all reasonable steps to prevent" the relevant contravention.[15]

Schedule 8 to the 2006 Act is an index of defined expressions, some of which are considered below.

"COMPANY"

By s.1, "a company" means: (i) a company formed and registered under the **14.4** Companies Act 2006, or (ii) an existing company which is one formed and registered under previous Companies Acts.[16]

---

[12] There are no indictable-only offences under the Companies Act 1985. A conspiracy to commit an offence, however, is always indictable only; this would include a conspiracy to commit a Companies Act offence.
[13] Which is derived from ss.730(5), 733(2) and 744 of the 1985 Act.
[14] s.1121(2)(a) and (b).
[15] s.1121(3).
[16] See also ss.616(1), 879(6) and 991(1), 2006 Act.

"BODY CORPORATE" AND "CORPORATION"

14.5 By s.1173(1) these terms include a company incorporated outside the United Kingdom (but not a corporation sole or a partnership that, whether or not a legal person, is not regarded as a body corporate under the law by which it is governed).

Section 256 contains a new definition of associated bodies corporate; bodies corporate are associated if one is a subsidiary of the other or both are subsidiaries of the same body corporate. Companies are associated if one is a subsidiary of the other or both are subsidiaries of the same body corporate.

"SUBSIDIARY", "HOLDING COMPANY" AND "WHOLLY-OWNED SUBSIDIARY"

14.6 By s.1159, a company[17] is a subsidiary of another company — its holding company — if that other company:

(a) holds a majority of the voting rights in it, or

(b) is a member of it and has the right to appoint or remove a majority of its board of directors, or

(c) is a member of it and alone controls a majority of the voting rights in it, pursuant to an agreement with other shareholders or members, or if it is a subsidiary of a company which is itself a subsidiary of that other company.

A company is a "wholly-owned subsidiary" of another company if it has no members except that other and that other's wholly-owned subsidiaries or persons acting on behalf of that other or its wholly-owned subsidiaries.

"DIRECTOR" AND "SHADOW DIRECTOR"

14.7 A "director" includes any person occupying the position of director, by whatever name he, she or it is called.[18] A company is required to have at least one director who is a natural person[19]; a private company must have at least one director, whilst a public company must have at least two.[20] "Shadow director", in relation to a company, means a person in accordance with whose directions or instructions the directors of the company are accustomed to act, but a person is not to be regarded as a shadow director

---

[17] For these purposes, "company" includes any body corporate.

[18] s.250(1). This definition is materially the same as its predecessor provision: s.741 of the 1985 Act.

[19] s.155(1).

[20] ss.155(1) and (2).

by reason only that the directors act on advice given by him in a professional capacity.[21] "Officer", in relation to a body corporate, includes a director, manager or secretary.[22]

INVESTIGATIONS UNDER PART XIV OF THE COMPANIES ACT 1985

It has long been recognised that abuses of corporate power cannot be **14.8** adequately constrained by leaving it to the company's members to ensure that those who control the company behave in accordance with the law. Those who deal with companies, whether as investors, suppliers or consumers, should be protected from misconduct or unscrupulous practices. Accordingly, the Secretary of State of the Department of Business, Enterprise and Regulatory Reform (BERR)[23] has wide-ranging statutory powers to investigate companies where misconduct is suspected and an investigation is considered to be in the public interest. The extent of the powers reflects the general principle that those who wish to enjoy the benefits of incorporation and invite investment from the public must accept the burden of being held accountable in law for the manner in which companies are operated.

In general terms, the Secretary of State has power:

(i) to appoint inspectors to investigate the affairs of a company (ss.432 and 432) or the ownership of a company (s.442); or
(ii) to require the production of documents and information (s.447).

Failure to comply with a request made by an inspector under s.434 (to inspect documents or for a person to attend before him to provide explanation) is treated as a contempt of court.

The power to set up an inspection is seldom used,[24] whereas the power to order an investigation under s.447 is commonly invoked. The Secretary of State may give directions requiring the company to produce documents or provide information as specified in the direction[25], or authorise an investigator (from the Companies Investigation Branch — now part of the Insolvency Service) to require the company or any other person to produce such documents[26] and provide such information as the investigator may specify.[27] A search warrant may be issued to an investigator to exercise his

---

[21] s.251(1) and (2).
[22] s.1173(1).
[23] which replaced the Department of Trade and Industry.
[24] Not least because an announcement that inspectors have been appointed is likely to result in damaging publicity to the company whatever the eventual outcome.
[25] s.447(2) Companies Act 1985.
[26] 'Document' is defined as information recorded in any form which would include records held on a computer: s.447(8) Companies Act 1985.
[27] s.447(3) Companies Act 1985.

powers under s.447.[28] Investigations are confidential and allow suspicions of misbehavior to be looked into without risk of harming the business. Where an explanation is sought by the Secretary of State (or a person acting on his behalf), questioning about any discrepancies between documents and/or explanations given, must be reasonably necessary to enable the investigator to discover whether there is any foundation for the concerns which led to the investigation.[29]

The privilege against self-incrimination does not extend to an investigation under s.447 (see *e.g. Saunders v UK*[30]). However, although a statement made by a person in compliance with an order under s.447 may be used against him, no evidence relating to the statement may be adduced by the prosecution in evidence in a criminal trial unless evidence is given or a question relating to it is asked in proceedings by the person charged.[31] This restriction does not apply to s.451 (see below) or an offence of perjury contrary to s.5 of the Perjury Act 1911. The power may be invoked in respect of a company or *any other person.*[32]

As with a refusal to comply with requests made by an inspector, so a person who fails without reasonable excuse to comply with the requirement of an investigator may be reported to the court which may deal with him as if he had been guilty of contempt of the court.[33]

14.9   Part XIV of the 1985 Act contains various criminal offences which underpin the exercise of the compulsory powers:

i. Obstruction: section 448(7)

Anyone who intentionally obstructs the exercise of any rights conferred by a warrant issued under s.448, or fails without reasonable excuse to comply with any requirement imposed on a person to explain a document or state where it may be found, commits an offence punishable on indictment by an unlimited fine.

Similarly, anyone who intentionally obstructs a person acting lawfully in relation to the power to enter and remain on premises in accordance with s.453A, commits an either way offence punishable on indictment by an unlimited fine.

---

[28] s.448 Companies Act 1985.
[29] *Att-Gen's Reference (No.2 of 1998)* [2000] Q.B. 412.
[30] (1997) 23 EHRR 313, ECHR.
[31] s.447A(1) and (2); inserted into the 1985 Act by s.25(1) of the Companies (Audit, Investigations and Community Enterprise) Act 2004.
[32] Section 21 of the Companies (Audit, Investigations and Community Enterprise) Act 2004 substituted a new s.447 which included this widened power.
[33] s.453C; inserted into the 1985 Act by s.24 of the Companies (Audit, Investigations and Community Enterprise) Act 2004.

ii. Destroying, mutilating or falsifying documents: section 450

It is an offence for an officer of a company to destroy, mutilate or falsify a document affecting or relating to a company's property or affairs or to make a false entry in such a document. Similarly, an officer commits an offence if he was "privy to" such activity. A document includes information recorded in any form and so includes electronic records held on computer. The offence is committed unless the accused proves that he had no intention to conceal the state of affairs of the company or to defeat the law. The words " ... unless he proves ... " clearly impose a legal burden on the defendant; once the prosecution proves that he has destroyed, mutilated or falsified a document (or was privy to it) he will be convicted unless he proves that he had no intention to conceal the state of affairs of the company or to defeat the law. It is submitted that to impose a legal burden on an officer in such circumstances does not offend the fundamental right of an individual to be presumed innocent[34] and complies with art.6(2) of the ECHR[35] because there is no question of conviction unless the prosecution proves that the officer has destroyed, mutilated or falsified a document relating to the company's property or affairs (or was privy to it). If a company officer has deliberately done such a thing, it will be peculiarly within his knowledge why he did so; to require him to prove, on a balance of probabilities, that he did not thereby intend to conceal the state of affairs of the company is justifiable in the corporate context.

A person convicted of the offence on indictment is liable to imprisonment for a term of up to seven years or a fine (or both) and on summary conviction to a maximum term of 12 months or a fine (or both).[36]

iii. Providing false information: section 451

It is an offence under s.451 of the 1985 Act for a person who, in purported compliance with a requirement under s.447, provides information which he knows to be false in a material particular or recklessly provides information which is in fact false in a material particular. The offence is triable either way; the maximum sentence on indictment is two years' imprisonment or a

---

[34] *R. v Johnstone* [2003] 1 W.L.R. 28, per Lord Nicholls at para.51.

[35] See, e.g. *Att-Gen's Reference (No.1 of 2004)* [2004] 2 Cr.App.R. 424; for a full discussion of the burden of proof in regulatory and other corporate contexts see Ch.12.

[36] By s.1131 of the 2006 Act, the maximum term on summary conviction is 6 months' imprisonment if the offence was committed before the commencement of s.154(1) of the Criminal Justice Act 2003. The maximum term of imprisonment that can be imposed by the magistrates was increased to 12 months by Sch.3 para5, Companies Act 2006.

fine (or both) and on summary conviction to a maximum term of 12 months or a fine (or both).[37]

A prosecution under any of sections 448, 450 or 451 requires the consent of the Secretary of State or the Director of Public Prosecutions.[38]

USING COMPANY'S MONEY TO ACQUIRE SHARES DIRECTLY OR INDIRECTLY

14.10 Generally, it is prohibited for a company to acquire its own shares.[39] Not only will the acquisition be void but criminal offences will be committed by the company, and also every officer in default (who will be liable to up to two years' imprisonment).[40] It is also an offence for a company (or its subsidiary) to give financial assistance directly or indirectly (i) either before or at the time of the acquisition, or (ii) for the purpose of reducing or discharging a liability incurred in order for another person to acquire shares in the company.[41] The offence applies only to public, not private, companies. The purpose of the legislation is to prevent fraudulent purchases of companies. A foreign subsidiary of an English parent company giving financial assistance for the acquisition of shares in its English parent company is not caught by the Act.[42] Financial assistance is defined by s.677 and is widely drawn; given the similarity between s.677 and its predecessor (s.152 Companies Act 1985), it is submitted that case law on the meaning of "financial assistance" under the 1985 Act will be relevant to the new offence. General exemptions are contained within each of the sections.[43] It is a defence to an allegation of financial assistance that it was given "in good faith in the interests of the company"; in *Brady v Brady*[44] Lord Oliver said the words form "a single composite expression and postulate a requirement that those responsible for procuring the company to provide the assistance act in the genuine belief that it is being done in the company's interest."[45] Certain specific exceptions are made by s.681. The sentence on indictment is a maximum of two years' imprisonment and/or a fine for an officer of the company and an unlimited fine for a corporation.[46]

---

[37] By s.1131, the maximum term on summary conviction is 6 months' imprisonment if the offence was committed before the commencement of s.154(1) Criminal Justice Act 2003. The maximum term of imprisonment that can be imposed by the magistrates was increased to 12 months by Sch.3 para5, Companies Act 2006.
[38] s.1126.
[39] s.658(1).
[40] s.658(2).
[41] ss.678(2) and (3).
[42] *Arab Bank Plc v Mercantile Holdings Ltd* [1994] Ch.71.
[43] At p.777.
[44] [1989] A.C. 755 HL.
[45] At p.777.
[46] s.680(2).

Accounting and Audit Offences

It is the duty of every company to keep adequate accounting records,[47] to **14.11** have the accounts independently audited (unless it is exempt),[48] and to submit accurate accounts and auditor's reports to the registrar of companies.[49] The directors must ensure that the accounts give a true and fair view of the assets, liabilities, financial position and profit or loss of the company.[50] "Accounting records" means:

> "the accounting records should comprise an orderly, classified collection of information capable of timely retrieval, containing details of the company's transactions, assets and liabilities. An unorganised collection of vouchers and documents will not suffice: whatever the physical form of the records, the information should be so organized as to enable a trial balance to be constructed."[51]

Failure to comply with these provisions will result in criminal sanctions[52] against: the company, any officer "who is in default" and, in respect of any auditing offences, the person purporting to be the auditor.[53] To be "adequate", the accounting records must be sufficient : "(a) to show and explain the company's transactions, (b) to disclose with reasonable accuracy, at any time, the financial position of the company at that time, and (c) to enable the directors to ensure that any accounts required to be prepared comply with the requirements of the 2006 Act. They must contain entries from day to day of all sums of money received and expended by the company and (b) a record of the assets and liabilities of the company."[54] Private companies must keep their accounting records for three years; public companies must keep them for six years.[55]

The statutory requirements are aimed at achieving these goals, both in respect of an individual company and, in certain circumstances, of a parent company for its subsidiary. Both the company and any officer in default will be guilty of an offence and liable to punishment. It is a defence for an officer to prove that he acted honestly and that in the circumstances in which the company's business was carried on, the default was excusable.[56]

The company auditor must be properly supervised and appropriately **14.12** qualified, and the audit must be "carried out properly and with integrity and

---

[47] s.386(1).
[48] s.475(1).
[49] s.441.
[50] s.393(1).
[51] This definition, from the Institute of Chartered Accountants, was approved by the Court of Appeal in *R. v Garvey* [2001] EWCA Crim 1365, paras 56–57.
[52] s.381.
[53] See generally the offences set out in Pts 15 and 16.
[54] s.386(2) and (3).
[55] s.388(4).
[56] s.389(2).

with a proper degree of independence".[57] The Companies Act 1989 Part II creates a number of offences penalising a failure to adopt these aims:

(i) An auditor who is ineligible for such an appointment commits an offence if he acts in contravention of the statute or if he fails to give notice of vacating his office as required. The offence is triable either way—on indictment he is liable to a fine.

(ii) A person who furnishes information which he knows is, or is reckless as to its being false or misleading in a material particular, in relation to, or in purported compliance with, a requirement imposed on him under Pt II of the Act (i.e. in relation to auditing activities) is guilty of an offence.[58]

(iii) A person whose name does not appear on the register of auditors but who holds himself out so as to indicate, or so that he could be reasonably understood to indicate, that he is a registered auditor commits a summary offence.[59]

Where an offence is committed by a body corporate with the consent or connivance of an officer or attributable to his neglect, he too is liable to prosecution and punishment.[60] An information for a summary only offence under this Part must be laid within 12 months after the date on which sufficient evidence to justify proceedings comes to the knowledge of the Director of Public Prosecutions or Secretary of State; the sufficiency is a matter for the Director of Public Prosecutions or Secretary of State's opinion.[61] It is submitted that the normal rules of abuse of process and the reasonableness of the opinion would make this susceptible to judicial challenge.

An auditor is entitled to the information necessary for him to conduct his statutory function.[62] He may require information from an officer or employee of the company or of any subsidiary, or any person holding the company's books, accounts or vouchers. A person who makes a misleading, false or deceptive statement in relation to such information commits an offence[63] triable either way with a maximum penalty of two years' imprisonment and/or a fine. A summary offence is committed by a person who fails to comply, or delays in complying, with a requirement to provide the auditor with such information.[64]

---

[57] s.24 Companies Act 1989.
[58] s.41(1) and (4) Companies Act 1989.
[59] s.41(2) and (5) Companies Act 1989.
[60] s.42 Companies Act 1989.
[61] s.43 Companies Act 1989.
[62] s.499.
[63] s.501(1).
[64] s.501(3).

INSOLVENCY

Insolvency is not itself defined by the Insolvency Act 1986 ("IA"), the **15.1**
principal statute which governs the demise of a corporation. By s.247(1):

> "'Insolvency' in relation to a company, includes the approval of a
> voluntary arrangement under Part I, the making of an administration
> order or the appointment of an administrative receiver."

By s.247(2):

> "...a company goes into liquidation if it passes a resolution for
> voluntary winding up or an order for its winding up is made by the
> court at a time when it has not already gone into liquidation by passing
> such a resolution."

A company may be wound up voluntarily[1] or compulsorily by the court in
the circumstances set out in s.122 including where it is "unable to pay its
debts",[2] or if the court considers it "just and equitable" to do so.[3]

The circumstances in which the company is "unable to pay its debts" are
clarified by s.123. Where the company is unable to pay it debts as they fall
due,[4] or where the value of its assets is less than its liabilities taking into
account its contingent and prospective liabilities,[5] the court may deem the
company to be unable to pay its debts. Evidence must be provided of the
inability to pay. Where the company genuinely disputes a debt, a winding up
order will not be made[6]; but where the dispute is not as to the existence, but
to the amount of the debt, a winding up order may be made.[7]

---

[1] There may be a members' voluntary winding up or a creditors voluntary winding up.
[2] s.122(1)(f) IA.
[3] s.122(1)(g) IA.
[4] s.123(1)(e) IA.
[5] s.123(2) IA.
[6] *Re Gold Mill Mines* (1883) 23 Ch D 210.
[7] *Re Tweeds Garages Ltd* [1962] Ch.406.

INVESTIGATIVE POWERS UNDER THE ACT 1986

15.2 Under either type of winding up, the company ceases to carry on business and the directors' powers cease. The court may appoint a provisional liquidator at any time after the presentation of the winding up petition. Chapter V of the Act enables the official receiver[8] to require company officers or other people who were employed by the company to supply him with a statement as to the affairs of the company.[9] Where a company is being wound up, the official receiver may apply to the court for the public examination of any person who is or has been an officer of or concerned in the management of the company.[10] A person whom the court has required to attend a public examination cannot rely on the privilege against self-incrimination[11] (on the basis that he may be charged with a criminal offence in respect of the matters subject of the examination) but a statement made in a statement of affairs (s.131) or in the course of the examination cannot be used in evidence in criminal proceedings against him[12] except for those under the Act (e.g. s.208(1)) specified in s.433(3) or for perjury.

The court may also order any person who has in his possession or control any property, books, papers or records to which the company is entitled to deliver up, surrender or transfer the property to the liquidator or provisional liquidator.[13] There is a corresponding duty on past and present officers or employees of a company in administration or liquidation to provide the liquidator or provisional liquidator with information concerning the company.[14] If the Secretary of State or official receiver is satisfied that material obtained under s.235[15] is required for the purpose of investigation by a prosecuting authority, he may disclose it without giving notice to the person who provided it;[16] accordingly, there is no "derivative use immunity" in respect of material disclosed under the duty upon company officers and other specified people under the section.[17] The court (on the application of, e.g. the liquidator) may also summon to appear before it any officer of the company or other person known or suspected of having in his possession any company property, or any other person the court thinks capable of giving information about the affairs etc. of the company and require him to submit an affidavit setting out his dealings with the company or to produce

---

[8] By s.132 the official receiver is given the duty of investigating the affairs of the company and why it has failed; and see *Re Pantmaenog Timber Co Ltd* [2004] 1 A.C. 158 HL.

[9] s.131.

[10] s.133.

[11] *Bishopsgate Investment Management Ltd v Maxwell* [1993] Ch.1 CA (Civil).

[12] s.433(2).

[13] s.234(2).

[14] s.235(2).

[15] Or under s.236; *Re RGB Resources Plc; Shierson v Rastogi* [2003] 1 W.L.R. 586 CA (Civ), and see below.

[16] *R. v Brady* [2005] 1 Cr.App.R. 5 CA.

[17] See Corporations and Human Rights.

any books, papers or records under his control concerning the company.[18] The examination takes place before a judge or registrar. The witness is entitled to know in advance in general terms upon what he is to be examined, but he cannot refuse to answer on the ground that he might incriminate himself, even if criminal proceedings have already been commenced against him.[19] However, a statement made by an examinee cannot be used in evidence against him in subsequent proceedings except in the circumstances set out above.[20] Section 236 extends to anything reasonably required by, e.g. the liquidator to carry out his function.[21]

CRIMINAL OFFENCES UNDER THE 1986 ACT

The Insolvency Act 1986 creates numerous criminal offences. We refer to those which seem most relevant to the subject matter of this book.[22] **15.3**

SUMMARY PROCEEDINGS: WHERE AND WHEN

As with the Companies Act[23] offences, the vast majority of offences relate to a failure to act as required by the statutory framework which is set out in order to provide as much transparency and accurate information to creditors, shareholders and customers of the company as possible. For the most part, these offences are summary only. Summary proceedings for any offence (whether summary only or triable either way) may be taken against a corporation at any place at which it has a place of business.[24] **15.4**

Proceedings may be commenced for an offence under the Act by an information laid within three years of the commission of the offence and within 12 months of the date on which evidence sufficient in the opinion of the Director of Public Prosecutions or the Secretary of State to justify proceedings came to his knowledge.[25]

---

[18] s.236.
[19] *Re Arrows Ltd (No.2)* [1992] Ch. 545, CA (Civ).
[20] s.433.
[21] *Re British & Commonwealth Holdings Plc (Nos 1 and 2)* [1993] A.C. 426 HL; and see *Re Pantmaenog Timber Co Ltd* [2004] 1 A.C. 158.
[22] Sch.10 of the Insolvency Act 1986 as amended contains all the offences; see Appendix B.
[23] 1985 and 1989 above.
[24] s.431(1). This includes a trade or profession—s.436.
[25] s.431(2); the date of such knowledge will be conclusively proved by a certificate issued by the Director of Public Prosecutions or Secretary of State—s.43(4).

CHAPTER 15

CRIMINAL LIABILITY OF INDIVIDUALS

15.5 Apart from a corporation's liability for an offence under the Act, an individual may be liable not only as a principal but also, in some circumstances, expressly as a secondary party. Section 430(5) defines an "officer who is in default" as "any officer of the company who knowingly and wilfully authorises or permits the default, refusal or contravention mentioned in the enactment".

CONSENT, CONNIVANCE AND NEGLECT

15.6 Section 432 provides that where an offence is committed by a body corporate with the consent or connivance of, or is attributable to neglect on the part of, any officer of the company (or person purporting so to act) he too is guilty of an offence. Certain offences under the Act are expressly excepted, including ss.206–211, in "Chapter X: Malpractice Before and During Liquidation".[26]

INSOLVENCY OFFENCES AND THE BURDEN OF PROOF

15.7 The criminal law applies different criteria to bankrupts and those involved with insolvent companies by virtue of their particular situation. The Report of the Cork Committee into Insolvency Law and Practice of 1982[27] noted the Law Commission's conclusion that insolvency cases should continue to be dealt with outside the general criminal law because:

> "being a bankrupt ... justifies the imposition of more stringent criminal liability than would be appropriate for solvent citizens."

A benefit of incorporation is that brings with it limited liability, but it does so on conditions, including those imposed when a company is insolvent, which are intended to protect the company's assets so they remain available to settle its debts. Insolvency law requires the safe-keeping of all the assets that should be comprised in the assets of an insolvent company (and in the estate of a bankrupt). In order to achieve this, the law imposes on an officer of an insolvent company obligations to disclose details of the whereabouts of, or any disposal of, company property and to deliver up to the liquidator any company property and any books and papers in his control. The law creates various criminal offences punishable by way of a fine or imprisonment for those who conceal or dispose of company assets; it provides a

---

[26] The other exceptions are ss.30, 39, 51, 53, 54, 62, 64, 66, 85, 89, 164 and 188.
[27] Cmnd. 8558.

defence for the person charged to prove he had no intent to defraud.[28] By way of example, s.352 of the Act provides:

> "Where in the case of an offence under any provision of this Chapter it is stated that this section applies, a person is not guilty of an offence if he proves that, at the time of the conduct constituting the offence, he had no intent to defraud or to conceal the state of his affairs."

The wording of such provisions plainly places the burden of proof on the defendant. Whether the imposition of a legal burden is compatible with art.6(2) of the Convention has frequently been considered in the context of various provisions of the Insolvency Act since the coming into force of the Human Rights Act 1998.

In *R. v Carass*,[29] the Court of Appeal, following the reasoning of the House of Lords in *R. v Lambert*,[30] held that the burden on the defendant imposed by s.206(1)(a) was evidential and not legal.[31] In *R. v Daniel (Anthony Lala)*[32] however, which concerned parallel provisions relating to bankruptcy,[33] the Court of Appeal held that, but for the fact that *Carass* was binding upon it, it would *not* have held the burden on the defendant to be evidential only. Auld L.J. stated:

> "30 ... The 1986 Act is aimed at a defined and circumscribed set of circumstances in which the law imposes duties upon an individual. When a person becomes bankrupt he is made aware of its purpose and the duties it imposes on him. Unlike citizens who are not bankrupt, he knows that he must make full disclosure of all material facts, that he is questioned and that he must answer the questions truthfully. Further he knows that the purpose of the disclosure is to protect the rights of his creditors...
>
> 31 ... Why should it be unreasonable to require a person, who has deliberately concealed a debt in circumstances where he knows he was obliged to disclose it, to prove that he did not intend to defraud or to conceal the state of his affairs. Such a burden does not seem to us, in the circumstances we have mentioned, to contravene Article 6(2)."

These decisions were both reviewed by the Court of Appeal in a consolidated appeal before a 5 judge court presided over by the Lord Chief Justice, Lord Woolf.[34] The Court considered the legislative policy and scheme of the Act, that it may be tempting for those involved in the

---

[28] The same applies to bankrupts.
[29] [2001] EWCA 2845.
[30] [2001] 2 Cr.App.R. 28.
[31] For a detailed discussion of this topic, see Reverse Burdens in Corporations and Human Rights, Ch.12.
[32] [2002] EWCA Crim 959.
[33] ss.354(1)(b) and 352 1.A.
[34] *Att-Gen's Reference (No.1 of 2004)* [2004] 2 Cr.App.R. 27.

management of an insolvent company (or a bankrupt) to conceal or dispose of such assets to the disadvantage of creditors, and in particular, the details and circumstances of any concealment or disposal may be known only to that person:

> "In our judgment, these considerations will normally justify the imposition on the defendant, who is proved to have deliberately acted in a manner that gives rise to an inference that he sought to defraud his creditors, of the burden of proving, on the balance of probabilities, that he did not intend to do so."[35]

The Court considered two provisions, both concerning bankruptcy, namely ss.353(1)(b) and 357(1). Under the latter, a bankrupt is guilty of an offence if he makes or causes to be made, or has, in the period of five years ending with the commencement of the bankruptcy, made or caused to be made, any gift or transfer of, or any charge on, his property. Given the width of the offence, the extended period it covers (when bankruptcy might not even have been on the horizon) and the fact that the prosecution does not have to prove anything unusual or irregular in relation to the gift or disposal, the Court considered that to require the bankrupt to prove he had no intent to defraud was not justified and infringed art.6(2).

However, s.353 is quite different in scope; to secure a conviction, the prosecution must prove (i) that the bankrupt failed to inform the official receiver of a disposal of property that, but for the disposal, would be comprised in the estate; and (ii) that the disposal was not in the ordinary course of business or made in payment of ordinary living expenses. It is "a normal inference from the failure to inform the official receiver of an unusual disposal that the bankrupt intended to defeat the claims of creditors or to conceal the true state of affairs".[36] In those circumstances, to impose a legal burden on the bankrupt to prove (on a balance of probabilities) that he did not intend to defraud was compatible with art.6(2). The legislature had attached insufficient importance to the presumption of innocence in creating this offence.

15.8   The Court did not follow the decision in *Carass* (an insolvency case), which it regarded as impliedly overruled by the decision in *R. v Johnstone*.[37] In *Sheldrake v DPP* Lord Bingham endorsed this approach, stating that *Carass* was wrongly decided.[38]

Thus, whether a provision in the Act imposes a legal (as opposed to evidential) burden on the defendant to prove he had no intention to defraud, will depend upon the context of the particular offence and whether the imposition of that burden is justified.

---

[35] at para.41.
[36] at para.43.
[37] [2003] 1 W.L.R. 1736 HL.
[38] [2005] 1 A.C. 264, 33.

Fraud etc. In Anticipation of Winding Up—Section 206

Under s.206(1), a past or present officer[39] of a company which is subject to a **15.9**
winding up order or has passed a resolution for a voluntary winding up is
deemed to have committed an offence if within the 12 months immediately
preceding the commencement of the winding up he has done any of the
following:

(a) concealed any part of the company's property to the value of
£500[40] or more, or concealed any debt due to the company;

(b) fraudulently removed[41] any part of the company's property to the
value of £500[42] or more;

(c) concealed, destroyed, mutilated or falsified any book or paper
affecting or relating to the company's property or affairs;

(d) made any false entry in any book or paper[43] affecting or relating to
the company's property or affairs;

(e) fraudulently parted with, altered or made any omission in any
document affecting or relating to the company's property or
affairs;

(f) pawned, pledged or disposed of any property of the company
which has been obtained on credit and has not been paid for
(unless the disposition was in the ordinary course of the company's business).

In *R. v Robinson*,[44] R, the director of a company which went into voluntary
liquidation, was charged, amongst other counts, with fraudulently removing
property within 12 months of the commencement of a winding up order. A
month before the voluntary liquidation and two months before the court
ordered the winding up, he had sent a cheque for £14,000 to a firm of
solicitors in respect of a prospective purchase of 50 per cent of the equity in
a transport company. The deal was not concluded and the money was sent
back to R who did not return it to the company. It was the Crown's case
that the whole transaction was part of an asset stripping plan and fraudulent
from the beginning. R was convicted and appealed on the ground that to
prove a fraudulent removal of property the fraudulent intention had to exist
at a time when the money (or cheque in this case) was originally sent for the
purchase. The Court of Appeal disagreed. Giving the judgment of the court,
Stuart Smith L.J. stated:

---

[39] Including a shadow director—s.206(3).

[40] This figure may be changed by statutory instrument.

[41] Removal of money includes money diverted elsewhere which should have been returned to
the company—*R. v Robinson* [1990] B.C.C. 656.

[42] This figure may be changed by statutory instrument.

[43] This expression has been held to include computer disks: *R. v McCredie* [2000] B.C.C. 617
CA.

[44] [1990] B.C.C. 656.

"The diversion of the debt owed to the company is just as much a removal of property of the company as if the original payment was direct to [the third party]. It is quite plain in our judgment that even if the fraudulent intent was only formed at the stage where the instruction was given to pay the money to [the third party], it was sufficient."[45]

By s.206(2) if, at any time *after* the winding up he does any of the things in (a)–(f), he is deemed to have committed an offence; moreover, such a person is deemed to have committed an offence if he is "privy to the doing by another" of the things mentioned in (c), (d) or (e) within 12 months of the winding up or at any time afterwards.

Section 206(4) provides defences for the person charged to prove: that he had no intent to defraud in respect of offences (1)(a) or (f) and (2); or that he had "no intent to conceal the state of affairs of the company or to defeat the law" in respect of offences (1)(c) or (d) and (2). The subsection imposes a legal burden on the defendant to prove (on a balance of probabilities) that he did not intend to defraud or to defeat the law.[46]

Each person who takes in pawn or pledge or receives company property in circumstances which amount to another person committing an offence under s.206(1)(f) knowing of those circumstances himself commits an offence.

All these offences are triable either way. On summary conviction a defendant is liable to six months imprisonment and/or the statutory maximum fine; on indictment the maximum sentence is seven years' imprisonment and/or an unlimited fine.

TRANSACTIONS IN FRAUD OF CREDITORS—SECTION 207

15.10 Under s.207(1) an officer[47] of a company which is subject to a winding up order or has passed a resolution for a voluntary winding up is deemed to have committed an offence if he has:

(a) made, or caused to be made any gift or transfer of or any charge on, or caused or connived at the levying of any execution against the company's property; or

(b) has concealed or removed any part of the company's property since or within two months before, the date of any unsatisfied judgement or order for the payment obtained against the company.[48]

---

[45] At p.662.
[46] *Sheldrake v DPP* [2005] 1 A.C. 264 per Lord Bingham at para.33; see paras 12.22 and 12.23.
[47] This section does not apply to shadow directors.
[48] The same maximum sentences apply as in s.206.

It is a defence for the officer to prove that, at the time of the conduct constituting the offence he had no intent to defraud the company's creditors.[49] In relation to s.207(1)(a), a person is not guilty of an offence if the relevant conduct occurred more than five years before the commencement of the winding up.[50] Applying the reasoning of the Court of Appeal in *Att-Gen's Reference (No.1 of 2004)*[51] it is likely that the burden in relation to s.207(1)(a) will be treated by the court as evidential only, whereas under (b) it is a legal burden.

MISCONDUCT IN COURSE OF WINDING UP—SECTION 208

By s.208(1) a past or present officer (including a shadow director) of any **15.11** company which is being wound up commits an offence if he:

(a) does not to the best of his knowledge and belief fully and truly discover to the liquidator all the company's property, and how and to whom and for what consideration and when the company disposed of any part of that property (except property disposed of in the ordinary course of business); or

(b) does not deliver up to the liquidator, or as he directs, all of the company's property which is in his custody or under his control, and which he is required by law to deliver up; or

(c) does not deliver up to the liquidator, or as he directs, all books and papers[52] in his custody or under his control belonging to the company and which he is required by law to deliver up; or

(d) knowing or believing that a false debt has been proved by any person in the winding up, fails to inform the liquidator as soon as practicable; or

(e) after the commencement of the winding up, prevents the production of any book or paper affecting or relating to the company's property or affairs.

Moreover, under s.208(2) such a person is deemed to have committed an offence if, in the 12 months preceding the commencement of the winding up, he has attempted to account for the company's property by fictitious losses or expenses; or if, after the commencement, he attempts so to account he commits an offence.

The past or present officers of the company are under a positive duty to comply with the Act's provisions; so the offences under s.208(1) of non-delivery up to the liquidator of company property and books and of non-

---

[49] s.207(2)(b).
[50] s.207(2)(a).
[51] [2004] 2 CAR 424.
[52] Following the case of *R. v McCredie, R. v French* (2000) B.C.C. 617 CA this includes computer disks.

discovery to the liquidator of company property do not depend on a prior request from the liquidator.[53]

The defence of lack of intent to defraud applies to s.1(a), (b) or (c). Similarly a person charged under s.1(e) will have a defence if he proves that he had no intention to conceal the state of affairs of the company or to defeat the law. This subsection imposes a legal burden on the defendant.[54]

Similar punishments apply to s.208 offences as to ss.206 and 207. In *R. v Bevis*[55] the Court of Appeal ranked this offence below fraudulent trading in terms of the seriousness, but decided that, since it goes to the root of company law and requires an element of dishonesty, it still warranted a sentence of imprisonment, the conduct passing the custody threshold.

FALSIFICATION OF COMPANY'S BOOKS—SECTION 209

15.12 Destruction, mutilation, alteration or falsification of books, papers or securities of a company which is being wound up, with intent to deceive anyone is an offence if done by an officer or contributory[56] of the company. It is also an offence to make or be privy to the making of any false or fraudulent entry in a register, book of account or document belonging to the company with a similar intent.

The punishment is seven years' imprisonment and/or an unlimited fine on indictment, and a maximum of six months or the statutory maximum fine in the magistrates' court. This offence is similar to false accounting contrary to s.17 of the Theft Act 1968.[57] Which of the two will be the more appropriate to charge will depend on the circumstances of the case.

MATERIAL OMISSIONS FROM STATEMENT RELATING TO COMPANY'S AFFAIRS—SECTION 210

15.13 Section 210(1) provides that it is an offence for any present or past officer of a company which is being wound up to make any material omission in any statement relating to its affairs. Where a company has been ordered to be wound up or has passed a resolution for a voluntary winding up such a person is deemed to have committed the offence if, prior to the winding up, he has made any material omission in a statement. The accused has a defence if he proves that he had no intent to defraud. Again, the maximum sentence on indictment is seven years' imprisonment.

---

[53] *R. v McCredie and French* [2000] B.C.C 617 CA.
[54] *R. (Griffin) v Richmond Magistrates' Court* [2008] EWHC 84 (Admin); [2008] W.L.R. (D) 13.
[55] [2001] 2 Cr.App.R.(S.) 49 CA.
[56] A contributory means every person liable to contribute to the assets of the company in the event of its being wound up—s.79(1).
[57] See Ch.18, False Accounting.

False Representations to Creditors—Section 211

By s.211 a past or present officer of a company being wound up commits an **15.14** offence if he makes any false representation or commits any other fraud in order to obtain the consent of the company's creditors to an agreement about the company's affairs or to the winding up. Such an officer is deemed to have committed an offence if, prior to the winding up, he so acts for that purpose. Officer includes a shadow director. On indictment the maximum punishment is seven years' imprisonment or an unlimited fine.

Restriction on Re-Use of Company Names—Section 216

Section 216 was introduced to meet the concerns raised in the Report of the **15.15** Review Committee (Insolvency Law and Practice—Cmnd 8558, June 1982) concerning the "Phoenix Syndrome". This syndrome typically occurs where an insolvent company is put into liquidation and its business bought, often at an undervalue, by a new company formed by the individuals who had owned and run the old one. Because of the principle of limited liability, they are shielded from the debts of the old company and can continue the same business as before under the new company's aegis, to the detriment of the old company's creditors. This section prevents the directors (and shadow directors) from using the old company name or a name by which it was known, or which is so similar to the name as to suggest an association with it; thus the prohibited name may be *any* name by which the business was known.

Section 216 provides:

(a) This section applies to a person where a company ("the liquidating company") has gone into insolvent liquidation on or after the appointed day and he was a director or shadow director of the company at any time in the period of 12 months ending with the day before it went into liquidation.

(b) For the purposes of this section, a name is a prohibited name in relation to such a person if—

   (i) it is a name by which the liquidating company was known at any time in that period of 12 months, or

   (ii) it is a name which is so similar to a name falling within paragraph (a) as to suggest an association with that company.

(c) Except with leave of the court or in such circumstances as may be prescribed, a person to whom this section applies shall not at any time in the period of five years beginning with the day on which the liquidating company went into liquidation—

   (i)   be a director of any other company that is known by a pro-
         hibited name, or
   (ii) in any way, whether directly or indirectly, be concerned or
         take part in the promotion, formation or management of any
         such company, or
   (iii) in any way, whether directly or indirectly, be concerned or
         take part in the carrying on of a business carried on (other-
         wise than by a company) under a prohibited name.

The section applies to any person who has been a director or shadow
director of a relevant company within the 12 month period ending on the
day prior to the company entering insolvent liquidation. Such a person may
not, for a period of five years beginning with the day on which the relevant
company went into liquidation, be a director or "shadow director" of a
company that is known by a prohibited name. The section is not aimed at
the new company itself, nor its shareholders.

15.16   The offence contrary to s.216 is one of strict liability; accordingly there is
no burden on the prosecution to prove knowledge or an intention to defraud
or deceive.[58] It is irrelevant whether the use of the prohibited name is
designed to misuse the name or assets of the old company or mislead
creditors of either company.

A person may seek the leave of the court to be a director of any other
company known by a prohibited name—s.216(3). Rules set out the procedure for such application.[59] Rule 4.231 itself contains an exception to the
prohibition where the new company with the prohibited name has been
known by that name throughout the 12 month period ending with the day
before the liquidating company went into liquidation.

In deciding whether to grant leave, the court[60] shall have regard to the
harm at which the provision is aimed:

> "First, the danger that the business of the old insolvent company has
> been acquired at an undervalue—or is otherwise to be expropriated—to
> the detriment of its creditors; and, secondly, the danger that creditors of
> the old company may be misled into the belief that there has been no
> change in the corporate vehicle. The 'phoenix' must be disclosed as
> that."[61]

On indictment the maximum sentence is two years' imprisonment and an
unlimited fine, six months and/or £5,000 on summary conviction; this
reflects the public concern at the mischief of the Phoenix Syndrome. Where

---

[58] *R. v Cole, Lees & Birch* [1998] 2 B.C.C. 87 234, 237–8 CA.
[59] Insolvency Rules 1986.
[60] The High Court or a county court in England and Wales, although not necessarily the one
   involved in the winding up or liquidation.
[61] *Penrose v Official Receiver* [1996] B.C.C. 311, 317 per Chadwick J., and see *Re Lightning
   Electrical Contractors Ltd* [1996] B.C.C. 950.

the court is satisfied that a defendant was not using a prohibited name with any dishonest or fraudulent intent, the offence falls into an entirely different category which should be reflected in the sentence passed. However, even in the absence of fraudulent intent, the offence will be serious enough to warrant a community penalty (as an alternative to custody).[62] In particular, in sentencing a defendant for this offence the court should not equate the situation with that in which a person is disqualified from acting as a director.[63]

DUTY TO CO-OPERATE WITH OFFICE-HOLDER IN A WINDING UP

Section 235 requires the persons set out in subs.(3) to co-operate with the **15.17** office-holder (i.e. the administrator, administrative receiver, liquidator or provisional liquidator, including the official receiver)[64] in the winding up process. Each person mentioned in subs.(3) shall:

> "(a) give to the office-holder such information concerning the company and its promotion, formation, business, dealings, affairs or property as the office- holder may at any time after the effective date[65] reasonably require, and
>
> (b) attend on the office-holder at such time as the latter may reasonably require."

If a person without reasonable excuse fails to comply with any obligation imposed by this section he is liable to a fine and, for continued contravention, to a daily default fine. The offence is triable either way.[66] Although the fine in the magistrates' court is limited to the statutory maximum, because there is provision for one-tenth of the statutory maximum fine to be imposed for continuing daily default, the available penalty in the lower court may well exceed the statutory maximum.

MORATORIUM OFFENCES

The Insolvency Act 2000 introduced the power of directors to obtain a **15.18** moratorium for the company when they propose a voluntary arrangement under the Insolvency Act 1986. A moratorium gives the directors a breathing space in which to reorganise the company's affairs in an effort to benefit the company and improve its financial position. A number of

---

[62] *R. v Cole, Lees & Birch* [1998] 2 B.C.C. 87.
[63] *Penrose v Official Receiver* [1996] B.C.C. 311.
[64] See s.234(1).
[65] s.235(4) defines the effective date.
[66] See Sch.10.

offences for misconduct during the moratorium provide not only for financial penalties, but also, in some instances, terms of imprisonment. Sch. 1, paras 41–42 set out a number of offences which correspond closely with ss.206–211 of the 1986 Act. Similar maximum sentences (a maximum of seven years' imprisonment and/or an unlimited fine) apply. There are, moreover, offences of failing to comply with the statutory scheme for a moratorium specified in the Act.

CHAPTER 16

FINANCIAL SERVICES & MARKETS ACT 2000

As a result of the burgeoning of financial instruments and investments **16.1** throughout the last century and into this, there has been increasing regulation of those who are involved in financial services. Originally, supervision was mainly self-regulatory, but, through piecemeal legislation, various areas were made subject to rules with disciplinary and/or criminal offences as sanctions for misconduct. Until recently, there was little common thread binding either the various financial institutions within the UK or across international borders. However, as a result of pressure from the European Union, and the European Convention of Human Rights there is now greater consistency between countries. The Financial Services & Markets Act 2000 ("FSMA") was enacted with the aim of providing consistency and certainty in approach to those involved in financial services irrespective of specific discipline or interest. The overriding purpose of the legislation is the protection of the consumer; powers granted by the Act to the regulatory body are designed to achieve this aim. FSMA provides for a system of authorisation and/or exemption, assistance and regulation. Contravention of regulations may result in private civil actions, disciplinary proceedings or criminal proceedings. Although two are outside the scope of this work, it is worth noting that, as a result of the ECHR, disciplinary proceedings, albeit classified by FSMA as non-criminal, may not be so categorised by the ECtHR.[1] It is certainly true that those drafting the statute had in mind the constraints of art.6 in delineating procedures to be followed.[2]

---

[1] See Corporations and The European Convention on Human Rights, Ch.12.
[2] For example, in disciplinary proceedings for market abuse, the availability of Legal Aid; the limitation on use of compelled statements; the clarification of what constitutes market abuse by the concept of "safe harbours".

FSMA provides for the setting up of the Financial Services Authority ("FSA") to regulate the financial system[3] with these objectives in mind:

(a) market confidence;

(b) public awareness;

(c) the protection of consumers; and

(d) the reduction of financial crime.

The FSA is tasked not only with regulation but also with giving guidance to those it is required to regulate and to consumers; the authority issues codes and policy statements as well as the FSA Handbook and is also required to give specific advice. For example, in an annual lecture delivered in March 2002, the criteria the FSA will use when considering action for alleged market abuse were set out as follows:

(a) Has there been an impact on market confidence or have consumers actually or potentially lost money?

(b) Will prompt action by the FSA prevent further damage?

(c) Will action by the FSA have the effect of deterring such behaviour in future?

The Chairman stated that the FSA:

"aims to prioritise rigorously, investigating only those cases which are material and significant"

and would not be interested in pursuing "technical or inadvertent infringements of the rules".[4]

16.2   Financial crime includes any offence involving fraud or dishonesty, misconduct or misuse of information relating to financial markets or handling the proceeds of crime.[5] By s.6(4) FSMA, jurisdiction for an offence specifically extends to an act or omission which would be an offence if it had taken place in the United Kingdom.

The FSA has power to prosecute offences under FSMA (s.402). The criteria it must apply to a decision to prosecute are subject to the Code for Crown Prosecutors. In particular, the FSA should consider whether, having regard to the seriousness of the offence, it is in the public interest to prosecute; it may be that civil intervention or enforcement would be more appropriate; in civil proceedings under the Act:

---

[3] Defined in s.3(2) as:

(a) financial markets and exchanges;

(b) regulated activities; and

(c) other activities connected with financial markets and exchanges.

[4] Worshipful Company of Chartered Secretaries and Administrators Annual Lecture 5.3.01, reported in Jordans Corporate Law Bulletin May 2002.

[5] s.6(3) FSMA 2000.

(a) an injunction can be imposed to guard against a likely or continuing breach[6];

(b) a restitution order can be made and monies distributed to those affected disadvantageously by the contravention[7];

(c) compulsory winding up/administrative/bankruptcy orders can be made[8];

(d) remedial orders, restraining orders and injunctions may be made not only against the principal who contravenes the provisions but also any other person who appears to have been knowingly concerned in the contravention.[9]

An offence committed by a body corporate which is shown: (a) to have been committed with the consent or connivance of an officer, or (b) to be attributable to any neglect on his part will amount to an offence by that officer—s.400(1). "Officer" is defined as:

"(a) a director, member of the committee of management, chief executive, manager, secretary or other similar officer of the body, or a person purporting to act in any such capacity; and

(b) an individual who is a controller of the body [corporate]".[10]

The purpose behind the regulatory scheme seems to be to prosecute only the most serious and intentional of contraventions, and moreover, to pursue employers (be they corporations, partnerships or otherwise) in preference to individual employees or officers. However, s.400 and the extension of remedial orders to individuals, demonstrate that officers of corporations (as defined) and indeed other individuals may, in the appropriate circumstances, be at risk of prosecution and punishment, as well as disciplinary action.[11] The latter may be:

(a) a public reprimand;

(b) prohibition from all or some involvement in a regulated activity (s.56);

(c) withdrawal of approval to perform a function if a person is no longer fit and proper (s.63);

(d) a fine (s.66).

---

[6] s.380 FSMA.

[7] s.382 FSMA.

[8] ss 367(1)(c); 359(1)(c); 372(1) and (7)(b) FSMA.

[9] ss.380(2) and (3); 382(1) FSMA.

[10] s.400(5) FSMA. The provisions also cover partnerships, a corporation managed by its members and unincorporated associations.

[11] Regulations may also extend liability pursuant to s.400 to foreign companies (s.400(7)).

Regulation

16.3 FSMA provides a general system for authorisation and exemption in the regulated field which is far broader than the Financial Services Act 1986.[12] Only those who are authorised or exempt can lawfully carry out regulated activity[13] (although the fact that an authorised person carries out regulated activity otherwise than in accordance with permission, "does not make a person guilty of an offence"[14]). All corporations involved in financial services must be aware of the boundary between regulated and non-regulated areas. If the line is crossed without authorisation or exemption, the possibility of criminal consequences will follow.[15] The punishment for contravention of the general prohibition is an unlimited fine or two years' imprisonment. A corporation may apply for permission to carry on a regulated activity (s.40).

A person who contravenes the general prohibition is guilty of an offence,[16] as is an unauthorised person who is not exempt, who describes himself as authorised or exempt, or who "behaves or otherwise holds himself out in a manner which indicates (or which is reasonably likely to be understood as indicating) that he is ..." either authorised or exempt.[17]

It is a defence to both sections that the person "took all reasonable precautions and exercised all due diligence to avoid committing the offence".[18]

Financial Promotion

16.4 By s.21 FSMA, a person must not, when acting in the course of business[19] communicate an invitation or inducement to engage in investment activity[20] unless he is authorised or the content of the communication is approved by an authorised person. A contravention of s.21 is an offence under s.25 subject to the defence "for the accused to show:

---

[12] ss.19–30 FSMA. See FSMA 2000 (Exemption) Order 2001 (SI 2001/1201) for exempt persons; FSMA 2000 (Carrying on Regulated Activities by Way of Business) Order 2001 (SI 2001/1177) for specific exemptions relating to deposit taking, investment business and occupational pension schemes.

[13] Regulated activities are defined as "activity by way of business relating to investment or property carried on in the UK"—FSMA Sch.2 Pts I and II.

[14] s.20 FSMA.

[15] s.23 FSMA.

[16] s.23 FSMA.

[17] s.24.

[18] See Regulatory Offences—Common phrases, Ch.20.17.

[19] Whether or not a person is acting in the course of business may be subject to an order of the Treasury—s.21(4).

[20] s.21(8)–(10) provide definitions of investment activity and controlled activities.

(a) that he believed on reasonable grounds that the content of the communication was prepared or approved for the purposes of section 21, by an authorised person; or

(b) that he took all reasonable precautions and exercised all due diligence to avoid committing the offence".[21]

Such an agreement may, distinct from criminal liability, be unenforceable against the other party and may be subject to compensation. It is to be noted that:

(a) financial promotion is wider than the scope of regulated activities by way of business and "investment advertising" (the term used under previous legislation);

(b) "In the course of business" will not normally apply to private individuals who communicate about investments via internet chatrooms outside of their regular activity, but does include cold calling and solicited calls;

(c) an activity is deemed to be caught territorially if a communication is made "in", "into" or "from" the UK;

(d) whether an activity is regulated or not is determined by FSMA 2000 (Regulated Activities) Order 2001.[22] If a person is in doubt he should contact the FSA for guidance. Failure to do so is likely to be evidence that "due diligence" was not exercised.

(e) The basic definition of financial promotion[23] is subject to approximately 60 exemptions.

The punishment on indictment for contravening the restriction on financial promotion is an unlimited fine or two years' imprisonment.

FALSE CLAIMS TO BE EXEMPT FROM THE GENERAL PROHIBITION

There is exemption from the general prohibition of certain professionals by **16.5** virtue of s.327. It is an offence for a person falsely to describe himself or hold himself out as such a professional person to whom the general prohibition in relation to a regulated activity does not apply.[24]

It is a defence for the person to show that he took all reasonable precautions and exercised all due diligence to avoid committing the offence.

Section 333 is a summary only offence subject to a level 5 fine (but with an additional daily multiplier reflecting the number of days a public display of offending material continued).

---

[21] s.25(2).
[22] (SI 2001/544).
[23] See s.21 FSMA.
[24] s.333 FSMA.

LISTING PARTICULARS

16.6 Listing particulars as defined by ss.80 and 81 must be delivered for registration to the registrar of companies as defined—s.83(1). If there has been a failure to comply with those provisions, the issuer of the securities in question and any person who is "a party to the publication and aware of the failure" is guilty of an offence and liable on summary conviction to a fine not exceeding the statutory maximum and on indictment to an unlimited fine (s.83(3) and (4)). Similar provisions apply to advertisements which are to be published in connection with an application for listing.[25]

PUBLICATION OF PROSPECTUS

16.7 Where a prospectus is required to be published prior to the listing of particular new securities on an official list, it is an offence for any of those securities to be offered to the public in the United Kingdom prior to publication of the prospectus—s.85. The punishment on summary conviction is up to twelve months' imprisonment[26] or a fine not exceeding level 5 on the standard scale; on indictment, the punishment is up to two years' imprisonment and/or an unlimited fine. It will not be regarded as a criminal offence merely because the prospectus does not fully comply with listing requirements in form or content, although this may affect a person's exposure to civil proceedings and/or compensation.

FAILURE TO COMPLY WITH REQUIREMENTS

16.8 It is likely that the FSMA will be used to a significant extent to investigate alleged contraventions and malpractice. The FSA, and other designated persons who are specified in the FSMA have power to require the provision of information or production of documents. If a person required to provide such relevant information or produce such documents, for example, to a person appointed by the Treasury to hold an inquiry, fails to comply with the requirement, or otherwise obstructs the inquiry, a certificate to that effect may be sent to the High Court by the person holding the inquiry. If the court considers (having heard both parties) that the person's conduct would have been a contempt of court had the inquiry been court proceedings, it may deal with him as if he were in contempt.[27]

Similar provisions cover a failure to comply with an investigator's requirements. Section 177:

---

[25] s.98 FSMA.
[26] As amended by CJA 2003 from a date to be ordered.
[27] ss.15–18 FSMA.

177.—(1) If a person other than the investigator ("the defaulter") fails to comply with a requirement imposed on him under this Part the person imposing the requirement may certify that fact in writing to the court.

(2) If the court is satisfied that the defaulter failed without reasonable excuse to comply with the requirement, it may deal with the defaulter (and in the case of a body corporate, any director or officer) as if he were in contempt.[28]

(3) A person who knows or suspects that an investigation is being or is likely to be conducted under this Part is guilty of an offence if—

(a) he falsifies, conceals, destroys or otherwise disposes of a document which he knows or suspects is or would be relevant to such an investigation, or

(b) he causes or permits the falsification, concealment, destruction or disposal of such a document,

unless he shows that he had no intention of concealing facts disclosed by the documents from the investigator.

(4) A person who, in purported compliance with a requirement imposed on him under this Part—

(a) provides information which he knows to be false or misleading in a material particular, or

(b) recklessly provides information which is false or misleading in a material particular,

is guilty of an offence.

(5) A person guilty of an offence under subsection (3) or (4) is liable—

(a) on summary conviction, to imprisonment for a term not exceeding six months or a fine not exceeding the statutory maximum, or both;

(b) on conviction on indictment, to imprisonment for term not exceeding two years or a fine, or both.

(6) Any person who intentionally obstructs the exercise of any rights conferred by a warrant under section 176 is guilty of an offence and liable on summary conviction to imprisonment for a term not exceeding three months or a fine not exceeding level 5 on the standard scale, or both.

By virtue of s.174, a compelled statement made by a person to an investigator is admissible in evidence in all proceedings in which he is charged save for criminal proceedings or market abuse proceedings. In criminal or market abuse proceedings, no evidence relating to the statement

---

[28] To include member of a limited liability company.

may be adduced and no question relating to it may be asked by the prosecution (or FSA) unless evidence in relation to it is adduced by or a question relating to it is asked on behalf of the person charged. Various exceptions to that rule apply by virtue of s.174(3), so that in criminal proceedings for providing false or misleading information to an investigator[29] or to the FSA[30] or perjury[31] the evidence may be adduced (subject to any argument on relevance or admissibility).

FAILURE TO NOTIFY CHANGES OF CONTROL

16.9 In order for the FSMA scheme to work, the FSA must have knowledge of and control over those who are, or who stand behind, authorised persons. So, where changes in control of an authorised person (typically a UK incorporated company) are proposed or occur, these must be notified to the FSA.[32] The FSA must be notified of increases and decreases in shareholdings and voting power not only in the authorised person but in any parent undertaking of the authorised person. The FSA must consider the proposal within three months of receipt of the notice. It may approve it, conditionally or unconditionally, or object. The FSA may also notify its objection to existing control of an authorised person pursuant to s.187. It may issue a restriction notice where shares have been improperly acquired so as to limit control over the authorised person—s.189. Failure to comply with the duty to notify acquisition of control[33] or reduction of control[34] are offences contrary to s.191(1) and (2) respectively. A person who carries out a proposal following the service of a notice of control before expiry of the notice period, whether notified of the FSA's determination or not, commits an offence. All offences are summary only except for s.191(5) which is triable either way with a maximum sentence of two years' imprisonment and/ or an unlimited fine.

Section 191(5) provides: "A person to whom a notice of objection has been given is guilty of an offence if he acquires the control to which the notice applies at a time when the notice is still in force."

It is a defence to s.191(1) for a person to show that, at the time of the offence, he had no knowledge of the act or circumstances by virtue of which the duty to notify the FSA arose. The burden of proof is on the defendant.[35]

---

[29] s.177(4) and 284(5).
[30] s.398.
[31] s.5 Perjury Act 1911.
[32] Pt XII FSMA 2000
[33] s.178.
[34] s.190.
[35] s.191(9).

If a person subsequently becomes aware of the act or circumstances and fails to notify the FSA within 14 days, he commits a summary offence.[36]

Consumer Credit Act Business

By s.203 FSMA, the Office of Fair Trading may impose a consumer credit **16.10** prohibition notice on a firm which it considers has contravened or is likely to contravene ss.25(2)(a)–(d) of the Consumer Credit Act 1974.[37] Once a notice is served (whether absolutely or not), a firm contravening the notice is guilty of an offence contrary to s.203(9) and is liable to be fined. Similarly, by s.204, the Office of Fair Trading may issue a notice imposing a restriction to a consumer credit EEA firm. A firm acting in contravention of that restriction will likewise be liable to conviction and fine.[38]

Providing Misleading Information

Persons are charged with investigating or inquiring and auditing authorised **16.11** persons and activities throughout the statute. It is within their powers to require persons, whether authorised or not, and whether individual officers or corporations, to attend and provide information or documentation. FSMA provides for a framework of offences, of failing to comply with or obstructing such requirements, and also of providing misleading information; e.g. to an appointed auditor or actuary[39]; or to the FSA[40]; or the Director General of Fair Trading[41]; or to an investigator appointed to investigate the affairs of a unit trust or collective investment scheme.[42]

A person who knowingly or recklessly gives an appointed auditor or actuary information which is false or misleading in a material particular is liable to an unlimited fine and/or up to two years' imprisonment. An authorised corporation's "officer, controller or manager" will also be liable if he is knowingly or recklessly involved.

Section 398 FSMA provides a "catch-all" offence of knowingly or recklessly providing the FSA with information which is false or misleading in a material particular, which is not covered by another provision. The maximum punishment is an unlimited fine on indictment.

---

[36] s.191(11).
[37] As amended by the Enterprise Act 2002.
[38] s.204(4).
[39] s.346.
[40] s.398.
[41] s.399 in relation to the Competition Act 1998.
[42] s.284.

MARKET RIGGING: MISLEADING STATEMENTS AND PRACTICES

16.12 By s.397 FSMA two methods of offending are addressed: making misleading statements (whether by act or omission) and engaging in a course of conduct or doing an act which gives a false or misleading impression. The conduct targeted in both offences must either occur or have an impact in the United Kingdom.

Section 397

(1) This subsection applies to a person who—

(a) makes a statement, promise or forecast which he knows to be misleading, false or deceptive in a material particular;

(b) dishonestly conceals any material facts whether in connection with a statement, promise or forecast made by him or otherwise; or

(c) recklessly makes (dishonestly or otherwise) a statement, promise or forecast which is misleading, false or deceptive in a material particular.

(2) A person to whom subsection (1) applies is guilty of an offence if he makes the statement, promise or forecast or conceals the facts for the purpose of inducing, or is reckless as to whether it may induce, another person (whether or not the person to whom the statement, promise or forecast is made)—

(a) to enter or offer to enter into, or to refrain from entering or offering to enter into, a relevant agreement; or

(b) to exercise, or refrain from exercising, any rights conferred by a relevant investment.

Section 397(1) defines what a person must do or say in making a misleading statement. By s.397(2) the acts or omissions in s.397(1) must be "for the purpose of inducing" or "being reckless as to whether it may induce another ..." to act in relation to a relevant agreement or relevant investment.

A relevant agreement is defined in s.397(9) as relating to a relevant investment, the entering into or performance of the agreement constituting a "specified" activity. Relevant investment includes any right, asset or interest as specified[43] or prescribed.

16.13   To be guilty of making a misleading statement contrary to subs.(1) and (2), a person must know[44] or be reckless[45] as to whether it is misleading, false

---

[43] "Specified" means one specified in an order made by the Treasury s.397(14).
[44] s.397(1)(a).
[45] s.397(1)(c).

or deceptive in a material particular.[46] A person need not be dishonest except in the concealment of facts as in s.397(1)(b). A reckless statement has been defined as a "rash statement ... with no real basis of fact to support it and not caring whether it was true or false".[47]

Where several statements are made, each of which is true, but which are cumulatively misleading, an offence is made out. What matters is the overall impact of the statements taken together.[48]

> "The statement of a portion of the truth, accompanied by suggestions and inferences which would be possible and credible if it contained the whole truth, but become neither possible nor credible whenever the whole truth is divulged, is, to my mind, neither more nor less than a false statement".[49]

Examples of misleading statements caught by the statute may be lies about the performance of a company by a person who wishes to raise the share prices in order to sell his shareholding at a higher price; or a statement issued by a person which deliberately or recklessly misrepresents the financial forecast for the company in order to induce shareholders to retain their shares; or circulating misleading or deceptive information in order to encourage investors.

Concealing material facts requires an element of dishonesty. If a person deliberately and dishonestly conceals a material fact, it matters not whether he does it in order to induce another or being reckless as to whether it may induce another to enter into or offer to enter into (or refrain from so doing) a relevant agreement[50]; or to exercise, or refrain from exercising any rights conferred by a relevant investment.

DEFENCES

The broad purpose of the statute is to protect consumers and to try to ensure openness within the market. Thus by s.397(4) it is a defence for the accused to show that the statement promise or forecast was made in conformity with price stabilising rules or control of information rules, so the statute acknowledges that there will be occasions where an accused may be able to show that he acted in compliance with FSA rules on price stabilisation or that there were effective 'Chinese walls' operating.

16.14

Since the Government is well aware of the need for compliance with the

---

[46] Material particular. See False Accounting, Ch.18.
[47] *R. v Page Holden Dunning & Bradshaw* [1996] Crim.L.R. 821, (a case concerning s.47(1)(b) of the Financial Services Act 1986).
[48] *Aaron's Reefs Ltd v Twiss* [1896] A.C. 273.
[49] per Lord Watson at p.287.
[50] s.397(2)(a).

jurisprudence of the European Court of Human Rights, the following may be inferred:

(a) Compliance with FSA and other professional guidelines and "safe harbours" as outlined in FSA literature will be taken into account in any decision to prosecute and would be likely to result in an acquittal[51] if criminal proceedings were instituted.

(b) The statutory provision will have to be capable of being read with a degree of certainty as to what does fall within the criminal ambit.[52]

(c) Dependent upon the circumstances, a burden on an accused to prove a defence may be read down as an evidential burden i.e. once a defence has been raised it is for the prosecution to prove beyond reasonable doubt that it does not apply.[53]

The Act also catches a person engaging in misleading conduct.

MISLEADING CONDUCT

16.15 Section 397(3) provides:

> Any person who does any act or engages in any course of conduct which creates a false or misleading impression as to the market, or the price, or value of any relevant investment is guilty of an offence if he does so for the purpose of creating that impression and of thereby inducing another person to acquire, dispose of, subscribe for, or underwrite those investments or to refrain from doing so, or to exercise, or refrain from exercising, any rights conferred by those investments.

The offence targets conduct which is done for the purpose of inducing another to act in particular ways in relation to relevant investments.[54] It is unnecessary for the Crown to prove dishonesty. This section will apply, for example, to those engaging in artificial trades in an investment to make it seem the object of more interest and thus more attractive to other potential investors, or perhaps to a share support operation. It is arguable that the Guinness/Distillers situation in which an indemnity given to those assisting in bolstering up the share price in a takeover battle, was just such a concealment of facts.[55]

---

[51] See Code for Crown Prosecutors—"realistic prospect of conviction"; *http://cps.gov.uk/publications/docs/code2004*.
[52] art.7 ECHR.
[53] See Reverse Burden of Proof, para.12.10.
[54] See definition above.
[55] For a brief factual resume, see the headnote in *R. v Spens* [1991] 4 All E.R. 421.

DEFENCES

It is a defence to a misleading practices offence (or "market manipulation" **16.16** as it has been called) for the accused to show that he reasonably believed that his act or conduct would not create a false or misleading impression.[56] The accused will need to prove not just his subjective belief, but that his belief was reasonable to an objective standard.

There are also defences of acting for the purpose of stabilising the price of investments and in conformity with price stabilising rules[57]; and acting in conformity with control of information rules or with the relevant commission Regulations.[58] Thus a person who engages in conduct which in fact creates a misleading impression for the purpose of inducing another to act in accordance with s.397(3) will be able to raise a defence that either he believed (reasonably) that no such false or misleading impression would be created by his acts or conduct, or that he acted in accordance with FSA price stabilisation rules.

DISCLOSURE OF INFORMATION

It is an offence to disclose or use confidential information provided to the **16.17** FSA, competent authority or Secretary of State pursuant to their powers under the FSMA (ss.348, 350, and 352). It is a defence for the accused to prove that he did not know and had no reason to suspect that the information was confidential information or disclosed pursuant to requirements by the Revenue and Customs; or that he took all reasonable precautions and exercised all due diligence to avoid committing the offence.[59]

CONSENT, CONNIVANCE AND NEGLECT

By s.400 where an offence is committed by a corporation with the consent or **16.18** connivance of an officer, or attributable to his neglect, the officer as well as the corporation shall be guilty and liable to punishment.[60]

It is thus clear that, although the scheme of the Act is very much designed to target corporations and bodies which are authorised persons and employers, where individuals of sufficient seniority within the primary target

---

[56] s.397(5)(a).
[57] s.397(5)(b).
[58] s.397(5)(c).
[59] Disclosing information contrary to s.352(1) carries a maximum sentence on indictment of two years' imprisonment and/or an unlimited fine. Other offences are summary only.
[60] Similar provisions apply to a corporation managed by its members, an unincorporated association and partnership—ss.400(2)–(4) & (6).

are shown to be responsible for the corporate acts, they too will be liable to prosecution. "Officer" is defined in s.400(5) as:

(a) a director, member of the committee of management, chief executive, manager, secretary or other similar officer of the body [corporate], or a person purporting to act in any such capacity; and

(b) an individual who is a controller of the body [corporate].

In *Boal*[61] (a case concerning fire regulations) "manager" in a similar provision was held to be limited to those in a position of control similar to a director, and not to include a deputy store manager.

INSIDER DEALING

16.19 The offence of Insider Dealing is created by s.52 of the Criminal Justice Act 1993. The section refers to "an individual who has information as an insider"; it follows that this is an offence that is only capable of being committed by human beings as principal offenders. Although a corporation can commit the offence as a secondary party (e.g. as an aider, abettor or counsellor) or as a party to a conspiracy, it is plain from the use of the term "individual" that Parliament intended the primary target to be the people misusing information. The purpose of the legislation is: (1) to try to ensure a level playing field for those trading or dealing in securities; and (2) to punish those who are blameworthy. The maximum sentence is seven years' imprisonment and/or an unlimited fine. Insider Dealing is a crime which is committed either by acquiring or disposing of price-affected securities armed with inside information[62]; or by encouraging a person so to acquire or dispose of them[63]; or by improperly disclosing inside information to another[64]:

Many of the principle terms used, for example "inside information", "dealing information" and "public information" are defined in Part V of the Criminal Justice Act 1993; "securities" and "regulated markets" are defined by statutory instrument.[65] Specific defences are also provided.

MARKET ABUSE

16.20 Separate from the crime of insider dealing is the regime introduced under the Act of "Market Abuse". This is behaviour which:

---

[61] (1992) 95 Cr.App.R. 272.
[62] s.52(1).
[63] s.52(2)(a).
[64] s.52(2)(b).
[65] Insider Dealing (Securities and Regulated Markets) Order 1994 (SI 1994/187).

(1) (a) occurs in relation to—

    (i) qualifying investments admitted to trading on a prescribed market,

    (ii) qualifying investments in respect of which a request for admission to trading on such a market has been made, or

    (iii) in the case of subsection (2) or (3) behaviour, investments which are related investments in relation to such qualifying investments, and

  (b) falls within any one or more of the types of behaviour set out in subsections (2) to (8).

(2) The first type of behaviour is where an insider deals, or attempts to deal, in a qualifying investment or related investment on the basis of inside information relating to the investment in question.

(3) The second is where an insider discloses inside information to another person otherwise than in the proper course of the exercise of his employment, profession or duties.

(4) The third is where the behaviour (not falling within subsection (2) or (3))—

  (a) is based on information which is not generally available to those using the market but which, if available to a regular user of the market, would be, or would be likely to be, regarded by him as relevant when deciding the terms on which transactions in qualifying investments should be effected, and

  (b) is likely to be regarded by a regular user of the market as a failure on the part of the person concerned to observe the standard of behaviour reasonably expected of a person in his position in relation to the market.

(5) The fourth is where the behaviour consists of effecting transactions or orders to trade (otherwise than for legitimate reasons and in conformity with accepted market practices on the relevant market) which—

  (a) give, or are likely to give, a false or misleading impression as to the supply of, or demand for, or as to the price of, one or more qualifying investments, or

  (b) secure the price of one or more such investments at an abnormal or artificial level.

(6) The fifth is where the behaviour consists of effecting transactions or orders to trade which employ fictitious devices or any other form of deception or contrivance.

(7) The sixth is where the behaviour consists of the dissemination of information by any means which gives, or is likely to give, a false or misleading impression as to a qualifying investment by a person

who knew or could reasonably be expected to have known that the information was false or misleading.

(8) The seventh is where the behaviour (not falling within subsection (5), (6) or (7))—

(a) is likely to give a regular user of the market a false or misleading impression as to the supply of, demand for or price or value of, qualifying investments, or

(b) would be, or would be likely to be, regarded by a regular user of the market as behaviour that would distort, or would be likely to distort, the market in such an investment,

and the behaviour is likely to be regarded by a regular user of the market as a failure on the part of the person concerned to observe the standard of behaviour reasonably expected of a person in his position in relation to the market.[66]

Market abuse is a civil offence for which a person could be fined, made subject to a restitution order or publicly reprimanded. The FSA also has power to seek an injunction where there has been market abuse or there is a reasonable likelihood of it continuing in certain circumstances. The FSA thus has a number of options in handling wrongdoings by those dealing in securities: it can prosecute an individual offender (subject to the Code for Crown Prosecutors) for insider dealing; it can implement market abuse proceedings against the individual and/or his employer (e.g. a corporation) or it can pass the matter to the person's regulated investment exchange to deal with as a disciplinary matter. If the FSA chooses market abuse proceedings (which, although categorised by the legislature as civil may well be viewed as criminal by ECtHR[67]) it would allow for the civil standard of proof and obviate the need for trial by jury.

The FSA has set out in its Handbook on Enforcement the criteria it will apply to the issuing of criminal proceedings; there are currently 13 considerations.[68] In addition to criminal proceedings, it is possible for the FSA to caution a firm for market abuse and/or to issue civil proceedings against it. It can also take measures to close the business down where it is in the interests of consumers to do so.

The FSA is also obliged to publish a policy statement on penalties for market abuse.[69] When considering whether to take action for a financial penalty or public censure, it must have regard to:

---

[66] s.118 FSMA 2000.
[67] The possibility that it may be viewed as a "criminal charge" has already led to a number of measures being implemented to meet any objection, e.g. the availability of legal aid; the setting up of "safe harbours" for greater certainty and appellate or review procedures.
[68] See *http://fsahandbook.info/FSA/extra/4755.pdf* at Ch.12.
[69] s.124 FSMA.

a.   whether the behaviour in respect of which the penalty is to be imposed had an adverse effect on the market in question and, if it did, how serious that effect was;
b.   the extent to which the behaviour was deliberate or reckless; and
c.   whether the person on whom the penalty is to be imposed is an individual.[70]

---

[70] s.124(2).

CHAPTER 17

FRAUDULENT TRADING

SECTION 993 COMPANIES ACT 2006—FRAUDULENT TRADING

Section 993 provides: **17.1**

"(1) If any business of a company is carried on with intent to defraud creditors of the company or creditors of any other person, or for any fraudulent purpose, every person who was knowingly a party to the carrying on of the business in that manner commits an offence.

(2) This applies whether or not the company has been, or is in the course of being, wound up."

This offence carries a maximum sentence of 10 years' imprisonment and/or an unlimited fine. The current offence has evolved from one which was first enacted over 50 years ago. The old legislation combined civil and criminal liability for those involved in the fraudulent trading of a company, so as to make them personally liable for the debts of the company and, on occasion, open to penalties including imprisonment. Now criminal and civil liability are separate. The new offence mirrors s.458 of the Companies Act 1985[1] and so old case law continues to be relevant. The offence is directed at those individuals in control of a company rather than a corporate defendant itself. It does not matter whether the company is operating or wound up.

There are two distinct criteria of liability.[2]

CARRYING ON OF BUSINESS

The "business of the company" strikes at the practical method and purpose **17.2** of the corporation's livelihood; it may be a single transaction within the corporate business.

---

[1] Except to raise the maximum term of imprisonment from two years.
[2] *Re Cooper Chemicals Ltd* [1978] 1 Ch.262.

Where a company accepted a deposit knowing that it could not supply the goods required and that the company was insolvent and not going to pay the deposit back, it was a fraud on a creditor perpetrated in the course of carrying on business. As long as the transaction could properly be described as "perpetrated in the course of carrying on business", it did not matter that it affected only one creditor and was made up of only one transaction.

FRAUDULENT INTENT

17.3 A fraudulent intent must be dishonest.[3] Where a person intends by deceit to induce a course of conduct in another which puts that other's economic interests in jeopardy, he is guilty of fraud even though he does not intend or desire that actual loss should ultimately be suffered by that other:

> "No distinction is to be drawn in English law between the state of mind of one who does an act because he desires it to produce a particular evil consequence, and the state of mind of one who does the act knowing full well that it is likely to produce the consequence although it may not be the object he was seeking to achieve by doing the act..."[4]

Thus, whereas a person may aim to continue the company's business, but knows that his method will produce the inevitable consequence that, e.g. a creditor will not be repaid, the person will be acting with fraudulent intent.[5] As Shaw L.J. observed:

> "Generally the primary objective of fraudsmen is to advantage themselves. The detriment that results to their victims is secondary to that purpose and incidental. It is 'intended' only in the sense that it is a contemplated outcome of the fraud that is perpetrated".[6]

It will be fraudulent and dishonest if an accused realised at the time when debts (e.g. buying potatoes on credit) were incurred that there was no reason for thinking that funds would become available to pay the debt when it became due or shortly thereafter.[7]

FRAUD ON CREDITORS

17.4 Where a count of fraudulent trading was indicted as: "... with intent to defraud the creditors of the said company or to defraud other persons by inducing them to grant credit to or to entrust properly to the said company

---

[3] *R. v Cox and Hodges* 1982.
[4] *R. v Grantham* (1984) 79 Cr.App.R. 86, per Lord Lane C.J. at pp.90–1.
[5] *R. v Allsop* (1977) 64 Cr.App.R. 29.
[6] At p.31.
[7] *R. v Grantham* (1984) 79 Cr.App.R. 86 per Lord Lane C.J. at pp.90–1.

when the said company was insolvent", it was not bad for duplicity.[8] The count related wholly to intent to defraud creditors or those in that position, and was merely detailing the methods by which the fraudulent trading manifested itself.

The definition of creditor has expanded over time. It had been interpreted narrowly so as to be limited only to those with a present right to sue. This is no longer the case. In *R. v Seillon*,[9] which concerned a conspiracy between S and his solicitor to defraud S's creditors, Lord Taylor C.J. stated:

> "That does not necessarily mean that the creditors existed then and there. It is sufficient ... if the creditor is a potential creditor because the crime relates to a time in the future".

He added that there was no need to add the word "potential" to qualify "creditor". It may have been thought a matter of common sense that, in the context of an agreement to commit future crime, the category of person to be defrauded could be widely defined. The courts have not, however, limited this interpretation of creditor to conspiracy alone but applied it broadly.

In *R. v Wallace Duncan Smith*,[10] the Court of Appeal enumerated the four elements the prosecution had to prove: (1) that S was knowingly a party to the carrying on of the business; (2) that there were creditors entitled to be paid; (3) that S intended that creditors should be defrauded in that he intentionally carried on its business to the prejudice of the rights of those creditors; (4) that he was acting dishonestly. The essence of this limb of the offence of fraudulent trading is:

> "keeping the business going with the dishonest intention of prejudicing the rights of its creditors".[11]

The Court of Appeal did not accept that the definition of "creditor" in *Seillon*[12] was based on the inevitable future element of a conspiracy charge. Rose L.J. emphasised that fraudulent trading was a continuing offence which might prejudice future as well as present creditors.

> "... the word 'creditor' in section 458, in its ordinary meaning, denotes one to whom money is owed: whether that debt can presently be sued for is immaterial ... we see no reason in principle why other kinds of creditors should not be within the scope of section 458 because such may come into existence after the fraudulent trading has first begun. Such a construction is consonant with the purpose of the first part of

---

[8] *R. v Inman* [1966] 3 W.L.R. 567.
[9] (1982) Crim.L.R. 676; and cited in *Kemp* (1988) 87 Cr.App.R. 95, 98.
[10] (1996) 2 Cr.App.R. 1 CA—unaffected on this topic by the subsequent HL decision in *R. v Wallace Duncan Smith (No.4)* [2004] 2 Cr.App.R. 17 HL.
[11] (1996) 2 Cr.App.R. 1, Rose L.J. approving the trial judge Tuckey J. at p.11.
[12] See above.

the section which is aimed at preventing insolvent trading to the prejudice of those who are induced to do business".[13]

Similar wording is found in the Insolvency Act 1986. It has been held that:

"...a business may be found to have been carried on with intent to
defraud creditors notwithstanding that only one creditor is shown to
have been defrauded, and by a single transaction. It is important to
keep in mind that the precondition for the exercise of the court's powers
under section ... 213 of the 1986 Act ... is that it should appear to the
court 'that any business of the company has been carried on with intent
to defraud creditors of the company'. Parliament did not provide that
the powers under those sections might be exercisable whenever it
appeared to the court "that any creditor of the company has been
defrauded in the course of carrying on the business of the company."[14]

ANY FRAUDULENT PURPOSE

17.5 The fraudulent purpose is not to be limited, and especially not to a fraud on
creditors which is already covered by the other limb of the offence. In
Kemp,[15] K, through two limited companies, carried out a number of frauds
in which he supplied paper to customers which they had not ordered but had
paid for. The customers, of whom there were over 20, did not pursue any
available civil remedy against the companies, but a charge of fraudulent
trading was brought against K. It was held that customers or potential
creditors were precisely the type of persons likely to be affected by the
mischief of fraudulent trading, and properly encompassed within the second
limb of the offence.

Moreover, in *Philippou*,[16] the fraudulent purposes of a travel company
were stated as being: (a) to conceal from the Civil Aviation Authority the
true financial position of the companies for which an ATOL licence was
sought; and (b) the transfer of funds beyond the reach of the company's
creditors and/or liquidators. The Court of Appeal recognised that a pre-
requisite to the company doing business was the holding of the ATOL
licence, and it was thus part of its business to apply for, maintain and renew
its licence. Similarly, where money was transferred out of the jurisdiction
two months before the company's liquidation, and was in fact beyond the
reach of creditors and liquidators, the Court of Appeal held that it was a
proper inference to draw that it was a transaction with a fraudulent purpose.

---

[13] At p.14.
[14] *Morphitis v Bernasconi* [2003] 2 W.L.R. 1521 per Chadwick L.J.
[15] (1988) 87 Cr.App.R. 95.
[16] (1989) 89 Cr.App.R. 290.

Party to Carrying On Business

The defendant must have participated in, taken part in or concurred in the **17.6** carrying on of the business. The section was aimed at those in controlling positions within the business. Those in a controlling or managerial position must be distinguished from those lower down the corporate scale, at least as principal offenders. In *Miles*[17] those "*running* the business" were the targets of the section. Where there is a factual dispute as to the level of the defendant within the corporate hierarchy, the judge must give clear guidance as to the meaning of the words.

A company secretary, who was a partner in a firm of accountants who were the company auditors, omitted to give advice to prevent the company trading fraudulently. It was held he could not be said to be a party to carrying on the business.[18] Pennycuick V.C. stated:

> "I do not think it can be said that someone is party to carrying on a business if he takes no positive steps at all. So in order to bring a person within the section you must show that he is taking some positive steps in the carrying on of the company's business in a fraudulent manner".[19]

Mere inertia or omission was insufficient to make out a case of being a party to the carrying on of a business fraudulently, although it might be sufficient for a negligence action or being implicated in a fraud if a person under a duty to speak remains silent; however, neither of those situations were covered by the offence fraudulent trading.

Although it is apparent that the courts have construed the phrase narrowly, it has been questioned whether there is any reason why secondary liability might not attach to those lower down the corporate scale as aiders and abetters.[20] In principle, although a possible and logical extension of general legal propositions, the authors suggest that this would undermine the precedents set by the courts in interpreting those who are parties to the business. If, as the courts have stated, this section is designed to punish those in control of the company's methods of trading, it would be at odds with the aim of the legislation, to widen liability to junior officers of the corporation.

Sentence

The Court of Appeal and the Sentencing Guidelines Council have reviewed **17.7** sentencing levels in theft and city fraud offences and provided guidelines for

---

[17] *Miles* [1992] Crim.L.R. 657.
[18] *Re Maidstone Buildings Provisions Ltd* [1971] 1 W.L.R. 1085.
[19] At p.1092.
[20] See commentary to *Miles* [1992] Crim.L.R. 657, 659.

sentencing courts.[21] Relevant considerations include: the amount involved, the manner in which the fraud was carried out, the period over which and the persistence with which it was carried out; the position of the accused in the company and any abuse of trust; the consequences of the fraud including the effect on City confidence and the integrity of commercial life. These principles reflect the importance attached to maintaining confidence in the City.

A charge of fraudulent trading resulting in a deficiency of a given amount is less serious than a specific charge of theft or fraud to an equivalent amount.[22] In a case of fraudulent trading, where there is, in reality, one continuous course of conduct, the Court of Appeal has made it clear that consecutive sentences should not be imposed.

---

[21] *Clark* [1998] 2 Cr.App.R. 137; *R. v Feld* [1999] 1 Cr.App.R.(S.) 1 and Sentencing Guidelines Council Guidelines.
[22] *Smith & Palk* [1997] 2 Cr.App.R. (S.) 167.

FALSE ACCOUNTING AND FALSE STATEMENTS

INTRODUCTION

Whilst most of the fraud provisions in the Theft Act—such as obtaining **18.1** property by deception—have been replaced by the Fraud Act 2006, false accounting and false statements by company officers, remain in force.

THEFT ACT 1968 SECTION 17

Section 17:   **18.2**

(1) Where a person dishonestly, with a view to gain for himself or another or with intent to cause loss to another,—

(a) destroys, defaces, conceals or falsifies any account or any record or document made or required for any accounting purpose; or

(b) in furnishing information for any purpose produces or makes use of any account, or any such record or document as aforesaid, which to his knowledge is or may be misleading, false or deceptive in a material particular; he shall, on conviction on indictment be liable to imprisonment for a term not exceeding seven years.

(2) For purposes of this section a person who makes or concurs in making an account or other document an entry which is or may be misleading, false or deceptive in a material particular, or who omits or concurs in omitting a material particular from an account or other document, is to be treated as falsifying the account or document.

The definition of "gain" and "loss" is found in s.34(2) of the Theft Act 1968.

(2)   For the purposes of this Act—

    (a)   "gain" and "loss" are to be construed as extending not only to gain or loss in money or other property, but as extending to any such gain or loss whether temporary or permanent; and—

        (i)   "gain" includes a gain by keeping what one has, as well as a gain by getting what one has not; and

        (ii)   "loss" includes a loss by not getting what one might get, as well as loss by parting with what one has.

DISHONESTY

18.3 This is an essential element of any offence under the Theft Act 1968. In *Eden*,[1] the jury was asked to explain verdicts of guilty in relation to several counts of false accounting when it had acquitted E in respect of linked theft offences in circumstances where the judge had directed them that the counts stood or fell together. "Not dishonest, but muddled" said the foreman. The Court of Appeal quashed the convictions. Sachs L.J. remarked "For my part I remain unable to understand ... how any ... court could come to think that he was punishing a man under the Theft Act for something which was not dishonest."[2]

WITH A VIEW TO GAIN FOR HIMSELF OR ANOTHER

18.4 The "gain" need only be temporary; indeed that is a distinguishing feature between false accounting and theft. In *Eden*,[3] Sachs L.J. said:

"... it is certainly not the law in cases of the type which are brought by the Post Office for theft and false accounting, that simply because the accused is not guilty of theft it follows that he is not guilty of false accounting. It could be perfectly proper for a jury, if properly directed, to find that an accused person who has deliberately made false entries with regard to the number of vouchers he has received for pensions and allowances in order to cover up a muddle guilty under section 17, whether or not at that time he committed a theft. The question for the jury would be whether he had dishonestly falsified the accounts for 'gain' within the meaning of that word as interpreted by section 34: that could obviously include temporary gains of many types. Such a gain could be constituted by putting off the evil day of having to sort out the

---

[1] (1971) 55 Cr.App.R. 193.
[2] At p.198.
[3] See above.

muddle and pay up what may have been in error kept within the sub-post office when it ought to have been sent to head office. There may well be other forms of *temporary* gain which could result in a verdict of guilty on a charge under section 17. Indeed it is not easy to think of a deliberate falsification of accounts done dishonestly that is not, in fact, aimed at some sort of gain and indeed some sort of monetary gain".

Thus, in *Lee Cheung Wing*,[4] a decision of the Privy Council on appeal from Hong Kong, the defendants had operated an account in a friend's name (with his consent) in the futures market. The company by whom they were employed prohibited trading by employees on their own account. The account in the friend's name was operated very successfully by the defendants. They operated the account in two ways: they either signed the friend's name and verified the signature by initialling it, after which the innocent chief cashier would approve payment upon receipt of the signed and initialled slip; alternatively, one defendant signed a cheque for withdrawal of funds in the friend's name and the other countersigned it to approve payment. The Privy Council rejected the argument that there was no gain from the falsification of the slips because the gain had in fact accrued on the sale of the futures contract; nor did it accept that there was no loss to the employer since the money had always belonged to the defendants. The court held that the profits which they sought to recover by means of the withdrawal slips were profits for which they were bound to account to their employer, F Co; had the slips been in their own names, F Co would have been entitled to refuse payment. The purpose of falsifying the withdrawal slips was to enable the defendants to recover from F Co funds to which they were not entitled and which, but for the falsification, they could not have recovered. Therefore they were falsified with a view to gain within the meaning of the section.

Although a gain can be shown by keeping money or other property that one already has, a distinction must be drawn between that situation and one in which the "gain" is the forbearance of another from enforcing their rights immediately or postponing the enforcement of an obligation. That would not constitute a gain within the statute.[5] It has been held that a gain is getting what a person has not, so that obtaining a service which then gave him some property which he had not had before, was such a gain.[6] "Gain" or "Loss" must relate to money or other property, so false accounting tending to show the account in a better light merely to improve relations with other directors was not a criminal offence.[7]

---

[4] (1992) 94 Cr.App.R. 355.
[5] *R. v Golechha & Choraria* (1990) 90 Cr.App.R. 241 per L.C.J. at pp.248–9.
[6] *R. v Bevans* (1988) 87 Cr.App.R. 64 (a blackmail case).
[7] *R. v Masterton* Unreported, April 30, 1996, CA (94 0221 × 5).

WITH INTENT TO CAUSE LOSS

18.5 Intent has its ordinary meaning of a willingness to produce the particular evil consequence to another by virtue of his acts (or omissions) as explained by Lord Diplock in *Hyam v DPP*[8] .

ANY ACCOUNT OR RECORD OR DOCUMENT MADE OR REQUIRED FOR ANY ACCOUNTING PURPOSE

18.6 The definition of account or record is wide enough to include a machine such as a turnstile which records those admitted.[9] It would be a falsification of such a record to permit it to be operated without counting the number of people passing through.

A complete failure to fill in a document made or required for an accounting purpose will fall within the definition. The account or record need not be identifiable in the sense of a specific piece of paper. Once an obligation to complete a document required for an accounting purpose arose, the omission came within the section, otherwise the ludicrous situation would occur that a failure to fill in part of a document would be caught by the Act whereas a complete failure to do so (which would usually be necessary to hide the dishonest conduct) would not.[10]

The information furnished must be "false in a material particular". This does not mean that it must be that information itself which is required for an accounting purpose.[11] The document must be looked at as a whole.

A document may fall within the ambit of the section if it is made for some purpose other than an accounting purpose but is required for an accounting purpose as a subsidiary consideration.[12]

Whether or not a document is made or required for an accounting purpose should usually be the subject of positive evidence called by the prosecution. In *Manning*[13] no such evidence was called, nor questions asked either of the prosecution witnesses or the defendant on that aspect of the case which concerned cover notes for maritime insurance. Each cover note stated on its face what and how the client had to pay. Buxton L.J. described the issue as "being close to the borderline" but concluded that it was a case where a reasonable juror could conclude simply by looking at the document that it was required for an accounting purpose in that it set out what the client owed.

---

[8] (1974) 59 Cr.App.R. 91, 110.
[9] *Edwards v Toombes* [1983] Crim.L.R. 43.
[10] *R. v Shama* (1990) 91 Cr.App.R. 138.
[11] *R. v Mallett* [1978] 1 W.L.R. 820.
[12] *Att-Gen's Reference (No.1 of 1980)* (1981) 72 Cr.App.R. 60.
[13] (1998) 2 Cr.App.R. 461, 465.

FALSE STATEMENTS BY COMPANY DIRECTORS AND OFFICERS

SECTION 19, THEFT ACT 1968

Provides: **18.7**

(1) Where an officer of a body corporate or unincorporated association (or person purporting to act as such) with intent to deceive members or creditors of the body corporate or association about its affairs, publishes or concurs in publishing a written statement or account which to his knowledge is or may be misleading, false or deceptive in a material particular, he shall on conviction on indictment be liable to imprisonment for a term not exceeding seven years.

(2) For purposes of this section a person who has entered into a security for the benefit of a body corporate or association is to be treated as a creditor of it.

(3) Where the affairs of a body corporate or association are managed by its members, this section shall apply to any statement which a member publishes or concurs in publishing in connection with his functions of management as if he were an officer of the body corporate or association.

An officer of a company includes a director, manager or secretary, or one purporting so to act.[14] The officers of a company are often enumerated in its articles of association or bye-laws. In *Boal*,[15] "manager" (for the purposes of the Fire Precaution Act 1971) was held to relate to one "who had the management of the whole affairs of the company", who was "intrusted with power to transact the whole of the affairs of the company" and was "managing in a governing role the affairs of the company itself". It is submitted that this interpretation applies to false accounting and s.19[16]; it also applies to the liability of company officers who have consented or connived in a breach of ss.2–4 of the Fraud Act 2006 by virtue of s.12 of that Act.

---

[14] s.1173(1) Companies Act 2006.
[15] (1992) 95 Cr.App.R. 272.
[16] by virtue of s.18 of the 1968 Act.

CHAPTER 19

CORRUPTION

INTRODUCTION

Corruption offences in the UK are currently covered by no fewer than four **19.1**
criminal statutes as well as the common law. There has been criticism of this
unsatisfactory state of affairs, which has led to inconsistency and injustice.
However, past attempts at reform, culminating in a Corruption Bill in 2003,
have not met with success. In the immediate past, there has been further
concern because of the need for the UK to comply with her international
obligations. At present there is a consultation paper "Reforming Bribery",[1]
the findings of which are anticipated at the end of 2008. In 1994 the Council
of Europe decided that corruption posed a serious threat to fundamental
values and by 1997 Ministers had adopted the "20 Guiding Principles for the
Fight Against Corruption" including the aim of "co-ordinated criminalisation of national and international corruption". The UK signed the
Convention on January 27, 1999 and ratified it in December 2003.This was
followed by the adoption of the Criminal Law Convention on Corruption
which came into force in the UK on April 1, 2004[2]. The two principal aims
are to harmonise the definition and criminalisation of corruption offences
and to facilitate effective means of international cooperation in the investigation and prosecution of these offences.

Offences of corruption are currently covered by the Public Bodies Corruption Act 1889 ("the 1889 Act") and the Prevention of Corruption Act
1906 ("the 1906 Act"), which are supplemented by the Prevention of Corruption Act 1916 ("the 1916 Act"); they are known collectively as the
Prevention of Corruption Acts. There is some overlap between the 1889 and
the 1906 Acts where the agents of public bodies are involved, but in essence,
corruption in local government and other public bodies is dealt with by the

---

[1] Law Commission Consultation Paper No.185, 2007.
[2] *http://www.conventions.coe.int/treaty/commun*; it is open to adoption by non-European
countries.

1889 Act and corruption of agents in general by the 1906 Act. Neither Act deals with corrupting a Member of Parliament. The Prevention of Corruption Acts have both been extended[3] to include corrupt acts having no connection with the United Kingdom and which are carried out in a country or territory outside the United Kingdom.

BRIBERY AND CORRUPTION AT COMMON LAW

19.2 At common law, "a man accepting an office of trust concerning the public ... is answerable criminally to the King for misbehaviour in his office ... by whomever and in whatever way the officer is appointed".[4] It is not entirely clear whether bribery at common law comprises a single general offence which may be committed in a variety of ways, or whether it comprises a number of distinct offences. A general definition is provided by Russell[5]:

> "Bribery is the receiving or offering [of] any undue reward by or to any person whatsoever, in a public office, in order to influence his behaviour in office, and incline him to an act contrary to the known rules of honesty and integrity."

The common law offence of misconduct in a public office applies generally to every person who is appointed to discharge "any duty in the discharge of which the public are interested, more clearly so if he is paid out of funds provided by the public".[6] A person in the position of trustee to perform a public duty who accepts a bribe to act corruptly in discharging that duty commits the common law offence of bribery, as does the person offering the bribe.[7] The mental element of common law bribery is an intention to influence the behaviour of a public officer with a view to that officer "acting contrary to the known rules of honesty and integrity".[8]

Prosecutions are occasionally still brought for the common law offence. In *Bowden*,[9] the Court of Appeal upheld the conviction of a local authority manager who corruptly used his position as chief building maintenance officer of the council to arrange for a gang of council workers to carry out work at his girlfriend's house. He misused his position to provide labour and materials to his girlfriend, both paid for by the council.

For the purposes of the common law offence of bribery, provided a "relevant act" occurs in England and Wales, it is now immaterial that the

---

[3] By s.108(3) and (4) Anti-terrorism, Crime and Security Act 2001.
[4] *Bembridge* (1783) 3 Doug 327 per Lord Mansfield.
[5] *Russell on Crime*, 12th edn (London, Stevens, 1964) p.381.
[6] *R. v Whitaker* [1914] 3 K.B. 1283. The defendant in this case was a colonel who accepted a bribe from a firm of caterers in return for giving the firm the tenancy of the regiment's canteen.
[7] *R. v Whitaker*. [1914] 3 K.B. 1283.
[8] *Russell on Crime*, 12th edn (London, Stevens, 1964).
[9] [1996] 1 W.L.R. 98.

functions of the person who receives or is offered a reward have no connection with the United Kingdom and are carried out in a country or territory outside the United Kingdom.[10]

THE PUBLIC BODIES CORRUPT PRACTICES ACT 1889

The 1889 Act was introduced following the revelations of malpractice that **19.3** emerged as a result of a Royal Commission appointed to inquire into the affairs of the Metropolitan Board of Works.[11] The Act makes the active or passive bribery of a member, officer or servant of a public body, a criminal offence. By s.1:

1(1) "Every person who shall by himself or by or in conjunction with any other person, corruptly solicit or receive, or agree to receive, for himself, or for any other person, any gift, loan, fee, reward, or advantage whatever as an inducement to or reward for, or otherwise on account of any member, officer, or servant of a public body as in this Act defined, doing or forbearing to do anything in respect of any matter or transaction whatsoever, actual or proposed, in which the said public body is concerned, shall be guilty of an offence."

(2) Every person who shall by himself or in conjunction with any other person corruptly give, promise, or offer any gift, loan, fee, reward or advantage whatsoever to any person, whether for the benefit for that person or of another person, as an inducement to or reward for or otherwise on account of any member, officer, or servant of any public body as is this Act defined, doing or forbearing to do anything in respect of any matter or transaction whatsoever, actual or proposed, in which such public body as aforesaid is concerned, shall be guilty . . . of an offence."

The offences created by s.1 are triable either way: punishable on summary conviction by imprisonment of up to a maximum of six months or to a fine not exceeding the statutory maximum or both; and on conviction on indictment by imprisonment of up to seven years, or to an unlimited fine or to both.[12]

The Court has additional powers of punishment in respect of public officers, including ordering the person to pay the amount or value of "any gift, loan, fee or reward received by him" to such body as the Court directs[13];

---

[10] s.108(1) Anti-terrorism, Crime and Security Act 2001. This provision came into force on February 14, 2002: (Commencement No.3) Order 2002 (SI 2002/228).

[11] P. Fennell and P.A. Thomas, "*Corruption in England and Wales: An Historical Analysis*" (1983) 11 Int J Soc Law 167, 172.

[12] ss.2(a)(i) and (ii).

[13] s.2(b).

disqualifying him from holding or being elected or appointed to any public office for five years for a first offence, and in the event of a second conviction for a like offence, for ever.[14] Where the convicted person is "an officer or servant" employed by any public body, he "shall, at the discretion of the court" be liable to forfeit his pension.[15]

The offence covers both the person soliciting or receiving the gift, loan, fee, reward or advantage and the person corruptly giving, promising or offering such gifts, etc. as an inducement or reward to any member, officer or servant of any public body. The person soliciting the bribe need not himself have any intention of passing it onto the requisite person, so long as he holds himself out as intending to do so.[16] "Giving, promising or offering" a bribe is the aspect of the offence that can be committed by a corporation. The expression "person" includes a body of persons, corporate or unincorporate.[17] It is no defence that the appointment or election of a person to a public office is invalid.[18]

PUBLIC BODY

19.4 "Public body" is defined by s.7:

> "The expression 'public body' means any council of a county, or county [*sic*] of a city or town, any council of a municipal borough, also any board, commissioners, select vestry, or other body which has power to act under and for the purposes of any Act relating to local government, or the public health, or to poor law or otherwise to administer money raised by rates in pursuance of any public general Act, *and includes any public body which exists in a country or territory outside the United Kingdom and is equivalent to any body described above.*" [emphasis added].

Public body does not include the Crown or any other government department; care must be taken to prosecute under the correct statute and with the appropriate consent.[19]

The expression "public office" means any office or employment of a person as a member, officer, or servant of such public body.

The words in italics were added by s.108(3) of the Anti-terrorism, Crime and Security Act 2001 with effect from February 14, 2002.[20]

---

[14] ss.2(c) and (d).
[15] s.2(e).
[16] *Jagdeo Singh v The State* [2006] 1 W.L.R.146 PC.
[17] s.7 of the 1889 Act.
[18] s.3(2).
[19] *R. v Natji* [2002] 2 Cr.App.R. 20.
[20] Commencement (No.3) Order 2002 (SI 2002/228).

"Public body" has been said to be "clearly ... confined to local authorities".[21] The definition of "public body" was extended by the Local Government and Housing Act 1989 to include companies which, in accordance with Part V of that Act, are "under the control of one or more local authorities".[22] This provision is still not in force. The 1889 Act does *not* apply to the Crown, or an officer serving under the Crown.[23] The Crown represents the State and carries out its duties on behalf of the State; a public authority is a body which has public or statutory duties to perform and which performs those duties for the benefit of the public, not for private profit[24] whether or not so described by legislation creating it (if any).

INDUCEMENTS AND REWARDS

In general terms, the offences require either the corrupt giving or receiving **19.5** of a "gift, loan, fee, reward or advantage". An inducement is bestowed *before* what is sought of the officer takes place; a reward is something bestowed *after* it has been done by him. A "reward" includes a gift for some favour already performed without there having been any agreement beforehand. Any payment will be covered provided it relates to something done or omitted by the recipient in respect of any matter or transaction in which the public body of which he is a member, officer or servant, is concerned.[25] Where an indictment alleged sums were corruptly accepted as an "inducement or reward" the counts were not bad for duplicity because:

> "The offence is the corrupt acceptance of the money. It is that act which constitutes the offence and the reference to 'inducement or reward' is simply a description of the criminality of the act and the character of the corrupt element".[26]

"Advantage" is also defined by s.7 of the Act and includes:

> "... any office or dignity, and any forbearance to demand any money or money's worth or valuable thing, and includes any aid, vote, consent, or influence, or pretended aid, vote, consent, or influence, and also includes any promise, or procurement of or agreement or endeavour to procure or the holding out of any expectation or any gift, loan, fee, reward, or advantage as before defined".

The term "any matter or transaction" does not mean the offer or inducement must relate to a specific act or omission; it is an offence under the 1889

---

[21] *R. v Joy* (1976) 60 Cr.App.R. 32 at 133 per HHJ. Rigg.
[22] Local Government and Housing Act 1989, Sch.11 para.3.
[23] *R. v Natji* [2002] 2 Cr.App.R. 312; 1 W.L.R. 2337.
[24] *The Johannesburg* [1907] p.65, as applied in *DPP v Holly* [1978] A.C. 43.
[25] *R. v Andrews-Weatherfoil Ltd* [1972] 1 W.L.R. 118; *R. v Parker* (1986) 82 Cr.App.R. 69.
[26] *R. v Richards* (unreported) October 6, 1994 CA No.94/0534/W4 per Hobhouse L.J.

Act to bribe an officer of a public body to "show favour" in a general, unspecific way because showing favour involves doing, or forbearing from doing something.[27]

CORRUPTLY

19.6 The word "corruptly" is not defined in either the 1889 or 1906 Act. Corruptly does not mean "dishonestly", but is purposely doing an act which the law forbids as tending to corrupt.[28] It is not necessary for the prosecution to prove a corrupt *motive* (although usually one will exist); where a defendant claimed to have offered a bribe to the mayor with a view to exposing him as corrupt, the judge had properly directed the jury that motive was irrelevant.[29]

In *R. v Harvey*,[30] a prosecution under the 1906 Act, W was a director of a company, BB Ltd, H was employed by the bank with whom the company had its account. W offered, and H accepted, an inducement to show favour to the company in various ways. W and H denied there was any corrupt motive behind the gift. The trial judge directed the jury that they had to be sure that when W agreed to give money to H he intended it to be a bribe (a payment with a tendency to corrupt) and when H took it, he knew it was intended to be such a payment. The Court of Appeal upheld the judge's direction; dishonesty was not an element of the offence. "Corruptly" meant deliberately offering money or other favours with the intention that it should operate on the mind of the person to whom it was made so as to encourage him to enter into a corrupt bargain. The test for corruption is the same in the private as in the public domain.[31]

It is no defence for the person accepting the bribe not to intend carrying out the corrupt bargain[32] or to say that the corrupt gift had no influence over the performance of his duties,[33] unless he accepts the money in order to expose the wrong-doing of the giver.[34] On those latter facts the defendant would neither be acting corruptly, nor inducing another person so to act. If a person accepts a corruptly offered payment which he believes to be gratuitous or in respect of an innocent consideration, he has a defence though

---

[27] *R. v Grierson* [1960] Crim.L.R. 773.

[28] *Cooper v Slade* (1857) 6 HL Cas. 746; the opinion of Willes J. related to the Corrupt Practices Prevention Act 1854; and see *R. v Wellburn* (1979) 69 Cr.App.R. 254, 265.

[29] *R. v Smith* [1960] 2 Q.B. 423, 424; Cr.App.R. 55 CCA.

[30] [1999] Crim.L.R. 70 CA.

[31] *R. v Godden-Wood* [2001] EWCA Crim 1586, *The Times* June 27, 2001.

[32] *R. v Mills* (1979) 68 Cr.App.R. 154. *Jagdeo Singh v The State* [2006] 1 W.L.R. 146 PC.

[33] *Parker* (1985) 82 Cr.App.R. 69.

[34] (1985) 82 Cr.App.R. 69; see also Lord Goddard in *R. v Carr* (1956) 40 Cr.App.R. 188, 189; cf. where the person offering the bribe does so to expose corrupt practices by the public body.

the giver does not.[35] Where a prosecution is mounted against A who offers, and B who accepts a bribe, the acquittal of one or other party does not necessarily render the conviction of the other unsafe; the cases do not necessarily stand or fall together.[36]

CORRUPTION OF AGENTS: THE PREVENTION OF CORRUPTION ACT 1906

This Act was the result of a report published in 1889 of the Secret Commissions Committee of the London Chamber of Commerce which recommended the extension of the criminal offence of corruption in the private sector. The recommendation was not universally popular; there were several unsuccessful attempts to introduce legislation before the 1906 Act finally reached the statute book.[37] The 1906 Act in essence extended to all *agents* the offences created by the 1889 Act in relation to public officers: **19.7**

Punishment of corrupt transactions with agents

"1(1) If any agent corruptly accepts or obtains, or agrees to accept or attempts to obtain from any person, for himself or for any other person, any gift or consideration as an inducement or reward for doing or forbearing to do, or for having after the passing of this Act done or forborne to do, any act in relation to his principal's affairs or business, of for showing or forbearing to show favour or disfavour to any person in relation to his principal's affairs or business; or

(2) If any person corruptly gives or agrees to give or offers any gift or consideration to any agent as an inducement or reward for doing or forbearing to do, or for having after the passing of this Act done or forborne to do, any act in relation to his principal's affairs or business, of for showing or forbearing to show favour or disfavour to any person in relation to his principal's affairs or business ... he shall be guilty of an offence."

Again, the offences are either way, punishable in the same way as the offences under the 1889 Act,[38] but without the specific penalties applicable only to public officers.[39] Imprisonment is the almost inevitable sentence in

---

[35] *R. v Millray Window Cleaning Co Ltd* [1962] Crim.L.R. 99.
[36] *R. v Andrews-Weatherfoil Ltd* 1 W.L.R. 118.
[37] P. Fennell and P.A. Thomas, "*Corruption in England and Wales: An Historical Analysis*" (1983) 11 Int J Soc Law 167, 172.
[38] On summary conviction by imprisonment of up to a maximum of six months or to a fine not exceeding the statutory maximum or both; and on conviction on indictment by imprisonment of up to seven years, or to an unlimited fine or to both.
[39] See ss.2(b)–(e) of the 1889 Act; see 19.4 above.

the event of conviction.[40] A prosecution requires the consent of the Attorney-General.[41]

AGENT

19.8 The expression "agent" includes any person employed by or acting for another; and the expression "principal" includes an employer.[42] Although aimed principally at private sector corruption, the definition is extremely wide and applies to the public, private and corporate fields. The Act applies to servants of the Crown; a person may be serving under the Crown even if he is not strictly an employee, provided the duties he performs are performed by him on behalf of the Crown.[43] A civil servant is an agent of the Crown and may be prosecuted under this Act but not the 1889 Act,[44] as may a police officer.[45]

If a person uses his position to get a payment corruptly, it does not matter whether the work in respect of which the bribe is paid is work to which his duties relate or not.[46] The words "in relation to his principal's affairs" in s.1 of the 1906 Act are to be widely construed.[47] Section 4 of the Prevention of Corruption Act 1916 extended the definition of agent to include a person serving under any "public body" including local and public authorities of all descriptions. The scope of the Act has been extended by s.108(4) of the Anti-terrorism, Crime and Security Act 2001 adding a subs.4 to s.1[48]:

> (4)   For the purposes of this Act it is immaterial if—
>
> > (a)   the principal's affairs or business have no connection with the United Kingdom and are conducted in a country or territory outside the United Kingdom;
> >
> > (b)   the agent's functions have no connection with the United Kingdom and are carried out in a country or territory outside the United Kingdom.

---

[40]   *R. v Dearnley* [2001] 2 Cr.App.R.(S.) 42. For cases of the utmost gravity see *Donald* [1997] 2 Cr.App.R.(S.) 272 and *Foxley* (1995) 16 Cr.App.R.(S.) 879. For sentencing in respect of a commercial corruption offence see *Wilson* (1982) 4 Cr.App.R.(S.) 337.

[41]   s.2(1).

[42]   s.1(2).

[43]   *R. v Barrett* [1976] 1 W.L.R. 946.

[44]   *R. v Natji* [2002] 2 Cr.App.R. 312; 1 W.L.R. 2337.

[45]   *Fisher v Oldham Corporation* [1930] 2 K.B. 364.

[46]   *R. v Dickinson and De Rable* (1948–49) 33 Cr.App.R. 5 CCA.

[47]   *Morgan v DPP* [1970] 3 All E.R. 1953 DC.

[48]   Commencement (No.3) Order 2002 (SI 2002/228); the amendment took effect from February 14, 2002.

GIFT OR CONSIDERATION

The wording of the 1906 Act differs from its predecessor: instead of "any **19.9** gift, loan, fee, reward or advantage whatever", the 1906 Act simply prohibits the offer or acceptance of "any gift or consideration". The expression "consideration" includes valuable consideration of any kind; it has a legal meaning,[49] namely:

> "some right, interest, profit or benefit accruing to the one party, or some forbearance, detriment, loss or responsibility given, suffered, or undertaken by the other ...".[50]

It is an offence under the 1906 Act to attempt to obtain gifts, etc., whereas the 1889 Act refers to "soliciting" such gifts.

THE "PRESUMPTION OF CORRUPTION"

The Prevention of Corruption Act 1916 was introduced as a result of dis- **19.10** satisfaction at the effectiveness of the law in combating corruption.[51] The Act placed a legal burden of proof on the defendant in certain situations. Where under either the 1889 or 1906 Acts, the prosecution has:

> "... proved that any money, gift or other consideration has been paid or given to or received by a person in the employment of [Her] Majesty or Government Department or a public body or from a person, or agent of a person, holding or seeking to obtain a contract from [Her] Majesty or Government Department or a public body, the money, gift or consideration *shall be deemed to have been paid or given and received corruptly* as such inducement or reward as is mentioned in such Act *unless the contrary be proved*".[52]
>
> [emphasis added]

Accordingly, in the case of public bodies, there is a presumption of corruption. This means that a benefit conferred on an employee of a public body by someone who holds or is seeking a contract with any such body is deemed to be corrupt unless it is proved to have been innocent. The presumption only applies to employees, not office holders, so local councillors are outside the ambit. Where a person makes a gift to a member of the planning committee in the hope of being granted planning permission, the presumption would not apply since it relates only to a person "holding or

---

[49] *R. v Braithwaite* (1983) 77 Cr.App.R. 34 CA.
[50] *Curry v Mica* (1875) L.R. 10 Exch.153, 162.
[51] See, e.g. the observations of Low J. reported in *Asseling, The Times*, September 10, 1916 and *Montague, The Times*, September 18, 1916. Both of these cases concerned corrupt conduct in relation to contracts with the War Office.
[52] s.2 Prevention of Corruption Act 1916.

seeking to obtain a contract".[53] The presumption has no application in relation to anything which is made an offence only by ss.108 or 109 of the Anti-terrorism, Crime and Security Act 2001.

In *R. v Braithwaite*,[54] Lord Lane C.J. explained that the section imposed a legal burden on the defence to prove, on the balance of probabilities, that "what was going on was not reception corruptly as inducement or reward", in other words, that a given payment was not corrupt. A jury may convict even if they are left with a reasonable doubt that the payment was corrupt.[55] The presumption applies to all payments made to employees and public bodies as defined by s.7 of the 1889 Act and s.4(2) of the 1916 Act, even if the charge is brought under the 1906 Act.

It is submitted that the imposition of a legal burden on the defence by s.2 of the 1916 Act is incompatible with art.6(2) of the European Convention of Human Rights.[56] The Law Commission doubted whether the presumption was either necessary or justifiable.[57] The presumption may be objected to on the grounds that it casts on the defendant the burden of disproving an essential element of the offence, the offences are "truly criminal" and carry a maximum sentence of seven years' imprisonment. As has been seen, to show that a legal burden on the accused is proportionate, it must be proved by the prosecution to be necessary, not merely reasonable.[58] In practice, as a result of the decision of the House of Lords in *Lambert*, where corruption is alleged, the prosecution accepts that there is an evidential rather than a legal burden on the accused.

CORPORATE LIABILITY FOR CORRUPTION

19.11 Where a corporation is prosecuted for corruptly offering or paying a bribe under either Act, the prosecution must prove that the company officer involved had the necessary status and authority to make his acts the acts of the company. In *R. v Andrews-Weatherfoil Ltd*,[59] the defendant company (a building firm) was convicted of corruptly offering bribes to S, chairman of the housing committee of Wandsworth LBC. The Crown alleged that the company was paying an emolument to S in return for preferment and council contracts. Three people within the company were involved in the corrupt scheme: Mr N, the managing director, Mr A, a "technical director" and Mr W the manager of the housing division.

---

[53] *Dickinson* (1948) 33 Cr.App.R. 5.
[54] [1983] 1 W.L.R. 385; 77 Cr.App.R. 34 CA.
[55] *R. v Evans-Jones* (1923) 17 Cr.App.R. 121.
[56] See Reverse Burdens, para.12.19 above.
[57] para.5, Law Commission report 248.
[58] *Grundy and Co Excavations Ltd v The Forestry Commission* [2003] EWHC Admin 272 per Clarke L.J.
[59] (1972) 56 Cr.App.R. 31.

The company's conviction was quashed on the ground that the judge failed adequately to direct the jury as to whether the employees of the company who made corrupt payments to S were acting "as the company" and not merely as the company's servants or agents. The court observed that:

"It is not every 'responsible agent' or 'high executive' or 'manager of the housing department' or 'agent acting on behalf of the company' who can by his actions make the company criminally responsible. It is necessary to establish whether the natural person or persons in question have the status and authority which in law makes their acts in the matter under consideration the acts of the company so that the natural person is to be treated as the company itself."[60]

Following the dictum of Lord Reid in *Tesco Supermarkets Ltd v Nattrass*,[61] the Court of Appeal held that the trial judge should have determined as a matter of law whether N or A or W were to be identified with and treated as the company.

BRIBERY AND CORRUPTION COMMITTED ABROAD

Corruption is an offence which, by its very nature, can take place in more **19.12** than one country, a fact reflected in various international treaties. In the preamble to the OECD Convention on Bribery and Corruption,[62] bribery is described as:

"...a widespread phenomenon in international business transactions including trade and investment, which raises serious moral and political concerns, undermines good governance and economic development, and distorts international competitive conditions."

The Convention called for effective measures to be introduced to "deter, prevent and combat the bribery of foreign public officials in connection with international business transactions". The Government's first response was to amend the existing law. The common law offence of corruption has been statutorily extended[63] and is now committed even if the functions of the person offered or accepting the bribe have no connection with the United Kingdom and are performed abroad. The scope of both the Prevention of Corruption Acts has also been widened to include a public body in a country or territory outside the United Kingdom. Section 109 of the Anti-terrorism, Crime and Security Act 2001 was introduced "to demonstrate the

---

[60] (1972) 56 Cr.App.R. 31, 37.
[61] [1971] 2 W.L.R. 1166 at 1176, 1179 HL; see Pt I, above for further discussion of this case.
[62] OECD Convention on Combating Bribery of Foreign Public Officials in International Transactions, 1997; signed on December 17, 1997.
[63] By s.108(1) Anti-terrorism, Crime and Security Act 2001.

United Kingdom's commitment to join with the international community in the fight against corruption":

(1) This section applies if—

    (a) a national of the United Kingdom or a body incorporated under the law of any part of the United Kingdom does anything in a country or territory outside the United Kingdom, and

    (b) the act would, if done in the United Kingdom, constitute a corruption offence (as defined below).

(2) In such a case—

    (a) the act constitutes the offence concerned, and

    (b) proceedings for the offence may be taken in the United Kingdom

(3) These are corruption offences—

    (a) any common law offence of bribery;

    (b) the offences under section 1 of the Public Bodies Corrupt Practices Act 1889 (corruption in office);

    (c) the first two offences under section 1 of the Prevention of Corruption Act 1906 (bribes obtained by or given to agents).

(4) A national of the United Kingdom is an individual who is—

    (a) a British citizen, a British Overseas Territories citizen, a British National (Overseas) or a British Overseas citizen,

    (b) a person who under the British Nationality Act 1981 is a British subject, or

    (c) a British protected person within the meaning of that Act.

The "presumption of corruption" does not apply to this section.

DOCUMENTS INTENDED TO DECEIVE PRINCIPAL

19.13 The third paragraph of s.1 of the 1906 Act makes it an offence for any person to give to an agent, or for an agent to use any receipt, account or other document intended to deceive the principal[64]:

> "If any person knowingly gives to any agent, or if any agent knowingly uses with intent to deceive his principal, any receipt, account, or other document in respect of which the principal is interested, and which contains any statement which is false or erroneous or defective in any

---

[64] There is no comparable offence under the 1889 Act.

material particular, and which to his knowledge is intended to mislead the principal; ... he shall be guilty of an offence."

This part of s.1 applies only to documents which were intended to pass between a principal and a third party, not to internal documents.[65] The offence may be committed by a third party or an agent or both, but the third party who gives a false document to an agent with a view to deceiving his principal commits the offence even if the agent is wholly unaware of its falsity.[66] "Knowingly" requires proof of the giving, and knowledge of the falsity, of the document. Proof of "wilful blindness" is sufficient.[67] It is not necessary to prove that the agent was bribed.

REFORM OF THE LAW OF CORRUPTION

In March 2003 the government introduced the Corruption Bill (Cm 5777)[68] **19.14** the aim of which is "to modernise and simplify the law replacing the overlapping and at times inconsistent provisions on corruption with a single clear statute". The existing legislation has been described by the Law Commission as "obscure, complex, inconsistent and insufficiently comprehensive".[69] Amongst the reasons why the law needs revising are the changes that have taken place as regards the nature of the public and private sector, especially in the last 20 years. In particular, many "public sector" functions are now carried out by private contractors or have been privatised completely; many public bodies wholly own limited companies which trade as commercial entities. However, the Bill failed to find favour with the Government and other agencies and it was dropped.

As discussed earlier, the whole process has started again with a further consultation paper.[70] The Law Commission advocates the implementation of two offences only, one of bribery generally and the other of bribing a foreign public official. It is submitted that the domestic offence proposed is cumbersome and complicated and that two offences, one aimed at the briber and the other at the bribee, set out in simple language would be a preferable manner to address the considerable problems which the current law undoubtedly poses. The Commission also proposes that consideration of the liability of corporations for corruption offences should be deferred until a wider review of corporate liability is undertaken. We suggest that there is no good reason why the law relating to corporate bribery cannot be modernised and clarified ahead of such a review. Indeed, irrespective of who it is that

---

[65] *R. v Tweedie* [1984] Q.B. 729; 79 Cr.App.R. 168 CA.
[66] *Sage v Eicholz* [1919] 2 K.B. 171 DC.
[67] *Westminster City Council v Croyalgrange Ltd* [1980] 1 W.L.R. 674.
[68] The Bill broadly follows the Law Commission Report "*Legislating the Criminal Code: Corruption*" (No.248, 1988).
[69] Law Commission Report 248: *Legislating the Criminal Code: Corruption*; March 3, 1998.
[70] Law Commission Consultation Paper No.185, 2007.

offers a bribe, bearing in mind that the beneficiary in the commercial sphere is often a company, postponing consideration of corporate criminality would be a wasted opportunity. Where an individual engages in corrupt conduct for the benefit of the company, criminal liability should not be restricted to that individual; if the corrupt behaviour was carried out on its behalf it too ought to be guilty of an offence; indeed, even if it does not "know" of the corrupt conduct but benefits, there is an argument that a financial and criminal deterrent will be effective and should be encouraged.[71] Whatever the eventual response to the Law Commission, the UK must comply with its international responsibilities which includes consideration of corporate liability in this field.

---

[71] See anti-competition legislation and, e.g. *Director General of Fair Trading v Pioneer Concrete (UK) Ltd; Supply of Ready Mixed Concrete (No.2), Re* [1995] 1 A.C. 456.

Part VI

REGULATORY OFFENCES

CHAPTER 20

REGULATORY OFFENCES

From the birth of the modern corporation, the legislature has sought to **20.1** control their conduct and activities through the enactment of regulations enforced by criminal sanctions.

Historically, it had been assumed that since a corporation could not have a criminal state of mind, it could only be guilty of an offence which did not include any mental element. The earliest corporate prosecutions were of companies engaged in major public works. These corporations were incorporated by Parliament so as to provide them with the statutory powers needed to fulfil their functions, such as compulsory purchase. They were creatures of statute, with rights and duties defined by statute. They could be prosecuted for failures to comply with their statutory duty (e.g. building railways) through offences of non-feasance or misfeasance.[1] Once it was possible easily to incorporate a limited liability company, the legislature saw that corporations quickly began to dominate all areas of commerce and to replace individual traders. Recognising that limited liability could leave the public unprotected from the unscrupulous, legislation was enacted in certain areas (including food, public health and transport, consumer protection and the like) to redress the imbalance between members of the public and the limited liability of those actually responsible for the conduct of the enterprise.

Parliament has provided two distinct but complementary schemes of legislation to regulate corporations. First, the various Companies Acts required a corporation to register and publish details of directors, shareholders, accounts, etc. so that those who might consider dealing with or investing in a company could make an informed decision, based on accurate information, as to its corporate structure and health.[2] Secondly, in areas such as public health and consumer protection Parliament enacted legislation to regulate and make corporations acting within those spheres

---

[1] See Early Development of Corporate Criminal Liability, Ch.2.
[2] See *Salomon v Salomon & Co Ltd* [1897] A.C. 22, 40 per Lord Watson.

accountable for the way in which their business is operated. Without such express provisions, those responsible, but protected by limited liability, would be immune from the coercive power of the State in precisely those areas in which the State has particular interest in protecting the public. Regulatory legislation puts pressure upon corporations in the field "to do their whole duty in the interests of public health or safety or morals".[3]

20.2 This principle has long been recognised by the courts as justification for a departure from the general principle that criminal liability depends on some mens rea.

In *Mousell Brothers v London & North West Ry*[4] Viscount Reading C.J. put the concept succinctly:

> "Prima facie, then, a master is not to be made criminally responsible for the acts of his servant to which the master is not a party. But it may be the intention of the Legislature, in order to guard against the happening of the forbidden thing, to impose a liability upon a principal even though he does not know of, and is not party to, the forbidden act done by his servant. Many statutes are passed with this object."

In the same case, Atkin L.J. suggested that in order to determine whether the offence in question was one of strict libility, it was necessary to have regard to: "the object of the statute, the words used, the nature of the duty laid down, the person upon whom it is imposed, the person by whom it would in ordinary circumstances be performed, and the person upon whom the penalty is imposed".[5] The courts have recognised that, were they not to interpret regulatory offences in this way, corporations would escape liability, thus rendering the legislation "ineffective for its avowed purpose".[6]

"CRIMES" AND "QUASI-CRIMES"

20.3 Because so much corporate business is regulated, companies are far more likely to be prosecuted for regulatory or "quasi- crimes" than for ordinary criminal offences. How have the courts distinguished between the two? In *Pearks, Gunston & Tee Ltd v Ward*,[7] the company was prosecuted under s.6 of the Sale of Food & Drugs Act 1875 for having sold to "the prejudice of the purchaser butter which was not of the nature, substance and quality demanded". The company argued that the section could not apply to a body corporate; the court disagreed. Explaining that decision in the light of the Interpretation Act 1889 and "having regard to the importance of the question", Channell J. gave some general guidance:

[3] Dean Roscoe Pound in "*Spirit of the Common Law*" 64 L.Q.R. 176.
[4] [1917] 2 K.B. 836, 844.
[5] At p.845.
[6] *Coppen v Moore (No.2)* [1898] 2 Q.B. 306 per Lord Russell at 314.
[7] [1902] 2 K.B. 1, 11.

"By the general principles of the criminal law, if a matter is made a criminal offence, it is essential that there should be something in the nature of *mens rea*, and, therefore, in ordinary cases a corporation cannot be guilty of a criminal offence,[8] nor can a master be liable criminally for an offence committed by his servant. But there are exceptions to this rule in the case of quasi-criminal offences, as they may be termed, that is to say, where certain acts are forbidden by law under a penalty, possibly even under a personal penalty, such as imprisonment, at any rate in default of payment of a fine; and the reason for this is that the Legislature has thought it so important to prevent the particular act from being committed that it absolutely forbids it to be done; and if it is done the offender is liable to a penalty whether he had any *mens rea* or not, and whether or not he intended to commit a breach of the law. Where the act is of this character then the master, who, in fact, has done the forbidden thing through his servant, is responsible and is liable to a penalty. There is no reason why he should not be, because the very object of the Legislature was to forbid the thing absolutely. It seems to me that exactly the same principle applies in the case of a corporation. If it does the act which is forbidden it is liable. Therefore, when a question arises, as in the present case, one has to consider whether the matter is one which is absolutely forbidden, or whether it is simply a new offence which has been created to which the ordinary principle as to *mens rea* applies."[9]

In *Sweet v Parsley*,[10] the House of Lords considered the provisions of the Dangerous Drugs Act 1965. By s.5, it is an offence for a person to be concerned in the management of any premises used for the purpose of smoking or dealing in cannabis. Miss Sweet sublet a farm to persons who, without her knowledge or permission, smoked cannabis when she was not there. The magistrates convicted her on the basis that mens rea was not an element of the offence; her conviction was upheld by the Divisional Court. The House of Lords unanimously overturned the conviction, Lord Reid rhetorically asking "How has it come about that the Divisional Court has felt bound to reach such an obviously unjust result?"

Consideration was given to the circumstances of absolute liability offences, and distinctions made between "real" and "quasi-crimes". Lord Diplock put it in this way[11]:

"Where penal provisions are of general application to the conduct of ordinary citizens in the course of their every day life, the presumption is that the standard of care required of them in informing themselves of

---

[8] This is no longer good law; see *DPP v Kent & Sussex Contractors Ltd* [1944] 1 K.B. 146, and *Tesco Ltd v Nattrass*.
[9] At p.11.
[10] [1969] 53 Cr.App.R. 221.
[11] ibid. at 246.

facts which would make their conduct unlawful, is that of the familiar common law duty of care. But where the subject matter of a statute is the regulation of a particular activity involving potential danger to public health, safety or morals, in which citizens have a choice whether they participate or not, the court may feel driven to infer an intention of Parliament to impose, by penal sanctions, a higher duty of care on those who choose to participate and to place on them an obligation to take whatever measures may be necessary to prevent the prohibited act, without regard to those considerations of cost or business practicability which play a part in the determination of what would be required of them in order to fulfil the ordinary common law duty of care. But such an inference is not lightly drawn, nor is there any room for it unless there is something that the person on whom the obligation is imposed can do directly or indirectly by supervision or inspection, by improvement of his business methods, or by exhorting those whom he may be expected to influence or control, which will promote the observance of the obligation."

In the context of regulatory offences, it is this last analysis which provides the foundation for many decisions on strict liability.

20.4   A criticism of the effect of this distinction between real crimes and quasi-crimes is that little or no moral blame or censure attaches to corporations for breach of regulatory offences, even though the consequences of such criminal acts or omissions can be fatal.

> "Both criminal law generally and regulation in particular can be regarded as exercises in harm prevention; what is lacking in the regulatory sphere is the element of social control and of denunciation or censure."[12]

Professor Celia Wells has argued that regulatory offences should not be viewed as a separate category from "real" crime. On the contrary, in order better to protect employees and the public, regulatory offences should be fully integrated into the criminal justice system. She argues that a consequence of the categorisation of offences as truly criminal or "quasi-criminal" is that serious or fatal accidents at work are not treated sufficiently seriously. Of the 241 workplace deaths in 2006–7,[13] the vast majority will probably not be the subject of *any* prosecution;[14] where there is

---

[12] Celia Wells, *Corporations and Criminal Responsibility*, 2nd edn (Oxford, OUP, 2001).

[13] According to the Health & Safety Executive: *http://www.hse.gov.uk/statistics*; (there has been a downward trend in fatalities in the last few years; for members of the public, excluding railway related incidents, the figure was 90).

[14] Fewer than 20% of workplace deaths are prosecuted—see Slapper & Tombs, *Corporate Crime* (Harlow, Longman, 1999). However, in 2007 the HSE Chief Executive indicated that in the past year 25% more prosecutions had been approved than the year before and HSE inspectors have served 1000 more enforcement notices. (No current statistics were available at the time of going to press.).

a prosecution it will almost inevitably be for breach of a regulatory offence, not corporate manslaughter.

Another effect of this distinction, she argues, is on sentence. On an analysis of fines imposed for regulatory breaches, it can be seen that, even up to the late 1990s, the level of penalty was relatively low. One explanation for this is that fines were not related to the *results* of the failure/breach of the regulation. Between 1996 and 1998, the average fine for an offence involving a work place death was £13,032.

RECENT CASES

The Court of Appeal[15] has given clear guidance in sentencing in regulatory **20.5** cases in order to achieve some consistency and to correct what even the judiciary perceived as inadequate penalties, and there is no doubt that fines are beginning to reflect the seriousness with which offences affecting public health are viewed.

One example concerns breaches of environmental protection legislation; the company, Eurocare Environmental Services Ltd,[16] a hospital waste disposal company which dealt with a quarter of the NHS clinical waste, pleaded guilty to 10 allegations spanning a period of six months. The charges mainly concerned contravention of provisions of the Environmental Protection Act 1990 in respect of keeping or depositing without a licence controlled special waste, and keeping such waste in a manner likely to cause pollution or harm to human health.[17] The company was fined £5,000 or £10,000 on each count. On the further charges of causing poisonous, noxious or polluted matter or waste to enter controlled water,[18] the company was fined £20,000. The company had emptied tanks of liquid chemical waste, including bodily fluids into a septic tank which discharged into the River Dee. The total sentence (including for offences of making false statements in relation to the licence) was £100,000. The company was also ordered to pay the costs of the Environment Agency which prosecuted the case in the sum of £114,818. In sentencing the judge remarked:

> "Over a period of time this company has fallen far short of the standard required ... in several instances ... this has led to some risk to public health and the health of employees, [with] the unlawful storage of clinical waste materials over long periods in grossly inadequate circumstances."

---

[15] *F. Howe & Sons (Engineers) Ltd* [1999] 2 Cr.App.R.(S.) 37. See Sentence, para.17.7 above.
[16] *The Times*, February 15, 2003.
[17] Contrary to s.33(1) of the Environmental Protection Act 1990.
[18] Contrary to s.85(1) Water Resources Act 1991.

In the later case of the Milford Haven oil disaster, the Port authority was fined £4 million at first instance, reduced on appeal to £750,000. The Port pleaded guilty to an offence when a tanker ran aground causing a devastating oil spill the effects of which were wide reaching for wildlife in the area. The Court of Appeal indicated the following factors were important to sentence: a low level of culpability—the plea of guilty was tendered and accepted on the basis of strict liability without admission of fault; no question of cutting corners or skimping on safety or operational requirements to maximise profit or of seeking to gain any competitive advantage; no record of previous offending; there was no history of non-compliance; there were no warnings which were said to have gone unheeded; there was no suggestion that the Port authority's behaviour in relation to this incident was in any way cavalier; once the incident occurred, the Port authority exerted itself to the utmost to mitigate the damage and thereupon initiated a searching review of all its operations to see how its procedures could be improved.

On the other hand, Bingham L.C.J. stated:

> "It is, however, important to bear prominently in mind a countervailing consideration. Parliament creates an offence of strict liability because it regards the doing or not doing of a particular thing as itself so undesirable as to merit the imposition of criminal punishment on anyone who does or does not do that thing irrespective of that party's knowledge, state of mind, belief or intention. This involves a departure from the prevailing canons of the criminal law because of the importance which is attached to achieving the result which Parliament seeks to achieve. The present case affords a very good example. The danger of oil pollution is so potentially devastating, so far-reaching and so costly to rectify that Parliament attaches a criminal penalty to breach of section 85 even where no lack of care or due diligence is shown."[19]

STRICT OR ABSOLUTE LIABILITY FOR QUASI-CRIMES

20.6 Many regulatory offences provide for strict liability, the rationale being that: (i) the activity to be prevented is so important that it justifies conviction even without proof of any criminal state of mind, and (ii) without absolute liability, the legislation would be rendered largely ineffective.

> "Since the Industrial Revolution the increasing complexity of life called into being new duties and crimes which took no account of intent. Those who undertake various industrial and other activities, especially where these affect the life and health of the citizen, may find themselves

---

[19] *R. v Milford Haven Port Authority* [2000] 2 Cr.App.R.(S.) 423, 432 per Bingham L.C.J.

liable to statutory punishment regardless of knowledge or intent both in respect of their own acts or neglect and those of their servants."[20]

In *Sweet v Parsley*,[21] their Lordships held that a criminal statute should be interpreted as requiring proof of mens rea, unless the contrary was the explicit and obvious intention of Parliament. Lord Pearce made the point that, since the nineteenth century, many such statutory provisions had been enacted by the legislature:

> "...the nature of the crime, the punishment, the absence of social obloquy, the particular mischief and the field of activity in which it occurs, and the wording of the particular section and its context, may show that Parliament intended that the act should be prevented by punishment regardless of intent or knowledge."[22]

A more recent explanation of the purpose of the regulatory regime was provided by Cory J. in the Canadian Supreme Court[23]:

> "The objective of regulatory legislation is to protect the public or broad segments of the public (such as employees, consumers and motorists to name but a few) from the potentially adverse affects of otherwise lawful activity. Regulatory legislation involves the shift of emphasis from the protection of individual interests and the deterrence and punishment of acts involving moral fault to the protection of public and societal interests. While criminal offences are usually designed to condemn and punish past, inherently wrongful conduct, regulatory measures are generally directed to the prevention of future harm through the enforcement of minimum standards of conduct and care.
>
> It follows that regulatory offences and crimes embody different concepts of fault. Since regulatory offences are directed primarily not to conduct itself but to the consequences of conduct, conviction of a regulatory offence may be thought to import a significantly lesser degree of culpability than conviction of a true crime. The concept of fault in regulatory offences is based upon a reasonable care standard and, as such, does not imply moral blameworthiness in the same manner as criminal fault. Conviction for breach of a regulatory offence suggests nothing more than that the defendant has failed to meet a prescribed standard of care."

Those who choose to carry on a regulated activity are in a different position from the general public[24]:

---

[20] *Sweet v Parsley* (1969) 53 Cr.App.R. 221, 236 per Lord Pearce.
[21] (1969) 53 Cr.App.R. 221, 236.
[22] At p.236.
[23] *Thomson Newspapers Ltd v Director of Investigation and Research* (1990) 54 C.C.C. 417.
[24] At p.228.

"...while in the criminal context the essential question to be determined is whether the accused has made the choice to act in the manner alleged in the indictment, the regulated defendant is by virtue of the licensing argument, assumed to have made the choice to engage in the regulated activity ... those who choose to participate in regulated activities have in doing so placed themselves in a responsible relationship to the public generally and must accept the consequences of that responsibility ... Those persons who enter a regulated field are in the best position to control the harm which may result and they should therefore be held responsible for it."

Ordinarily a master is not criminally liable for the acts of his servants done without his knowledge or authority. In cases of strict liability, the term vicarious liability has been used by the courts to explain the responsibility of the employer and to fix the employer with liability for acts done by an employee within the scope of his employment. It is suggested that this is a misuse of the term; in reality the employer is liable directly because it is his responsibility to ensure (often subject to reasonable practicability or due diligence, etc.) that the regulation in question is not breached. In *Mousell Bros v London & North Western Railway Co*,[25] Viscount Reading C.J. rationalised the decision on the basis that "the Legislature intended to fix responsibility for this quasi-criminal act upon the principal if the forbidden acts were done by his servant within the scope of his employment".[26]

Where a person is a licence-holder he may have an additional liability for criminal acts committed by another if that other is his *delegate*. If a licensee chooses to delegate his powers and responsibilities to another, "... what that other does or what he knows must be imputed to the person who put that other into that position".[27] This is quite distinct from vicarious liability; it depends not on the wording of the offence, but on the nature of the licence and the fact of delegation.

DELEGATION

20.7 It has long been the position in licensing cases where a licensee has delegated his powers and duties, that even where the licensee is personally ignorant of the prohibited behaviour by his delegate, he is legally responsible for the wrong of the delegate. The courts developed the "doctrine of delegation" to give effect to legislation imposing particular responsibilities on a licensee. According to the ordinary rule, a person is not liable for acts or omissions committed by another without his knowledge or authority. A licensee is in a different position because, by the terms of the licence, he is permitted to do

---

[25] [1917] 2 K.B. 836.
[26] At p.845.
[27] Lord Goddard C.J. in *Linnett v Commissioner of Metropolitan Police* [1946] K.B. 290, 296.

acts which would otherwise be unlawful, e.g. sell liquor. If a licensee could avoid liability simply by handing over the running of his licensed premises to another, the intention of Parliament to control the licensed activity would be thwarted. This was particularly important where a delegate would not normally be guilty of a licensing offence as he could not be described as, e.g. "the keeper of licensed premises" or "the licensee".

Thus, in *Linnett v Commissioner of Metropolitan Police*,[28] a licensee who had handed over control of licensed premises to his co-licensee was guilty of an offence of knowingly permitting disorderly conduct in a public house. The two elements that had to be proved (it being conceded that there was disorderly conduct) were: (a) that the accused was the keeper of the house— being a licensee was held to be sufficient in the circumstances; and (b) that he knowingly permitted the disorderly conduct. It was accepted that he was neither present nor aware of the conduct. However, because he was responsible in law under the terms of the license, where he chose to entrust another (be it servant or joint licensee), with the sole management and conduct of the licensed premises, he had delegated his powers and duties and was thus fixed with the knowledge of that person, his delegate.

Whether a licensee has delegated his rights and responsibilities to another depends on the relationship between the licence-holder and the person who committed the offence. Once the facts are established, it is a question of law whether or not a person is the licensee's delegate. Thus in *Vane v Yianno-poullos*,[29] the House of Lords held that where the licensee was away from the premises and, without his knowledge and contrary to his instructions, a waitress served drinks without food in breach of the terms of the license, he was not guilty of "knowingly selling intoxicating liquor to persons to whom he is not permitted by the terms of the licence to sell". He had not delegated his powers, duties and responsibilities; the waitress was simply his employee and so her knowledge could not be imputed to him. It is inevitable that a licensee will employ others to carry out certain tasks for him in the performance of his licensed trade, e.g. serve customers. Employment of itself is not indicative of any delegation. Whether the doctrine applies in a particular case depends upon whether the licensee has handed over his responsibilities to another.

A licensee who absented himself from the premises and delegated control of them to a manager could not avoid his duties and responsibilities under the Licensing Act; where the manager knowingly contravened the terms of the licence, his knowledge was imputed to the licensee. In *R. v Winson*,[30] the Appellant was the holder of the licence of a club and director of the limited company which owned it. The club was managed by a Mr McBride, who had been appointed by the managing director of the company with the

---

[28] [1996] K.B. 290.
[29] [1965] A.C. 486.
[30] *R. v Winson* [1969] 1 Q.B. 371.

approval of the Board on which the appellant sat. Despite his absence and, his ignorance of a contravention of the licence, it was held that the appellant had been correctly convicted. Lord Parker C.J. put it thus[31]:

> "... a man cannot get out of the responsibilities and duties attached to a license by absenting himself. The position of course is quite different if he remains in control. It would only be right that he should not be liable if a servant behind his back did something which contravened the terms of the licence. But if he wholly absents himself leaving somebody else in control, he cannot claim that what has happened has happened without his knowledge if the delegate has knowingly carried on in contravention of the licence."

20.8   However, in *Howker v Robinson*[32] the offence was one of knowingly selling alcohol to a person under the age of 18. The licensee was working in the public bar at the time. He had given the barman complete control over the sale of alcohol in the lounge of the public house, including ensuring that no alcohol was served to the underage. In fact, the barman served a 14 year old with alcohol knowing that it was in breach of the licence. The licensee was convicted by the magistrates who found as a fact he had effectively delegated the "managerial functions and responsibilities in respect of the lounge bar" to the barman. The House of Lords upheld the conviction on that factual foundation, although they recognised that the situation may be anomalous.

It is surely a matter of policy (in this case the social policy to curb under age drinking) as well as degree, whether a licensee will be held, in any given scenario, to have delegated his powers and responsibilities to another. The principle of delegation, although still applied in licensing cases, has caused the courts anxiety and is not to be extended.[33]

A new scheme of licensing has been introduced by recent legislation in respect of both liquor and gaming licences. Corporations may be granted premises licenses for the sale of liquor and operating licenses for gaming. However for both types of license it is necessary for there to be an individual in a supervisory or managerial role who holds the personal license. This individual will be subject to checks as to his/her suitability to hold a license, and will, in the event of a breach of license be guilty of "relevant offences" under both Acts[34]; the principle of delegation will still apply in respect of subordinate employees.[35]

---

[31] At p.385.
[32] [1973] Q.B. 178.
[33] See *Howker v Robinson* at p.186 per James J.
[34] Licensing Act 2003 and Gambling Act 2005.
[35] See Paterson's Licensing Act 2008.

STRICT LIABILITY

Statutes do not usually announce the introduction of an offence of strict **20.9** liability, rather the policy behind the legislation, as well as the words and construction of it will determine the nature of the liability. In a precursor to the present Food Safety Act 1990, two decisions in the late nineteenth century exemplify this proposition. At that time, there were many instances of adulteration of dairy produce against which the Sale of Food and Drugs Acts were, in part, concerned to legislate. In *Brown v Foot*[36] a vendor of milk was liable for the unauthorised act of his servant in selling watered-down milk to an inspector. He had given warnings that any servant found to be in possession of milk for sale which did not match the sample he had extracted from each can, was liable to dismissal. Section 6 of the 1875 Act provided: "No person shall sell to the prejudice of the purchaser any article of food or any drug which is not of the nature, substance and quality of the article demanded by such purchaser under a penalty not exceeding twenty pounds". The servant was admittedly employed in the general business of the appellant, namely selling milk by retail. It was, therefore, the responsibility of the appellant to see that the servant acting within the scope of his authority, did not contravene the Act.[37] Moreover, the defendant was the seller since it was his milk.

The strictness of the liability is demonstrated by the old case of *Parker v Alder*,[38] in which a milk supplier near Challow, Berkshire was contracted to supply pure milk to a London association via the railway. Pure, unskimmed, new milk in good condition was to be delivered to Paddington Station. An inspector at Paddington Station took a sample from a milk churn, which was fastened in the usual way. The milk was found to be watered down. The magistrates found as a fact that when the churn was delivered by the Appellant to his home station it contained pure milk and the seller was not party, directly or indirectly, to the adulteration which must have occurred during the journey from Challow to Paddington.

The Divisional Court held the seller had committed the offence although he was morally innocent and had no means of protecting himself from the adulteration of the milk in transit by a stranger. Lord Russell C.J. stated:

> "When the scope and object of these Acts are considered, it will appear that if he were to be relieved from responsibility a wide door would be opened for evading the beneficial provisions of this legislation."[39]

The court observed that there was no material difference between the situation of a dishonest servant acting against the instructions of his master,

---

[36] 66 L.T. (N.S.) 649.
[37] See also *Coppen v Moore*, discussed above.
[38] *Parker v Alder* [1899] 1 Q.B. 20.
[39] p.25.

as in *Brown v Foot*, and that of a stranger acting fraudulently. The offence was absolute. The court, however, questioned whether the decision to prosecute in the circumstances was appropriate, and reminded the magistrates' court (to which it remitted the case) of its power to discharge on conviction.

This case is interesting because the court did not criticise the system employed by the Appellant, there was nothing further he could do to protect his milk from adulteration in transit by a stranger. It is submitted that he was rightly convicted because: (i) it was a strict liability offence and (ii) the statute provided no "due diligence" or "reasonable steps" defence. Whether it was appropriate to prosecute in the first place is a moot point.

20.10 The opposite result occurred in *Reynolds v GH Austin & Sons Ltd*,[40] a case of causing or permitting a vehicle to be used as an express carriage without a road service licence.[41] A women's guild organised an outing and arranged with the defendant company, which operated coaches, to hire a coach from it at a fixed price per passenger. Unbeknownst to the defendant company, the organiser of the trip advertised in a shop window: "Few tickets left. Apply within". The remaining tickets were sold to members of the public who were not part of the woman's guild. The defendant had not told the organiser that the trip should not be advertised, and the court found as a fact that it had no reasonable means of discovering that the advertisement had, in fact, been placed. By reason of the advertisement, the outing did not constitute a "special occasion". The prosecution asserted that the coach company had therefore contravened the statute. The Divisional Court disagreed. It held that since the defendant neither knew nor could reasonably have known of the advertisement, it did not have a guilty mind. Lord Goddard C.J. observed[42]:

> "Unless compelled by the words of the statute so to hold, no court should give effect to a proposition which is so repugnant to all the principles of criminal law in this Kingdom. This is not to throw any doubt on the well-established principle that if there is an absolute prohibition and the prohibited act is done a penalty is incurred, but hitherto that doctrine has never been applied, as far as I know, to a case where the prohibited act was not that of the defendant, but of some person over whom he had no control and for whom he had no responsibility, I am not now considering the cases of delegated management or of a shopkeeper's liability under such Acts as the Food and Drugs Act for sales by his servants."

As Devlin J. expressed it[43]:

---

[40] [1951] 2 K.B. 135.
[41] An offence contrary to s.72 of the Road Traffic Act 1930.
[42] At p.144.
[43] At p.149.

"... a man may be made responsible for the acts of his servants, or even for defects in his business arrangements, because it can fairly be said that by such sanctions citizens are induced to keep themselves and their organisations up to the mark. Although, in one sense, the citizen is being punished for the sins of others, it can be said that, if he had been more alert to see that the law was observed, the sin might not have been committed. But if a man is punished because of an act done by another, whom he cannot reasonably be expected to influence or control, the law is engaged, not in punishing thoughtlessness or inefficiency, and thereby promoting the welfare of the community, but in pouncing on the most convenient victim."

Parker v Alder was apparently not cited to the court. It is submitted that strict liability will not be imposed unless firstly, it is clearly expressed, and secondly, the policy of the statute requires it for the public good.[44]

The courts rightly remain reluctant to see a defendant convicted for the conduct of a stranger over whom he had no control acting without his knowledge or authority, and in circumstances in which he could not reasonably anticipate the intervention. The cases in which convictions in such circumstances have been upheld are limited to those in which protection of the public is paramount.

These two cases demonstrate that different decisions can be made on similar facts depending on the purpose of the legislation. In *Parker v Alder*, the court decided that the seller of milk to the public had the absolute responsibility of ensuring it was not adulterated because protection of the public in, e.g. health, food and drugs was paramount.[45] Whilst it can be argued that all legislation is for the general good of society, different levels of protection are required in different areas of life. So, in *Reynolds v G.H. Austin & Sons Ltd*, where the legislation did not have an overt "public welfare" characteristic, the court was not prepared to extend "no fault" liability to the acts of a stranger.

Where there is true strict liability extending to the acts of strangers, the **20.11** courts must rely on the discretion of the prosecuting authority not to prosecute those cases where there is no fault in the system nor possible control over the events which led to an otherwise lawful operation breaching a statutory provision.[46] The courts can only signal their disapproval of the bringing of such a prosecution by discharging (absolutely or conditionally) the defendant corporation and refusing to award the prosecution its costs.

---

[44] *B v DPP* [2000] 2 A.C. 428 C-D per Lord Nicholls.
[45] See also *Hobbs v Winchester Corporation* [1910] 2 K.B. 471, 481 per Farwell L.J.
[46] See *R. v British Steel Plc* [1995] 1 W.L.R. 1356, 1363 per Steyn L.J. for a more recent exposition on the exercise of the discretion.

CHAPTER 20

PURPOSIVE INTERPRETATION OF REGULATORY PROVISIONS

20.12 A review of the authorities demonstrates that when it comes to statutes in the regulatory field, the courts have generally adopted a purposive interpretation. That is to say, the courts have looked at the reasoning behind the legislation, the harm the provision is designed to prevent, or the good it is intended to engender, and interpreted the particular provision in accordance with that aim. So, liability for regulatory offences attaches to corporations (or employers) in a variety of ways: sometimes vicariously, sometimes as a personal, non-delegable duty and sometimes dependent upon what the directing mind and will of the corporation has or has not done. Although the courts have not always expressly recognised this, the approach is essentially a practical and pragmatic one, and it is only by concentrating on the purpose of the legislation that it is possible to find consistency in judicial approach.

Tesco Supermarkets Ltd v Nattrass[47] is the leading case which explains the doctrine of identification in fixing corporate liability for crimes. *Tesco* concerned an offence under s.11(2)[48] of the Trade Descriptions Act 1968, a strict liability offence subject to a specific statutory defence set out in s.24(1) which provides:

> "In any proceedings for an offence under this Act it shall, subject to subsection (2) of this section,[49] be a defence for the person charged to prove (a) that the commission of the offence was due to a mistake or to reliance on information supplied to him or to the act or default of another person, an accident or some other cause beyond his control; and (b) that he took all reasonable precautions to avoid the commission of such an offence by himself or any person under his control."

The Tesco store at Northwich was selling washing powder at a price higher than that advertised by the store. The store manager was unaware that the lower priced packets were not on display because, although he instructed his staff to inform him if they ran out of the lower price powder, the assistant who replenished the shelves had not done so. Unless the company could bring itself within s.24, the offence, being strict, was made out. The company served a s.24(2) notice on the prosecutor naming the store manager as "another person", and blaming him for the admitted breach.

---

[47] [1972] A.C. 153. For the detailed facts and a full consideration of the case, see Ch.4, Pt I above.

[48] "If any person offering to supply any goods, gives, by whatever means, any indication likely to be taken as an indication that the goods are being offered at a price less than that at which they are in fact being offered, he shall, subject to the provisions of this Act, be guilty of an offence." This section has now been superceded by s.20 of the Consumer Protection Act 1987.

[49] s.24(2) requires notice to be given to the prosecutor if the accused is blaming another for the offence.

Viscount Dilhorne encapsulated the question for the court in two sentences:[50]

> "Here the question is not whether the company is criminally liable and responsible for the act of a particular servant but whether it can escape from that liability by proving that it exercised all due diligence and took all reasonable precautions and that the commission of the offence was due to the act or omission of another person. That, in my view, is a very different question from that of a company's criminal responsibility for its servants' acts."

It was found as a fact in the magistrates' court that the company had **20.13** taken all reasonable precautions to avoid the commission of an offence. The issue was whether the store manager was "another person", i.e. different from the company who employed him. The House of Lords held that the company could mount a "due diligence" defence if it showed that those in the position of "director, manager, secretary or other similar officer" in the sense of those managing the affairs of the company and identified with it, had acted with due diligence. It was not necessary that every single employee be proved so to have acted. The store manager was "another person" and not identified with Tesco itself. Lord Reid considered the purpose of the legislation:

> "And if I look to the purpose and apparent intention of Parliament in enacting this defence, I think that it was plainly intended to make a just and reasonable distinction between the employer who is wholly blameless and ought to be acquitted, and the employer who is in someway at fault, leaving it to the employer to prove that he was in no way to blame.

> What good purpose could be served by making an employer criminally responsible for the misdeeds of some of his servants but not for those of others? It is sometimes argued—it was argued in the present case—that making an employer criminally responsible, even when he has done all that he could to prevent an offence, affords some additional protection to the public because this will induce him to do more. But if he has done all he can, how can he do more? ... The purpose of this Act must have been to penalise those at fault, not those who were in no way to blame".

The purposive element can also be found in the judgment of Lord Diplock:[51]

> "Consumer protection, which is the purpose of statutes of this kind, is achieved only if the occurrence of the prohibited acts or omissions is prevented ...

---

[50] p.185.
[51] At p.194.

Where, in the way that business is now conducted, they are likely to be acts or omissions of employees of that party and subject to his orders, the most effective method of deterrence is to place upon the employer the responsibility of doing everything which lies within his power to prevent his employees from doing anything which will result in the commission of an offence..."

This was the rational and moral justification for strict liability offences in the realm of consumer protection, health and safety.

"But this rational and moral justification does not extend to penalising an employer or principal who has done everything that he can reasonably be expected to do by supervision or inspection, by improvement of his business methods or by exhorting those whom he may be expected to control or influence to prevent the commission of the offence ... What the employer or principal can reasonably be expected to do to prevent the commission of an offence will depend upon the gravity of the injury which it is sought to prevent and the nature of the business in the course of which such offences are committed."

In *Tesco Stores Ltd v Brent London Borough Council*,[52] the Divisional Court was concerned with an offence of supplying a video recording to an under-age person, contrary to s.11(1) of the Video Recordings Act 1984. By s.11(2)(6), it was a defence for the accused to prove that he neither knew nor had reasonable grounds to believe that the person supplied was under-age. On the direction of a local Trading Standards Officer, a fourteen year old boy had gone into the Tesco store in Brent Park, selected a video with an "18" classification certificate and paid for it at the checkpoint operated by a cashier. The magistrates found that the cashier had reasonable grounds to believe that the boy was under eighteen years and convicted the company of the offence. The question for the Divisional Court was whether s.11(2)(b) was concerned with the knowledge and information of the employee supplying the video, or only with that of those representing the directing mind and will of Tesco Stores Ltd as with s.24 of the Trade Descriptions Act 1968, above. Staughton L.J. was robust in rejecting the latter:[53]

"It is ... absurd to suppose that those who manage a vast company would have any knowledge or any information as to the age of a casual purchaser of a video film. It is the employee that sells the film at the checkout point who will have knowledge or reasonable grounds for belief. It is her knowledge or reasonable grounds that are relevant. Were it otherwise, the statute would be wholly ineffective in the case of a large company, unless by the merest chance a youthful purchaser were

---

[52] [1993] 2 All E.R. 718.
[53] At p.721.

known to the board of directors. Yet Parliament contemplated that a company might commit the offence...

By contrast, the single-handed shopkeeper would be less readily able to rely on the defence section, although he would fare better if he had an assistant serving at the counter while he was in the back of the shop. I cannot believe that Parliament intended the large company to be acquitted but the single-handed shopkeeper convicted".

The court considered a number of authorities, including *Tesco v Nattrass*, but ultimately looked to the wording and purpose of the section and the parameters of the specific defence available.

This approach was also followed in *The Director General of Fair Trading v* **20.14** *Pioneer Concrete (UK) Ltd*, also known as *Ready Mixed Concrete (No.2)*.[54] This case concerned injunctions obtained under the Restrictive Trade Practises Act 1976 by the Director- General against four companies which supplied ready mixed concrete. The injunctions were to prohibit the companies from unlawful price fixing and allocating work between themselves. In breach of the injunctions and in disobedience of express instructions of the companies, their employees met together and entered into precisely such unlawful arrangements. The court found as a fact that, as well as expressly prohibiting their employees from acting in breach of the injunction, the companies had adopted reasonable systems to ensure compliance. Nevertheless, the companies were held to be in contempt of court. The House of Lords explained that the purpose of the Restrictive Trade Practices Act was to eradicate restrictive practices which had the effect of pushing up prices for consumers and limiting fair competition from industries engaged in the supply of goods and services. The court found that the arrangements between the employees were implemented by and for the benefit of the companies, albeit without the knowledge or approval of the "directing minds" of the companies.

Having quoted from the judgments in *Tesco v Nattrass*, Lord Nolan articulated the purposive approach in this way[55]:

"The Act is not concerned with what the employer says but with what the employee does in entering into business transactions in the course of his employment. The plain purpose of [the section] is to deter the implementation of agreements or arrangements by which the public interest is harmed, and the sub- section can only achieve that purpose if it is applied to the actions of the individuals within the business organisation who make and give effect to the relevant agreement or arrangement on its behalf ... Liability can only be escaped by completely effective preventive measures. How great a burden the devising

---

[54] [1995] 1 A.C. 456.
[55] At p.475.

of such measures will cast upon individual employers will depend upon the size and nature of the particular organisation."

It is clear that a company can be convicted of an offence, committed on its behalf by servants who bind the company, even if the company has expressly forbidden the conduct. In *Ready Mixed Concrete (No.2)*, although acting in flagrant disregard of the express instructions of the company, the employees bound the company. They were obviously on one level seeking to act in its interests. It was the company who would benefit from their misconduct.

It does not follow, however, that where the company does not benefit, or even where it is the victim of the crime, there will be no liability. In *Meridian Global Funds Management Asia Ltd v Securities Commission*[56] ("Meridian") the employees were perpetrating a fraud on the corporation, but it was held to be liable for their unlawful conduct. The corporation, an investment management company, was charged with an offence of failing to comply with s.20 of the Securities Amendment Act 1988,[57] which required a sub-stantial security holder in a public issuer to give notice of that fact to: (a) the public issuer and (b) any stock exchange on which the securities of the public issuer are listed. The chief investment officer and the senior portfolio manager, both of whom, in the ordinary course of business had authority to bind the company, used funds managed by the company to acquire shares in a public issuer. The board of directors and manager director were unaware of the transaction which was carried out for the fraudulent purposes of the two employees. The employees deliberately did not give notice. Before the Privy Council, it was common ground that Meridian was, for a short period, a substantial security holder in a public issuer. The company argued that the fraudulent actions of the employees could not be attributed to the company.

20.15   Lord Hoffmann, giving the judgment of the Court, stated that the primary rules of attribution (by which to determine whether an individual's acts were attributable to the company) were normally to be found in the company's constitution (its memorandum and articles of association), and implied by company law or the general rules of agency, but where the application of those primary rules would defeat the intended application to corporations of a provision, a *special rule of attribution* would be necessary:

> "This is always a matter of interpretation: given that it was intended to apply to a company, how was it intended to apply? Whose act (or knowledge, or state of mind) was *for this purpose* intended to count as the act etc. of the company? One finds the answer to this question by applying the usual canons of interpretation, taking into account the language of the rule (if it is a statute) and its content and policy."[58]

---

[56] [1995] 2 A.C. 500.
[57] A New Zealand statute.
[58] At p.507.

Lord Hoffmann described the policy of s.20 as being "to compel, in fast-moving markets, the immediate disclosure of the identity of persons who become substantial security holders in public issuers".[59] He determined that the person whose knowledge was to count as the knowledge of the company should "surely" be the person who, with the authority of the company, acquired the relevant interest. If that were not so, the policy of the Act would be defeated; it would encourage the board of a company to pay little attention to their investment managers' actions. He made it plain, however, that this did not mean that whenever an employee had authority to act on behalf of the company, his knowledge would be attributed to the company. It would always be a question of construction of the particular rule.

The principle to be gleaned from *Meridian* is that the primary rules of attribution will not necessarily provide an answer to questions of corporate liability for statutory offences. The court must look at the purpose of the particular piece of legislation and if the ordinary rules of attribution would defeat that purpose, or render it nugatory, the court will look to see how that purpose can be fulfilled by a different interpretation. As can be seen from the facts in *Meridian*, the actions of an employee can bind the corporation even if their motive and aim was to defraud their employer.[60] As Lord Hoffmann said,:

> "Their Lordships would therefore hold that upon the true construction of section 20(4)(e), the company knows that it has become a substantial security holder when that is known to the person who had authority to do the deal. It is then obliged to give notice under section 20(3). The fact that Koo did the deal for a corrupt purpose and did not give such notice because he did not want his employers to find out cannot, in their Lordships' view, affect the attribution of knowledge and the consequent duty to notify."[61]

In *R. v British Steel Plc*,[62] Steyn L.J. dismissed the company's argument **20.16** that liability under s.3 of the HSWA 1974 depended upon the doctrine of identification. The court adopted a purposive approach to the legislation.

> "If it be accepted that Parliament considered it necessary for the protection of public health and safety to impose, subject to the defence of reasonable practicability, absolute criminal liability, it would drive a juggernaut through the legislative scheme if corporate employers could avoid criminal liability where the potentially harmful event is committed by someone who is not the directing mind of the company. After all, as Stuart-Smith L.J. observed in *R. v Associated Octel Co Ltd*, at p292, s.3(1) is framed to achieve a result, namely, that persons not

---

[59] At p.511.
[60] See *Moore v I Bresler* [1944] 2 All E.R. 575 discussed in Pt I.
[61] At p.511.
[62] *R. v British Steel Plc* [1995] 1 W.L.R. 1356, 1362–3.

employed are not exposed to risks to their health and safety by the conduct of the undertaking. If we accept British Steel Plc's submission, it would be particularly easy for large industrial companies, engaged in multifarious hazardous operations, to escape liability on the basis that the company through its "directing mind" or senior management was not involved. That would emasculate the legislation."

COMMON PHRASES IN REGULATORY OFFENCES

20.17 It is an ancient canon of construction that "where there are different statutes *in pari materia* though made at different times, or even expired, and not referring to each other, they shall be taken and construed together, as one system, and as explanatory of each other".[63] So, where a similar phrase or defence appears in different statutes, the courts will be assisted by authorities on one provision in interpreting the other. Contrarily, where one case explains a defence of due diligence, it will not help the court to interpret a defence of knowledge or reasonable grounds to believe a fact in another.[64] As is now abundantly clear, the courts must look to the provision itself and construe it in accordance with its purpose, whilst giving consistency to the interpretation of particular words or phrases. In the following section, a number of words and phrases which frequently appear in regulatory offences are examined.

"UNDERTAKING"

20.18 In *R. v Mara*,[65] the issue on appeal was the scope of "undertaking" in s.3(1) of the Health & Safety at Work Act 1974. In that case, a cleaning company (CMS) of which Mr Mara was a director (the other being his wife), was contracted to clean a store every weekday between 7.30–9.00am. The cleaning equipment was left at the store for its employees to use at other times. To the knowledge of Mr Mara, one such machine had a damaged cable. It was used on a Saturday morning by one of the store's employees who was electrocuted and killed. The store pleaded guilty to an offence contrary to s.2(1) HSWA 1974. Mr Mara, as a director of CMS was convicted of an offence under s.3(1) by consenting to or conniving[66] at a breach by CMS of its duty to conduct its corporate undertaking in such a way as to ensure that persons not in the company's employment were not thereby exposed to risks to their health and safety. It was argued that CMS were not

---

[63] *Loxdale* (1758) 1 Burr 445.
[64] *Tesco Stores Ltd v Brent LBC* [1993] 2 All E.R. 718, 721 per Staughton L.J.
[65] [1987] 1 W.L.R. 87.
[66] s.37(1) of the HSWA 1974.

"conducting the company's undertaking" at all on a Saturday morning. The court held that the section should not be treated as being applicable "only when an undertaking is in the process of being actively carried on".[67] The "undertaking" continued even whilst it was not operating to fulfil its primary purpose. Parker L.J. gave an illustration of such a scenario[68]:

> "A factory, for example, may shut down on Saturdays and Sundays for manufacturing purposes, but the employer may have the premises cleaned by a contractor over the weekend. If the contractor's employees are exposed to risks to health or safety because machinery is left insecure, or vats containing noxious substances are left unfenced, it is, in our judgment, clear that the factory owner is in breach of his duty under s.3(1). The way in which he conducts his undertaking is to close his factory for manufacturing purposes over the weekend and to have it cleaned during the shut down period. It would clearly be reasonably practicable to secure machinery and noxious vats, and on the plain wording of the section he would be in breach of his duty if he failed to do so".

The "undertaking" not only included situations where the company used its own staff to clean, but also where it arranged to "have the factory cleaned". Similarly, in *R. v Associated Octel Co Ltd*,[69] the House of Lords, approving the judgment in *R. v Mara*, held that "undertaking" covered the situation where the company's plant was shut down for repairs.

Lord Hoffmann concluded as a matter of fact that part of the undertaking in Octel was the repair of its chlorine tank by outside workers. The employer (Octel) was under a duty to "take reasonably practical steps to avoid risk to the contractor's servants which arise, not merely from the physical state of the premises ... but also from the inadequacy of the arrangements which the employer makes with the contractors for how they will do the work".[70] There should be no rigid formula for determining whether something is or is not a part of an undertaking; it is a question of fact. Lord Hoffmann stated, however, that the place where the activity takes place will normally be very important and possibly decisive in making that determination.

"EXPOSED TO RISKS OF HEALTH AND SAFETY"

20.19 The word "risk" has been held to bear its ordinary meaning of "possibility of danger" and not "actual" or "real danger". In *R. v Board of Trustees of the Science Museum*,[71] the Appellants were charged as employers with failing

---

[67] [1987] 1 W.L.R. 87, 90.
[68] ibid.
[69] [1996] 1 W.L.R. 1543.
[70] p.1548.
[71] [1993] 1 W.L.R. 1171.

to discharge their duty under s.3(1) Health & Safety At Work Act 1974, to conduct their undertaking in such a way as to ensure, so far as was reasonably practicable, that persons not in their employment were not exposed to risks to their health as a result of the inadequate system for maintenance of the air conditioning. The air conditioning system was inspected by HSE officers and found to contain a high concentration of the bacterium causing legionnaire's disease which could become air bound and a risk to the health of passing members of the public. The appellants did not regularly pump fresh water into the system. Where any cooling tower in operation poses a risk to persons in the vicinity, the risk was increased by the failure to maintain efficient water treatment. It was unnecessary to show that a person had been exposed to a real danger to their health.

The Court of Appeal approved the direction of the trial judge as follows:

> "The key word ... which the prosecution have to prove, is 'risk'. Risk is a different word from the word 'danger' and it has a different meaning. It means, in the circumstances of this case, a possible source of danger ... It is common ground that in certain circumstances and under certain conditions, ... that [the L.P. virus] is a risk to health. The prosecution do not have to prove that members of the public actually inhaled [L.P.] or that [L.P.] was actually there to be inhaled. It is sufficient if there was a risk of it being there; that is the risk to which the public must have been proved to have been exposed."[72]

However, a risk has to be real and not fanciful or hypothetical. There is no 'objective standard' but "one way or another there would be important indicia or factors, none of which might be determinative but many might be of importance, e.g. evidence of any previous accident in similar daily circumstances".[73]

"So Far as is Reasonably Practicable"

20.20 This phrase appears in many regulatory offences[74]; it is a non-delegable duty.[75] The phrase mitigates the rigour of what is otherwise an offence of strict liability. Since it appears as a defence, it is for the defendant to prove[76] on the balance of probabilities.[77] The Court of Appeal has held that the reverse burden contained in s.40 HSWA 1974 does not violate the

---

[72] At p.1176.
[73] *R. v Porter* [2008] EWCA Crim 1271 per Moses L.J.
[74] See, for example, s.2 and 3 of the HSWA 1974.
[75] *R. v Mersey Docks & Harbour Company* (1995) 16 Cr.App.R.(S.) 806.
[76] *R. v Carr-Briant* (1943) 29 Cr.App.R. 76.
[77] *R. v Dunbar* (1957) 41 Cr.App.R. 182.

presumption of innocence in art.6(2) of the European Convention on Human Rights and the Human Rights Act 1998.[78]

Section 40 of the HSWA 1974, provides that in any proceedings for an offence consisting of a failure to comply with a duty or requirement to do something:

"... so far as is practicable or so far as is reasonably practicable, or to use the best means to do something, it shall be for the accused to prove (as the case may be) that it was not practicable or not reasonably practicable to do more than was in fact done to satisfy the duty or requirement, or that there was no better practicable means that was in fact used to satisfy the duty or requirement".

So, in *R. v Associated Octel Co Ltd*,[79] during its annual shut down, the appellants' "major hazard site" was being repaired by a contractor's employees. They had used acetone without a special lamp or a closed container; the acetone caught fire, severely burning one of the men. The prosecution had adduced evidence of the "perfunctory" work system operated by the appellants. The appellants called no evidence and were convicted, a conclusion the House of Lords considered inevitable. In explaining the ambit of s.3, Lord Hoffmann said[80]:

"Section 3 requires the employer to [operate a system] in a way which, subject to reasonable practicability, does not create risks to people's health and safety. If, therefore, the employer engages an independent contractor to do work which forms part of the conduct of the employer's undertaking, *he must stipulate for whatever conditions are needed to avoid those risks and are reasonably practicable*. He cannot, having omitted to do so, say that he was not in a position to exercise any control" [emphasis added].

In *Gateway Foodmarkets Ltd*[81] (which concerned s.2(1) of the HSWA 1974), the company contended on appeal that it was not liable, because the head office personnel of the company who represented the "directing mind" had done all they should; it contended that the store manager had himself developed a different, and in the event, fatal system. Evans L.J. giving the judgement of the court, disagreed:

"The duty ... is broken if the specified consequences occur, but only if 'so far as is reasonably practicable' they have not been guarded against. So the company is in breach of duty unless all reasonable precautions have been taken, and we would interpret this as meaning 'taken by the

---

[78] *Davies v HSE* [2002] EWCA Crim 2949. See Reverse Burdens in Regulatory Offences, para. 12.19.
[79] [1996] 1 W.L.R. 1543.
[80] ibid. 1547.
[81] [1997] 2 Cr.App.R. 40.

company *or on its behalf*. In other words, the breach of duty and liability under the section do not depend upon any failure by the company itself, meaning those persons who embody the company, to take all reasonable precautions. Rather the company is liable in the event that there is a failure to ensure the safety etc. of any employee, unless all reasonable precautions have been taken, as we would add, by the company *or on its behalf*". (emphasis added)

A similar result was achieved in the earlier case of *R. v British Steel Plc*[82] in which an engineer employed by the appellant was responsible for supervising two labourers (sub-contractors) in repositioning a platform. It was apparent that the engineer had failed to supervise the work; had he done so, the risk would have been avoided. The company could not delegate the duty by saying that it had appointed a person who was experienced and best qualified to supervise the job. If he, in that position, did not do all that was reasonably practicable to ensure that others were not exposed to risks to their health or safety, the company could not avail itself of the defence.

20.21   The fact that the acts or omissions of employees have exposed members of the public to risks to their health or safety is not, of itself, sufficient to establish a failure on the employer's part to conduct its undertaking, *so far as is reasonably practicable*, in such a way as to avoid such risks occurring. In other words, conduct by an employee which constitutes the strict liability offence does not preclude the employer from raising and proving the defence of reasonable practicability. What is "reasonably practicable" is a question for the jury.[83] In *R. v Nelson Group Services (Maintenance) Ltd*,[84] which concerned a gas appliance installation, the company which was responsible for maintenance, and its fitters were charged with offences contrary to s.3(1) of the HSWA 1974 and the Gas Safety (Installations & Use) Regulations 1994. Roch L.J., giving the judgment of the court, explained the ambit of the statutory defence as follows[85]:

> "...it is sufficient obligation to place on the employer in order to protect the public to require the employer to show that everything reasonably practicable has been done to see that a person doing the work has the appropriate skill and instruction, has had laid down for him safe systems of doing the work, has been subject to adequate supervision, and has been provided with safe plant and equipment for the proper performance of the work".

---

[82] [1975] 1 W.L.R. 1356.

[83] *Austin Group Ltd v Inspector of Factories* [1990] 1 A.C. 619; the relevant factors are the foreseeable risk of injury and the cost of the preventative measures. These must relate to a relevant risk.

[84] [1999] 1 W.L.R. 1526.

[85] ibid. at 1549.

This dictum, it is submitted, provides a succinct and workable test for the *reasonably practicable* defence. It encapsulates all of the responsibilities of the employer, whilst leaving open the possibility of acquittal (as Parliament, by the terms of the defence, must have intended), where the employer has done all it reasonably practicably could and is not to blame, whether by acts or omissions, or as a result of defects in its system. Moreover, if the event which happened was wholly unknown and unexpected, it would not be reasonable to require a defendant to take measures against it when it was not foreseeable.[86]

"ALL REASONABLE STEPS/PRECAUTIONS"

The phrase "all reasonable steps" was considered in *Seaboard Offshore Ltd v Secretary of State for Transport*[87] in the context of failing to take all reasonable steps to secure that the defendant corporation's ship was operated in a safe manner, contrary to s.31 of the Merchant Shipping Act 1988.[88] The complaint was essentially that the ship's engineer had had insufficient time to familiarise himself with the vessel before it took to sea. The facts were apparently not thoroughly investigated during the magistrates' court trial. The magistrates simply found that the ship was operated in an unsafe way in that the engineer was only allowed a short time to familiarise himself with it.
Lord Keith of Kinkel explained the offence under s.31[89]: **20.22**

> "It consists simply in failure to take steps which by an objective standard are held to be reasonable steps to take in the interests of the safe operation of a ship, and the duty which it places on the owner, charterer or manager is a personal one. The owner, charterer or manager is liable if he fails personally in the duty, but is not criminally liable for the acts or omissions of his subordinate employees if he has himself taken all such steps."[90]

It is to be emphasised that it is for the defendant to prove that he has taken *all* reasonable steps. This is a stringent test to pass—even if a defendant has taken some reasonable steps, if he could have taken more, or other steps which objectively might, for example, have made a difference to safety or the

---

[86] *Austin Rover Group Ltd v Inspector of Factories* [1990] 1 A.C. 619. Applied by Stanley Burnton J. in *R. (on the application of Hampstead Heath Winter Swimming Club) v London Corporation* [2005] 1 W.L.R. 2930.

[87] [1994] 1 W.L.R. 541.

[88] "It shall be the duty of the owner of a ship to which this section applies to take all reasonable steps to secure that the ship is operated in a safe manner".

[89] ibid. at 546.

[90] Lord Keith's analysis of the section is entirely consistent with the House of Lord's decision in *Tesco Supermarkets Ltd v Nattrass* [1972] A.C. 153.

discovery of a false trade description, the defence will not be made out.[91] This principle was stated in the recent case of *DEFRA v Keam*[92]:

> "In a case in which the keeper defendant employs an independent contractor to take care of his animals and does nothing more, whether in these circumstances he has taken all reasonable steps is a matter for a trial court. In many cases, if not most, one would expect the keeper (a) to have ensured that his independent contractor was indeed competent, and (b) to take steps to ensure that his independent contractor was doing that which ought to be done in caring for the animals. In many, if not most, and possibly all, cases, simply to appoint an independent contractor .... to care for his animals may well not amount to the taking of all reasonable steps. Conversely, the fact that an independent contractor fails to take all reasonable steps does not, of itself, involve criminal liability on the part of the person .... who has employed the independent contractor, if that [person] has taken all reasonable steps to ensure that the [regulations are complied with], that is to say there is no vicarious liability for the default of an independent contractor in circumstances in which the keeper can show that he himself did take all reasonable steps. On the other hand there will be cases in which both the independent contractor has defaulted and the keeper has failed to take all reasonable steps."

"DUE DILIGENCE"

20.23 It is for the accused to prove on the balance of probabilities that it has exercised due diligence.[93] A corporation cannot rely on this defence if it has delegated its responsibilities to another who has failed to act with due diligence. The failure of the delegate is the failure of the principal, which, in cases involving corporations, will be the company.[94]

In *Tesco Supermarkets Ltd v Nattrass*,[95] the magistrates' court heard much detailed evidence in support of the due diligence defence, a summary of which can be found in the judgment of Lord Morris of Borth-y-Gest at p.177. Suffice it to say that the magistrates were satisfied that Tesco had taken all reasonable precautions and exercised all due diligence. The appellate courts emphasised that this type of evidence was necessary to discharge the burden on the defendant company.

What is sufficient is a question of objective fact; compliance with recognised trade codes of practice may be evidence of due diligence, but may not

---

[91] For many examples see Butterworths *Law of Food and Drugs*.
[92] [2005] EWHC 1582 Admin.
[93] [1994] 1 W.L.R. 541, 546.
[94] *R. v Mersey Docks and Harbour Company* (1995) 15 Cr.App.R.(S.) 806.
[95] [1972] A.C. 153.

alone be sufficient to satisfy the burden of proof. Non-compliance with such codes of practice, on the other hand, is likely to lead to the defence being rejected. If a simple independent test could be carried out to check a warranty given by a supplier, the defendant who does not take such steps (but without more, relies on the supplier's assertion) will not have exercised due diligence. Adequate checking, recording of inspections and details of training and supervision, are all elements which will go towards proving the exercise of all due diligence.

"USING"

Although the driver of a vehicle must, of necessity, be a human being, it is **20.24** beyond doubt that a corporation can, in certain circumstances, also be said to be *using* a vehicle.[96]

> "While the driver of a vehicle on the road uses that vehicle within the meaning of [the particular regulation] so also, if he be a servant, does his master whether that master be a private individual or a limited company, provided always that the servant is driving on his master's business. It cannot be said that only the servant uses and that the master merely causes or permits such use. In common parlance a master is using his vehicle if it is being used by his servant on his business."[97]

Where use of a vehicle by the corporation is a necessary ingredient of liability in the case, the prosecution must prove, at the very least, that: (i) it owns the vehicle, (ii) it employs the driver, and (iii) the employee was driving on his employer's business.[98]

As Lord Widgery C.J. put it in *Bennett v Richardson*[99]:

> "A man cannot be convicted of using a motor vehicle which he is not personally driving unless he is the employer of the driver. If the owner is driving the vehicle, then, good enough, he can be charged with using it. If the owner's employee, in the strict sense of the master–servant relationship, is driving the vehicle, again the employer can be regarded as vicariously being responsible and can be convicted on an information. But if the relationship between driver and would-be defendant is any other than those to which I have referred, then it is not possible to convict the person not driving of these offences."

---

[96] *Richmond upon Thames LBC v Pinn and Wheeler* (1988) 87 L.G.R. 659 DC.
[97] *James & Son Ltd v Smee* [1955] 1 Q.B. 78, 90 per Parker J.
[98] *Mickleborough v BRS (Contracts) Ltd* [1977] R.T.R. 389 per Boreham J. at p.394.
[99] [1980] R.T.R. 358, 361.

The words "use" or "using" which occur in many statutory provisions, particularly those concerning vehicles, have been considered by the courts on a number of occasions. How the words are interpreted has followed two different routes according to whether the word appears on its own or whether it appears together with the alternative provisions of causing or permitting the use.

"The Narrow Definition"

20.25 A corporate defendant which owns a vehicle, driven by its employee on its business "uses" that vehicle. Where the provision creates alternative offences of "using" and "causing or permitting the use", "using" has been narrowly construed.

> "The position quite simply is that where regulations provide ... for an offence of using and also an offence of causing or permitting the use, the verb 'use' should be restricted in its meaning to reflect the fact that causing or permitting are separately and independently mentioned in the regulation."[1]

It is submitted that, although this interpretation has resulted in some illogical decisions, the foundation for the distinction is sound. Where the alternative of causing or permitting another to use (for example, a vehicle in a certain way) is provided by the statute, the owner should be charged with one of those offences and the driver with the using offence. Lord Widgery described the offence of "using" as "the driver's offence, whereas permitting and causing are, as it were, the owner's offences".[2]

Where the owner's *servant* was driving on the owner's business that was "equivalent to driving by the owner himself" and was thus capable of coming within the term "using". Both the driver and owner may be convicted. In *Howard v GT Jones & Co Ltd* the driver was supplied to the defendant company by an agency by whom he was employed. The Divisional Court upheld the magistrates' decision that he was not the defendant's servant and thus the defendant company was not using a vehicle which he was driving for it. The defendant company conceded that, on the same facts, if the charge had been one of causing the vehicle to be on the road, it would have pleaded guilty.[3] In charging "using", the prosecution had picked the wrong offence; it should have proceeded under the "causing" alternative providing by the section. Where, however, the defendant company was in business hiring out vehicles with drivers, and had hired out the offending vehicle and driver exclusively to the hirer's company for five years,

---

[1] *Garrett v Hooper* [1973] R.T.R. 1, 3 per Widgery C.J.
[2] *Howard v GT Jones & Co Ltd* [1975] R.T.R. 150, 154.
[3] [1975] R.T.R. 150.

and, during that period and under the hirer's livery and control, the vehicle was used on a road in contravention of weight regulations, the defendant had used the vehicle and was guilty of the offence.[4] In this situation the hirer would be guilty of "causing" the offence.

Where in a business one partner was driving and the joint owner of the vehicle was prosecuted for the contravening use of the vehicle, the joint owner was not using the vehicle.[5] The court interpreted the provision strictly, acknowledging in its judgment the illogicality of the fact that:

> "A man may use a vehicle through his servant but cannot use it through the hands of someone specifically authorised to drive it on the day in question ... [and further] a co-partner does not use a vehicle merely because it is driven by his partner on partnership business."[6]

Where liability for "using" or "permitting" or "causing" is strict, once it is proved that the vehicle was used by the defendant corporation's servant in the course of his employment, the corporation charged with "using" a vehicle in contravention of a regulation is guilty of an offence; but where the defendant corporation is charged with *permitting* a user in contravention of the provision, it must be proved that the corporation "permitted" as opposed to "committed" the offence. "Permit" requires some mens rea, and, as Parker J. spelt out in *James v Smee, Green v Burnett*[7] the need for proof of the mental element applies equally to a corporation as to an individual person. In those circumstances some person for whose criminal act the company is responsible must be proved to have permitted the crime. "Permit" connotes an active, conscious decision to allow the particular conduct. A person who does not know, does not *permit*.

"THE WIDE DEFINITION"

Where the statutory provision includes the term "using" in isolation, (and **20.26** there is no offence of permitting or causing the use), the courts have held that the class of persons who may be guilty of the offence is more widely drawn. In *Richardson v Baker*[8] the defendant was a road haulage contractor. He owned a tractor unit which had been undergoing repairs and was being used only within the confines of his yard. The excise licence for the vehicle had expired. An employee, whose regular vehicle was suddenly unavailable, took the tractor unit without the knowledge or authority (express or implied) of the defendant, to carry out the haulage job on behalf of the defendant. As a consequence of the vehicle being taken out, the driver was

---

[4] *Mickleborough v BRS (Contracts) Ltd* [1977] R.T.R. 389.
[5] *Garrett v Hooper* [1973] R.T.R. 1.
[6] [1973] R.T.R. 1 per Widgery C.J. at p.3.
[7] [1955] 1 Q.B. 78, 92.
[8] [1976] R.T.R. 56.

dismissed. The defendant was summonsed for using the vehicle on a road without a current vehicle excise licence. The Divisional Court held that the employer was indeed using the vehicle. It made no difference that the employer had not authorised the employee to undertake the use; what mattered was that the employee was engaged on his master's business. If, however, the vehicle was being used by the servant "on a frolic of his own",[9] or being used by a thief who had stolen the vehicle and used it for his own purposes, the master would not be using the vehicle at all. Likewise, unlawful use of a company vehicle out of office hours by an employee does not render the company liable for his driving offences. In summary, where the vehicle is being used on behalf of the employer by its employee it is no answer for the employer to say that the use by the employee at the time was not authorised. In that case the fact that the vehicle was unlicensed did not prevent its being used on the master's business—the offence was absolute and the vehicle was being used on the master's business at the relevant time and thus was being used by him.[10]

This accords with common sense. An offence has been committed. Since no employer is likely to admit to having authorised his employee to commit that offence, if the employer could escape liability by relying on lack of authority, the regulatory scheme would be emasculated.[11]

In the earlier case of *Quality Dairies (York) Ltd v Pedley*,[12] a distributor of milk to a hospital was guilty of contravening the duty to ensure that "every vessel used for containing milk shall be in a state of thorough cleanliness immediately before use by him". The distributor had engaged a sub-contractor to buy, bottle and deliver the milk to its customers; it had never touched the milk or bottles. Parker J., giving the judgment of the court, held that the regulations were designed to ensure, so far as possible, that milk delivered to consumers was as clean as possible, and that the duty imposed was absolute; accordingly, the principal would be liable for the acts of his servant or agent done within his authority. For the purposes of the Act, the person who delegated his duties, powers and authority to another, could not escape liability by the delegation.[13]

20.27   This line of authority was followed in *Charman (FE) Ltd v Clow*,[14] a case concerning weights and measures legislation. The brief facts were as follows: O ordered 14 cubic yards of ash from C. H, on C's instructions, delivered the

---

[9] [1976] R.T.R. 56, 60.

[10] Although the provision did not have the alternatives of causing or permitting, Widgery C.J. decided this case on a "narrow" basis—at p.59F–G.

[11] In *R. v Robert Millar (Contractors) Ltd* [1970] 2 Q.B. 54 the employer sought to avoid conviction as a secondary party by blaming the driver and denying it had authorised his use of its vehicle with defective tyres. In reality, the driver was carrying out his employer's business, not his own. The court found as a fact that the employer knew full well the state of the vehicle and convicted the employer at trial.

[12] [1952] 1 K.B. 275.

[13] At pp.278–9. The position was similar to that of a licensee under the Licensing Acts.

[14] [1974] R.T.R. 543.

ash. In fact, only nine cubic yards were delivered. The lorry, which was owned, operated and used by H, contravened the weights and measures regulations. C engaged sub-contractors for delivery of its orders. One of two hundred such sub-contractors was H; H did not work exclusively for C. C believed H's vehicle to be appropriate but had not checked it, nor was there any system for doing so. The Divisional Court held "with reluctance" and "regret"[15] that the absence of the words "causing or permitting" were crucial. Their absence compelled the court to give "using" the wider meaning and so to include C, because the vehicle was operating in pursuance of their own trade as suppliers of ash.

On analysis, whether the court will apply the narrow or the wide construction of "use" or "using" to a corporate defendant will depend (a) on the wording of the regulation/provision concerned, and (b) on the purpose of the legislation. If the purpose is to impose strict liability on a person in the course of whose business an offence is committed, then, in the absence of "causing or permitting" provisions, the wider definition is most likely to apply. The rationale behind this interpretation, which is draconian at first blush, is that some obligations are too serious to enable the principal to evade liability by a delegation of his duties.

"CAUSING/PERMITTING"

Just as "using" has a different meaning according to whether or not the **20.28** word stands alone in a provision, so the interpretation of "causing" or "permitting" depends on whether the words appear together or separately. It is another example of the purposive approach to statutory interpretation.

Where the three phrases appear together, mens rea is generally a necessary ingredient of a "causing" offence. In those circumstances the prosecution must prove that the defendant knew the facts making the use of, e.g. a vehicle unlawful. In the case of a corporate defendant, the individual with the requisite knowledge must be a person in the position of the directing mind of the company.[16] So where a corporation was summonsed for causing a vehicle to be used on a road with excess rear axle weight contrary to s.40(5)(b) of the Road Traffic Act 1972 (which provided alternative offences of "using, causing or permitting the use") the prosecution had to prove that those directing the affairs of the company knew of the factual situation. In the absence of such knowledge, even if someone within the company knew, the company could not be guilty of "causing the use", although it may have been guilty of "using" the vehicle unlawfully.

Where the prosecution is uncertain whether the company can be shown to have "used" the vehicle on the one hand, or "caused or permitted its use" on

---

[15] per Lord Widgery C.J. and Melford Stevenson J. at p.549.
[16] *James & Son Ltd v Smee* [1955] 1 Q.B. 78; *Ross Hillman Ltd v Bond* [1974] R.T.R. 279.

the other, it should lay informations in the alternative.[17] It is crucial to lay the correct information as the courts will have to acquit a defendant who is guilty of one variant but charged with another.

20.29 "Causing" requires at least the positive, if not the express, authorisation of the person causing the use to the user. In the case of a corporation, the person authorising must be identified with the company. In *Rushton v Martin*[18] the general manager of five depots was charged with causing a vehicle to be on a road in a dangerous condition. Each depot had a vehicle superintendent. In those circumstances he was not guilty of the "causing" offence and he had no knowledge that the vehicle was on a road.

Redhead Freight Ltd v Shulman[19] concerned an offence of causing an employee to use a vehicle fitted with a tachograph on a road contrary to s.97(1) of the Transport Act 1968. The transport manager knew that one of the company's drivers regularly failed to fill in the necessary records. The court held, however, that, in spite of that knowledge, the company had not "caused" the offence. It had not done any positive act, it had merely acquiesced in the driver's failure to keep records. If such acquiescence was insufficient to establish that it had "caused" the offence, the company would, however, have been guilty of the "permitting" offence.

Where the statute provides only for "causing or permitting", "causing" requires some positive act, although it may not require mens rea. Deliberately pouring toxic material into a drain, which unbeknownst to the defendant, ran into a stream, "caused" the pollution of the stream; even though the defendant thought the material would run into the sewage system, he had done a positive act which in fact *caused* the pollution.[20]

Where "causing" appears on its own in a statutory provision, the offence may be absolute, particularly where it requires a person "to cause" something to be done; where the thing is not done, no mens rea is necessary on the part of the person whose duty it is. There may be a statutory defence— usually for the defendant to prove—but the offence is still one of strict liability. Thus, the requirement to cause proper records to be kept is one of absolute liability, subject to the availability of a defence that an employer gave proper instructions to the driver and took reasonable steps to ensure that those instructions were put into effect.[21]

---

[17] *Ross Hillman Ltd v Bond* above; *R. v Newcastle JJ. Ex p. Bryce* [1976] R.T.R. 325.
[18] [1952] W.N. 258.
[19] [1988] Crim.L.R. 696.
[20] *F.J.H. Wrothwell Ltd v Yorkshire Water Authority* [1984] Crim.L.R. 43.
[21] s.98(4) Transport Act 1968, as amended.

"PERMITTING"

The meaning of "permitting" was considered by the Divisional Court in **20.30**
James & Son Ltd v Smee.[22] The defendants were charged with permitting the
use of a vehicle which was not properly maintained in contravention of a
regulation. The "using" offence was strict:

"Permitting the use ... at once imports a state of mind. The difference
in this respect was pointed out as long ago as 1894 by Collins J. in
Somerset v Wade where he pointed out the difference between an
absolute prohibition against a licensee selling to a drunken person and
a prohibition against permitting drunkenness. In the latter case he must
be shown to have known that the customer was drunk before he can be
convicted ... knowledge, moreover, in this connexion includes the state
of mind of a man who shuts his eyes to the obvious or allows his
servant to do something in the circumstances where a contravention is
likely, not caring whether a contravention takes place or not ... In the
present case there is no evidence that the defendants by any responsible
officer permitted in any such sense the user by [the driver] in contravention of the regulation."

"Permitting" has been interpreted in different ways depending on the harm
at which the statutory provision is directed. Generally "permitting" requires
some mens rea but permission does not require express authorisation; permission may be inferred.[23] Equally, permitting may be constructive, as where
a person deliberately shuts his eyes to what is happening[24]; or is reckless, not
caring whether the breach will happen or not.[25] Negligence however, is not
sufficient to prove permitting, and if recklessness is relied on by the prosecution, there must be evidence to prove that the defendant's behaviour was
indeed reckless.[26]

Where the defendant is a corporation, a person identifiable with the
company must have permitted the conduct. In *James & Son Ltd v Smee*
Parker J. stated:

"before a company can be held guilty of permitting a user in contravention of the regulation it must be proved that some person for whose
criminal act the company is responsible permitted as opposed to
committed the offence."

---

[22] [1954] 3 W.L.R. 631 applied in *Driver & Vehicle Testing Agency v McNicholas Construction
Services Ltd* [2003] NICA 9.
[23] *McLeod v Buchanan* [1940] 2 All E.R. 179.
[24] *James & Son Ltd v Smee* [1954] 3 W.L.R. 631.
[25] [1954] 3 W.L.R. 631; and see *Grays Haulage Co Ltd v Arnold* [1966] 1 All E.R. 896.
[26] *Hill & Sons (Botley & Denmead) Ltd v Hampshire Chief Constable* [1972] R.T.R. 29, in which
the Divisional Court overturned a conviction based on the alleged recklessness of the
defendants, where there was no evidence to support such a conclusion.

That "permission" may be inferred by a failure. In *Browning v JWH Watson (Rochester) Ltd*[27] the company was charged with permitting a coach to be used as an express carriage without the appropriate licence. The coach was carrying members of a football club to a match. Unbeknownst to the company, the driver had allowed two members of the public on board; this brought the use outside the terms of its licence. The Divisional Court held that the failure of the company's responsible officer to take any precautions to ensure that only club members boarded the coach constituted permission by the company, albeit in the absence of "wilful violation".[28]

20.31   It has been suggested that if a corporation delegates its duties through its directors to a junior, an inadequately trained employee who himself could not be described as "a responsible officer" or "the brains" of the company, the corporation might still be liable for permitting a contravention on the basis of recklessness.[29]

In some legislation, Parliament has clearly intended that liability, even for a "permitting" offence be absolute. Mens rea will not need to be proved, for example, in permitting a vehicle to be used without insurance. Once permission is proved, the fact that the defendant genuinely believed that the user had insurance is no defence[30]; nor was the genuine but mistaken belief that the user is covered by the defendant's insurance.[31] Permission applies to the use of the vehicle; there is no need to prove that permission was actually given to use the vehicle without insurance. In short, once the person is proved to have given permission, under whatever misapprehension, the offence is proved, regardless of any intention or efforts to avoid committing an offence.

Finally, as with many regulatory offences, the courts will look at the purpose of the legislation and seek to give effect to it. If, in order to do so, it is necessary to interpret a particular word or phrase in a way which is different from its meaning in another context, the courts will do so.

SECONDARY PARTIES

20.32 A person who aids, abets, counsels or procures an offence is generally guilty as a secondary party and may be punished equally to the principal offender. Even where a person cannot in law be a principal offender, he, or in the case of a corporation, it, may incur secondary liability. In this way a corporation cannot avoid liability for an offence to which it has been a party but in respect of which it could not be a principal offender.

---

[27] [1953] 1 W.L.R. 1172.
[28] ibid. 1176.
[29] *Wilkinson's Road Traffic Offences*, 23rd edn (London, Sweet & Maxwell, 2007).
[30] *Tapsell v Maslen* (1967) Crim.L.R. 53.
[31] *Baugh v Crago* [1975] R.T.R. 453; nor was a belief induced by the misrepresentation of the driver *Lloyd-Wolper v Moore* [2004] EWCA Civ 766.

The Accessories and Abettors Act 1861 provides:

"s.8 Whosoever shall aid, abet, counsel or procure the commission of any indictable offence, whether the same be an offence at common law or by virtue of any Act passed or to be passed shall be liable to be tried, indicted and punished as a principal offender."[32]

In the case of *National Coal Board v Gamble*, Devlin J. held:

"A person who supplies the instrument for a crime or anything essential to its commission aids in the commission of it, and if he does so knowingly and with intent to aid, he abets it as well and is therefore guilty of aiding and abetting."[33]

There is no doubt that a corporation can aid and abet criminal offences through the acts of its servants in the course and operation of their employment. In *National Coal Board v Gamble*, the employee of a firm of hauliers, who was delivering coal from the NCB to an electricity authority with whom the NCB had a contract, took his lorry to be filled with coal and then to the weighbridge. It was operated by an NCB employee who told the haulier the lorry was overweight. The lorry driver said he would risk taking the overload, took the ticket and left. The weighbridge operator knew that if the lorry driver drove on a road, he would inevitably be committing an overweight load offence. The driver was stopped by police and subsequently both he and the hauliers were convicted of contravening the Motor Vehicles (Construction & Use) Regulations. NCB was prosecuted for aiding and abetting the firm in the commission of the offence.

Lord Goddard C.J. identified the object of the legislation as being "to protect the roads of the country from damage to which the Board would directly contribute if they allow excessive weight to be taken from their premises". He found as a fact that the Board could have insisted on the excess being removed but once it knew (through the weighbridge employee) that the lorry was overweight and about to be driven on the road, and yet still completed the sale (i.e. gave the driver the ticket and allowed him to leave carrying the excess) it had aided and abetted the very offence it contemplated happening.

In *John Henshall (Quarries) Ltd v Harvey*,[34] another weighbridge case, **20.33** *NCB v Gamble* was relied upon as a correct statement of the law, although the result on the facts was quite different. The company had a weighbridge operated by an employee, B, but regularly supervised by its office manager. The company and the office manager were normally meticulous in observing the regulations and would send back overloaded lorries. On this occasion, B weighed a sub-contractor's lorry which was overweight, but, by an

---

[32] For summary offences see s.44 of the Magistrates' Courts Act 1980.
[33] *National Coal Board v Gamble* [1959] 1 Q.B. 11, 20 per Devlin J.
[34] [1965] 2 Q.B. 233.

oversight, allowed the lorry to be driven away. The driver was stopped and in due course convicted and fined. The company was prosecuted for aiding and abetting the sub-contractor to use the lorry in excess of the permitted weight. The first that the management of the company knew of the matter was when the prosecutor told the office manager. The company was acquitted. Lord Parker C.J. distinguished between absolute offences where "a master, whether an individual or a company, is criminally liable for the acts of any servant acting within the scope of his authority ..." and liability through aiding and abetting:

> "It is however, quite clear that when one is dealing with aiding and abetting, as has been often said, the master must know of the facts out of which the offence arises, albeit he does not know that an offence is committed".[35]

The court emphasised that there is no difference in principle between an individual or corporate employer, and that in either case, were the master to have *delegated* his responsibilities to the servant, he would be fixed with the knowledge of the servant.

In *R. v Robert Millar (Contractors) Ltd*,[36] a limited company with its registered office and place of business in Scotland had instructed (through M, the managing director) an employee to drive one of its lorries to England.[37] Both the managing director of the company and the driver knew that the lorry had a defective and dangerous tyre. On a motorway in England, the tyre blew out causing a head-on collision and the death of the six people in the oncoming car. The driver, the company and M were all prosecuted for dangerous driving; M and the company were found guilty of the offence of aiding, abetting, counselling and procuring the causing of the death of six people by dangerous driving. The Court of Appeal, dismissing the appeal, approved the words of Fisher J. in the Crown Court:

> "Where an employer with actual or imputed knowledge of the defective mechanical state of the vehicle permits an employee to take that vehicle out on the road, he is ... counselling and procuring the employee to drive that vehicle in that state and it seems to me that the common sense of the matter is that that counselling and procuring is a continuous act which persists so long as the driver is driving the vehicle in that condition on the road."[38]

So it is clear that for there to be liability for aiding, abetting, counselling or procuring an offence, even an offence of strict liability, knowledge (actual or imputed) must be proved. The prosecution may rely on all the surrounding

---

[35] At p.240.
[36] [1970] 2 Q.B. 54.
[37] There was a preliminary separate argument on jurisdiction.
[38] At p.73.

circumstances to prove the mental element, but the mere fact of the offence will not be sufficient of itself to result in a conviction.

REMEDIAL ORDERS

Some regulatory offences permit prosecuting authorities to issue and serve **20.34** on a corporation a remedial order by way of notice.[39] In many cases where an offence is committed, the prosecuting authority will serve a notice requiring a business to implement certain measures, or to stop doing a particular activity.[40] This power demonstrates the dual functions of the bodies charged with enforcing regulations but also the dichotomy inherent in these regulatory authorities: on the one hand working *with* corporations to improve practises (by cooperation and encouraging self-regulation), and on the other, having responsibility for *prosecuting* corporations for breaches of the regulations, so damaging or destroying that relationship.

Once a notice has been served, it must be complied with within a given time frame. Failure to do so may in itself give rise to an offence.[41] It is also possible for a court to order remedial work to be done as a sentencing option.[42] This is a sensible means of improving the level of safety and compliance in business/work undertakings. It has been argued that it is a more constructive use of corporate resources than substantial fines. The balance struck by regulatory authorities between prosecuting regulatory failures and assisting in compliance remains somewhat uneasy.

"STOP NOW" ORDERS

Stop Now Powers were brought into force[43] in order to provide a stronger **20.35** mechanism for enforcing existing legislation in the field of consumer protection, in line with EC Directives. Although the powers are not exercisable in criminal courts, the repercussions of such orders may be very serious and include proceedings for contempt of court. The areas covered are:

(a) package holidays;
(b) doorstep selling;
(c) misleading and comparative advertising;
(d) timeshares;
(e) unfair contract terms;

---

[39] e.g. an improvement notice pursuant to s.10 Food Safety Act 1990 or s.21 HSWA 1974.
[40] s.22 HSWA 1974.
[41] e.g. s.33(1)(e) HSWA 1974.
[42] e.g. s.42 HSWA 1974 provides for such a power instead of or in addition to another form of sentence.
[43] The stop Now Orders (EC Directive) Regulations 2001 (SI 2001/1422); brought into force 1.6.2001.

- (f) consumer credit;
- (g) distance selling;
- (h) sale of goods rights;
- (i) TV broadcasting;
- (j) advertising of medicinal products for human use.[44]

Power to take action over breaches of the relevant consumer protection legislation is granted to the OFT and 10 specified public bodies known as Public UK Qualified Entities ("QEs"),[45] including every weights and measures authority in Great Britain.

There are four types of action that the OFT or one of the QEs can take against a company breaching a relevant piece of legislation:

- (a) an informal undertaking;
- (b) a formal undertaking;
- (c) Stop Now orders;
- (d) contempt of court proceedings.

None of these are matters which are dealt with in the Crown Court but, in principle, they provide the foundation for a far greater level of control; which course of action is taken will depend on the gravity of the breach.

Usually, a QE will allow a corporation in breach 14 days[46] in which to agree voluntarily (in writing) to stop the offending behaviour and to comply with the law in future—an informal undertaking. Any further breach is likely to result in a formal undertaking being required or, depending on the circumstances, a Stop Now order.

20.36   A formal undertaking given to a QE is a serious step, to be viewed in a similar way to an undertaking given to the court. Breach of that undertaking may give rise to contempt of court proceedings, and/or proceedings for a Stop Now order.

A Stop Now order will be sought where a business has breached consumer protection law covered by the powers and either fails to agree to an undertaking, whether formal or informal, or looks likely not to honour such an undertaking. A Stop Now order may also be granted if the business is likely to infringe the legislation.[47]

A Stop Now Order is a court order either requiring the cessation of, or prohibiting the infringement of the legislation.[48] Breach of a Stop Now order will also amount to contempt of court. Breach of an informal undertaking will not give rise to contempt of court proceedings, but may provide evidence in support of an application for a Stop Now order.

---

[44] Sch.1 for the 10 EC directives.
[45] Sch.3.
[46] "A consultation period"; this may be waived if urgent action is required in the consumers' interests.
[47] Sch.2 reg.3, para.7.
[48] ibid. at para.6.

Proceedings may be brought not only against the business in breach but **20.37**
also, in the case of a corporate defendant, against any person "consenting to
or conniving at" an infringement which has occurred or is likely to occur.[49]
Moreover, an individual who gives a formal undertaking may be proceeded
against for contempt of court. The punishment for contempt is a fine or
imprisonment.

Guidance is given in the Explanatory Note to the regulations.[50] Proportionality is crucial to the level of response by the QE to the breach. The
QE must endeavour to get the voluntary agreement of the business to stop
any breach before taking the more serious steps, subject to the urgency of
the action required to protect consumers.

---

[49] ibid. at para.11.
[50] The Director General of the Office of Fair Trading was required to publish advice and
information on the effect of the regulations and how they were likely to operate, see the OFT
website for guidance.

352

Appendix A

COMPANIES ACT 2006

There follows a table listing all offences in the 2006 Act, their mode of trial, their maximum penalties and their origins, if any. The key to the mode of trial and penalties and derivation columns is as follows:

A	Summary (level 2 fine)
B	Summary (level 3 fine)
C	Summary (level 5 fine)
D	Summary (51 weeks' imprisonment, or a level 5 fine, or both (but where offending involves public display of the offending description, maximum fine is level 5 multiplied by the number of days))
E	(1) Indictment (fine); (2) Summary (fine not exceeding one tenth of the statutory maximum for each day that the contravention continues)
F	(1) Indictment (fine); (2) Summary (fine not exceeding statutory maximum)
G	(1) Indictment (two years' imprisonment, or a fine, or both); (2) Summary (12 months' imprisonment, or a fine not exceeding the statutory maximum, or both)
H	(1) Indictment (seven years' imprisonment, or a fine, or both); (2) Summary (12 months' imprisonment, or a fine not exceeding the statutory maximum, or both)
I	(1) Indictment (10 years' imprisonment, or a fine, or both); (2) Summary (12 months' imprisonment, or a fine not exceeding the statutory maximum, or both)
Y	Daily default fine of one tenth of the penalty on summary conviction
Z	Daily default fine of one fiftieth of the penalty on summary conviction
C.A.	Companies Act
B.N.A.	Business Names Act

Section of Act	General nature of offence	Mode of trial and penalties		Derivation (where applicable)
Part 3	**A company's constitution**			
26(3)	Company, and every officer in default, failing to send registrar copy of amended articles	B	Y	*C.A.* 1985, s.18(3)
30(2)	Company, and every officer in default, failing to forward resolutions or agreements affecting company's constitution to registrar	B	Y	*C.A.* 1985, s.380(5)
32(3)	Officer of company in default by failing to send constitutional documents to member when requested by the member	B		*C.A.* 1985, s.19(2)
34(5)	Company, and every officer in default, failing to give registrar notice of changes made to company constitution by enactment	B	Y	*C.A.* 1985, s.18(3)
35(3)	Company, and every officer in default, failing to give registrar notice of changes made to company constitution by court order	B	Y	New offence
36(3)	Officer of company in default by failing to incorporate, *etc.*, documents in copies of articles issued by company	B		*C.A.* 1985, s.380(6)
Part 4	**A company's capacity and related matters**			
45(3)	Company with a common seal, and every officer in default, failing to have company name engraved on seal	B		*C.A.* 1985, s.350(1)
45(4)	Officer of company, or person acting on behalf of company, using, *etc.,* seal purporting to be seal of company on which its name is not engraved	B		*C.A.* 1985, s.350(2)
Part 5	**A company's name**			
63(2)	Company, and every officer in default, amending its articles so that it ceases to be exempt from requirement to have "limited" in its title	C	Y	*C.A.* 1985, s.31(5)
64(5)	Company, and every officer in default, failing to change name on Secretary of State's direction so that it has "limited" at the end	C	Y	*C.A.* 1985, s.31(6)

Section of Act	General nature of offence	Mode of trial and penalties		Derivation (where applicable)
68(5)	Company, and every officer in default, failing to change name on Secretary of State's direction in case of similarity to existing name	B	Y	*C.A.* 1984, s.28(2), (5)
75(5)	Company, and every officer in default, failing to change name on Secretary of State's direction following provision of misleading information, *etc.*	B	Y	*C.A.* 1985, s.28(3), (5)
76(6)	Company, and every officer in default, failing to change name on Secretary of State's direction on grounds that is misleading as to its activities	B	Y	*C.A.* 1985, s.32(4)
Part 7	**Re-registration as a means of altering a company's status**			
99(4)	Company, and every officer in default, failing to give registrar notice of application to court to cancel resolution to re-list public company as private company, or failing to give notice of court's order on such application	B	Y	*C.A.* 1985, s.54(10)
108(4)	Company, and every officer in default, re-registered as limited company and failing to deliver statement of capital to registrar of companies	B	Y	New offence
Part 8	**Part 8: A company's members**			
113(7)	Company, and every officer in default, failing to keep register of members and their particulars	B	Y	*C.A.* 1985, s.352(5)
114(5)	Company, and every officer in default, failing to give notice to registrar of place where register of members is kept	B	Y	*C.A.* 1985, s.353(4)
115(5)	Company having more than 50 members, and every officer in default, failing to keep index of members and have it available for inspection	B	Y	*C.A.* 1985, s.354(4)
118(1)	Company, and every officer in default, refusing to allow person to inspect its register or index of members' names or making default in providing copy of register	B	Y	New offence
119(1)	Person making request containing false, *etc.* statement, to inspect company register or index of members' names	G		New offence

Section of Act	General nature of offence	Mode of trial and penalties		Derivation (where applicable)
119(2)	Person provided with access to company register or index of members' names using or disclosing information obtained for an improper purpose	G		New offence
120(3)	Company failing to provide person inspecting register or index of members' names with details of amendments	B	Y	New offence
123(4)	Single member company, and every officer in default, failing to comply with requirement as to register of members containing a statement that company has only one member	B	Y	*C.A.* 1985, s.352A(3)
130(2)	Company, and every officer in default, failing to give notice to registrar of location of overseas branch register, *etc.*	B	Y	*C.A.* 1985, s.365 and Sched. 14, Pt II, para. 1(3)
132(3)	Company, and every officer in default, failing to keep overseas branch register, or a copy, available for inspection at place in United Kingdom where main register kept	B	Y	*C.A.* 1985, s.362 and Sched. 14, Pt II, para. 4(2)
135(4)	Company, and every officer in default, failing to give notice to registrar of discontinuance of overseas branch register	B	Y	New offence
Part 10	**A company's directors**			
156(6)	Company, and every officer in default, failing to comply with Secretary of State's direction to comply with requirements as to appointment of directors	C	Y	New offence
162(6)	Company, and every officer in default, failing properly keep of register of directors containing requisite information, failing to keep it available and open for inspection, or failing to give notice to registrar of place where kept	C	Y	*C.A.* 1985, s.288(4)
165(4)	Company, and every officer in default, failing to keep separate register of directors' residential addresses	C	Y	New offence
167(4)	Company, and every officer in default, failing to give notice of change of directors or change of registered particulars	C	Y	*C.A.* 1985, s.288(4)
183(1)	Director failing to disclose interest in existing transaction or arrangement entered into by company	F		*C.A.* 1985, s.317(7)

356

Section of Act	General nature of offence	Mode of trial and penalties		Derivation (where applicable)
228(5)	Officer of company in default by failing to keep directors' service contracts, *etc.*, available for inspection	B	Y	*C.A.* 1985, s.318(8)
229(3)	Officer of company refusing to allow member of company access to directors' service contracts	B	Y	*C.A.* 1985, s.318(8)
231(3)	Officer of company with sole member as a director failing to record terms of contract	C		*C.A.* 1985, s.322B(4)
237(6)	Officer of company defaulting by failing to keep copy of qualifying indemnity provision available for inspection	B	Y	New offence
238(3)	Officer of company defaulting by failing to keep copy of qualifying indemnity provision available for inspection by company members or by failing to supply copy to member on request and payment of prescribed fee	B	Y	New offence
246(5)	Company, and every officer in default, failing to comply with requirements as to putting director's residential address on its register	C	Y	New offence
248(3)	Officer of company defaulting by failing to record and retain minutes of all proceedings at meetings of its directors	B	Y	*C.A.* 1985, s.382(5)
Part 12	**Company secretaries**			
272(6)	Company, and every officer in default, failing to comply with Secretary of State's direction to appoint company secretary	C	Y	New offence
275(6)	Company, and every officer in default, failing to keep register of secretaries and make it available for inspection	C	Y	*C.A.* 1985, s.288(4)
276(3)	Officer of company failing to notify registrar of change of details as to company secretaries	C	Y	*C.A.* 1985, s.288(4)
Part 13	**Resolutions and meetings**			
291(5)	Officer of company in default by failing properly or at all to send written resolution proposed by directors to members of company	F		New offence

Section of Act	General nature of offence	Mode of trial and penalties		Derivation (where applicable)
293(5)	Officer of company in default by failing properly or at all to send written resolution proposed by member of company to other members	F		New offence
315(3)	Officer of company in default by failing to circulate members' statement with respect to business to be dealt with at general meeting of company	F		*C.A. 1985, s.376(7)*
325(3)	Officer of company in default by failing to include statement of members' rights when giving notice of meeting	B		*C.A. 1985, s.372(4)*
326(3)	Officer of company in default by not issuing company-sponsored invitations to appoint proxies to all members	B		*C.A. 1985, s.372(6)*
336(3)	Officer of company in default by failing to hold annual general meeting	F		*C.A. 1985, 366(4)*
339(4)	Officer of public company in default by failing to circulate members' resolutions for company meetings	F		*C.A. 1985, 376(7)*
341(3)	Officer of company in default by failing to make certain information available on its website following poll at meeting	B		New offence
343(4)	Director failing to obtain independent report on poll or polls when required to do so	C		New offence
350(1)	Person failing to provide information when requested to do so by independent assessor	B		New offence
350(3)	Person making false or misleading statement to independent assessor	G		New offence
351(3)	Officer of company in default by failing to make available on its website information about appointment of independent assessor	B		New offence
355(3)	Officer of company in default by failing to keep records of resolutions and meetings, *etc.*	B	Y	*C.A. 1985, s.382(5)*
357(3)	Sole member of company failing to provide company with details of decision	A		*C.A. 1985, s.382B(2)*

Section of Act	General nature of offence	Mode of trial and penalties		Derivation (where applicable)
358(5)	Officer of company failing to allow inspection of records of resolutions and meetings or to give registrar notice of where inspection may take place or to provide member with copy on payment of prescribed fee	B	Y	*C.A.* 1985, s.383(4)
Part 15	**Accounts and reports**			
387(1)	Officer of company in default by failing to keep accounting records	G		*C.A.* 1985, s.221(5)
389(1)	Officer of company failing to comply with requirements as to keeping of accounting records (where to be kept)	G		*C.A.* 1985, s.222(4)
389(3)	Officer of company failing to take steps for compliance by the company, *etc.*, with requirements as to keeping of records (how long to be kept)	G		*C.A.* 1985, s.222(6)
410(4)	Company, and every officer in default, failing to annex information about related undertakings to annual return	B	Y	*C.A.* 1985, s.231(6)
412(6)	Director failing to provide company with matters about himself to enable company to provide information about director remuneration	B		*C.A.* 1985, s.232(4)
414(4)	Directors approving and signing defective accounts	F		*C.A.* 1985, s.233(5)
415(4)	Directors failing to prepare directors' reports	F		*C.A.* 1985, s.234(5)
418(5)	Directors approving report containing false statement as to disclosure to auditors	F		*C.A.* 1985, s.234ZA(6)
419(3)	Directors approving report which does not comply with requirements of the Act	F		*C.A.* 1985, s.234(5)
420(2)	Directors failing to prepare directors' remuneration report	F		*C.A.* 1985, s.234B(3)
421(4)	Director failing to give prescribed information about himself for purposes of directors' remuneration report	B		*C.A.* 1985, s.234B(6)
422(2)	Directors knowingly or recklessly approving directors' remuneration report which does not comply with requirements of Act	F		*C.A.* 1985, s.234C(4)

Section of Act	General nature of offence	Mode of trial and penalties		Derivation (where applicable)
425(1)	Company, and every officer in default, failing to send out copies of reports to those entitled to receive them	F		C.A. 1985, s.238(5)
429(1)	Company, and every officer in default, failing to comply with requirements as to summary financial statements	B		C.A. 1985, s.251(6)
430(6)	Officer of company in default by failing to make annual accounts and reports available on website	B		New offence
431(3)	Unquoted company, and every officer in default, failing to make copies of accounts and reports available to members or debenture holders	B	Y	C.A. 1985, s.239(3)
432(3)	Quoted company, and every officer in default, failing to make copies of accounts and reports available to members or debenture holders	B	Y	C.A. 1985, s.239(3)
433(4)	Company, and every officer in default, failing to state name of signatory in published copies of reports or accounts	B		C.A. 1985, ss.233(6) and 234A(4)
434(4)	Company, and every officer in default, failing to comply with requirements as to publication of statutory accounts	B		C.A. 1985, s.240(6)
435(5)	Company, and every officer in default, failing to comply with requirements as to publication of non-statutory accounts	B		C.A. 1985, s.240(6)
438(1)	Directors of public company failing to lay accounts and reports before members before general meeting	C	Y	C.A. 1985, s.241(2)
440(1)	Officer of company in default by failing to comply with procedure for approval of directors' remuneration report	B		C.A. 1985, s.241A(9)
440(2)	Director failing to put resolution to approve directors' remuneration report to vote	B		C.A. 1985, s.241A(10)
450(4)	Directors approving abbreviated accounts which do not comply with prescribed requirements	F		C.A. 1985, s.233(5)
451(1)	Directors failing to comply with section 441 (duty to file accounts and reports)	C	Y	C.A. 1985, s.242(2)

Section of Act	General nature of offence	Mode of trial and penalties		Derivation (where applicable)
458(4)	Person contravenig restrictions on disclosing or using information disclosed by Commissioners for Revenue and Customs	G		*C.A.* 1985, s.245E(3)
460(4)	Person contravening restrictions on disclosing information obtained under compulsory powers	G		*C.A.* 1985, s.245G(7)
Part 16	**Audit**			
486(3)	Private company, and every officer in default, failing to give Secretary of State notice of non-appointment of auditors	B	Y	*C.A.* 1985, s.387(2)
490(3)	Public company, and every officer in default, failing to give Secretary of State notice of non-appointment of auditors	B	Y	*C.A.* 1985, s.387(2)
501(1)	Person making false, misleading or deceptive statement to auditor	G		*C.A.* 1985, s.389B(1)
501(3)	Person failing to comply with auditor's request for information or explanation	B		*C.A.* 1985, s.389B(2)
501(4)	Parent company, and every officer in default, failing to obtain from overseas subsidiary undertaking information for purposes of audit	B		*C.A.* 1985, s.389B(4)
505(3)	Company, and every officer in default, laying, circulating or delivering auditor's report without stating name of auditor	B		*C.A.* 1985, s.236(4)
507(1)	Person knowingly or recklessly causing auditor's report on company's annual accounts to include misleading, false or deceptive matter	F		New offence
507(2)	Person knowingly or recklessly causing auditor's report on company's annual accounts to omit required statement	F		New offence
512(2)	Company, and every officer in default, failing to give notice to registrar of resolution removing auditor from office	B	Y	*C.A.* 1985, s.391(2)
517(2)	Company, and every officer in default, failing send auditor's notice of resignation to registrar	F	Y	*C.A.* 1985, s.392(3)
518(6)	Directors failing to convene meeting requisitioned by resigning auditor	F		*C.A.* 1985, s.392A(5)

Section of Act	General nature of offence	Mode of trial and penalties		Derivation (where applicable)
519(5)	Person ceasing to hold office as auditor failing to deposit statement at company's registered officer as to the circumstances connected with his ceasing to hold office	F		*C.A.* 1985, s.394A(1)
520(6)	Officer of company in default by failing to comply with requirements as to distribution, *etc.*, of statement of person ceasing to hold office as auditor	F		*C.A.* 1985, s.394A(4)
521(3)	Person ceasing to hold office as auditor, depositing statement under s.519, but failing to send copy to registrar	F		*C.A.* 1985, s.394A(1)
522(5)	Person ceasing to hold office as auditor failing properly or at all to notify appropriate audit authority when ceasing to hold office	F		New offence
523(4)	Company, and every officer in default, failing to notify and give reasons to audit authority of auditor ceasing to hold office	F		New offence
530(1)	Officer of company in default by failing to comply with requirements as to website publication of members' statement of audit concerns	F		New offence
Part 17	**A company's share capital**			
542(4)	Officer of company in default by purporting to allot shares without fixed nominal value	F		New offence
549(4)	Directors exercising company's power to allot shares without authority	F		*C.A.* 1985, s.80(9)
554(3)	Company, and every officer in default, failing to register allotment of shares	B	Y	New offence
557(1)	Officer of company in default by failing to make return of allotment of shares by limited company, or of new class of shares by unlimited company	F	Y	*C.A.* 1985, s.88(5)
572(2)	Person knowingly or recklessly authorising or permitting inclusion of misleading, false or deceptive material in directors' statement under s.571 (disapplication of pre-emption rights by special resolution)	G		*C.A.* 1985, s.95(6)
590(1)	Company, and every officer in default, contravening prohibitions (in Pt 17, Chap. 5) as to payment for shares	F		*C.A.* 1985, s.114

Section of Act	General nature of offence	Mode of trial and penalties		Derivation (where applicable)
597(3)	Officer of company in default by failing properly or at all to deliver valuer's report under s.593 to registrar for registration	F	Y	C.A. 1985, s.111(3)
602(2)	Company, and every officer in default, failing to deliver copy of resolution under s.601 and valuer's report to registrar	B	Y	C.A. 1985, s.111(4)
607(1)	Company, and every officer in default, contravening s.593 (public company allotting shares for non-cash consideration) or s.598 (public company entering into agreement for transfer of non-cash asset)	F		C.A. 1985, s.114
619(4)	Company, and every officer in default, exercising power under s.618 (sub-division or consolidation of shares) but failing properly or at all to give notice to registrar of shares affected	B	Y	C.A. 1985, s.122(2)
621(4)	Company, and every officer in default, exercising power under s.620 (reconversion of stock into shares) but failing properly or at all to give notice to registrar of stock affected	B	Y	C.A. 1985, s.122(2)
625(4)	Company, and every officer in default, failing properly or at all to give notice to registrar specifying redenominated share capital	B	Y	C.A. 1985, s.122(2)
627(7)	Company, and every officer in default, passing resolution under s.626 (reduction of capital in connection with redomination) but failing properly or at all to give notice to registrar	F		C.A. 1985, s.122(2)
635(2)	Company, and every officer in default, failing to forward to registrar copy of court order upon an application under s.633 or 634 (objection to variation of class rights)	B	Y	C.A. 1985, s.127(5)
636(2)	Company, and every officer in default, assigning name or other designation (or new name or designnation) to class of shares and failing to give notice to registrar	B	Y	C.A. 1985, s.128(5)
637(2)	Company, and every officer in default, varying rights attached to shares and failing to give notice to registrar	B	Y	C.A. 1985, s.128(5)

Section of Act	General nature of offence	Mode of trial and penalties		Derivation (where applicable)
638(2)	Company, and every officer in default, creating new class of members and failing to give notice to registrar	B	Y	*C.A.* 1985, s.129(4)
639(2)	Company, and every officer in default, assigning name or other designation (or new name or designation) to class of members and failing to give notice to registrar	B	Y	*C.A.* 1985, s.129(4)
640(2)	Company, and every officer in default, varying rights attached to class of members of company not having a share capital and failing to give notice to registrar	B	Y	*C.A.* 1985, s.129(4)
643(4)	Directors making solvency statement and delivering it to registrar without having reasonable grounds for opinions expressed in it	G		New offence
644(7)	Officer of company in default by delivering solvency statement to registrar without providing copy to members	F		New offence
644(8)	Company, and every officer in default, failing properly or at all to deliver to registrar solvency statement and statement of capital and directors' statement as to the timing of the solvency statement and its provision to members	F		New offence
647(1)	Officer of company intentionally or recklessly concealing name of creditor or misrepresenting nature of debt	F		*C.A.* 1985, s.141
656(4)	Directors failing to convene general meeting of company on serious loss of capital	F		*C.A.* 1985, s.142(2)
Part 18	**Acquisition by limited company of its own shares**			
658(2)	Company, and every officer in default, contravening general rule against acquisition of its own shares	G		*C.A.* 1985, s.143(2)
663(4)	Company, and every officer in default, failing properly or at all to give notice (and accompanying statement of capital) when cancelling shares in order to comply with s.662 (duty to cancel shares in public company held by or for the company)	B	Y	New offence

Section of Act	General nature of offence	Mode of trial and penalties		Derivation (where applicable)
667(2)	Public company, and every officer in default, failing to comply with duty under s.662 to cancel shares in company held by or for the company, or to apply for re-registration as a private company	B	Y	C.A. 1985, s.149(2)
680(1)	Company, and every officer in default, contravening prohibitions in s.678 or s.679 as to financial assistance	G		C.A. 1985, s.151(3)
689(4)	Company, and every officer in default, failing properly or at all to give notice to registrar of redeemed shares	B	Y	New offence
703(1)	Officer of company in default by failing to comply with duty under s.702 to keep contract for purchase of shares available for inspection and to notify registrar of place where inspection may be made, or refusing to allow inspection	B	Y	C.A. 1985, s.169(7)
707(6)	Officer of company in default by failing properly or at all to make return to registrar of purchase of shares by company	F	Y	C.A. 1985, s.169(6)
708(4)	Company, and every officer in default, failing to give notice to registrar of cancellation of purchase of its own shares in accordance with s.724 or s.729	B	Y	C.A. 1985, s.169A(4)
715(1)	Directors of private company making statement under s.714 (as to permissible capital for redemption or purchase of its own shares) without having reasonable grounds for opinions expressed in it	G		C.A. 1985, s.173(6)
720(5)	Company, and every officer in default, failing to give notice to registrar as to place where directors' statement and auditors' report kept, or failing to allow inspection by member of company or creditor	B	Y	C.A. 1985, s.175(7)
722(4)	Company, and every officer in default, failing to give notice to registrar of making of application under s.721 (application to court to cancel resolution), or failing to forward copy of order of court to the registrar	B	Y	C.A. 1985, s.176(4)

Section of Act	General nature of offence	Mode of trial and penalties		Derivation (where applicable)
728(4)	Officer of company failing properly or at all to deliver return to registrar where treasury shares sold or transferred for purposes of employees' share scheme	F	Y	C.A. 1985, s.169A(4)
730(6)	Officer of company failing properly or at all to deliver return to registrar where treasury shares cancelled	B	Y	C.A. 1985, s.169A(4)
732(1)	Company, and every officer in default, failing to comply with general requirements under Pt 18, Chap. 6, as to treasury shares	F		C.A. 1985, s.162G
Part 19	**Debentures**			
741(2)	Company, and every officer in default, failing to register allotment of debentures	B	Y	C.A. 1985, s.399(3)
743(4)	Company, and every officer in default, failing to give notice to registrar of place where register of debenture holders kept	B	Y	New offence
746(1)	Company, and every officer in default, refusing to allow inspection of register of debentures or failing to provide copy	B	Y	C.A. 1985, s.191(4)
747(1)	Person making request containing false, *etc.* statement, to inspect company register of debenture or share holders	G		New offence
747(2)	Person provided with access to company register of debenture or share holders using or disclosing information obtained for an improper purpose	G		New offence
749(2)	Officer of company in default by failing to comply with request of debenture holder to be provided with copy of trust deed	B	Y	C.A. 1985, s.191(4)
Part 20	**Private and public companies**			
767(1)	Company doing business or exercising borrowing power in contravention of s.761 (public company: requirement as to minimum share capital)	F		C.A. 1985, s.117(7)
Part 21	**Certification and transfer of securities**			
769(3)	Officer of company in default by failing to complete certificates of shares and debentures allotted	B	Y	C.A. 1985, s.185(5)

Section of Act	General nature of offence	Mode of trial and penalties		Derivation (where applicable)
771(3)	Company, and every officer in default, failing to register transfer of shares or debentures or give transferee notice of refusal to do so and reasons why	B	Y	*C.A.* 1985, s.183(5)
776(5)	Officer of company in default by failing to complete certificates of shares and debentures transferred	B	Y	*C.A.* 1985, s.185(5)
780(3)	Officer of company failing to complete certificates of shares specified in warrant for cancellation	B	Y	New offence
Part 22	**Information about interests in a company's shares**			
795(1)	Person failing to comply with notice under s.793 (notice requiring information about interests in company's shares) or making false statement in connection therewith	G		*C.A.* 1985, s.216(3)
798(2)	Person holding shares subject to restrictions imposed by order under s.794 (notice requiring information: order imposing restrictions on shares) seeking to exercise certain rights	F		*C.A.* 1985, s.455(1)
798(3)	Company, and every officer in default, issuing shares in contravention of restrictions imposed under s.794	F		*C.A.* 1985, s.455(2)
804(2)	Officer of company in default by failing to exercise powers under s.793 (notice requiring information about interests in company's shares) when requested to do so by members under s.803	F		*C.A.* 1985, s.214(5)
806(1)	Company, and every officer in default, failing to comply with s.805(5) (notice to registrar of place at which report to members on outcome of investigation into interests in shares under s.803 available for inspection)	B	Y	New offence
806(3)	Officers of company failing to comply with any other provision of s.805 (report to members on investigation under s.805)	F		*C.A.* 1985, s.215(8)
807(3)	Company, and every officer in default, refusing to allow inspection of report prepared under section 805	B	Y	*C.A.* 1985, s.219(3)
808(5)	Company, and every officer in default, failing properly or at all to keep register of information received in pursuance of requirement under s.793	B	Y	*C.A.* 1985, s.211(10)

367

Section of Act	General nature of offence	Mode of trial and penalties		Derivation (where applicable)
809(4)	Company, and every officer in default, failing to keep register of interests disclosed available for inspection	B	Y	*C.A.* 1985, s.211(10)
810(5)	Company, and every officer in default, failing to keep associated index of names entered in register of interests disclosed	B	Y	*C.A.* 1985, s.211(10)
813(1)	Company, and every officer in default, refusing to allow inspection of register of interests disclosed and associated index or making default in providing a copy	B	Y	New offence
814(1)	Person making request containing false, *etc.* statement, to inspect company register or index of interests disclosed	G		New offence
814(2)	Person provided with access to company register or index of interests disclosed using or disclosing information obtained for an improper purpose	G		New offence
815(3)	Company, and every officer in default, improperly removing entry in register of interests disclosed or failing to restore improperly removed entry	B	Y	*C.A.* 1985, s.218(3)
819(2)	Company ceasing to be public company but failing to keep register of interests disclosed and associated index for six further years	B	Y	*C.A.* 1985, s.211(10)
Part 24	**A company's annual return**			
858(1)	Company, its directors and secretaries, any other officer in default, failing to deliver annual return within 28 days of return date	C	Y	*C.A.* 1985, s.363(3)
858(5)	Every officer not guilty of an offence under s.858(1) (*ante*) in default in relation to continued contravention	C	Y	*C.A.* 1985, s.363(3) and (4)
Part 25	**Company charges**			
860(4)	Company, and every officer in default, creating charge but failing properly or at all to deliver particulars and instrument to registrar	F		*C.A.* 1985, s.399(3)
862(4)	Company, and every officer in default, acquiring property subject to registrable charge and failing to deliver particulars and certified copy of instrument to registrar	F		*C.A.* 1985, s.400(4)

Section of Act	General nature of offence	Mode of trial and penalties		Derivation (where applicable)
865(3)	Person knowingly or wilfully permitting delivery of debenture or certificate of debenture stock without copy of certificate of registration of charge endorsed upon it	B		*C.A.* 1985, s.402(3)
871(4)	Person obtaining order for appointment of receiver, *etc.*, failing to give notice of that fact to registrar	B	Y	*C.A.* 1985, s.405(4)
876(3)	Officer of company in default by knowingly and wilfully permitting omission of entry in company's register of charges	F		*C.A.* 1985, s.407(3)
877(5)	Company, and every officer in default, failing to give notice to registrar of place at which documents creating charges and register of charges are kept available for inspection or refusing to allow inspection	B	Y	*C.A.* 1985, s.408(3)
Part 26	**Arrangements and reconstructions**			
897(5)	Company, and every officer in default, failing to make explanatory statement to creditors when giving notice summoning meeting of creditors for proposed compromise or arrangement	F		*C.A.* 1985, s.426(6)
898(2)	Directors and trustees for debenture holders failing to give notice of matters necessary for giving explanatory statement under s.897	B		*C.A.* 1985, s.426(7)
900(7)	Company, and every officer in default, failing properly or at all to deliver copy of order under s.899 (court sanction for compromise or agreement) to registrar	B	Y	*C.A.* 1985, s.427(5)
901(5)	Where court order under s.899 (order sanctioning compromise or arrangement) or 900 (order facilitating reconstruction or amalgamation) alters company's constitution, company, and every officer in default, failing to ensure that copy order sent to registrar accompanied by articles as amended and that every copy of articles accompanied by court order	B		*C.A.* 1985, s.425(4)

Section of Act	General nature of offence	Mode of trial and penalties		Derivation (where applicable)
Part 28	**Takeovers, *etc.***			
949(1)	Unauthorised disclosure of information relating to the private affairs of individual, or any particular business, provided to the Takeovers Panel in connection with exercise of its functions	G		S.I. 2006 No. 1183 (CLW061818), reg. 8
953(2)	Person making bid failing to comply with bid offer document rules	F		S.I. 2006 No. 1183 (CLW061818), reg. 10(2)
953(4)	Directors and others officers of company failing to comply with bid response document rules	F		S.I. 2006 No. 1183 (CLW061818), reg. 10(4)
970(3)	Company passing opting-in or an opting-out resolution and failing to notify Takeovers Panel of that fact	B	Y	S.I. 2006 No. 1183 (CLW061818), reg. 24
980(6)	Person failing properly or at all to give notice of right to buy out minority shareholders ("squeeze out"); failure to accompany notice with statutory declaration that conditions satisfied; knowingly making false statement in such declaration	G	Z	S.I. 2006 No. 1183 (CLW061818), Sched. 2
984(5)	Person failing properly or at all to give notice, *etc.*, of rights of minority shareholders to be bought out ("sell out")	F	Z	S.I. 2006 No. 1183 (CLW061818), Sched. 2
Part 29	**Fraudulent trading**			
993(1)	Fraudulent trading	I		*C.A.* 1985, s.458
Part 30	**Protection of members against unfair prejudice**			
998(3)	Company, and every officer in default, failing to deliver copy of amended articles to registrar following order of court on complaint by member that affairs of company being conducted in unfairly prejudicial manner	B	Y	*C.A.* 1985, s.461(5)
999(4)	Company, and every officer in default, failing to annex to articles order of court on complaint by member that affairs of company being conducted in unfairly prejudicial manner	B		New offence

Section of Act	General nature of offence	Mode of trial and penalties		Derivation (where applicable)
Part 31	**Dissolution and restoration to the register**			
1004(5)	Person making improper application under s.1003 (application for voluntary striking off of company name from register) on behalf of company when activities of company preclude striking off	F		*C.A.* 1985, s.652E(1)
1005(4)	Person making improper application under s.1003 (application for voluntary striking off of company name from register) on behalf of company when other proceedings not concluded	F		*C.A.* 1985, s.652E(1)
1006(4)	Person applying on behalf of company for its name to be struck off register failing to give copy of application to existing members, employees, *etc.*	F		*C.A.* 1985, s.652E(1)
1006(4)	Person applying on behalf of company for its name to be struck off register failing to give copy of application to existing members, employees, *etc.* (offence aggravated by intention to conceal making of application from person concerned)	H		*C.A.* 1985, s.652E(2)
1007(4)	Director of company failing to give copy of application for company name to be struck off register to person who becomes member, employee, *etc.*, after application was made	F		*C.A.* 1985, s.652E(1)
1007(4)	Director of company failing to give copy of application for company name to be struck off register to person who becomes member, employee, *etc.*, after application was made (offence aggravated by intention to conceal making of application from person concerned)	H		*C.A.* 1985, s.652E(2)
1009(5)	Director of company failing to withdraw application for company name to be struck off register after company name changed, *etc.*	F		*C.A.* 1985, s.652E(1)
1033(6)	Company, and every officer in default, failing to comply with requirements as to its name upon restoration to the register	C	Y	New offence

Section of Act	General nature of offence	Mode of trial and penalties		Derivation (where applicable)
Part 35	**The registrar of companies**			
1093(3)	Company, and every officer in default, failing to deliver documents to registrar in connection with request for replacement document where information inconsistent with register	C	Y	New offence
1112(1)	Person knowingly or recklessly delivering documents, or making statements, to register which are false or deceptive	G		New offence
Part 37	**Companies: supplementary provisions**			
1135(3)	Company, and every officer in default, failing to comply with requirements as to form in which company records must be kept	B	Y	*C.A.* 1985, s.722(3)
1138(2)	Officer of company in default by failing to comply with duties to guard against, and facilitate discovery of, falsification of company records	B	Y	*C.A. 1985, s.722(3)*
1145(4)	Company, and every officer in default, failing to send document or information in hard copy form to member or debenture holder on request	B	Y	New offence
1153(2)	Person knowingly or recklessly making misleading, false or deceptive statement to person carrying out valuation	G		New offence
1155(1)	Judicial factor failing to notify registrar of his appointment	C	Y	New offence
Part 41	**Business names (this part does not fall under the umbrella of the "*Companies Acts*")**			
1193(4)	Person without approval carrying on business with name likely to give impression that business is connected to the government or a public authority	B	Y	B.N.A. 1985, s.2(4)
1194(3)	Person without approval carrying on business under name including specified word or expression	B	Y	B.N.A. 1985, s.2(4)
1197(5)	Person carrying on business in contravention of regulations as to words conveying inappropriate indication of company type or legal form	B	Y	*C.A.* 1985, ss.33-34A
1198(2)	Person carrying on business using name which is misleading as to its activities in such a way as to cause harm to the public	B	Y	New offence

Section of Act	General nature of offence	Mode of trial and penalties		Derivation (where applicable)
1203(4)	Large partnership refusing access to list of partners names during office hours	B	Y	B.N.A.1985, s.4(6)
1205(1)	Person failing to comply with requirements as to display of business name on business documents and premises, *etc.*	B	Y	B.N.A.1985, s.4(6)
Part 42	**Statutory auditors (this part does not fall under the umbrella of the "*Companies Acts*")**			
1213(3)	Person purporting to act as statutory auditor when ineligible to do so or without giving notice to audited person that he has resigned as a statutory auditor	F		*C.A.* 1989, s.28
1213(5)	Person convicted of offence under s.1212(3) (*ante*) through indelibility and continuing to act as statutory auditor	E		*C.A.* 1989, s.28
1213(6)	Person convicted of offence under s.1212(3) (*ante*) through failure to give notice and continuing to fail to give notice	E		*C.A.* 1989, s.28
1215(2)	Person continuing to act as statutory auditor when independence requirement no longer met, or failing to give notice to audited person that he has resigned by reason of his lack of independence	F		*C.A.* 1989, s.28
1215(4)	Person convicted of offence under s.1215(2) through acting when independence requirement no longer met yet continuing to act as statutory auditor	E		*C.A.* 1989, s.28
1215(5)	Person convicted of offence under s.1215(2) through failing to give notice yet continuing to fail to give notice	E		*C.A.* 1989, s.28
1248(5)	Company failing to retain person to carry out second audit or review accounts when directed to do so by Secretary of State	C	Y	*C.A.* 1989, s.29
1248(7)	Company failing to send report prepared by appropriate person as to whether second audit required to registrar, or failing to take steps referred to in report as to carrying out of second audit	C	Y	*C.A.* 1989, s.29
1250(1)	Person knowingly or recklessly furnishing false, misleading or deceptive information in connection with application or requirement under this part	G		*C.A.* 1989, s.41(1)

Section of Act	General nature of offence	Mode of trial and penalties		Derivation (where applicable)
1250(2)	Person whose name does not appear in register of auditors describing, *etc.*, himself to be a registered auditor	D		*C.A.* 1989, s.41(2)
1250(3)	Person whose name does not appear in register of auditors describing, *etc.*, himself to be a registered third country auditor	D		*C.A.* 1989, s.41(2)
1250(4)	Body which is not a recognised supervisory body or a recognised qualifying body describing itself, *etc.*, as such	D		*C.A.* 1989, s.41(3)

Appendix B

INSOLVENCY ACT 1986

Schedule 10

Punishment of Offences Under this Act

Section creating offence	General nature of offence	Mode of prosecution	Punishment	Daily default fine (where applicable)
12(2)	Company and others failing to state in correspondence etc. that administrator appointed.	Summary.	One-fifth of the statutory maximum.	
15(8)	Failure of administrator to register office copy of court order permitting disposal of charged property.	Summary.	One-fifth of the statutory maximum.	One-fiftieth of the statutory maximum.
18(5)	Failure of administrator to register office copy of court order varying or discharging administration order.	Summary.	One-fifth of the statutory maximum.	One-fiftieth of the statutory maximum.
21(3)	Administrator failing to register administration order and give notice of appointment.	Summary.	One-fifth of the statutory maximum.	One-fiftieth of the statutory maximum.

Section creating offence	General nature of offence	Mode of prosecution	Punishment	Daily default fine (where applicable)
22(6)	Failure to comply with provisions relating to statement of affairs, where administrator appointed.	1. On indictment. 2. Summary.	A fine; The statutory maximum.	One-tenth of the statutory maximum.
23(3)	Administrator failing to send out, register and lay before creditors statement of his proposals.	Summary.	One-fifth of the statutory maximum.	One-fiftieth of the statutory maximum.
24(7)	Administrator failing to file court order discharging administration order under s. 24	Summary.	One-fifth of the statutory maximum.	One-fiftieth of the statutory maximum.
27(6)	Administrator failing to file court order discharging administration order under s. 27.	Summary.	One-fifth of the statutory maximum.	One-fiftieth of the statutory maximum.
30	Body corporate acting as receiver.	1. On indictment. 2. Summary.	A fine; The statutory maximum.	
31	Undischarged bankrupt acting as receiver or manager.	1. On indictment. 2. Summary.	2 years or a fine or both; 6 months or the statutory maximum; or both.	
38(5)	Receiver failing to deliver accounts to registrar.	Summary.	One-fifth of the statutory maximum.	One-fiftieth of the statutory maximum.
39(2)	Company and others failing to state in correspondence that receiver appointed.	Summary.	One-fifth of the statutory maximum.	
43(6)	Administrative receiver failing to file office copy of order permitting disposal of charged property.	Summary.	One-fifth of the statutory maximum.	One-fiftieth of the statutory maximum.

Section creating offence	General nature of offence	Mode of prosecution	Punishment	Daily default fine (where applicable)
45(5)	Administrative receiver failing to file notice of vacation of office.	Summary.	One-fifth of the statutory maximum.	One-fiftieth of the statutory maximum.
46(4)	Administrative receiver failing to give notice of his appointment.	Summary.	One-fifth of the statutory maximum.	One-fiftieth of the statutory maximum.
47(6)	Failure to comply with provisions relating to statement of affairs, where administrative receiver appointed.	1. On indictment. 2. Summary.	A fine. The statutory maximum.	One tenth of the statutory maximum.
48(8)	Administrative receiver failing to comply with requirements as to his report.	Summary.	One-fifth of the statutory maximum.	One-fiftieth of the statutory maximum.
51(4)	Body corporate or Scottish firm acting as receiver.	1. On indictment. 2. Summary.	A fine. The statutory maximum.	
51(5)	Undischarged bankrupt acting as receiver (Scotland).	1. On indictment. 2. Summary.	2 years or a fine or both; 6 months or the statutory maximum, or both.	
53(2)	Failing to deliver to registrar copy of instrument of appointment of receiver.	Summary.	One-fifth of the statutory maximum.	One-fiftieth of the statutory maximum.
54(3)	Failing to deliver to registrar the court's interlocutor appointing receiver.	Summary.	One-fifth of the statutory maximum.	One-fiftieth of the statutory maximum.
61(7)	Receiver failing to send to registrar certified copy of court order authorising disposal of charged property.	Summary.	One-fifth of the statutory maximum.	One-fiftieth of the statutory maximum.

Section creating offence	General nature of offence	Mode of prosecution	Punishment	Daily default fine (where applicable)
62(5)	Failing to give notice to registrar of cessation or removal of receiver.	Summary.	One-fifth of the statutory maximum.	One-fiftieth of the statutory maximum.
64(2)	Company and others failing to state on correspondence etc. that receiver appointed.	Summary.	One-fifth of the statutory maximum.	
65(4)	Receiver failing to send or publish notice of his appointment.	Summary.	One-fifth of the statutory maximum.	One-fiftieth of the statutory maximum.
66(6)	Failing to comply with provisions concerning statement of affairs, where receiver appointed.	1. On indictment. 2. Summary.	A fine. The statutory maximum.	One-tenth of the statutory maximum.
67(8)	Receiver failing to comply with requirements as to his report.	Summary.	One-fifth of the statutory maximum.	One-fiftieth of the statutory maximum.
85(2)	Company failing to give notice in Gazette of resolution for voluntary winding up.	Summary.	One-fifth of the statutory maximum.	One-fiftieth of the statutory maximum.
89(4)	Director making statutory declaration of company's solvency without reasonable grounds for his opinion.	1. On indictment. 2. Summary.	2 years or a fine or both; 6 months or the statutory maximum, or both.	
89(6)	Declaration under section 89 not delivered to registrar within prescribed time.	Summary.	One-fifth of the statutory maximum.	One-fiftieth of the statutory maximum.
93(3)	Liquidator failing to summon general meeting of company at each year's end.	Summary.	One-fifth of the statutory maximum.	
94(4)	Liquidator failing to send to registrar a copy of account of winding up and return of final meeting.	Summary.	One-fifth of the statutory maximum.	One-fiftieth of the statutory maximum.

Section creating offence	General nature of offence	Mode of prosecution	Punishment	Daily default fine (where applicable)
94(6)	Liquidator failing to call final meeting.	Summary.	One-fifth of the statutory maximum.	
95(8)	Liquidator failing to comply with s. 95, where company insolvent.	Summary.	The statutory maximum.	
98(6)	Company failing to comply with s.98 in respect of summoning and giving notice of creditors' meeting.	1. On indictment. 2. Summary.	A fine. The statutory maximum.	
99(3)	Directors failing to attend and lay statement in prescribed form before creditors' meeting.	1. On indictment. 2. Summary.	A fine. The statutory maximum.	
105(3)	Liquidator failing to summon company general meeting and creditors' meeting at each year's end.	Summary.	One-fifth of the statutory maximum.	
106(4)	Liquidator failing to send to registrar account of winding up and return of final meetings.	Summary.	One-fifth of the statutory maximum.	One-fiftieth of the statutory maximum.
106(6)	Liquidator failing to call final meeting of company or creditors.	Summary.	One-fifth of the statutory maximum.	
109(2)	Liquidator failing to publish notice of his appointment.	Summary.	One-fifth of the statutory maximum.	One-fiftieth of the statutory maximum.
114(4)	Directors exercising powers in breach of s.114, where no liquidator.	Summary.	The statutory maximum.	
131(7)	Failing to comply with requirements as to statement of affairs, where liquidator appointed.	1. On indictment. 2. Summary.	A fine. The statutory maximum.	One-tenth of the statutory maximum.

Section creating offence	General nature of offence	Mode of prosecution	Punishment	Daily default fine (where applicable)
164	Giving, offering etc. corrupt inducement affecting appointment of liquidator.	1. On indictment. 2. Summary.	A fine. The statutory maximum.	
166(7)	Liquidator failing to comply with requirements of s.166 in creditors' voluntary winding up.	Summary.	The statutory maximum.	
188(2)	Default in compliance with s.188 as to notification that the company being wound up.	Summary.	One-fifth of the statutory maximum.	
192(2)	Liquidator failing to notify registrar as to progress of winding up.	Summary.	One-fifth of the statutory maximum.	One-fiftieth of the statutory maximum.
201(4)	Failing to deliver to registrar office copy of court order deferring dissolution.	Summary.	One-fifth of the statutory maximum.	One-fiftieth of the statutory maximum.
203(6)	Failing to deliver to registrar copy of directions or result of appeal under s.203.	Summary.	One-fifth of the statutory maximum.	One-fiftieth of the statutory maximum.
204(7)	Liquidator failing to deliver to registrar copy of court order for early dissolution.	Summary.	One-fifth of the statutory maximum.	One-fiftieth of the statutory maximum.
204(8)	Failing to deliver to registrar copy of court order deferring early dissolution.	Summary.	One-fifth of the statutory maximum.	One-fiftieth of the statutory maximum.
205(7)	Failing to deliver to registrar copy of Secretary of State's directions or court order deferring dissolution.	Summary.	One-fifth of the statutory maximum.	One-fiftieth of the statutory maximum.

Section creating offence	General nature of offence	Mode of prosecution	Punishment	Daily default fine (where applicable)
206(1)	Fraud etc. in anticipation of winding up.	1. On indictment. 2. Summary.	7 years or a fine or both; 6 months or the statutory maximum, or both.	
206(2)	Privity to fraud in anticipation of winding up; fraud, or privity to fraud, after commencement of winding up.	1. On indictment. 2. Summary.	7 years or a fine or both; 6 months or the statutory maximum, or both.	
206(5)	Knowingly taking in pawn or pledge, or otherwise receiving, company property.	1. On indictment. 2. Summary.	7 years or a fine or both; 6 months or the statutory maximum, or both.	
207	Officer of company entering into transaction in fraud of company's creditors.	1. On indictment. 2. Summary.	6 months or the statutory maximum, or both.	
208	Officer of company misconducting himself in course of winding up.	1. On indictment. 2. Summary.	7 years or a fine or both; 6 months or the statutory maximum, or both.	
209	Officer or contributory destroying, falsifying etc. company's books.	1. On indictment. 2. Summary.	7 years or a fine or both; 6 months or the statutory maximum, or both.	
210	Officer of company making material omission from statement relating to company's affairs.	1. On indictment. 2. Summary.	7 years or a fine or both; 6 months or the statutory maximum, or both.	
211	False representation or fraud for purpose of obtaining creditors' consent to an agreement in connection with winding up.	1. On indictment. 2. Summary.	7 years or a fine or both; 6 months or the statutory maximum, or both.	

Section creating offence	General nature of offence	Mode of prosecution	Punishment	Daily default fine (where applicable)
216(4)	Contravening restrictions on re-use of company in insolvent liquidation.	1. On indictment. 2. Summary.	2 years or a fine, or both. 6 months or the statutory maximum, or both.	
235(5)	Failing to co-operate with office-holder.	1. On indictment. 2. Summary.	A fine. The statutory maximum.	One-tenth of the statutory maximum.
389	Acting as insolvency practitioner when not qualified.	1. On indictment. 2. Summary.	2 years or a fine, or both. 6 months or the statutory maximum, or both.	
429(5)	Contravening s.429 in respect of disabilities imposed by county court on revocation of administration order.	1. On indictment. 2. Summary.	2 years or a fine, or both. 6 months or the statutory maximum, or both.	
Sch.7, para.4(3)	Failure to attend and give evidence to Insolvency Practitioners Tribunal; suppressing, concealing, etc. relevant documents.	Summary.	Level 3 on the standard scale within the meaning given by section 75 of the Criminal Justice Act 1982.	

INDEX